What we hope to give you is more insight, a few new approaches, and a handful of ways to make peace. We are not little yes-men, who dutifully listened to 2,102 women and now come marching back to you to present their demands. But we're not trying to pick a fight either. We're trying to build a bridge.

Our goal is that you'll come away with two or three things that you'll do differently. Believe us: If you do, that will go a long way. Most women, deep down, just want you to try. Stop being overwhelmed. This is not about miracles. You're not going to change who you are. But you can reach out to her. And you will both be happier for it. Who knows, your life together may just get better and better from there.

With that hope, we've written this book.

—THE AUTHORS

WHAT WOMEN WANT

What Every Man Needs to Know about Sex, Romance, Passion, and Pleasure

Laurence Roy Stains
and
Stefan Bechtel

BALLANTINE BOOKS • NEW YORK

A Ballantine Book
Published by The Ballantine Publishing Group
Copyright © 2000 by Laurence Roy Stains and Stefan Bechtel

www.ballantinebooks.com

ISBN 0-345-44341-1

This edition published by arrangement with Rodale Inc.

Manufactured in the United States of America

First Ballantine Books Edition: January 2001

10 9 8 7 6 5 4 3 2 1

Acknowledgments

Men need women—and, man, we needed a lot of women to write this book. A special thanks, first of all, to the 17 interviewers who gathered the voices for parts three and five: Andrea Adams-Miller, Lisa Osherow Bergman, Adrienne Carlish, Markie Christianson, Kris Croteau, Shirley Helman, Loriann Jamka, Kristin Lang, Megan Marshall, Megan Pera, Sara Roeber, Jill Rudick, Nena Sandoval, Lydia Sausa, Claudia Six, Kayla Warner, and Wendy Weise.

For their help in gathering small groups of women together, we thank Heather Ascher, Kathy Craigmile, Mary Sandy Hingston, Ellen Kane, Sonia Laudi, Susan Lewis, Priscilla Pfohl, Becky Pfohl, and Kathy Taylor.

Thanks to our wives, Kay and Cyndi, for their insights, laughter, and support.

Many, many thanks to all of the people at Rodale who worked their magic: Cathie Grozier and Julie White for the Magellan Poll; Kathryn C. LeSage, our copy editor; Joanna Reinhart and Charles Beasley for the design; and Jane

Unger Hahn, Sandra Salera-Lloyd, Lucille Uhlman, and Terry Sutton-Kravitz for research. Thanks to Jackie Dornblaser for shepherding the transcripts. A salute to Jack Croft for his help in getting this project off the ground, and to Ken Winston Caine for making it soar. And a warm thanks, finally, to Neil Wertheimer for his continued support and care.

Contents

Part Six: The Breadwinner She Respects

Part Seven: The Father She Admires

Part Eight: A Hassle-Free Home

Part Nine: Going for the Golden

Welcome

WE INTERVIEWED 2,102 WOMEN—REAL, REGULAR WOMEN, LIKE THE ONE YOU'RE WITH. We did it scientifically; we did it in person; we did it with female sociology students. We asked specific, detailed questions. Whoa, did we get answers. And are you ever gonna be glad.

A guy is walking along the beach in Malibu when he finds a lamp half-hidden in the sand. He picks it up, gives it a rub. Out pops a genie. The genie looks him over and says, "You're my third master this week. I'm giving you only one wish."

The guy says, "I've always wanted to go to Hawaii, but I'm afraid to fly. Could you build me a highway so I can drive there?"

The genie frowns. "A highway across 3,000 miles of ocean? Hey, buddy, I'm a good genie, but not *that* good. Gimme another wish."

So the guy says, "Okay, just tell me something, then. I've always wanted to know: What do women want? Can you answer that?"

The genie looks out at the ocean. Then he turns and asks, "You want two lanes or four?"

We, your friendly authors, worked on this book for the better parts of 1998 and 1999. Most of the time, we felt like that genie.

"What do women want?" is a question that men have asked forever. Men with far better minds than ours have come away shaking their heads.

But we asked anyway—because each and every generation has the right to puzzle it out for themselves, and because the answer keeps changing.

When we told people about this project, we were often asked, "Why are two guys writing that book?" Simply because this is a book for men. So we wrote this in male speak. Whenever possible, we avoided words like "intimacy" and "communication." But it's more than that. If two women wrote this book, you know what would happen. In a nicey-nice, soft-spoken way, they'd end up yelling at you. "Do the dishes! Learn to talk! Pick up your socks!" What guy wants to read 519 pages of that?

If you're like us, you've been yelled at enough. You want to know what to do. You want to know what she means when she starts talking about "good communication." You want to know why your sex life isn't what it used to be.

You want to know why she's mad, and, most maddening of all, why she won't tell you why she's mad.

And this is a woman who loves you! Even when men and women have the best of intentions, confusion rules. Time and again in this book, we quote a woman, only to ask ourselves, "What guy would ever say such a thing?" We were especially impressed by the vast differences between male and female sexuality. She is not like you in so many ways, and don't let anyone tell you different. As you'll see, good sex has to happen in her head—and her heart. And it's much more of a front-end deal. If you want to make love tomorrow night, start by warming up to her tomorrow morning.

For this project, we interviewed women like the woman you know. We talked to women who basically like men, *not* women who regard men with bug-eyed hostility. Because, no matter what you do, you will never please those women.

Why would you even want to?

Stefan was in his neighborhood copy shop the other day when he ran into a friend of his. With this friend was another woman. When she overheard Stefan telling his friend about this project, she turned toward him, bore down on him like a mighty frigate, and issued her challenge:

"What I would like is for men to treat Earth with as much respect as they treat their own power."

Well, excuuuuuuse us!

Hello and good-bye.

Some women want men to be just like them. There's no way . . . We hereby pledge: This book will not turn you into a woman.

Instead, what we hope to give you is more insight, a few new approaches, and a handful of ways to make peace. We are not little yes-men, who dutifully listened to 2,102 women and now come marching back to you to present their demands. But we're not trying to pick a fight, either. We're trying to be a bridge. That highway to Hawaii, maybe.

Our goal is that you'll come away with two or three things that you'll do differently. Believe us: If you do, that will go a long way. Most women, deep down, just want you to try. Stop being overwhelmed. This is not about miracles. You're not going to change who you are. But you can reach out to her. And you will both be happier for it. Who knows, your life together may just get better and better from there.

With that hope, we've written this book.

You know and we know that you're not going to read this book from cover to cover. First, you'll turn to the part called The Lover She Wants.

And when you're done, maybe you'll peek at the part that addresses the biggest problem in your relationship right now. So go ahead. We've designed this book for the wandering eye, so to speak. Just read this so you don't get confused along the way.

Here's a brief backstage tour and reading guide.

The raw material for this book was gathered chiefly from four major sources.

1. We placed a one-page survey in the September 1998 issue of *New Woman* magazine, a now-defunct national magazine that had a circulation of one million. We asked 15 questions and received 785 replies. We also posted these 15 questions, plus others, on the New Woman Web page and received replies from around the globe.

2. A 69-question formal survey conducted by a professional polling firm was mailed to 3,000 females under age 50 who have been buyers of Rodale health books. This survey, which we came to call our Magellan Poll, was mailed in September 1998, and by late October of that year, 1,148 replies had been received, for a response rate of 40 percent.

3. For the intimate material in part five, The Lover She Wants, we hired female graduate students in human sexuality. We sent them 90-minute cassette tapes and a list of 52 suggested questions. They selected the interviewees. Thus, we got in-depth sexual interviews with 80 women from Newport Beach, California, to Newfoundland, Canada.

4. We conducted interviews with nearly 100 women, often in small groups in home settings, where we shamelessly plied them with white wine and French pastries.

And that is how we came up with the figure on this book's

cover: We heard from 2,102 women across the United States and Canada.

The two surveys, in the magazine and in the mail, provided a greater depth of response than we had expected. In the case of the magazine survey, respondents usually tore the page out of the magazine, filled it out, and sent it to us, but they also faxed it, e-mailed their replies, and wrote long, beautifully penned letters on lilac-scented stationery. They also gave us phone numbers and e-mail addresses, allowing us to ask follow-up questions and get a dialogue going. In the case of the mail survey, we left space at the end and asked respondents to "use it to give a final word of advice to the men who will read our forthcoming book." The resulting missives filled a 59-page, single-spaced supplemental report.

The in-the-mail survey of 69 questions proved to be such a treasure trove of data that we christened it the Magellan Poll, in honor of the Magellan Mission to Venus. In 1990, NASA launched the first data-gathering probe of that planet. The satellite circled Venus for 4 years until the day, late in 1994, when it got too close, plunged through the dense atmosphere, and met a fiery demise.

You might say we felt its pain.

The results of our Magellan Poll are presented throughout the book in charts furnished with the kicker The Facts of Life.

When we first conceived of this book, we believed that our toughest hurdle would be gathering women's voices for the section on love, sex, and intimacy, The Lover She Wants. What woman would want to talk to two middle-aged guys about her sex life? We had loads of questions, and we needed answers that were honest and candid and jargon-free (because those are the answers that *you* need). We finally hit upon a solution: We canvassed female student members of the two national organizations representing the field of human sexuality, the American Association of Sex Educators,

Counselors, and Therapists (AASECT) and the Society for the Scientific Study of Sex (SSSS). These young women, we hoped, would be able to ask the most personal of questions without embarrassment—and elicit frank replies. The interviewers conducted 80 highly professional, very substantial interviews, and we thank them.

Frankness exacts a price, and that is anonymity. We identify women by first names only, and we allowed them to choose pseudonyms. In part five, for instance, you can safely assume that all first names are pseudonyms. Elsewhere in the book, real first names mix with masked identities. Ages are roughly accurate. Locations sometimes reflect home states rather than current residences.

> "Men and women, women and men: It will never work."
>
> —ERICA JONG

At times, we felt that honesty and strong opinion were not enough. On certain subjects, we thought, the guidance ought to come from an expert. Who can't use a little professional coaching? So we interviewed female experts. Our question-and-answer sessions with them are presented throughout the book under the heading Can She Explain It?

Now you're ready to surf the book. You can get the gist of each chapter by reading the summaries at the beginning. Oh. There's one last thing we should tell you.

We've highlighted our major points in bold type.

Like that.

PART ONE

Crossing
the Great Divide

CHAPTER ONE

More Different Than Alike

YOU STILL CAN'T FIGURE OUT WOMEN?
Well, guess what: They still can't fathom you. Of all
of the differences between the sexes, there are three
that annoy most women, most days of the week.
They have to do with talking and feeling and, well,
talking about feelings.

Most women like men. Really. Despite the Bobbitt jokes,
and despite the fact that they read books with titles like *How
to Dump a Guy*, *No Good Men*, and *Why It's Always the Guy's
Fault*.

They want us, and they want to get along with us. Just as
we want them. Despite the fact that they like to watch *Ally
McBeal* once a week.

But how? On that point, they're stuck. They're as clueless
as we are.

They are stumped by the Great Divide, and most of them
have come to the sorry conclusion that men and women are
more different than alike.

Take "Vanessa," for instance. She's a 42-year-old interior
designer from California. For her, the Great Divide is as clear
as Rocky Mountain air.

My last husband was a doctor. We liked to ski. We were
skiing in Aspen one Christmas, and we had just gotten on the

hill when I blew my knee on a mogul field. I fell, and all of a sudden I hear this big "pow!" I try to stand on it and I can't. And I'm looking at the bottom of the mogul field, and he's there waving me down. "C'mon! Hurry up! We just got here!"

So I slid all the way down on my good knee and said, "I think I blew my knee. I mean, I can't stand on it or anything."

And he says, "Lay down. Take off your ski." He's rotating my whole leg 360 degrees, then he says, "Yeah! You tore your ACL."

I say, "What are we gonna do?"

He says, "Ski down to the next chairlift." So I skiied down on one leg while he was waiting very impatiently for me to catch up with him. "Okay," he says, "take the chairlift up to the top so they can put you on the gondola—and I'll see you later."

And I said, "Wait a minute: If you leave me here, when I get down to the bottom, I'm not seeing a doctor—I'm seeing a lawyer."

He finally helped her down the hill, but the incident was the beginning of the end of that marriage. "There was no sympathy there at all," Vanessa said, looking back on it. "If that had been a woman I was skiing with, she'd have said, 'Oh my God, your arm is hurt too! Let's get the ski patrol.' She would have been sympathetic. Women talk to each other. They're caring. They're listeners. They discuss each other's problems. Men talk about sports. That's it. Sports or their jobs."

And she has come to a conclusion that goes straight to the heart of this book: "Men are totally different from women—and the only way we can deal with each other is by trying to communicate as much as possible."

Women don't understand us. Now you know why she always wants you to talk to her. Maybe, just maybe, she'll come away a teeny bit less flabbergasted.

We mystify women. We all do. And at times, we seem so alike in our differences from them that they invent crazy theories for why this is so. Here's Vanessa's.

> From day one, fathers give their little boys a book to read. It's called *The Book of Dicks*. It teaches you how to be a guy. That book is given to every little boy in the world. Now, I've never read it. But you can tell when a kid finally has. He changes over from a cute little boy to a guy—a guy who has read *The Book of Dicks*.

Now that we've suffered through 30 years of feminism, are relations any better? Hardly. Now we have a new generation of women who grew up playing soccer and basketball, who wear men's boxers and Gap T-shirts and CK One cologne. And they ponder the age-old question: What makes men tick? As Cristin in Baltimore told us, "Men are foreigners to us sometimes."

How swell if everyone could smile and say, "*Vive la différence.*" As a rule, people don't. Instead, someone starts sleeping on the sofa. Someone like you.

Sorry, but you cannot ignore the Great Divide.

Ignoring the Great Divide doesn't work. If it did, you wouldn't be reading this book.

So we're going to tackle it right here, right now. You're about to learn that—surprise—it isn't as big or as awful as some women make it out to be. Women, as we know all too well, can generalize and "awfulize" about men like nobody's business. We'll spare you all that and just break down this dilemma into some approachable pieces.

Let's begin by recognizing that men and women are different in some ways more than others. This is exactly what

THE FACTS OF LIFE

THE STRANGER IN HER BEDROOM

In our Magellan Poll of nearly 1,200 women, we asked a point-blank, no-wiggle-room question about gender difference. The question: "In your opinion, men and women are . . ."

More different than they are alike ⇨ 70%

More alike than they are different ⇨ 30%

Women in their thirties and women who are dissatisfied with their relationships and sex lives answered "more different" in even higher percentages. But no matter how we sliced it, our numbers showed that the vast majority of women remain mystified by men.

one anonymous respondent wrote in the blank space at the end of her form.

In terms of basic needs, personalities, habits, etcetera, I think men and women are more alike than different. However, when it comes to dating, sex, and some marital expectations, men and women are more different than alike.

Good point. Such a good point, in fact, that you'll see this book zero in on those very subjects that produce the most friction. We talked to women about dating; we talked to them about sex; and we examined the major roles in a married man's life: husband, father, and breadwinner.

We probed for ways in which men could make little adjustments and get big results. After all, you can no sooner change your ways than the leopard can change his spots.

But you're more apt to make a few changes if you understand why you're making them and if you're pretty sure it won't kill you.

In our *New Woman* magazine poll, our first questions read "What is it that men just don't get about women? What is it that women just don't get about men?"

Several hundred women took the time to reply. Their gripes—and, oh, can they gripe—pretty much come down to a few big concerns. Think of these as the daily sore spots. And let's be thankful that the battle of the sexes can be broken down, at least for starters, into these three approachable problems.

1. Talking. Or, to use her favorite word for it, *communication*. In essence, women talk and men don't. Or if you do, you interrupt her with some solution to the problem that she has placed before you. As we'll say again in chapter 14, don't do that. Let go of the burden of fixing it, because that's not why she's telling you all of this stuff anyway. She's telling you as a way to think out loud and to feel closer to you. Women talk to create intimacy. When you simply listen, she feels that you're taking her seriously.

Here are some representative remarks on the subject from the women we surveyed.

- "Women need to talk. It's that simple."
- "When women talk, they aren't bitching; they just need to vent or discuss."
- "Listen and let me vent."
- "Our need to talk . . . it makes us feel connected."
- "We think out loud and we just want you to listen."

It's definitely true that some men don't talk enough. (That used to be a good thing—the strong, silent type.) It's also true that some women, and we all know who they are, talk too much. They will not shut up. So when we read so many women commenting, "Listen to my problems without being judgmental and without giving advice unless asked," we have to wonder. . . . If you're enduring a steady stream, maybe she needs five little words of advice: Say less. Be heard more.

2. Feelings. Women show emotions; men hide emotions. At least, that's the way they see it. Her emotions are more complicated. And she's more sensitive to the feelings of others. Whereas you're not as sensitive, especially when it comes to *her* feelings. You blurt and you hurt. You tease her about her feelings; you even tease her about expressing her feelings to her girlfriends.

Again, some representative commentary:

- "Women are more emotional. Men are more practical."
- "Men don't get how emotional women are about things. Women don't get how men aren't."
- "Women are emotionally connected to everything."
- "A lot of men tend to not want to discuss emotions and feelings, and that's what most women thrive on."
- "They expect us to just 'suck it up,' like they do."

> "Men really are different in many respects. We shouldn't try to fit them into a mold that we have in our heads."
> —Lynn, Texas

One anonymous respondent makes an excellent point: "Men are notoriously quiet when something is bothering them, until they finally blow up, run away, or look for an escape." So when she talks vaguely about "good communication," maybe all she means is, tell her what's really bugging you before you go postal on her. Of course, she'd much rather hear nice feelings. Feelings like, you sure missed her when she went away last weekend. You can't read her mind; don't expect her to read yours.

3. Romance and intimacy and relationships. She wants

to be wooed. She wants to be that special someone. She wants attention. She wants time together. She wants affection, both physical and verbal. She needs the emotional security that comes of your constant reassurances. She needs to feel close to you—and you seem to have a spiteful determination not to fulfill her need.

A sampling of the messages:

- "We like sex, too, but what we really like is romance."
- "We just want to be adored."
- "Worship us!"
- "We need a lot more attention than they think we need."
- "We don't understand the way they express their love for us—*lack* of cards, *lack* of gifts, *lack* of worry, etcetera."
- "Listen to the radio. What women want is being broadcast daily."

And here are helpful hints from Cindy in Naperville, Illinois: "Women need to be hugged or simply touched. In the video store or grocery store, give a little squeeze on the arm, or throw your arm around her waist." You're right, Cindy. That's not so hard. If it is, then she's not really the right gal for us, is she?

There's one catch: your suggestion that we not be embarrassed to "talk in goofy voices" in public. There we draw the line. Can't we compromise? We'll squeeze you in the video store if you promise to stop the baby talk.

Now, gentlemen, let us pause to ask you something. Have you noticed anything about this list? If you add item one together with items two and three, you realize what happens, don't you?

You get a guy's worst nightmare—that moment when a woman wants you to *talk* about your *feelings* about the *relationship*.

Many women will ask, but few will receive. Most guys

simply cannot do that. We were not engineered to process the question. Depending on our particular wiring, we either shut down or blow up.

If she suddenly asks this ultimate of female questions, it's probably because she's thinking of having coffee with that guy in the art department and she's been checking your commitment level lately and you're 2 quarts low. But if she's consistently asking and you're consistently shutting down, try this.

Give her pieces of what she wants. Tonight, make her feel special. Tomorrow, don't dismiss her feelings. This weekend, let her vent.

Maybe then the ultimate question won't come up as often.

Women, of course, had lots more to say about lots of other things. Here are some of the biggies.

- "Women always worry."
- "Women can't come every time."
- "It is the little things that count."
- "We get bitchy sometimes."

Whoa! Back up! Let's talk about that rhymes-with-witchy thing. Women want guys to know two things about PMS. First, PMS is hell.

"PMS is real," we heard.

"You just don't understand PMS," said Maria in Miami.

"PMS means *go away*," warned a lady in North Carolina.

Second, don't blame every angry reaction on PMS. "Every time I get mad, my boyfriend blames it on PMS," said Edith, a 23-year-old student in Maine. "I do believe in PMS, but there are times when I get angry and it's not because of my hormones."

ADVANCE WARNING SYSTEM

If PMS is a fact of life at your house, consider a PMS calendar. Not for her. For you.

Sue, who is 32 and has been married for 8 years, told us that her husband watches her calendar and then marks a calendar that he keeps next to his tool bench in the basement. "I mark my days with a little star, so that's what he does, too," she said. "It's always a week before, and so he's warned. He knows how to deal with me that week. He won't argue with me or pick a fight; and if I pick a fight, he'll step around me or stay away. To me, it's something very considerate. He is kinder to me and he understands my needs more at that time of the month."

Beyond what women wish we understood about them, our *New Woman* survey also asked what women don't get about men. Here's the litany of their woes. Basically, they want to know why we have such big egos and why we're so selfish and where we get off having such an inflated sense of self-worth. (Oh, yeah? We'll address who's selfish in the next chapter.) They want to know why we're so full of blarney. Why we have to compete with everyone, everywhere, every day. Why we're so controlling, yet so helpless in the kitchen. Why we can't tell them how we feel about anything, how it seems we really don't feel anything, and how they can acquire our nonchalance. They want to know why we have friends if we don't tell them anything. And why on Earth *can't* we read their minds?

They'd love to know when science will discover the gene sequence that causes men to scream at the TV during sporting events. "If you'd get as excited about us as you do about sports, you'd have it made," advises a lady in Long Beach, California.

If modern science ever solves that one, perhaps the answers

to these enigmas are not far behind. (1) What is the deal with pro wrestling? And, (2) do we really think the Three Stooges are funny?

There you go. Invaluable advice. You can wave it off as silly or sexist. You can ignore everything. But then what will happen?

You'll be the guy sleeping on the sofa.

CHAPTER TWO

What Women Want: Everything

FOR THE LAST 30 YEARS, MEN HAVE BEEN
TOLD THAT THEY JUST DON'T GET IT.
Women don't get it, either. Men will never be
women. Maybe it's time her expectations
came down out of the blue.

In the 1993 movie *Groundhog Day*, Bill Murray plays an egocentric TV weatherman, Phil, and Andie MacDowell plays his young producer, Rita. They have breakfast in a diner, and Phil hits on her. "Who is your perfect guy?" he asks. She begins ticking off the qualities. . . .

"Well, first of all, he's too humble to know he's perfect. He's intelligent, supportive, funny. He's romantic and courageous. He's got a good body, but he doesn't have to look in the mirror every 2 minutes. He's kind, sensitive, gentle. He's not afraid to cry in front of me. He likes animals. Children. He'll change poopy diapers. Oh! And he plays an instrument. He *loves* his mother. . . ."

Close to the end of this, Phil interrupts to double-check something. "This *is* a *man* we're talking about, right?"

When it's Andie MacDowell rattling off this list of particulars, most guys fall completely under the spell of her beauty and basically agree to everything. "Whatever you say, Andie!

(Sigh.)" Printed here in black and white, however, it's a different story. Hers is a tall order.

This scene is a perfect reflection of our times because it's not just Andie MacDowell's character who expects all this and more. Most women expect all this and more.

At no time in human history have women expected so much from men.

And, as Phil's joke makes clear, this is an androgynous list. If it sounds to you like women want you to be the perfect man *and* the perfect woman, you're right. They do. And they're unashamed to say so. Listen to a few remarks from our *New Woman* magazine survey.

- "Men, recapture the feminine part of you."
- "Men need to get in touch with their feminine sides."
- "Men should have more 'female' characteristics across the board."

THE SHORT ANSWER

ARE MEN GETTING BETTER OR WORSE?

- "We're all getting worse together."
- "Very, very, very, very slowly better."
- "I have two sons. I am committed to men getting better."
- "Men are getting better. Oh, yeah. Look at the men from the old days, grunting all the time. Women had it bad. Men are so much fun to be with—they're your buddies now. You can do things with them. Men are changing."
- "Men are the same—but our expectations are higher. So therefore, they're relatively worse."

Uh, yeah, right away, ladies. With some women, you don't get any sense that they are aware of the pie-in-the-sky nature of their desires. They're not dreaming up a wish list. They're presenting nonnegotiable demands. Listen to Anne in Schenectady, New York: "I want a man who can cook and also can fix things around the house . . . a man to be sensitive and also secure within himself. I want and need it all. I don't want to settle for less."

One of the big surprises for us, in writing this book, was the extent of the rage that some women carry around with them each and every day. In a way, it's no wonder. These expectations are impossibly inflated. How can men live up to that?

How can life possibly measure up? No wonder they're angry.

If any women are reading this now, we don't want you to get angrier. So we're politely asking you to leave. Please, skip ahead to the next chapter, or peruse the index or something, because we're going to display some emotion. And even though you say that you want us to show our feelings, what you really mean is, you want us to show loving feelings about you. If it's anything else—if it's not about you—you get that smirk. You ask us if we've been beating our drums in the woods lately. So, we'll catch up with you later, okay?

Guys, we need to talk. We need to get it all out on the table, right here, right now: the blatantly contradictory things they ask of us, the hypocrisy, the narcissism, the ways they drive us just plain nuts. For just this one chapter, we have to be honest about years and years of frustration. Then we can move on.

> "Most women set out to change a man, and when they have changed him they do not like him."
> —MARLENE DIETRICH

Subject numero uno on which we must set the record straight: the male ego. Or, as women habitually say, the fabled male ego.

Yes, there are plenty of men with inflated egos in this world. Women have a love-hate relationship with the male ego; when they love it, they call it *confidence*. If nothing else, a big ego comes in handy as armor in the competitive workplace. We can sympathize with Amanda in Ohio when she wrote, "What women don't get about men is the overwhelming sense that they have to be right, all of the time."

It takes a secure guy to think that Amanda is not belittling him or one-upping him by pointing out that he's not exactly on the mark. But there are plenty of women who get equally prickly at the mere suggestion that they may not be right. That's exemplified by this joke: "If a man talks in the forest and a woman isn't there to hear him, is he still wrong?"

What irks us is when a woman does her little superior dance, when she wags her finger at us and says, "For goodness sake, realize that you are not the center of the universe."

What she really wants us to realize is, *she* is the center of the universe.

Introducing: the fabled female ego.

The female ego is not blustery, like the male ego. So you might not recognize it instantly if you were to define "big ego" strictly in male terms. But it's there, catlike. The key feature of the female ego is an insatiable need for adoration.

Men have to realize that in a relationship a woman wants and needs to feel as if she is the only woman—the most beautiful woman, the sexiest woman, the sweetest, most wonderful woman in his life. A woman needs to be number one.

That's a workable definition.

But it is not enough to be adored.

THE FACTS OF LIFE

WAS IT EVER BETTER?

Given the discontent with men, we wondered whether women think that their mothers had it any better? No. In fact, women today think they lead happier love lives. We asked a long-winded question: "It's often said that people today enjoy more fulfilling relationships than ever before. And yet both sexes are busier and more stressed these days. Here's a tough question: If you had to guess, who do you think has enjoyed more fulfilling romantic relationships, you or your mother?"

Me ⇨ 76%

My mother ⇨ 24%

Women without partners were much more likely to answer, "My mother" (no surprise, there). Married women and women who are very satisfied with their relationships and sex lives were much more likely to answer, "Me."

The fabled female ego wants to be adored by the perfect man.

"My ideal man would be tall (6 feet and over), sensitive, sweet, caring, spiritual, honest, understanding, and will love me until the day I die," wrote an anonymous respondent to our Magellan Poll. Note, by the way, that sometimes women distract our attention from their egos by bashing our egos. This woman started her response by saying, "Men should be less selfish." And not a trace of irony followed.

Here's another survey respondent with a long, long list for Santa Claus.

I like men who are tall, dark, and handsome; give me compliments; pay attention to me and only me; are

monogamous, have no children, and want a long-term relationship. I am looking for someone who makes me feel special and has never been married. Someone who doesn't
drink, smoke, or do drugs or alcohol. I want a special man.

Then she leaves her address and phone number. She'll
probably be furious with us because we declined to pass it
along. Oh, were we supposed to turn ourselves into a free
dating service, just for her? What an ego.

> "Women don't really want
> a man to be sensitive—
> just sensitive to <u>their</u>
> feelings."
> —DR. LAURA SCHLESSINGER

"I wish men would sur-
prise their women more," said
Stephanie in Connecticut. "I
wish men would listen more.
I wish men would make love
when and how we want, even
when they don't want or like
how we want it."

Calling all love slaves! Stephanie wants *you*. Bring your
own handcuffs.

Another key feature of the fabled female ego is its desire
that men be able to read her mind and read between the lines.
You'll read more about this in chapter 15. But here and now,
listen to this honest self-assessment from "Trixie," a 28-year-
old single lawyer in Philadelphia.

I can be very demanding at times, but I also like to feel like
I'm not demanding. So pampering me without my realizing
it is always a nice thing. Without me saying, "I want this."
You know what I mean. I want a mind reader, basically.
That's the best kind of pampering.

Anybody care to step up to the plate for Trixie? Anybody
out there who believes that someday she'll be satisfied?

To be fair, not all of the desire for us to read between
the lines is ego driven. There's a component that is just . . .
feminine.

Women converse in cushioned ways. It smooths their interactions with other women, but it complicates their interactions with men.

In fact, one woman spoke to us of "womaneeze," the language that women use to talk to one another. And it teases us with a wonderful idea. Why couldn't we just have a male-female dictionary? Then everyone's problems would be solved! Right? Every guy dreams of

> "Fifty years, (Freud) spends analyzing women. And he still can't figure out what they want. So this makes him the world's greatest expert on female psychology?"
> —CLARE BOOTHE LUCE

this. Our friend Joe wanted us to forget this whole book and just do a big wall chart, "When she says X, she means Y."

Ah, if only.

The trouble is, when she says X, she could mean A through Z. If she says, "Why don't you meet me for lunch today?" it could mean:

1. "I'm down to $2 and some pennies."
2. "I'm bored."
3. "I miss you lately."
4. "I'm still mad about last month, and you haven't apologized."
5. "I don't want to have lunch with Ann again."
6. "My boss is hitting on me."

This indirection is especially characteristic of the South, according to southern writers and our personal experience.

But wherever you live, you tend to listen to a conversation for the subject matter and ignore half of the details. Whereas women want to hear all of the details. Not only that, they want *you* to hear all of the details and then, out of all of those details, figure out which two, added together, make her secret point. When you don't, some women are disappointed. Other women take it personally.

The fabled female ego believes that "womaneeze" is the only language on Earth.

When men don't speak it, women get mad. They get downright insulting. Oh, it can get ugly.

- "Men really don't think about things as deeply as we like to think they do," said Sandra in Washington, D.C.
- "Women don't get how simply men's minds work," said a woman in Pensacola, Florida.
- "Women need to understand: Guys are morons," claimed a trash-talker in Queens, New York.
- "Face it, women will inherit the Earth and you will be caged," wrote a real sugarplum of a gal in Richmond, Virginia.

Apparently, she doesn't think we'll ever recapture our feminine sides.

The feminine hope to turn every man into the perfect man/perfect woman may just possibly be part of her hardwiring. A study of 104 British and Japanese women found that the ladies preferred the looks of manly men during the week when they were ovulating. When they were shown the same set of hunky photos during the other 3 weeks of the month, they thought that the smoother, softer, more sensitive-looking guys were handsome.

By comparison, yes, men are simple. Henceforth, we'll take that as a compliment.

If contradiction is inherent in women, there's nothing in our culture right now to dissuade them from thinking that it's perfectly normal and okay and maybe even politically correct to flaunt it.

Women now proudly say they want us to be a certain quality—and they want us to be its opposite.

You know, rugged but sensitive? Get a load of this request from an anonymous survey respondent.

Men should be more sensitive and not so rough, more gentle. Men should never take sex for granted, should be more romantic, and should always be the aggressive one.

Gentle and unassuming, but always aggressive. Got it. Here are a few other examples.

- "Be totally in love with us—but at the same time, don't be a wimpy pushover!" wrote a lady in Juneau, Alaska.
- "Always be honest (unless we don't want you to be)," wrote another survey respondent.
- Tina in Youngstown, Ohio, told us not to drool over other women in her presence ("Is that clear?"). But apparently, it's perfectly okay for her to sleep with other men. "Yes, we like bad boys on the side," she said.
- Dana in Texas told us, "Women want equality, we want to be treated fairly. But we also want to be treated like goddesses. That's what I want."

> "Women don't want to be dominated and bullied, but neither do they want a man to be a baby. They want him to be a 'man.' Then, when he's a man, they don't like it because that means he's too controlling and they're afraid of him. They all want heroes, but they want warm, tender, loving heroes. Oh, what a fantasy that is!"
>
> —OLGA SILVERSTEIN, therapist, in VOGUE magazine

Who wouldn't?

Dana's sentiment, we would wager, is at the very center of so much male/female misunderstanding. Is this not a setup for trouble? When you get down to the nitty-gritty, it usually means things like: He has to do half the laundry, but she won't mow the lawn. She can earn more than him, but he should still spend more on her.

This is all perfectly straightforward to most women, who can't for the life of them figure out why we don't get it. "It seems as though the more we tell them, the more confused they become," wrote a woman in Flint, Michigan, incredulously.

If you're not dizzy by now, if you can stand one more contradiction, here it is. Invariably, after women rattle off their lists of opposing qualities that we should strive to achieve in order to be worthy of them, they will tell us, as did Sarah in Rio Linda, California, "Just be yourself."

A-a-a-a-a-a-a-a-a-a-a-arrrrrrrrrgggggggh!

Jane, a woman in one of our living-room chats, had an interesting suggestion: "I think women should marry gay men, and then just have boyfriends."

Jane, you're on.

CHAPTER THREE

Beyond Mars and Venus

GET OVER ANGER, AND REMEMBER,
NOBODY WINS AN ARGUMENT. Make that
okay, and make it a practice that both of you say
what you mean so you aren't playing constant
guessing games. Accept each other as the
fascinating, faulty human beings that you are. If you
were perfect, you would know better than to
criticize her imperfections—but until then, quit it.

Did you catch the last chapter? It sure felt good to get that off our chests. We feel better now.

Luckily, there were no women around to hear it. (They all stopped reading, as per our request, of course.) The answer to all of the male bashing that we've endured over the last few decades is not to weigh in with some equally mean-spirited female bashing. Where would that get us? Nowhere. You guys who want to live in a world without women, you can just leave now and go off ice fishing together. The rest of us guys will stay behind, thanks. We're still trying to attract women. We want to live with them. We confess: We can't live without them.

For us, the ultimate question is: How are a bunch of badly flawed men and women supposed to get along in this imperfect world? Let's start by agreeing on a few basic rules of engagement.

1. Anger goes nowhere and accomplishes nothing.

It's emotional wheel spinning, that's all. It digs a deeper rut.

When she gets angry, what do you usually do? You get defensive. That's exactly where most men are, most of the time. That's the average guy's way of keeping peace. But that's just a setup for a closed loop: You do something, she gets mad, you make amends, you do it again.

No one is the wiser. And nothing changes.

> "Trying to understand is a gift to your lover."
> —LEE, Salt Lake City

When you get angry, you start to argue with her. And that's generally the most fruitless tack that you can take. Women, due to their generally superior verbal skills, are more likely to win the argument. Repeat this mantra: "If I argue, I will lose."

Avail yourself of the wisdom contained in a folktale passed down among African-Americans in the South and retold by the novelist Zora Neale Hurston. A character named George Thomas opens the story with this nugget: "Don't you know you can't git de best of no woman in de talkin' game?"

But let us assume, for a moment, that you can match her in the argument department, that you can thrust and parry and foil and win? Exactly what have you won, Mister Big Shot? You win the right to live in a shabby apartment and eat your dinners out of a can. Oh, you were absolutely right. And now you're absolutely alone.

2. Deal with the differences.

Nothing is more transparently obvious, nor more in need of saying: Men and women are fundamentally different. You didn't make the world. That's just the way it is.

Listen to Mary, who scribbled the following advice at the end of her Magellan Poll survey.

It's a known fact: Men and women think differently. The sooner you come to grips with this, the better your relation-

ship is. Say what you want and mean it up front, and quit
with the guessing games and mind reading.

It's all too easy to get trapped while only halfway to this
realization, to get stuck in the mental prison of gender stereotypes. We know because we met women who seemed unable
to break free of their rigid attitudes and could not use the
word "men" without putting an "all" in front of it. They took
a perverse comfort in the walls that separate the sexes. These
women were black holes of negative energy. And, big surprise, we couldn't help but notice that they were usually
single or bitterly divorced.

They've never gotten beyond the Mars-and-Venus mind-
set, the notion that men and women are so different that it's as
though we're from different planets. In saying this, we're not
criticizing the *Men Are from Mars, Women Are from Venus*
books of John Gray, Ph.D.—he has dedicated his life to
bringing couples together. We're talking about the rigid
mind-set that frames every person and every behavior as
male or female, good or bad. (If it's your gender it's good; if
it's their gender it's bad.)

By contrast, we also met women who have learned to accept, and even celebrate, the guyness of guys. Despite the occasional self-centered yearning for a new, sappy, neutered
male, most women can deal with the Great Divide. "We fully
accept that men and women are different," said Lisa, a
24-year-old student in Arizona. "We acknowledge the differences and we try to work with that. We don't need Mr. Sensitive, Ponytail-Head Man. But we do need men who are true to
themselves and respectful."

Are you ready to accept the maddening, complicated
womanliness of women?

If so, then you've already embraced the third rule of
engagement.

THE SHORT ANSWER

WHAT DO WOMEN REALLY WANT?

- "Companionship."
- "Respect."
- "The ability to compromise."
- "I want a husband who treats me like his girlfriend, not his wife."
- "I want to get the most out of life that I can. If I have someone to share it with, it's all that much better."
- "I would like men to like women more. Not love women, like women."
- "A decent partner, someone you really can walk through life with."
- " 'Partner' is a good word."

---

3. Don't expect so much.

We tip our hats to Tami in Colorado, who makes this brilliant point:

> Men want women to be strong but feminine, capable but sexy, and a virgin but a hooker. Women want men to be macho but sensitive, quietly strong but communicative, and reliable but boyish. Neither sex has figured out that nobody's perfect. You have to accept certain vices because you appreciate certain virtues.

If you expect perfection from her and she expects perfection from you, what happens? Neither of you ever enjoys those sunny moments when you feel really and truly appreciated by your mate. In this life, there is nothing sweeter than those moments.

Alas, "we were raised to believe in fairy tales, which is why we're disappointed to find reality," wrote a *New Woman* magazine survey respondent.

Man, oh man. Can you imagine being compared to Sir Lancelot on a daily basis?

The bottom line, said Shirley in Atlanta, is this: "The perfect man can only coexist with the perfect woman." To the extent that we're shy of that ideal, we need to bring our expectations down from the blue. As one woman told us, "Just like it's unfair for us to expect you to be all things, the same goes for you."

4. Learn to accept what you cannot change.

One of the oldest and wisest lessons that people learn from long-term marriages is that you can't really change your partner. That's like trying to stop the wind. Life is easier when you give up trying.

Fran, a 43-year-old mother in Pennsylvania, put it this way:

> Stop believing in your own head that you can make anybody do anything. You can't. If my husband doesn't want to, he doesn't want to, and it really irks me if he says, "Yes, dear" and he doesn't mean that—he's just humoring me. I don't want to be humored. If you mean no, tell me no. And tell me no now.

But here's another bit of wisdom that we heard: Both men and women change over time. Some, quite a lot. Although you can't force someone to change, there is a deep, slow, natural transformation that occurs with maturity and age. In fact, if you want to ask the question "What do women want," you're led to another question: "What age are we talking about?" What women want changes with time.

Cindy, a 50-year-old painter from New York City, said it best.

> Women and men want different things at different times in their lives. It's not like you can say, "Women want this or that." In high school, I wanted to be adored. When the nesting urge hit and nature said, "Go have kids," I wanted

someone dependable. When I had kids, I wanted to find my-self again and have respect for my own self-worth. When I started getting older, I wanted a companion. And eventually, you come all the way back around again because, finally, you want someone to adore you just like in high school, be-cause who else is going to stay with you when you're old?

Many women feel that the Great Divide narrows with age. "By the time the hormones are gone, the men become a little gentler and the women become a little meaner, a little tougher, a little stronger," said Stephanie, a 48-year-old lawyer and mother in Philadelphia.

JUST DO IT

WELL, AREN'T YOU NICE?

Men need women. And more particularly, you need *her.* Show her that you do. Give her compliments more often. Don't stop at looks. Praise something that she's done.

Guys tend to be bad at paying compliments and way too good at handing out criticism. Think about the last time you sincerely complimented another guy. What was his reaction? Did you get a weird look, a look that said, "Hey, what's your angle?"

If your gal gives you the same reaction, you're already in trouble.

"Women tend to need many compliments for each criticism," writes Warren Farrell, Ph.D., a men's-movement guru, San Diego-area psychologist, and author of several books on men's issues, in his latest book, *Women Can't Hear What Men Don't Say.* He even suggests a ratio of four to one. You'd better get busy.

Compliments make her feel appreciated and loved. Criticism doesn't change anything; it just makes her feel defensive, which leads to fights, life-long grudges, and sexual withdrawal. Take your pick.

5. Accept that we need each other.

Here's an attitude that usually gets ignored in the over-heated, media-fanned battle of the sexes. "Women need men and men need women," said Sherry in Denver.

We need each other precisely because of our differences, not in spite of them. The women whom we love and admire are the women who can revel in the differences. Who can appreciate us and show that appreciation and know the depth of the need—theirs and ours.

Carry this message from Karen in Florida as you continue on your journey through this book.

> Know that as much as we may not always understand you, that's exactly why we love you. We love the very fact that you're so different from us and it draws us in every way. Also know that we watch you, too, when you walk by, and we smile.

Karen, you are beautiful. That's an attitude that will lift men and women across the Great Divide.

PART TWO

Our Good Points and Our Bad Points

CHAPTER FOUR

Our Good Points: What Women Secretly Admire about Us

IN A WORLD WHERE EVERYBODY HAS SEEN THOSE "SAVE THE MALES" BUMPER STICKERS, it's easy to forget that lots of women actually like men. They like our physical and emotional strength, our self-confidence, our chivalrous manners, our "selfishness," and, of course, our butts.

Unless you've had your head in a hole for the past two decades, you've probably noticed that all men are either brutes, boors, deadbeats, turkeys, or chauvinists (take your pick). When we're not out starting wars, wolf-whistling at babes, cheating on our taxes, harassing female coworkers, abusing power, or yelling too loud at ball games, we're torturing small animals.

You get the picture.

But cheer up. Although the thousands of women who responded to our surveys did have their fair share of complaints about male behavior, we were pretty amazed at the fact that lots of these ladies actually *like* us. Some of them really, really like us. Imagine that. (How come you never hear this stuff anymore?) These women looked us over and found lots to love and admire—our strength, our willpower, our confidence, even our hands. Shoot, it was enough to make us blush. When we asked, "What do you admire most about men?" they came back with stuff like this:

"I love men's strength and their beautiful, artful bodies. . . . I worship them!" (That was Marina, in San Jose, California. And no, darn it, we didn't get her phone number.)

They even recognized the fact that, without men, the human race would pretty quickly go the way of the dinosaurs. They not only like us, they need us. As Sherry put it, "Women need men and men need women, for sure."

> "I must say, as a feminist since the age of 12, when I began reading <u>Ms.</u> magazine, I love men."
> —ANONYMOUS

Good press for the endangered male is in such short supply these days that we figured we'd share some of the good news with you. It made us feel so good about ourselves that we thought maybe it would make you feel good too. Consider the following pages the literary equivalent of a chorus of wolf whistles from a big crowd of great women from across the United States, Canada, and abroad.

Lots of women still genuinely like men. This is real news!

"I would like to say that all men have a sexiness about them," said Cynthia, of Whittier, California. "If they are bold or if they have blue eyes or if they have big muscles. Whatever it is, they are sexy just like women, just in a different way. Men are great. They can be great friends more than a woman; you can trust men more than women."

"There is nothing more sexy than a freshly showered man wearing a magnificent cologne and dressed in snug jeans and a front-button sport shirt, showing just a hint of chest hair," another enthused. "Or a well-tailored suit, showing pride in self and an air of sophistication, yet not acting holier-than-thou (no gaudy expensive Rolexes or bracelets)."

Another woman said, "I still hear a great deal of hostility from men toward feminists and the women's movement. It seems they're reacting to a perceived hostility toward men. I must say, as a feminist since the age of 12, when I began reading *Ms.* magazine, I love men. I still love to receive the little gestures that men can give to demonstrate their consideration or manners (holding the door, giving up a seat on the train), just as I enjoy giving the little gestures that women give to demonstrate their consideration for men or their manners (we still like to feed them and see that they're comfortable)."

Other women seemed to be as attracted to men's bodies as men are to women's bodies. Vicki, in McMinnville, Oregon, said that what she loves about men is "dark hair, dark eyes, chest hair, and a nice-looking penis."

> "There is nothing more moving than gentleness in a big, strong man."
> —STACIE, Pittsgrove, New Jersey

Quite a few other women went on and on about their long-time mates or husbands. "My husband is great," said one, simply. "We've been married for 26 years. Sex is great. He's an all-around good guy."

Despite what you may have read or heard, being an old-fashioned gentleman has not gone out of style.

One recurrent theme in all of these men's-fan-club letters was how much women like an old-fashioned gentleman. That could mean dressing well, being courteous and considerate, or even merely being a man who is gentle. As Stacie, in Pittsgrove, New Jersey, put it, "I have always been awed by those men who combine intelligence and grace with good old-fashioned brute strength. For instance, hockey players fascinate me—so graceful, yet so powerful. I deeply respect those men who go soldiering on, supporting their kids, being supportive of their wives or lovers, and seldom asking for much in the way of sympathy or applause or even thanks. There is nothing more moving than gentleness in a big, strong man."

Respect for gentlemanliness has not always been the norm, of course. There were times over the past 2 decades when men were rightfully confused about whether opening the door for a woman was (a) chauvinist bullying, (b) an implication that she couldn't open it herself, (c) condescending, or (d) just a nice, polite thing to do. Now it turns out that "d" was very often the correct answer (though women sure made us guess).

- "Call me old-fashioned, but when a man treats me like a lady, I cannot help but be attracted to him," said Lasca, in Dallas. She adds, with that telltale edge in her voice, "It turns me off when a guy obviously does not know he is being a schmo when I have to open my own door. Also, bad table manners is a sure sign of no-second-date syndrome."
- "Most women like the old-fashioned gentleman," another woman said. "If he's being caring, protective, and attentive, a woman knows that he'll be attentive in bed too."
- "I find it a turn-on for men to show concern," another woman said. "I like men to open doors, walk me to the door, and pick up the check. It's very, very nice when he makes an effort, especially when he doesn't expect something in return. Men become gracious to me when they are 'human.' When they look into your eyes, not at your chest. When they talk to you, not at you. When they treat you like a person, not a dumb woman. That is sexy to me."
- "A class-A classy man is usually a gentleman," a woman in Imperial, Missouri, told us. "Keep wearing those suits."

(Just as an aside here: In our survey, when we asked "What is the sexiest clothing a man can wear?" the most common answer, by far, was "a finely tailored suit.")

Physical strength, you may think, is a virtue that only counted in bygone days. Not so! Women still love it.

During the great gender debates of the 1970s, 1980s, and 1990s, the point was often made that men's generally superior physical strength had become completely irrelevant in a society where almost nobody has to chop wood and carry water anymore. Well, sure, that may be true. But women still go for bulging biceps, no matter what they say. Apparently, judging from our survey results, they're not too crazy about the human-marshmallow model of maleness—sweet, skinny, self-effacing Alan Alda types. Nor are they too keen about the brutal, ironclad terminators of the world—Schwarzenegger and Stallone. They want both physical strength and gentleness, which may explain why Mel Gibson is one of the world's biggest heartthrobs (at least for now).

- "I admire men's physical strength," wrote Tami. "I worked as a certified nurse's assistant in a nursing home for a while, and I could lift some fairly hefty patients. But I had a partner named John who could lift the biggest patient in the hospital without even breaking a sweat. It impressed me."

> "I love to watch men walk, and I love the way they are physically strong but usually just as much mush as we are, privately."
> —KAYE, Little Rock, Arkansas

- "I love to watch men walk, and I love the way they are physically strong but usually just as much mush as we are, privately," wrote Kaye, in Little Rock, Arkansas. "I admire the way that most men are not afraid to say what they want, and then they take full responsibility to ensure that they get what they want. They, for the most part, are risk takers, and taking risks takes guts. . . . I admire that. . . . I think everything about a guy is sexy." (Drat, no phone number again.)

> "I love men's strength and their beautiful artful bodies. . . . I worship them."
> —MARINA, San Jose, California

- A woman in Atlanta said that she admires "how strong and brave they are. It's really a good feeling for a woman to

know she has a man who will take care of her and defend
her against anyone or anything."

- A woman in Des Moines, Iowa, said she admired the fact
that men "are stronger than me. They are generally taller
than me. They are hairy on their chests. They have great
moustaches. They are not women."

Women admire that men have self-confidence even if it's completely unwarranted.

> "I admire how man can
> get away with murder
> because they are men. He
> has sex with another girl.
> His response: 'She put it in
> my face; what was I
> supposed to do?' "
> —ANONYMOUS

Ever wonder why women need
to attend all those assertiveness-
training, confidence-boosting,
buck-up-kid courses? Well, for
reasons that it would take too
long to explain, those are attrib-
utes that many women (not all
of them, of course—*some*) lack.
And when women look at men,
they often see and admire the
fact that lots of us have assertiveness and self-confidence
out the wazoo. Even if it's mostly show, they still seem to admire it.

Our favorite female comment about all that was this, from
Tarita, a 29-year-old California housewife: "I admire the fact
that a man can have a beer belly, a bald head, yellow teeth,
bad breath, athlete's foot, and no job and still think he's the
best catch in the sea." Ahem . . . We chose to take this as a
compliment.

Here are some slightly kinder comments.

- "I admire men's ability to believe they are just like John
Wayne or Mel Gibson. Men seem to have such high self-
esteem."
- "I admire men's ability to be cool and debonair in situa-
tions that would drive women crazy."
- "Men have such self-esteem. It seems like most women

look in the mirror and only see their faults, but men only seem to see the good stuff."

Some of the things they say they admire about us are the very same things they say they don't like about us. Go figure.

That was a real shocker—and at first we thought these women were joking. After all, after all these years of being criticized, excoriated, castigated, and denounced for being unemotional, it's a little startling when women say they can see the advantages of being like that. But when we asked, "What do you admire most about men?" so many of our respondents said such things that eventually we decided to take them at their word.

- "What I admire most about men," Sherry wrote, is "their selfishness. Sometimes I'd love to be as selfish as they so I could have more time to myself."
- ". . . the way they can have sex and not care. I wish I could be like that."
- ". . . how detached they can be. How they can keep their lives *and* have a relationship, instead of where our relationships become our lives."
- A woman in New York City observed that "men are so easily able to do anything they damn well please without being self-conscious, physically and emotionally. They can walk down the street without care of being gawked at. Women don't get how men can be readily unfaithful to their partners, leave children unsupported financially and emotionally, and go off on new adventures seemingly easily and without the guilt that would consume women."
- "They don't worry; they keep it inside. Also, they can blow things off. We can't."
- A woman in Kennewick, Washington, wrote, ". . . the way they can just leave, no explanations, no cares, no worries."
- ". . . their ability to get away with being immature."

- "I admire men for their beauty, strength, and ability to handle a difficult situation without losing control," a woman in Baltimore wrote. "Also, how they can get away with murder because they are men. He has sex with another girl. His response: 'She put it in my face; what was I supposed to do?' " (Is that a good line or what?)
- "I admire their wit and sense of humor—their ability to separate sex and emotion," said Sandy, in Morganton, North Carolina. "I would have saved myself a lot of pain in the past if I could have learned how."

> "I admire the fact that a man can have a beer belly, a bald head, yellow teeth, bad breath, athlete's foot, and no job and still think he's the best catch in the sea."
>
> —TARITA, California

- "I envy them for being more secure, less sensitive."
- ". . . their ability to have sex with whoever and not feel guilty."
- Leann, at Drake University in Des Moines, Iowa, said that her male friends "seem to move from relationship to relationship with an ease that neither myself nor my girlfriends can do."
- Monique, in Riverside, California, said she admired "men's ability to conduct business and have sex without emotion."
- ". . . that they don't let things get to them. Just once, I wish something could hurt my feelings and I would not cry about it."

Many of these women do not seem entirely conscious of the inherent contradiction in admiring something that they tell us they hate about us. Other women we heard from were aware of the contradiction, and they weren't quite sure what to make of it. On one level, these are things they really do hate about men; on another, they love the very same things. (Hey, nobody ever said it was easy to be a woman . . . or a man.) Take this comment from Chris, a 39-year-old home-maker and mother of two in Canada.

There are some men who think that the main purpose of a woman is to have sex. And every woman they see walking by, they imagine having sex with. Oh, I hate their posturing. "Look at the tits on that one!" And just saying it for the benefit of each other. I've known men like that. And then I've known men like my husband, who are very sensitive. When somebody calls a woman a chick, he takes umbrage. He's very much a feminist in some ways.

Intellectually, I find that really attractive, that attitude. Somebody who thinks we have equal rights and women are to be respected, blah, blah, blah. And if they do think a woman is attractive, they don't feel the need to tell the world about it when they see her walking down the street.

But on the other hand, I like to be submissive in some ways. And I like the male thing, essentially. On a one-to-one level, I like to feel like a man is a protector and a little more aggressive sexually than me. So it really doesn't coexist well.

She wants him to be forceful and manly; she wants him to be the sexual aggressor; she wants to submit to him. But she doesn't like men who are *too* sexually aggressive, *too* domineering, *too* overt in their sexual admirations of women. If they think a woman looks terrific, they're supposed to keep quiet about it, but still be sexually aggressive. Is it any wonder that guys are confused?

Other things that women say they admire about men are the same things they say they don't like about women.

Just as an aside to any woman who may be reading this: Look, we did not ask for this stuff. We weren't setting some sort of cunning trap in order to elicit all the dirt about women. We did not offer them cookies or a free weekend in Las Vegas or anything else. Our respondents merely offered these frank and unflattering observations about themselves and their female friends, as a way of saluting men. We appreciate their candor, we really do.

One of our female respondents offered this, for instance: "What I admire most about men is they do not have the incredible need to put other men down. They are not in competition with one another. They are not afraid of one another. They don't size up the competition and degrade each other the way women do. They don't let women get in the way of their friendships with other men. Women will drop their best friends from second grade just to get a man, it seems."

- "It seems to me that men are good at making a decision and sticking to it without flip-flopping back and forth like a lot of women do," said Connie, in Strasburg, Pennsylvania. "They seem to make decisions based on logic rather than emotion."
- "I admire men's confidence and that they aren't petty like women and that they tell a friend when they are mad at them."
- Clarise, in San Mateo, California, told us, "Men don't seem to go through the whole, 'Does she really like me? What does she mean when she says I look good in this? Does saying she likes my hair today mean she didn't like it yesterday?' thing." Uh—yeah, we know. And thank you for that, Clarise.
- ". . . that they can usually say what's on their minds to their friends without them analyzing their clothes, mannerisms, etcetera."
- "I think men take a lot from women. I mean, we can be real bitches sometimes. You have to admire anyone who can put up with that."
- "I admire men's patience; the fact they're nonjudgmental, and they usually don't gossip. Women are frequently jealous and catty (especially if you're clever) or petty."
- "I admire that men don't bitch and they don't talk about their friends."

- "I like the way men can get mad at each other, argue about it, and be best friends again the next day," said a woman in Bear Creek, Pennsylvania. "They don't stay mad. When something goes wrong, they consider all of the facts and do what needs to be done to make it right."
- "I admire how down-to-earth men are—not gossipy or backstabbers."
- "Men seem to have a great ability to get mad and be done with it. Women stay mad."

Lots of women appreciate the fact that men are not obsessed with their own physical appearance, like—well, women.

As Fran, in Pottstown, Pennsylvania, put it, "I'm jealous that my husband can walk around in the nude and not give a shit. He likes being in his skin."

"I admire men's chests and butts, and the fact that they don't worry about their appearance," said Deb, in Prenacook, New Hampshire.

"I like the fact that most men don't really care what they look like, and look great because of it," echoed another.

> "Men don't seem to go through the whole, 'Does she really like me? What does she mean when she says I look good in this? Does saying she likes my hair today mean she didn't like it yesterday?' thing."
>
> —CLARISE, San Mateo, California

Lots of women really don't like being in their own skin, apparently, judging from the relentless monthly onslaught of women's magazines that all promise to show women how they can be different than what they are (skinnier, prettier, more desirable, with a bigger this or a smaller that). Of course, let's face it: Women have a lot tougher time of it than we do, since advertising, the media, and women's magazines are forever holding up the most fabulous-looking 17-year-old girls in the world and implying that all women should look like that. Nobody really expects the average guy to look like a 17-year-old bodybuilder named Brutus.

But here's something else that many women appreciate: Lots of guys don't care about women's minor imperfections, either. They don't hold themselves up to the standard of Brutus the muscle man, nor do they hold the women in their lives up to the standard of that busty, pubescent bombshell in the lipstick ad.

As Jamie, a 24-year-old theater director in Baltimore, told us, "I think that what the media makes look sexy is unrealistic." And, she adds, most guys don't fall for it. "Girls worry about it more than guys do. Most of the guys that I talk to don't expect girls to look like Pamela Anderson Lee and are very turned on by girls who don't."

Jamie, on behalf of decent dudes everywhere, we thank you.

A surprising number of women mentioned how much they like men's hands.

Guys tend to think of their hands as exceptionally useful tools, like cordless drills or meg-loaded laptops, not as something that can add a little shine to their sex appeal. Too bad. Because many women love how expressive men's hands can be. What is it that they like? Here's the killer combo: Power combined with gentleness.

- Teri, in Nashville, said it beautifully: "I admire men's hands, how much bigger they are than mine. How much power is there, yet they can be so incredibly gentle, especially with a much smaller, softer woman's body. How such a powerful, much larger human being can melt, defenseless, when he's with a woman he really likes."
- "I just love men—the fact that they are male. Strong arms, good hands, nice smiles," said Deborah, in Long Island, New York.
- "I love men's hands," said a woman in Pittsburgh. "Also, how they don't judge like women do."

- "What turns me on? A man who puts my pleasure first, or at least equal, is definitely a turn-on. A man with ambition is also good because who wants to date someone who is going nowhere? A good job doesn't hurt. And to conclude this answer, I leave you with this: sexy hands!"

It's also true that women really do love the part of you that they see when you're leaving.

In our scientific survey, we asked women what they considered to be a man's most attractive physical feature. The three most common answers were all above the Adam's apple: eyes, face, and smile.

> "I just love men—the fact that they are male. Strong arms, good hands, nice smiles."
> —DEBORAH, Long Island, New York

That may well be true. But the next most common answer—and one that our female magazine-survey respondents mentions so often that we couldn't ignore it—lies slightly to the south of your smile.

Theresa, in Richmond, Virginia, told us that the first thing she looks at when she looks at a man is "his butt, then his eyes." Hmmm, how does she see both at once?

Another woman said that the thing she admires most about men is "a sense of humor, brains, and a tight butt."

"What I admire most in men (besides nice round butts) is the self-discipline to reach their personal goals no matter what the obstacle, while being trustworthy and kind at the same time," said a self-described happily married 29-year-old woman in Fort Payne, Alabama.

Quite a few women these days say they prefer a man's posterior in boxers rather than briefs. Amy, a 24-year-old admissions director at a Baltimore nursing home, said of her new boyfriend: "Some times he wears his sexy little boxer shorts that are tight, and he looks good in them. They look really cute on his butt. I like him and I like his butt, and every time he turns around I look at it and try to grab some."

And a woman in Santa Ana, California said, "Their eyes, their physiques, their butts. Okay, everything." Gosh, we're starting to feel like sex objects.

How do they love thee? Let us count the ways.

There was a sort of grab bag of assorted comments about what women like about us, from a whole lot of women we'd love to get to know better.

- "I love the combination of strength with softness," purred a woman in Seattle. "Physical beauty, especially long dark hair (clean) and steely eyes. I love to release his long hair from a tieback and watch it fall over his shoulders, tangle my fingers in his hair, etcetera."
- "I love how sexy men look asleep. I love when they love someone or something very much and try not to show it but it's obvious."
- A woman in Long Island, New York, said she admired "how most men believe they can conquer the world because they have penises."
- "I like men's humor, their friendships with other men, and, usually, their ability to be responsible (when they are)," said Tess, of Santa Clara, California. "I admire men who are strong inside without being macho or arrogant. Physically, I love men's legs, and a nice set of wide shoulders always turns my head (unless my partner is there)."
- Cheryl, in Newark, New Jersey, said, "Men can be very macho, and then turn around and be boyish within seconds. I like that a man can show both sides to a woman. It's very sexy."
- "I admire men who are so secure in themselves that they can give freely and openly without insecurity in their manhood," said Gloria, a therapist. "I know I will get a thump on the head for this, but I like how it feels to be hugged by strong arms and hands when I need the security. Being an independent woman, I don't need a man to take care of me emotion-

ally or financially, so I don't care about their caretaking abilities. Basically, I see men with as much admiration as women for the great people they are, rather than a gender."

- Connie, in Barnes, Texas, said she liked men's "ability to be hard towards life and soft towards their families."
- ". . . that they can pee standing up."
- Mary, in Sarasota Florida, said, "their strength, compassion, and ability to be so sweet and gentle while still being incredibly macho."

Some women—God bless 'em—really do appreciate the bind that men are in these days.

You come up behind a strange woman just as both of you are getting ready to pass through a door. Is it more politically incorrect to (a) hold the door open for her or (b) let her open the door herself?

The answer is, both are politically incorrect. If you allow her to open the door herself, are you affirming her power and independence as a person or just being rude? And if you open the door for her, are you being an old-fashioned gentleman or just an old-fashioned chauvinist pig? After all, doesn't opening the door put her in a subservient position, as if she were a child incapable of doing it herself, as if by opening the door you were giving her permission to pass through? Aren't you, in some ways, implicitly demanding an imperial tribute in the form of a thank-you, whether she asked for the favor or not? Isn't there . . . ?

Oh, just forget it. For decades now, the safest thing for men to do has simply been to use a different door. Courtesy is too complicated.

We'd like to end this chapter with some heartening news: Lots of women out there really do understand and appreciate

> "I love how sexy men look asleep. I love when they love someone or something very much and try not to show it but it's obvious."
>
> —ANONYMOUS

how difficult it can be to be a guy these days. They recognize the conflicts and contradictions inherent in all of the things that women seem to be asking of us.

- Lorraine, in South Bend, Indiana, said she admires the fact that men "haven't given up on us. In this feministic age of picking up the check ourselves but still wanting the car door held for us, I really respect the fact that they do try to find that delicate balance between classic courtesy and classic chauvinist, no matter how many millions of ways their actions may be misinterpreted."

- Rosie, in South Carolina, said she "admires men's ability to live in a society that is not 100 percent fair to them. For example, women can wear men's clothing, no problem; but let a man put on a dress and he is considered homosexual. Women who hold 'male' jobs are admired; but men who are dancers, nurses, stewards, or hairstylists are assumed to be less of a man."

- "It's more difficult to be a man these days," said Teri, in Nashville. "The double standard applies to them, too. They shouldn't be too emotional, yet they should be sensitive enough not to be branded an insensitive clod. They're still expected to be macho in some circumstances, yet have to turn it off when around the modern woman."

- Gale, in Philadelphia, told us, "I admire men's ability to find the strength to go on and do what has to be done, in terms of working overtime or tackling hard projects at home when they know their family is counting on them and needs them to take charge. I admire the huge effort they're making now to understand women better, and their willingness to go out of their way or do something totally out of character in order to keep the woman in their life happy. And I admire their ability to maintain some sense of their own masculinity in a society that's pressuring them to become more like women ('sensitive,' emotional, etcetera)."

So there you have it guys. Feel better now?

CHAPTER FIVE

Our Bad Points: What Women *Don't* Love about Us and How We Could Do Better

YOU WANT TO KNOW HOW TO PLEASE A WOMAN? For starters, make sure you smell clean. Shut up about the details of your past relationships. Don't move things toward the bedroom too fast. And when you ogle other women, be very, very discreet. Did we say very, very discreet?

Well, sure, buddy, we understand your position: You didn't buy this book to get a bunch of grief from women. If you needed somebody to criticize your every waking move, you could get it for free at home.

We know, we know. Same with us. We're on your side, pal.

But you have to understand this: We decided to include the following laundry list of female complaints because we figured that there has to be a way to turn them to your advantage. If you can just bear with these whining, complaining women for a moment and listen without getting defensive, you may learn something useful about how to attract, keep, or please a woman. That would be worth the trouble, wouldn't it?

More than likely, she has a better sense of smell than you do. So try a little harder to keep clean.

This is a biggie, fellas. A real biggie. In fact, we heard so many complaints about malodorous males that eventually we had to admit that we probably do smell worse than we realize. Check yourself right this moment, just to make sure.

Cheri, in Michigan, complained that her biggest problem with her man was "not being clean (showering, etcetera). Smell is important!"

"When I first start dating a man, it turns me off if he is not well-groomed or doesn't smell good," said another. "I put a lot of thought into what I wear, how my hair is done, etcetera. A man who shows up and doesn't smell good or look like he's put an effort forth may as well go home."

When asked about the source of her biggest arguments or misunderstandings, a woman in Juneau, Alaska, said "our biggest arguments and hard times have been over his personal hygiene."

You get the picture. We won't beat you over the head with it (though she might).

If you take a moment to consider the biology of human mating, all this is not too surprising. "Every person smells slightly different; we all have a personal 'odor print' as distinctive as our voices, our hands, our intellects," writes Helen Fisher, Ph.D., an anthropologist at Rutgers University in New Brunswick, New Jersey, in her book *Anatomy of Love*. When two humans kiss or cuddle each other (just like when two dogs sniff each other), they are in effect checking out each other's "odor print" to make sure they'd make a suitable mate. If they smell like overripe cheese, the message is pretty clear: no.

People are also hardwired to react emotionally to smells. That's because when you detect an incoming aroma, it's transmitted via olfactory nerves to the olfactory bulbs and thence to the limbic system, a primitive part of the brain that controls both emotions and sex. Anatomically, your emotional reactions and your sexual reactions are linked. So if you stink, it's no wonder that women get turned off. On the other hand, if you smell like oiled leather, fine cognac, and cologne, your chances improve dramatically. Not for nothing are perfume and cologne called sex in a bottle.

It's easy to turn women's superior sense of smell to your advantage. Just make a more devoted effort to wash, shower, and stay clean. Consider soap the world's cheapest, most readily available aphrodisiac. As Cindy, from Naperville, Illinois, told us, "It definitely turns me on when a man looks and smells clean, like he just stepped out of the shower."

Hey, how difficult could that be?

Shut up about the details—particularly the sexual details—of your past relationships. Women absolutely hate hearing them. (Don't you?)

The big mystery is why so many guys simply can't resist waxing rhapsodic about their ex-lovers when in the presence of their current ones. Think about it: What message, exactly, is this supposed to convey? That the woman you're with is just another fish in the sea? That her physique and performance are constantly being compared to somebody else's? That you yourself are the studliest of studs, whether she knows this or not?

Actually, the usual effect is to make her think of you as "el jerko maximo."

- "For me, a big sexual turnoff is the man who seems to have to brag about his past conquests; for instance, 'The last lady I was with looked like Heather Locklear,' " said Lynn, in Midlothian, Texas.
- "I get really turned off by a man talking about his ex-relationships right away in a new relationship, especially while in bed," one woman complained.
- "Any time men talk about their past relationships when you first get to know them is terrible," said Cindy. "What she looked like or her age is not important. Also, making up huge stories about their careers or activities just to build up their egos can actually make them look like less of a man."

We know you're great; you know you're great. So shut up about it. Women hate men who brag too much.

They want to feel secure that you are competent, that you can take care of them, that they aren't going to get stuck carrying you across the desert on their backs or paying your bills. But they don't want to hear about all that money you make and how important you are.

- "Bragging about money will turn me off quicker than anything," said Sherry. "I lose interest real quick when I start hearing how much was spent on this or how much is in the bank. I'm totally uninterested in his money. I can earn my own. A man who is gentle with children and animals is a big turn-on. When he wants to take time to pay attention to them, I'm there. If my brain isn't turned on, my body won't be, either."

- "Egotism is a huge turnoff for me," said Tami, a twice-divorced mother of four living in Broomfield, Colorado. "A man who sits there and waxes eloquent about his accomplishments and how wonderful he is makes me believe two things: (1) He's trying to convince himself that he's wonderful and (2) if I get out of this date without 'hurling,' I'll never date again."

- "To me, the biggest turnoffs are smoking, excessive drinking, drugs, lack of hygiene, false bravado (sports, machismo), egomania, trying to make out to be something you are not . . . that peacock thing," said Laurie, in British Columbia.

- "Arrogance is a major annoyance," offered another woman. "I can tolerate many things, but a man who talks too much of himself or is more concerned with how he looks than how I look is a turnoff."

Whoa, partner! Don't move things toward the bedroom too fast.

For more on this particular story, see chapter 9. But we also include a few women's comments here because this is

probably the oldest female complaint of all, undoubtedly pre-
dating the pyramids. It's not necessarily that she doesn't want
to roll in the hay with you. It's just that she needs to make a
personal, emotional connection with you first.

- "It really turns me off for him to be blatantly sexual during
  the first few dates," wrote a woman from Des Moines,
  Iowa. "A woman wants to be romanced and cared about.
  A lot of men want a prostitute without having to pay! One
  man started asking me about
  where we were going to have
  sex before he pulled out of
  the driveway on our first date!
  He was a handsome doctor,
  but I never went out with
  him again. If I want a pelvic,
  I'll pay for it in-office. What
  turns me on is gentleness,
  asking what I would like to
  do, flowers, and long, deep kisses that last 3 days."

  > "For me, a big sexual
  > turnoff is the man who
  > seems to have to brag
  > about his past conquests;
  > for instance, 'The last lady
  > I was with looked like
  > Heather Locklear.'"
  > —Lynn, Midlothian, Texas

- "Real turnoffs are pressuring me to get involved sexually
  too fast (makes me think that's all he's after) or trying to
  make the relationship move too fast in general (for example, calling every day after our first date)."
- "First kiss: tongue down throat. . . . I don't know you that
  well, honey!" said a woman in Winnipeg.
- "When a man shows me that his interests are merely
  sexual, it can be a major turnoff."
- "He tells you he is madly in love with you, you are just the
  greatest woman he has ever met, and you are the best in
  bed, within the first few days of the relationship," complained one woman in Atlanta. "You know that he is lying
  and just saying what he thinks you want to hear. Wrong!"
- "In the start of a relationship, the thing he can do to turn me
  off is be more concerned about the outside, not taking time
  to ask questions and get to know the real person living

within," said Betty, of Port Charlotte, Florida. "And being interested in sex so early in a relationship. . . . He would need to be slow and learn to know me. What might turn me on would be the opposite, taking that time to get to know who I am and what I am all about."

Sure, you're going to keep on ogling women, whether she likes it or not. Just remember, when you're with her, be sure to do it very discreetly.

"Ogling" is a crude word that doesn't quite do justice to the ancient male practice of treating women who are not one's wife as eye candy. We're not going to tell you to stop doing it. And most reasonable women won't tell you to stop doing it, either. For one thing, they know that telling you to cut it out wouldn't do any good. For another, nobody spends more time ogling women than women do. Why else are women's magazines packed from cover to cover with images of fabulous female bods? (Okay, it's not precisely the same thing, but it's close enough to count.)

> "If men would look at the women they are with the same way they look at the women they aren't with, they would be amazed at the result. Men always seem to be looking for something better, and we notice that."
>
> —ALLISON, Billings, Montana

The bottom line is, just don't let her see you do it. A woman named Susan explained the proper technique: "If a guy ogles other women in a really obvious way, I know he is just too pathetic for words. But if a guy can manage to be utterly charming, polite, and discreet at the same time, I'm hooked."

Another woman put the whole thing considerably more bluntly: "It's a big turnoff if a guy comes off as cocky, like you're so lucky he's spending any time on you, so don't bitch if he's distracted by the big set of knockers that just walked by."

Passing gas may impress your friends, but it doesn't impress your girlfriend.

If you're one of those guys who likes to crow, "Greetings from the interior!" after you pass gas, you'd better read this. Most women just don't think it's funny (especially after the 25th time). In fact, breaking wind, spitting, and belching probably didn't even impress women back in Neanderthal times. Women mentioned these, uh, indelicacies so often that we felt it was our duty to pass along their views on the subject. Here's what one anonymous survey respondent had to say, which basically sums up the collective female position on bodily functions.

"In the early stages of a relationship, it's easy to weed out the losers. Come on, guys, the obvious answer here is: If you burp, blow your nose, or make any other 'natural' body sound, have the decency to try to do it out of the room, or at least don't feel the need to announce it. Sure, all guys say they'd never do that, but think back: You've done it before at least once. That does not get us hot and bothered, just bothered."

If you want her to stay slim and fit, and look good, you ought to do the same yourself.

At the heart of feminist gripes against men is the issue of fairness. Women don't think it's fair if men get paid more for the same work, or if men don't pick up their fair share of the housework. But women also don't appreciate it if they're the only ones who go to great lengths to keep up appearances.

"I think that men should make an effort to eat healthy and stay in shape, especially if their wives keep their weight down and work out regularly so they can look good for their husbands and themselves," one woman told us. "Just because a man marries, he shouldn't get so comfortable with his relationship that his appearance doesn't matter anymore."

Another woman, equally peeved, put it this way: "There are, without a doubt, two things that women in our circle of friends agree drive them crazy regarding men: (1) Like a pea-cock, they preen to catch their bait, and once caught, let themselves go with no regard for themselves or for their mate; and (2) men have a tendency to disregard their health, waiting until it's almost too late to prevent some illness. Women, on the other hand, go to the doctor at the first sign of trouble."

Lots of women say that they really don't like "that macho-man thing."

> "A man who is gentle with children and animals is a big turn-on. When he wants to take time to pay attention to them, I'm there. If my brain isn't turned on, my body won't be, either."
>
> —SHERRY

In the previous chapter, women told you how much they love men's hands, especially if those hands are both strong and gentle. Strength combined with gentleness: It's an unbeatable combination. (In fact, that's the combo that's implied in the word "gentleman.") On the other hand, if you get strength without gentleness—with a little bound-less male ego thrown in—what you get is "that macho-man thing" that women told us about. And we can tell you one thing for sure: They don't like it.

"Being selfish sexually is the biggest turnoff for me," said Tarita. "The whole macho-man thing is really outdated, and of course, it runs over to their personalities. You can't be a selfish, self-centered jerk outside the bedroom and turn into Don Juan in the bedroom."

"Most women, I feel, will always wonder why so many men have to put on a macho front to be a man," said Vicki. "Some men go too far with it. It's not attractive. I feel that it is a sign of immaturity."

Let's face it, sometimes women object to things for reasons that only Albert Einstein could ever figure out.

We got our fair share of women who strongly disliked things that it would be hard for even the most reasonable of men to anticipate. For instance, one woman told us that what really turned her off was "when he talks about himself incessantly and has a 1960s attitude. He actually liked the '60s." Marital therapists are fond of saying that communication is the key to a long-lasting relationship—and when it comes to something like this, you have to admit that it's probably true. How else are you supposed to figure out that the reason she doesn't want to go out with you again is that she can't stand Grace Slick?

Here are a couple of other gripes that you probably wouldn't have guessed in a thousand years.

- Karen, from West Trenton, New Jersey, told us her top-three turnoffs: "Brags, no sense of humor, and thanks me after sex."
- Another said, "Releasing bodily functions, picking nose, or wearing socks while having sex."
- "Turnoff: longish nails. I don't care if they are squeaky clean; it still conjures up images of drag queens, coke freaks, and pedophiles. I also can't stand racists, fascists, loud and arrogant men."
- "I am turned off when men are easy to get. I like the hunt."
- "Well, I'm married, so it's been a while. But thinking back, a real personal turnoff would be a man being overly nice. Yes, I think there is a limit to how nice a man should be. For example, when I was in high school, I went to the prom with one guy and I wanted to get pictures with another guy (who was a friend). The guy who took me to the prom offered to pay for the pictures of me with the other guy. I thought that was a real turnoff—way too much. Of course, I paid for my own pictures."
- "I cannot stand it if someone seems overwhelmed by my

mythical greatness. I haven't got a problem with self-esteem; that's not the issue here. No one is a goddess, everyone has issues, and it's that much harder to talk about your issues with someone who thinks you have none."

- "Too much contact is a turnoff," said Jeanette, of Albuquerque, New Mexico. "Holds my hand or keeps an arm around me constantly, calls every day and talks too long, makes a point at the end of each date to nail down the time and place we'll next be getting together. Makes me feel flattered, but also trapped."

Finally, we present the gimme-a-break file.

We told you at the beginning of this chapter that we were on your side, pal—and we are. Just to prove it, and just to add a bit of balance to the foregoing dismal riff of male bashing, we'd like to share to a few choice tidbits from something we came to call the gimme-a-break file. That is, stuff that practically knocked us off our seats.

Men have their fair share of flaws, granted; you just heard about some of them. But to be entirely fair, women are not exactly angels, either, and some of them were candid enough to admit it. (To our female readers: Hey, we didn't say this stuff. They did.)

Sandy, in Morganton, North Carolina, was kind enough to send us this one, for instance: "When most women get together, all we talk about is sex and how awful we treat you just because we can." That's funny, we seem to have had that same conversation ourselves.

A darker confession came from a woman who wouldn't give her name.

I am very evil in my manipulation, though I hate to admit this. I have done some very conniving things in my day. I have picked on his most vulnerable parts before, things I know he is sensitive about. Normally, control is the game with me. I would even go so far as to say I would fake pregnancy to hold on to my man. Or duke it out with another woman who is getting in the way.

Whoa! And women complain that men talk about their exes too much?

A couple of these women took the Gatling-gun approach to communication—basically just hosing all men, their hubbies included, for everything.

Stephanie, in New Haven, Connecticut, complained, "I wish men would say, 'I love you' more and not let it be something we just know. It's nice to hear it. And last but not least, would it kill a man to call when he says he'll call? We always wait by the phone and expect that call. That goes for beepers too."

Another woman wrote, "Turn-offs: cheap with money (doesn't have to spend tons, but don't study the check—just see what the total is and pay it); doesn't

> "When most women get together, all we talk about is sex and how awful we treat you just because we can."
>
> —SANDY, Morganton, North Carolina

call/arrive on time; thinks that sex is over after he has come, when I still haven't; too little kissing; not giving me oral sex unsolicited; excessive swearing (I'm not a buddy; I'm a woman); feeling threatened if we have different opinions about politics, etcetera; being condescending; not accepting my sexual limits, but trying to take it further too early."

Other women were of the opinion that men must have nothing but mashed potatoes between their ears, whereas they themselves will surely be nominated for a Nobel Prize any day now. Like Carol in Saint Peters, Missouri, who said, "What do women not get about men? Well, if you ask me, I think we have a pretty damn good take on the situation! We can read men, we know what their thought process is. I think that drives most men to insanity because they themselves are not equipped with a high-tech database like a woman's mind."

A woman in Salt Lake City added, "Men don't understand

that a woman's mind is constantly thinking, observing, reflecting, etcetera. Women don't understand that men's minds do not do this."

Then there's the sister from hell. "I live with my parents and three brothers. So with four men in the house, I have a lot to say, as each one has different faults. Personal hygiene, lack of table manners, not picking up after themselves, not cleaning up messes that they make, bad language, playing with the remote control, smoking and not dumping out the ashtray, lack of regular manners, not saying 'please' and 'thank you,' leaving the seat up in the bathroom, not showing up for meals, or being very late without calling. . . ." Uh, listen, lady, we'd love to talk, but we gotta go.

CAN SHE EX?LAIN IT

Dealing With the Dark Side of the (Female) Force
—KATE FILLION

Nobody's perfect, but the general impression is that women are more perfect than men. Nurturing, gentle, supportive, morally superior—you get the picture. Except that picture is not only incomplete and untrue but it also deeply complicates men's relationships with women, according to Kate Fillion, author of the Canadian bestseller *Lip Service: The Truth about Women's Darker Side in Love, Sex, and Friendship.* Fillion won a National Magazine Award, has written for the *Globe and Mail* in Toronto, and contributes to many magazines and newspapers.

Q: *You write, "According to an extensive body of research on love, sex, and friendship, men and women do not behave as differently as we tend to think; women are not mythic creatures of sweetness and light, but flesh-and-blood mortals who are capable of all the negative feelings and behavior we currently associate with masculinity." What do you think both men and women are missing by failing to acknowledge this fuller picture of women?*

A: We miss opportunities to get along better and enjoy ourselves more when we get entrenched in these positions that all men are doing horrible things to women or that women are somehow morally superior to men. Those ideas get integrated into our everyday interactions with each other on a really basic level. We lapse into talking about the so-called opposite sex very casually; it's almost second nature to most of us.

And what happens is that when we interact with men or women, we misread the other person's signals. Rather than seeing their behavior as indicative of their individuality or feelings, we see it as being indicative of gender. When it doesn't fit what we think of as masculine behavior, we can somehow twist the evidence to make it seem to ourselves, "Oh, he's just being a man; men are all pigs." Or "She's just being a woman; women are oversensitive." So we miss a lot of opportunities to understand each other better and enjoy each other's company more.

Q: *You also write, "Just like men, women can be aggressive, competitive, cruel, and exploitive. And just like women, men can be nurturing, cooperative, and submissive." Why is it that it seems surprising, even shocking, to say this?*

A: Women, in particular, have so much invested in what we think is our good reputation for being moral people, people who care about others and are sensitive and compassionate, that we ignore a lot of evidence that conflicts with that image. When we read in the newspaper that a woman has gotten into a bar brawl, say, we immediately look for evidence that a man provoked her. We think, "That's not really what she would have done if she'd had her choice."

When we see behavior that doesn't fit gender stereotypes, we try to explain it by blaming it on the opposite gender. That's why when you see a man being supersensitive and caring and all those things a woman is supposed to be, people often cast aspersions on the man's masculinity. "Oh, he's gay," or "He's a mama's boy," that kind of thing.

Q: *In many ways, what you describe has long been described in fairy tales, which are the respositories of ancient human psychological wisdom. In fairy tales, the dark side of the male is depicted as a giant who will stomp you or rip you limb from limb. But there's also the dark side of the female—the witch who will give you a poisoned apple. How did we manage to forget the truth of these ancient stories?*

A: Well, obviously, it's not politically correct. I also think the media tends to report on what confirms their own assumptions. It's much easier to write a story or do a radio broadcast that just confirms assumptions or affirms existing stereotypes, rather than challenging them. If you're mainly concerned about sound bites and getting the message out in 25 seconds, you don't have time to address the complexity of behavior. You need yes-or-no answers, black-and-white scenarios. And when you start breaking things down into polarities, you come up with "male" and "female" behavior. I really do believe that a lot of these stereotypes are promoted and sustained by the way news is reported.

What's most damaging about this way of thinking about men and women is that it allows women to avoid any sense of personal responsibility for their own behavior. Because nothing is ever your fault. You're a sharing, sensitive, wonderful person. Your biggest flaw is that you are too caring, too sensitive, and too wonderful; and therefore, anything bad that happens to you must be somebody else's fault. It can never be that you made a bad choice.

Q: *Over and over again, we heard women say, either openly or in a veiled way, "Why can't men be more like women? Why is it so hard to have deep, intimate friendships with them?" But according to you, female friendships are often based on a fundamentally adversarial relationship* *toward men. You write, "Women's sharing and caring frequently involves swapping stories about what jerks men are, and diminishing men to shore each other up." So there are enormous barriers to forming genuine friendships between men and women, aren't there?*

A: That's true. It's also true that women tend to define those "deep, intimate friendships" as involving only certain kinds of behaviors. To women, intimacy means revealing secrets; talking about deep, dark things; laying your soul open to someone. But I don't think that that's always healthy. Too much of that can be a lot like sitting around navel gazing with another person. There's a bit of a hot-house effect when you're always sitting around talking about your feelings. You tend to create problems or to magnify really small problems to the point where they seem absolutely insurmountable. You can ruin a relationship if you're always examining your feelings. You're never actually living life. It can be narcissistic, almost as if you're keeping an ongoing verbal diary of what's going on in your head—a form of mutual masturbation.

By contrast, men tend to think of intimacy as doing things together, sharing activities. I think that in some ways that can be a very healthy kind of intimacy because you're pursuing something together, you have a connection to the outside world. And frankly, I think women's friendships could benefit from more of that.

Q: *You write about the "supportive dishonesty" in female friendships, where a woman will always try to agree with or support or validate a female friend, even when she's tired of hearing her complain about something instead of actually doing something about it. Yet one of the things we heard most often from women, talking about men, was, "I just want him to listen to me without offering solutions." Doesn't this put men in a real bind?*

A: I understand why women say that—and they say it about some of their women friends too. You start talking about your bad day at work, and someone says, "Here's what you should do." It has the effect of making you feel that the other person won't let you finish your thoughts, that they're not interested in what you have to say. They're trying to shut you down and change the topic of conversation.

On the other hand, I know from giving dinner parties that you see women doing that to men all the time. The man will start to talk and the woman will shut him down, either with a witticism or with a solution: "Well, you should do this." It never gets remarked upon, however. Women don't have a reputation among social scientists for being people who offer solutions instead of listening. I know I do it to my husband at the end of the day if I'm really tired and he wants to have some long, involved discussion about something that happened at work. I will try to immediately curtail the discussion by offering a solution.

In fact, one of the reasons I wrote this book was that the whole prevailing notion that women can do no wrong didn't reflect what I knew about myself and other women that I know.

Also, I honestly don't think it's particularly supportive to simply listen to a woman go on and on for years about how she can't stand her job, for instance. I think a more supportive thing is to say, "Well, do something about it. Look for a new job."

Q: *As a practical matter, what can men learn from under-standing the darker side of females? What would help us in our relationships with women?*

A: First, women need to accept that they do have a darker side. And I think the conundrum that men find them-selves in is being with women who don't accept that they have any capacity for aggression or competition or even ambition, so they're with women who are really in denial about fundamental aspects of themselves and their desires. I don't know what a man in that situation does, because everything in the culture is supporting that woman in believing what are, in essence, lies about herself. I don't think she's going to take it very kindly when the man says, "Hey, I've noticed that you have the capacity for aggression."

You see women's inability to appreciate or acknowledge their desires when it comes to talking about sex. So many women find it hard to admit that they want to have sex. They talk about men in excruciating sexual detail, but rarely do they say, "I felt so horny that I just had to have sex right that second." It's usually, "He really wanted it" or "I was drunk" or "I was crazy about him." It's very rare that women talk about their physical desire for sex, as opposed to their emotional desire for it.

When I was interviewing women for the book, I'd talk to them for a couple of hours and eventually they'd really begin to start sounding like men, without even being aware of it. Sometimes, they'd wind up talking about chasing or hounding men in the same way that men are said to hound women. And yet it was like they walked the walk but they couldn't talk the talk. They were just in denial about very fundamental aspects of human behavior. And I understand why. It's because there's so much cultural pressure to be a good woman, a nice person, to not be that kind of girl, so it's very difficult for them to admit they do have those kinds of feelings. To me, this is one of the big difficulties between men and women now.

Q: *But if a man is in a relationship with a woman who is in complete denial about the fact that she has a darker side at all, it's very difficult for him to know what he's supposed to do. I don't want to argue and have this big discussion about feminism. That will go nowhere. Is it my job to try to change her? I'm not sure that I can or even want to.*

A: Well, the point is that you're not allowed to anymore. You're a man. I think this is what men are fumbling with right now. Even offering advice and giving solutions and being supportive in that way can be read as being oppressive or controlling. And I really don't know what you do about it. I really don't have an answer to that. I think it's a very fine, almost impossible line that men are expected to walk.

But at the same time, the standard that's been set up for being a woman is so impossible to meet that, inside, I think most women feel like cross-dressers. They feel like female impersonators. The standard for being a woman is really so tiresome on a day-to-day basis. You have to be this nice, sweet, wonderful, lovely person (all things that are going to get you totally screwed over in an office situation, things that will guarantee you'll be on the phone being whined at round the clock). And you're supposed to look very sexy and attractive and alluring all the time, but you're not really supposed to want sex. It's such a recipe for women to feel bad about themselves.

Maybe this explains why women sometimes give off such mixed messages, why they fly into these inexplicable rages. They feel they aren't living up to some cultural ideal of what women are supposed to be like. Sometimes, what they're really angry at is themselves.

PART THREE

The Dating Game

CHAPTER SIX

Across a Crowded Room

SHE'S OVER THERE. You're over here.
How do you meet? By keeping it simple. Don't get
clever or cocky. Have confidence in your
attractiveness. And if she wants to play the hard-
to-get game, well, you gotta play to win.

"I met my husband outside a bar at closing time, and he bravely approached me," recalled Andrea, a 29-year-old hairdresser in Canada. "He wasn't overbearing. He was really kind of shy, but yet he took the chance to come over and say hello. He just struck me as kind of different from the rest of the guys in the bar. And that's what I liked."

The sweetest stories of romantic connection all start out that way. Rarely is the hero dashing and bold. More often, he's the shy guy who screws up his courage. And what every guy has to learn, after much trial and error, is: There's no magic place or article of clothing or pickup line that will help you meet the woman of your dreams. Try those tactics, and you're likely to fail.

If you come off as honest and sincere, not haughty and sarcastic, that's what women want. Remember, they're nervous too.

And if you're relaxed, they can relax.

Amanda, a 21-year-old college student in Maine, recalled the best opening line she ever heard. It was hardly presump-

---

THE FACTS OF LIFE

THE EYES HAVE IT

Women say they want soul mates, so we shouldn't be surprised that they choose the windows to the soul as a man's most attractive physical feature. As for all that work on your abdominals—hey, it's not a *bad* thing.

Feature	%
Eyes	27%
Face	24%
Smile	22%
Butt	7%
Chest	6%
None of these	4%
Height	3%
Arms	3%
Legs	2%
Abs	1%
Hair	1%
No answer	4%

tuous. "This guy said he saw me walking around campus and wanted to get to know me, and it took him a while but he finally got the nerve up and just came over and started talking and broke the ice that way. It was relaxing."

There are opening lines that are funny. Leslie in California recalled her favorite: "I've lost my phone number. Can I have yours?" Some women told us that a humorous opening line, delivered as a joke, can be a fun way to meet someone. But mostly, it's a bomb.

More than one woman used the word "cheesy" to describe pickup lines. For most women, they send out huge signals that the guy is insecure, at best, and untrustworthy, at worst. Markie, 24, from Alaska, told us, "I'd much rather handle a 'Hi.' It's simple, to the point, and it's the person; it's not somebody trying to be anybody."

Carolyn, 29, of Chicago, agreed: "If they're just themselves and they admit to being nervous or whatever . . . I think a lot of guys have trouble showing their weakness and vulnerability. When they do, it's very touching. I mean, you don't want to hear everything that's wrong with them on the first date, but it's nice to see that they don't always have to be tough guys."

If you haven't quite gotten the message yet, Danielle of Philadelphia will explain it to you once again.

> Guys will ask me, "Should I go over and say this?" I've seen the 50 most used pickup lines, and they all suck, by the way. The best thing you could do, seriously, is be honest to someone, and be honest in the way that women like to be complimented. If you see a girl and you think she's pretty, pick one of her features and tell her. There is no woman in the world who wouldn't at least give you a smile and say thank you. And if she doesn't, she's a bitch and she's not worth it anyway.

Maybe we won't get anywhere by telling you to be secure if you're insecure. But we're going to try. We're going to give you some confidence boosters, straight from the women you're dying to impress.

- "It's not necessarily how he looks or what he is wearing," said Beth in Missouri. "I am more attracted by his attitude and how he carries himself. He should have enough confidence in who he is to turn his attention to others and not be the center of attention."

- "Each man has his own most attractive feature," said Sharon, in eastern Washington. "Some, their faces; some, their butts; some, their arms. . . . Don't get so hung up on the exterior. Be true to yourself, and don't be afraid to let your true colors show."

> "Some people like the chase, and some people don't. I like being chased."
> —Amy, Pittsburgh

- "All men have a sexiness about them," said Cynthia, in Whittier, California. "If they are bold or if they have blue eyes or if they have big muscles. Whatever it is, they are sexy, just like women, only in a different way. Men are great!"

- "If a man is comfortable with what he's wearing, whether it's a tuxedo or a pair of shorts, he exudes a state of sexiness," wrote a respondent to our *New Woman* magazine survey.

- "I find that when I'm attracted to a personality, the looks become attractive," said Chris in Canada. "Unless they're Quasimodo or something."

There. Consider your confidence bolstered—because you're going to need it. You know the rules: Most women won't speak until spoken to. You're going to have to risk rejection and make the first move. And the second, and third, and fourth, because if she's like a lot of women, she's going to play hard to get. You have to be astute enough to not just listen to her words but also to be aware of her body language and other cues to discern whether she's giving you the brush-off or just testing your resolve.

Leslie, 27, of California, explained how she plays the game.

THE FACTS OF LIFE

THE DRESS CODE

It's hard to look bad in a good suit, but three out of four women would rather see you in something else. The point is, clothes do not make the man. If you're on a date, wear whatever is appropriate, comfortable, and, most of all, clean. Here is how women completed the sentence "The sexiest clothing a man can wear is . . ."

A finely tailored suit	25%
Jeans and a sweatshirt	18%
A black tuxedo	16%
Khakis and a blazer	9%
A dark turtleneck	5%
A military uniform	4%
Your birthday suit	4%
Boxers	3%
A leather jacket	2%
Baggy shorts and a polo shirt	2%
A bathing suit	2%
Workout gear	1%
Other	9%
No answer	1%

I like playing hard to get. He's got to come up to me; he's got to make that first move. It's not cat and mouse, but it is a tug-of-war kind of thing between a guy and a girl.

"Can I get your number?"

"No, I'm not giving you my number."

"C'mon. Give me your number."

"What do you want my number for?"

I don't think it's ever backfired. They show more interest. They realize it's a game, and that they need to be a little persistent.

Often, the game begins before the first word is spoken.

Carolyn in Chicago explained how the game can work with eye contact—so well, in fact, that it led to dating guys she really didn't want to date.

In college, if I sensed a guy was interested in me, I would keep eye contact going with him, but kind of play it cool and not act too interested. It was totally convoluted—I would want them to notice I'm looking at them, but think that I'm not really looking at them. I look, but I don't look. It's like I'm aware of them and aware of them aware of me, but I'm not looking at them directly.

It really worked a lot, especially with guys who also play that way. But what would inevitably happen is, it would be a really bad relationship. We would never get very far because there was nothing real there. It was all a stupid game.

That is exactly why some women, like Sara in Texas, can't stand those games. Show interest in her, and she'll give you a thumbs-up or thumbs-down, with no messing around. "I can't do it," she said. "When I like somebody, I have a hard time pretending I don't like them."

Sara, we wish all women were like you. Unfortunately, they are not. In fact, many women are exactly the opposite.

The weird truth is, the more she's interested, the more she may pretend that she's not.

Listen to this snippet of conversation between Leah, 25, and Jane, 28, both of Canada.

LEAH: If it's a guy I really like, I'll be less apt to make a move. He'll walk into the room, and I might just act like I don't even notice he's there, if it's a guy I really like. If it's someone that I just think is all right and I don't kind of care either way, I'm more forward. I'll just walk up to him and ask him to dance.

JANE: You don't want to make it look like you're too interested, so you'll do that backing away. It's a wonder people get together!

LEAH: Everyone is afraid of being rejected. I think that that's the bottom line.

THE FACTS OF LIFE

WHAT ARE YOU WIGGED OUT ABOUT?

Okay, you're back in the saddle again. This time, you have more money, more sense, and . . . less hair. Don't let it undermine your self-assurance. We asked, "If a man starts to lose his hair, what should he do?" Women over 40 were especially inclined to say, "Fuggedaboutit."

Not worry about it ⇨ 91%

Shave his entire head bald ⇨ 4%

Use toupee, hair plugs, The Hair Club for Men, anything ⇨ 3%

Comb it over ⇨ 1%

Find another woman ⇨ 1%

But these ladies are so afraid that they become their own worst enemies. That's a feeling that every shy guy knows all too well.

When Leah and Jane were asked what guys should do about this, they shrugged. But we have a modest suggestion. Read "Maybe She Wants to Meet You Too" on page 125.

If you'd like to meet someone who doesn't seem to want to meet you, be on the lookout for her body language. Is she simply being nervous (a good thing) or is she sending out wave upon wave of rejection signals? If you're not getting the wrong cues, maybe you should give it one more shot. In the mixed-up world of the dating game, a little polite persistence is no big crime.

CHAPTER SEVEN

First Dates

ARE YOU GETTING PLENTY OF FIRST DATES,
BUT FEWER SECOND AND THIRD DATES?
Maybe you'll recognize your fatal error among the
sad-sack tactics described below. May we present
the definitive list of dating do's and don'ts.

Women talk so big. They say they won't settle for anything less than the perfect guy, blah, blah, blah. But when it comes down to the nitty-gritty of first-date etiquette, most women's expectations are surprisingly low.

Maybe that's because most of the men they date are cavemen.

Oh, the horror stories we heard. In our *New Woman* magazine poll we asked, "When you've just met a man, what things might he do that really turn you off? What really turns you on?" We thought we'd get a few advanced-level tips. You know, some real inside stuff. A little coaching from the big leagues.

There's no big secret to success on a first date. All you have to do is not be a psychopath or a slob.

Let's put it this way. If you can take a shower, hold a door open, and chew with your mouth closed, you've dusted 80 percent of your competition.

First, we'll run through the turnoffs. These are the things that guys consistently get wrong. After compiling the answers to more than 700 survey forms, we can safely say that there are five big mistakes. We'll describe them, and then we'll supply some typical female commentary. Here they are, ranked in order of mention (the most common first).

1. He is sexually pushy or grabby.

It's the first date, and the guy is talking dirty; he's all innuendo. He is just way too horny.

"The biggest turnoff in a new relationship is rushing. Rushing to tell you things they think you want to hear, rushing the issue of sex, rushing to try and be who they weren't in past, failed relationships."

2. He lacks a certain savoir faire in the personal-hygiene department.

Okay, let's be blunt: He stinks. He has body odor. Or bad breath. Or both. Also included in this category is, as one woman noted, "stuff stuck in his teeth." He never even looked in a mirror before walking out the door.

"If he has bad breath on the first date, I don't care if he's gorgeous. Bye-bye!"

3. He displays no manners. He's just plain gross.

He belches, farts, talks with his mouth full, scratches himself in public, and picks his nose.

4. He's arrogant and egotistical. He's full of himself. A guy who, said one woman, "talks about himself all night." Or, in the words of another respondent, "It's all about him."

He interrupts her; he dominates the conversation. Actually, if we included in this category those guys who brag about and, worse yet, invent stuff about themselves, this category would be the number one complaint.

"Any man who is too full of himself when he is nothing unique is an instant turnoff."

"Let's just say that I *do* fall for your macho act. I get to know you and we go out a few times. I ask about the ranch in Wyoming that your family owns, and your mouth drops open. You realize that you lied to impress me—now I'm really turned off."

"If you find out that something they said was not true or even not quite right, you'll never, ever give them a second thought."

5. He spends the evening talking about his ex-wife or old girlfriends.

"Ex talk," as one woman put it. What's the problem here? Haven't you gotten over them? Are you still angry? Or do you want to prove that lots of women want you?

"Sexual turnoff: Any talk of previous women."

Those five mistakes clearly outdistance all the others.

Then there are a bunch of mistakes that all got at least 10 mentions apiece. This is the sort of stuff you may have learned to hide well. And she won't spot it on the first date. But she has her antennae out, and when she sees it, she'll stop seeing you.

- He has a cocky, too-cool, macho, or he-man attitude ("that peacock thing").
- He flirts with or blatantly ogles other women ("If he does that, I know he's just too pathetic for words.").
- He's cheap.
- He drinks too much.
- He puts others down.
- He's possessive, overprotective, and jealous.
- He has a sloppy appearance ("the I-still-live-in-my-parents'-basement look").
- He swears, curses, and uses crude language ("I'm not just one of the guys, okay?").

- He's rude to people.
- He's controlling or bullying and neglects to ask her what she wants.

What's this one about? Listen.

It was pretty much a blind date. We had met once, for a short time, previously. He took me to a family-style restaurant and asked me to share a plate with him, not even asking me what kind of food I liked or anything. So he got what he wanted and I shared it and I never wanted to talk to him again.

Here's another example.

On the phone, he was just too pushy. I suggested going for coffee, but no, he wanted to go to a movie. I said, "What about Thursday night?"

He said, "What about tomorrow night?" He just got on my nerves.

We have a long, long list of things to keep in the back of your mind as you head out the door. Try not to . . .

- Appear desperate (an example: "telling you he loves you on the second date," said Lynda in La Junta, Colorado)
- Sport a know-it-all attitude
- Be insecure and clingy
- Be showy or obsessed with money
- Overdo the compliments (you'll seem manipulative)
- Dump your problems on her ("I am not a therapist.")
- Try to be someone other than who you really are
- Be disrespectful of women generally
- "Stick your tongue in my mouth on the first kiss. Yuck!"

Oh, by the way, if you say you'll call her tomorrow, call her tomorrow.

Last and definitely least, we heard about some minor stuff that's in the pet-peeves category.

- Sloppy kisses
- Negativity
- Bikini underwear
- Gold teeth
- Toe sucking
- Dirty fingernails
- Too much cologne
- No friends, no life
- The I'm-not-ready-for-a-relationship speech
- Chewing on ice cubes

Did you clear all of those hurdles? Then you are definitely call-back material. Having eliminated the major negatives, you can relax and subtly stress your positive qualities.

So what are women hoping to find on the first date? Seven characteristics clearly stood out from the pack.

1. Instead of talking about himself all the time, he focuses on her. He's genuinely interested in her and her life.

He asks questions and listens to the answers. Ideally, they end up having a good conversation together. About anything, women said. (There's no magic topic.)

"He's more interested in me than in what's going on around us."

"He asks me about my day before telling me about his."

"I like a man who listens. If he really listens, he'll pick up on little things that he can do to make me happy, things that come from the heart, not the wallet."

2. He's an old-fashioned gentleman. He's polite and courteous. He opens doors for her or pulls out her chair.

"A complete gentleman. Opening doors, going out to dinner, a movie. Being very polite and still able to be himself."

"Doesn't even glance over at me when he picks up the check at dinner."

THE FACTS OF LIFE

DO'S AND DON'TS ON A FIRST DATE

In our Magellan Poll of nearly 1,200 women, we posed a series of questions about potential pitfalls on a first date. For each of the following nine situations, we asked, "Is it a requirement, would it impress you, or would it turn you off if . . ." The bottom line here is that old-fashioned chivalry is in vogue again. And they were pretty easy on you: Your only requirement is that you show up on time. The trickiest calls are holding hands on the first date and ordering her dinner.

What if:

He arrives on time?

Required ⇨ 66%

Would impress you ⇨ 34%

Turns you off ⇨ 0%

He brings you flowers?

Required ⇨ 1%

Would impress you ⇨ 96%

Turns you off ⇨ 3%

He has the evening planned?

Required ⇨ 16%

Would impress you ⇨ 78%

Turns you off ⇨ 6%

He holds the door for you?

Required ⇨ 30%

Would impress you ⇨ 69%

Turns you off ⇨ 1%

He holds your hand?

Required ⇨ 6%

Would impress you ⇨ 73%

Turns you off ⇨ 21%

He opens the car door for you?

Required ⇨ 26%

Would impress you ⇨ 73%

Turns you off ⇨ 1%

He orders dinner for you—after asking what you'd like?

Required ⇨ 4%

Would impress you ⇨ 72%

Turns you off ⇨ 24%

He rises when you return to the table?

Required ⇨ 4%

Would impress you ⇨ 86%

Turns you off ⇨ 9%

He walks you to the door?

Required ⇨ 55%

Would impress you ⇨ 45%

Turns you off ⇨ 0%

THE FACTS OF LIFE

ALERT! ALERT! DEADLY DATE TRAP AHEAD!

Dinner is finished. The waiter places the check on the table. You made this date, you'd love to see this woman again, you have the highest respect for her, and you're trying not to do anything boorish. So when she says, "Let me split that with you. . . . I insist," you freeze. What's the right move here? She has her own career. You don't want to appear pushy or patronizing. So you say, "Uh, okay, whatever. . . ."

Bam! You're finished, pal! No matter how much money she makes, you're supposed to grab the tab. In fact, the more she makes, the likelier she'll want to see you step up to the plate. (She's suspicious of freeloaders.) Our advice: Avoid a tussle. Get up and head for the rest room; then slip the waiter your credit card.

We asked, should he:

Offer to pick up the check, and not relent when
you insist? ➪ 59%

Offer to pick up the check, but relent when
you insist? ➪ 32%

Accept your offer graciously? ➪ 9%

What if she asked you to dinner? In that case, most women will expect to pick up the check. But almost 1 in 10 would want you to split it, at least. Our advice: Whatever you do, leave a generous tip. (That's another test.) Here's how women see the issue when they made the first move.

I would expect to pick up the check ➪ 88%

I'd expect us to split the check ➪ 8%

I'd expect him to pick up the check ➪ 4%

"Women appreciate a man being a true gentleman, not just on the first date, but always."

3. He's not too embarrassed to indulge her in a little of the traditional courtship stuff. He courts her by bringing flowers, holding her hand, sending cards, and wining and dining her.

Women still love the "simple, small romantic gestures," as one woman said.

"It's nice to bring a flower. Stuff like that, guys don't do—at least in this town. A date isn't really a pitcher of beer and a game of pool."

> "I love men opening doors and treating me like a lady. Any women who don't like this are insane."
> —KARIN, Minneapolis

4. He has a sense of humor.

That doesn't mean he has to be a stand-up comic. But a shared laugh, early on, signifies a chance at a real connection.

5. He's what women variously describe as considerate, thoughtful, kind, and caring. Not just to her—most women want a man who displays this attitude to the world at large.

If a man is "caring and attentive, a woman knows that he'll be caring and attentive in bed too."

6. He's affectionate. He's not pawing her, but he is physically tender.

Women like to be touched. "Please touch me!" said Irene, in Kansas.

7. He's honest and open. He doesn't put on airs. He acts himself. He shares his feelings, which is not to say that he sits around and cries on her shoulder, but he reveals a little of what is inside him.

It's not seen as a weakness. In fact, one woman called this trait "strength of character."

"Guys, just be respectful and be true. Don't put on a show. Girls can usually sense insincerity."

"He knows what he likes, and isn't afraid to tell me and show me."

"Trust is sexy."

Here are the attractive traits that were mentioned at least 10 times.

- He's dependable, part of which means he shows up on time.
- He's friendly to others.
- He's intelligent.
- He smells good.
- He makes eye contact when he talks to her.
- He's patient with the relationship. He takes it slow, both sexually and in the overall getting-to-know-you way.
- He respects her.
- He has self-confidence without being overconfident or cocky.
- He's a good kisser.

What does that last one mean? Just how are you supposed to kiss her, besides not jamming your tongue in her mouth on the first kiss? Here are some descriptions.

- "Kisses that leave you breathless"
- "Long, deep kisses that last 3 days"
- "Warm, soft, no-pressure-to-go-further kisses"

Get the point?

Here are some other traits that women like to see in a guy, right from the get-go.

> # THE SHORT ANSWER
>
> ## DOES SHE DO THE ASKING?
>
> We asked women in their twenties, "Have you ever asked a guy out?" We'd heard that women were doing more of that, these days.
>
> - "The past few guys I've dated, I've made the first move."
> - "I think some guys get intimidated by that. Uh-oh! Strong female! What to do, what to do?"
> - "I've asked guys out after they've asked me out first. It takes some of the stress off."
> - "I'm not real good at taking risks in that area. It's very scary. So I try to put the interest out there and hope he picks up on it."
> - "I asked a guy to my senior prom. But that was when I was 18. I'm not quite as brave as that now."
> - "We were hanging out for a month before I mentioned to him that I was attracted to him."
> - "It's really nerve-racking. I can't imagine how guys do it all the time."

A man with a plan. Show up with at least an idea about what the two of you can do that evening and where you can go. She's a date, not a poker buddy.

"It's okay to ask, 'What do you want to do,' but if she says that she wants you to pick, then do it."

"Being in health care, I'm in the nurturing role, and I just really like it when someone else takes over and directs the whole thing and I don't have to know anything."

"There is no surer recipe for disaster than a guy who shows up on my doorstep and then asks, 'So . . . ummmm . . . what should we do tonight?' "

A man who's sensitive. But not sensitive and weak—that's a loser. She would like you to be sensitive and strong—the artistic type, underneath it all. She appreciates a man who gives compliments freely and in a genuine way.

A man who has passion for something outside himself. She'll be interested in someone who is "interested in the world." Someone who has a life.

And it always helps to be flexible enough to try something new, be affectionate in public, be well-groomed, give her "a secret wink," and be nonjudgmental. Keep in mind that if you can't say anything nice about someone, you shouldn't say anything at all. At least, not on the first date.

We hope you saw something of yourself in all that. If so, don't hide your light under a bushel. Since you have so many endearing qualities, we'd hate to see you strike out in the dating game because you flubbed the initial inspection. You're not crude, really you're not. You're just . . . absent-minded sometimes.

So here's a little reminder list to tape to the inside of your medicine cabinet. Call it the 12 commandments of the first date.

1. Take a shower.
2. Brush your teeth.
3. Wear something clean.
4. Arrive on time.
5. Don't make fun of the waiter.
6. Don't flirt with the waitress.
7. Be sure that some of your sentences end in a question mark.
8. Don't talk about any other woman, unless it's your mom.
9. Smile.
10. Make eye contact.
11. Mind your manners.
12. Pick up the check.

CHAPTER EIGHT

Did You Pass the Test?

YOU ARE BEING WATCHED. And she's taking notes. You don't see her clipboard, but it's there, inside her head. If she needs more data, she might just have to make a scene, embellish an emotion, make it up. Just to see if you're being totally honest with her.

"His mom doesn't like me," said Amanda, a 21-year-old student in Maine, referring to her boyfriend of 6 months. "So I wanted to see if he would stand up for me in front of her. I kind of changed the words she'd said to me a little bit. And he did; he told his mom off. I made it a little worse than it actually was. I said I was *so* upset when, really, I was just a little pissed. But I really needed to know that his mother wasn't going to be in our relationship."

Women run circles around men in some ways, and this is one of them. We can only speak for ourselves, here, but we will say two things about this anecdote: (1) If we were Amanda's boyfriend, we would have had no idea we were being set up, and (2) we never did this to our girlfriends. Not that we're so morally superior; it just would not occur to us. Like most men, we're a little too simpleminded in these matters. To use the euphemism that women commonly use to describe their mates, we're "pretty basic."

And women are not. If you're a young man playing the

dating game, let us ask you something: Has your girlfriend's behavior ever left you feeling totally confused? Does she overreact on occasion? Do sudden crises just as suddenly disappear? Then you need to understand a basic fact.

Women test men. Some women test for sport, some test to see how much control they have over you, and some test because they're unsure about you in some way.

Sometimes they test you simply to see how much you care. Megan in Chicago is one of these women.

> "I ask things or say things to kind of see how they react."
>
> —LEAH, Canada

Once in college, nearly 9 years ago, I had been dating a guy for a year or so and we were on the rocks. What I really wanted from him was some attention, so I told him that my physician felt a lump in my breast. I completely exaggerated the story, but I was willing to go to that length just for some attention. Anyway, it completely backfired. He just did not get it. I'm glad it wasn't serious because he acted like a complete idiot.

Most women won't pretend they have cancer to test your love for them. But they might leave in a huff to see if you'll run after them. It often fails because we're too dumb to realize what's up. Listen to Emma, 29, of Washington, D.C., who matter-of-factly recalled that tactic: "I've pulled the storm-out-of-the-bar, pretending-you're-mad thing to see if they follow. Ten minutes later, I had to come back, humiliated."

Playing hard to get can be another test.

It may work on you if you know she's really interested. But it won't work if she's a little klutzy at this game and does it too well, too soon. Edith, a 23-year-old student in Maine, learned that lesson the hard way.

> I met this guy one time, and we went to a bar. I really liked him, but I was playing hard to get. I don't know if I was just nervous or what. But I guess I played too hard, because he ended up leaving with somebody else. It really backfired.

Most of the younger women we interviewed admitted to having tested a guy at some point. Some, like Amy, 26, of Pittsburgh, said that they don't realize it at the time, or they realize it only in the middle of setting up the test.

> I didn't really realize what I was doing until I was doing it. And then I was, like, "Yeah, I did this on purpose, didn't I?" I was a little worried that it was just about sex, and I sort of wanted to test that notion. I got a hot new dress. I looked good in it. And I wore that to work on a day when I knew he was going to be in. "Oh, is he going to call me after this?" Well, he saw me, and he said he'd call tomorrow—and then he ended up not calling. So it wasn't a very good test, was it? I guess we both kind of failed it, although there was no way for him to win it.

Carolyn in Chicago made the same point about testing being only a semiconscious thing.

> When I test my boyfriends, I don't test them in ways that I know I'm testing them. I'll pick fights sometimes or try to prove to them that they don't actually like me, which is really stupid. But it's just when I'm feeling insecure about the relationship. So the greatest thing for me is when someone doesn't take me that seriously. Like, they can see past that, and they can see that I'm just feeling insecure. And they can give me reassurance.

Some women say that they do not create tests. "I never set the person up to see how they're going to react," said Jane, a 28-year-old Canadian. Other women told us that formal testing of their boyfriends was something they did when they were younger, more insecure, or less adept at judging character.

Once they are older and wiser, they learn to test more subtly. They simply let life do the testing, and watch the results.

"Observational testing" is what Lisa in Arizona called this method. She explained:

You can sit back and watch guys and see how they are with other women or other men. And how they are with family. I mean, a really great test is seeing how they interact with their own families. If they treat their parents like crap or treat their siblings like crap, they're probably going to treat you the same way. Those people have certainly been around a lot longer than you have.

> "The truth in a relationship is like food and water to life. With it, you grow and stay well. When you begin lying, you choke off the life and continuously live in turmoil."
>
> —ANONYMOUS survey respondent

Sara in Texas said everyone does it.

We all do little tests, especially when you first start dating someone. Like, how is he going to react to my friends? There are certain things that come up, and you kind of like make a mental note of how they react to it. Like, the first time you cry, the first time you have an issue you want to talk to them about. That's how I test people.

You've heard it said of women that they "read into everything." What they're reading is often a grander statement concerning your character, or lack thereof. More observational testing.

They're looking at the little things you do and reading bigger things into them.

"I look at strange stuff," admitted Nedina in Philadelphia. "I want to know how well you tip. If the person does a good job and you do not even show your appreciation to them, then how are you going to show your appreciation for me? If you took someone for granted after 2 hours, what will happen by the time you've been married to me for 5 years?"

That's not sneaky. That's just plain smart. Megan, who as a college kid once lied about the results of a breast exam, said she still tests guys, but now she uses the observational method.

> When I meet someone, I tell them what I do, which is teach medical students how to perform breast and pelvic exams. If they sound genuinely interested and mature, like they can handle it, then I'm interested in them. If they start making stupid jokes like they're 5 years old, which is what usually happens, then I run the other way.

Surely, some women do more man testing than others. And there's another factor at work here too.

Some guys are tested more than others. Do you bring it on yourself? Maybe.

Is your relationship out of balance? Are you staying in it because it's easy and convenient? Does she care about the relationship more than you do? Has she hinted that you could be more demonstrative in your affections? Does she use the expression "like pulling teeth" to describe your conversational style? Do you act one way when you're around her and another way when you're with your friends?

Just checking.

If you answered all those questions with "no," Markie in Alaska would like to date you. "Is he being true to himself? That's the biggest issue for me," she said. "If a guy knows well enough who he is, he's going to be the same person with everyone and have a good sense of himself. Guys like that don't really need a test."

Well, maybe one little test. Just to be sure.

CHAPTER NINE

Getting Physical

SHOW YOUR DESIRE FOR HER, AND THEN ACCEPT THE FACT THAT SHE SETS THE PACE. She has more to do in order to be ready for love. You have only a couple of things to do. Meanwhile, here's what you *don't* say about your sexual past.

It was the worst line that Dana had ever heard.

"We'd hung out for a little while that evening, and then we went back to my place," recalled the 27-year-old Texan. "This was only the second time I'd been out with this guy. We were on my couch; and one thing was leading to another kind of fast; and I knew I didn't want it to go further. Plus, my roommates would be walking in any minute. So I told him, 'I think you need to be going now.' And he said, 'Well, I need to give you at least three orgasms before I go.' "

Let's give this guy the benefit of the doubt. Maybe he wanted her to know just how, uh, unselfish he was. But that's not how he came off. After all, Dana and a girlfriend were hooting about him years later. What an overconfident jerk! He came off as a guy with way too much sexual ego, a guy who was looking for a conquest, and, furthermore, a guy who knew nothing about female sexuality. His orgasms may be a matter of simple friction, but hers aren't.

"It didn't impress me," Dana said, with understatement. "If

he was trying to impress me, he wasn't. I don't know what he thought. It was a flop. I'd prefer to give myself those three orgasms."

When we asked women to tell us their worst dating experiences, most of those experiences involved sex. They had a common thread.

Guys pushing and pawing too fast, too hard, too soon. Women hate that. Yes, even women who like sex.

These were not prudish young fogies we interviewed, believe us. Women will put up with a lot—like Leslie, for instance, whose date showed up late to take her out for her birthday and then stuck her with the check. "But that's . . . whatever," she

> "I usually ask him, 'How do you know you're ready to sleep with a woman?' "
> —NEDINA, 36, Philadelphia

said, chalking it up. "It's not one of the worst." The worst is when a guy tries to get physical on his schedule, not hers. Admit it: Most of us guys start with physical attraction and go from there. So we're ready within hours or even minutes. But women are usually much more cautious. They're not ready for weeks or even months.

The stories we heard reinforce the feedback that we got in our *New Woman* magazine survey. Those readers told us that sexual aggressiveness during the initial dating phase is the biggest turnoff.

Our interviews also fell in line with the results of our Magellan Poll of nearly 1,200 women. According to that survey, most women want you to wait at least a month or two before trying anything—and one in four said she'll let you know when she is ready.

Okay, go ahead. Say it. We know. You're thinking about the time with that girl with the tattoo. You met in a bar, and an hour later you were back at her place having wild sex on the floor. The only reason it took an hour is that you had to stop at the Piggly Wiggly for Reddi-Wip. You can't get her out of your mind, can you?

Sorry, we can't tell you where she's living now or why she turned out to be such a psycho. But we can tell you about adventurous women. Basically, they are few and far between. There is a much greater percentage of women, however, who are adventurous for a few months or a few heady years in their youth. Their only two criteria are (1) "Is this guy cute?" and (2) "Is anyone going to walk in on us?" Call it their sexual awakening. Catherine, a 28-year-old single graduate student in Chicago, said she remembers those days well.

> When I was in college, it was about feeling my independence. It gave me a new sense of self, a sort of sexual self. It felt really good and free, and I felt independent. But I am less invested in that part of me now. I have calmed down about it. I don't need to prove anything any more.

These days, she no longer indulges in sex as a weekend sport. She's cautious.

She protects her heart.

When asked if she has any personal rules that must be met before she has sex with someone new, she replied, "I have to feel safe. There are not rules like, 'You have to do this and you have to do that.' It is more like how I feel. I want to feel safe, I want to feel cared about, and I want to love a person."

Some women do have a timetable. It may seem arbitrary, but that's what they're comfortable with, and there's no quibbling or wondering or nagging or doubt. Susi, 42 and a mother of two in Philadelphia, recalled that she always had a 3-month rule. It worked for her.

> I like a partner to really want me. I mean, really want me. I would be right up front about it and say, "It's worth waiting for, so don't even complain. And if you're not man enough to

THE FACTS OF LIFE

YOU WEREN'T IN A HURRY, WERE YOU?

When it comes to getting physical, every woman has a different timetable. We asked, "When you're steadily seeing someone new, how long should he wait before initiating sex?" (Note: You can be physically affectionate sooner, and it's usually appreciated. Just don't paw.)

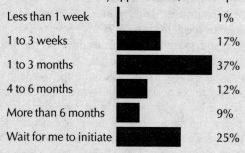

Less than 1 week	1%
1 to 3 weeks	17%
1 to 3 months	37%
4 to 6 months	12%
More than 6 months	9%
Wait for me to initiate	25%

wait, then walk away. Then you'll always wonder." And by the time we made love, they were nuts. They felt very appreciative. And I felt very valued.

Other women aren't watching the clock. Hey, this is love, not a bus route! But they are no less careful. Listen to "Trixie," a 28-year-old single lawyer in Phildelphia:

It can happen on the first date or it can happen 5 months down the line. Most people sort of know it when they feel it. For me, it's more of a culmination: We've reached a certain point in the relationship in terms of trust and openness and vulnerability. Sex is a very vulnerable thing for me. I mean, once I'm deep into a relationship, I can divorce the physical from the emotional, but that's because it's part of the context of the relationship. But the first time I have sex with someone,

it's not just a straight banging kind of thing. For me, it builds
up, and then you can have a lot of banging later on.

What Trixie assumes that you realize is something that,
say, Austin Powers had a very difficult time with: Women
want one-woman men.

Part of the waiting is for her to become emotionally committed to the relationship. And the other part is making damn sure that you are too.

"I need a commitment," said Jennifer, a 29-year-old single
human-resources specialist in New York. "I need to know that
you will not date or be intimate with any other person. I need
to come to that agreement before we have sex."

Some women, like Jennifer, will be quite up-front with you
and tell you they're not ready yet. And others, like Jodi, 26, a
divorced mom in Wisconsin, will rely on nonverbal cues and
hope you pick up on them. "There's that personal space kind
of thing. How close I sit to that person. How we sit on the
couch together—you know, things like that. I think there are a
lot of nonverbal ways to communicate that I'm just not comfortable yet."

If you think the go-slow rule is intended to make you crazy,
wait till you hear the corollary.

The more she likes you, the longer you'll have to wait.

You think we're kidding? Amy, 24, of Baltimore told us flat
out, "If I really like the person, I try not to have sex with him
right away."

Let's put it another way: The more seriously she regards
you, the more she will want to take the time that's necessary
for both of you to open your hearts, get to know each other,
and develop a deeper attraction for each other. She's not
playing games, necessarily. She recognizes the potential for a
terrific connection, and she's building up to it. (Think romance novel.) In theatrical terms: She doesn't see you as a
walk-on. You're being auditioned for the lead.

Here's the ironic part: She may have slept with some sleazeball just last week. He may be just a "fuck buddy," as Ronnie, a 25-year-old bartender in Fort Worth, Texas, calls these guys. She admitted to having two different standards. "It differs, depending on the guy. If I'm really intellectually stimulated by him, chances are, I would probably wait longer to have sex. Just because I would want to get to know him better as a person and the ultimate sex experience is going to be better in the long run. Whereas, if it's just somebody I'm sexually attracted to in the beginning, I'd probably have sex pretty fast, you know. Sometimes, the first time I meet him."

It was the same story with Andrea in Ohio. Andrea started having sex at 14; by 15, she was engaging in threesomes. She was married and divorced while in her early twenties. Then, when she was 26, she met the man who was to become her second husband. And suddenly, she was this little Rules Girl. This was not recreational sex, which she'd had plenty of and from which she had gotten herpes along the way. As she later told him during our interview, "This was going to be emotional sex, where I was expecting something from you. I had expectations of a future, so therefore, you're not getting any."

We could get grouchy about this.

We could say it's the female version of the old double standard. Warren Farrell, Ph.D., a men's-movement guru, San Diego psychologist, and author of several books on men's issues, called it the Club Med Syndrome, back in the days when Club Med still offered vacation sex for singles instead of day camps for toddlers whose parents are going parasailing. In essence, women would pair off like bunnies at Club Med, but when they got home and met Mr. Right, they claimed that they just couldn't "open up" without a commitment from him.

Dr. Farrell allows as how this reluctance "may appear manipulative to a man." He says that she's just feeling torn by the

THE FACTS OF LIFE

SHE'LL LET YOU KNOW

One of the biggest surprises in this book is the percentage of women who said that the new men in their lives should wait for them to initiate the first sexual encounter. Once they're in a relationship, most women prefer the traditional sexual scenario where the man makes the moves. It makes them feel attractive. But when they're dating, many women hate being pestered about sex before they're emotionally ready. The older she is, the truer this rule.

Under 30 ⇨ 17%

Ages 30–39 ⇨ 22%

Ages 40–49 ⇨ 28%

culture's mixed messages. Whatever. We were encouraged to hear women being honest about this contradiction, at least.

Women are complicated—have you noticed?

In the end, the truth is simply this: We didn't hear from one woman who looked back on her love life and said, in effect, "Darn it, I wish I'd slept with more guys on the first date." We did hear from women who regretted not having higher standards. Women like Dee, a 32-year-old single professor in Chicago.

I wish I had more rules than I do. Sometimes, when I talk to people and they say, "Here is my absolute minimum," I feel like they must have a questionnaire. They wait a really long time. They discuss all the possible ramifications; they discuss birth control; they discuss testing. They discuss all this stuff before they will even consider having sex. I admire that. I sort of feel, like, wow. I have done semi-risky things; and I have definitely slept with people before I felt like it was a good idea to do so. So I tend to err on the side of, "Oh, what the heck." And that's just the technical stuff. On an emotional level, I feel like, with every relationship I've ever been in, we have had sex too soon. In every case, I can say that I think it would have been better to wait.

Dee, we suspect, is more honest about her intimate life than most. By now, a new generation of women has grown up being told that any unprotected sexual encounter, any slipup, could literally kill them. Some young women say that "safer sex" is the big lie, the politically correct behavior to espouse to all of your friends or a female interviewer, but that fear of AIDS hasn't really done away with risky behavior. Single women still have unplanned, unprotected sex. They're just more reluctant to admit it. If they were really so careful all the time, then why did so many of our interviewees get tested for AIDS so often—as many as 10 times, in one case?

But some behaviors surely have changed. From what we heard, the sexual progression seems to be: Use condoms until she's really sure that you're committed to her. Then, she'll switch to birth control pills after you both get AIDS tests. It's not uncommon, at this point, for a woman to ask a guy to go get tested with her. Mating rituals of our times . . .

Because the modern woman has been told to worry about where you've been, there's probably more probing of past sex lives these days.

Some women say they want to know everything you've ever done, and they mean it. Other women say they want to know everything, and they don't really mean it.

"I do always want to know," said Jamie in Baltimore. "Although I am usually sorry once I know."

Can you walk the fine line? Talking to new girlfriends

THE SHORT ANSWER

SHOULD WE TALK ABOUT THIS?

What's supposed to happen the first time you make love? Does she want to have it all unfold tenderly and wordlessly, like a scene out of a romance novel? Or does she want to hash it out first?

- "It would be nice, but not required."
- "I have never been in a relationship where we talked about it before it happened. It happened, and then we talked about it later."
- "It takes away from the romance. I'd rather talk about it after it happened the first time."
- "I prefer it to be spontaneous, but with everything out there, I'd rather talk about it and know what I'm getting into. With my current boyfriend, we had started dating and talking about sex, and I sat down and asked him exactly, 'What were your past relationships and what are we going to do about what types of birth control and protection?' "
- "It can be kind of fun just to talk about sex first. It is kind of a turn-on."
- "I want to know what I'm getting into. I don't want to be just swept away."

about old girlfriends is a minefield. You have to know what to say and, even more important, what not to say.

There's such a thing as too much information.

"I don't want graphic descriptions," said Lori, 28, a computer consultant in Fort Lee, New Jersey. "It gets stuck in my memory and, as he's going down on me, I'll be thinking, 'He did this to such and such. I remember, he told me on the second date that he did that.' It ruins it for me because I'm thinking of the other woman."

Jane in El Cajon, California, completely agreed. "We compare ourselves to other women," she explains. "I would rather not know, because I'd feel like I'm taking way too many people into the bedroom with me."

Here's a little tip from Amy in Baltimore. Don't brag. If you can, shyly admit your inexperience. "I like knowing that he hasn't done things, which is the best part."

Now that we've gotten you safely past all of the verbal hurdles, we'd like to pass along a few snippets of advice about having sex for the first time in a new relationship.

It's okay to have condoms; she's hoping you will.

That's nice. That's appreciated. You've put thought into this, and you're being responsible. But if you fear fumbling with it in your nervousness, do not pre-open it under any circumstances. That's just too geeky. Or too weird. Or too suspicious. Said Laura, a 32-year-old Web site designer in New York City, "I would probably think, 'Well, that means he was with somebody else and they changed their minds.' I can't imagine somebody pre-opening a condom."

Nor is it cool to pull a condom out of your wallet. "I have had men pull them out of their wallets, and I'm like, 'No, you go buy them,' " said Nedina, 36, a social worker in Philadelphia. "I don't know how long that thing's been there. You've sat on it; your wallet's been hot; you won't be popping stuff in me and that sucker breaks."

Don't complain to her about condoms as if she can do something about it.

It's not like she loves condoms, said Mandy, who's 35 and single. "Everybody hates them, guys. You hate them. We hate them too. I don't like reaching through that plastic, either. I mean, honestly, who does?"

Keep it simple. Don't try to impress her with your circus tricks.

"I certainly wouldn't want him to try all those acrobatic things the first time, you know what I'm saying? Just go traditional," said Diane, a 24-year-old teacher. "Be on the safe side. Don't try anything crazy, talk to each other, then work your way into it."

After all, it could be the start of something big.

As guys, we hate to feel sexually frustrated. When we're behaving badly, we blame women for our frustration. We say they're being teases; we think they want us to trade commitment for sex. Women see this in us all the time. Even in the best of us. Sometimes they're helpless to say, "We're different. We are not built like you." But the good ones out there want you to know that they need to move at their own pace, and they're not trying to be spiteful or manipulative.

"Just because a woman says she just wants to be friends, that doesn't mean it's a roll-your-eyes, kiss-of-death situation," a *New Woman* reader told us. "Perhaps it just means that she would like to be able to relate to you on a different level. Dating can be so contrived. I'm now married to the guy I 'just wanted to be friends with,' and I strongly believe that our friendship led to the very intense sex life we have now. The whole friendship, getting-to-know-each-other thing turned out to be like a drawn-out session of foreplay."

Anna, who's 40 and lives in Huntington Beach, California, was even more eloquent on this point.

I would like for men to know that if they take the time to be with a woman and let her sexuality kind of awaken in its own time, the payoff is going to be just awesome for them. Let me be the one to decide when it's time to have sex, when I'm ready, rather than him figuring, "Okay, we had the third date. Should I make the move?" Sit back and let my sexuality unfold.

Note: All of the above makes it sound like we've never heard of virginity and saving yourself for marriage. Let us just say that people make that decision, and we honor that. After reading about all of the risk and regret that can accrue, you may be less inclined to scoff at virginity, at least. But we wrote this chapter for men who've decided to have sex before marriage. As for those who intend to wait, they skipped these pages, right?

CHAPTER TEN

Where Is This Going?

EARLY ON, SHE WANTS TO KNOW
IF YOU'RE PLAYING GAMES. Later on, she
may look for more commitment than you're
willing to give. Is it time to break up?
Just how do you do that? Here women give advice
on that subject, and it turns out that breaking up
is easier said than done.

"I have not seen anything that's made me believe that a single word he's ever told me isn't accurate or is false," said Mandy, 35, of the new man in her life, "which is great because it allows me to relax. It allows me to feel more comfortable."

Let's say you're in the head-over-heels stage of a new love. You've only known her for a little while, but you're having a terrific time. After a wonderful evening out together, we'll bet a hundred dollars that you don't go home and start reexamining the night's conversation for inconsistencies. She's your date, not a defense witness, right? And if you couldn't relax after the date, it's only because you had four bean burritos for dinner.

But Mandy is like most women. If they've been around the block a few times, they are watchful of your intentions. Their antennae are wiggling like crazy.

Their code word is "honesty"; they talk about a guy being what he seems.

What they really mean is, they are incredibly afraid of falling for a guy who doesn't even respect them or, worse yet, who only pretends to be falling for them.

This is a theme we heard over and over and over again.

"Trixie," a 28-year-old Philadelphia lawyer, made a typical plea:

> Show me who you are. If it's meant to be, the sparks will be there. Don't create fireworks if there aren't fireworks for real. It doesn't help you and it doesn't help me. Facades take a lot of time and energy. As I get older, I have less patience for that.

Emma and Carolyn are two 29-year-old friends in Chicago who got together for an interview for this book. And they, too, are wary at the beginning of relationships. "If I sense any dishonesty or player-ish type behavior, that's a turnoff," said Emma. "Trust is just the biggest thing. When a person says things that make you feel so good, then you find out it's not sincere, that's just the worst thing. That is so hurtful. I hate that. I've only had two guys be like that in my life, so that says a lot for men."

Unlike some women, Emma did not accuse all men of being dirty rotten liars. Male dishonesty is not common, but it is uncommonly painful. Her friend Carolyn explained what Emma meant by "player-ish"; to their generation, a "player" is a guy who's popular with women because he's charming and attractive—but especially charming. "He is usually very self-assured because he can woo a woman and make her fall for him. But very soon afterward, she discovers that he was not sincere. This type of guy is known for moving quickly, sexually, and being commitment-phobic. He charms a woman for a week or two or even a few months, and then moves on.

"Most women I know have fallen for the player type at

some point," said Carolyn. "And I think there's that developmental stage to dating where, when you're younger, you want to date somebody who makes a certain impression—like, they're cool or there's some quality about them that's attractive, but they're not really genuine. From my end, I try to stay away from that kind of guy now because he'll probably hurt me."

Carolyn, being perfectly fair, said this playing-games, playing-the-field behavior of the player is not strictly limited to the male sex. Despite what some very bitter women may say, not all men are lying dogs on the prowl, nor are all women belles above reproach. Women pull this stuff.

Cathy, a 30-year-old in California, was bluntly honest with one of our interviewers in the field.

> When I met him, it was important for him to feel like he was in a relationship. And he didn't want to have sex too quickly; and really, I was just getting out of a bad relationship. I was just looking to have a rebound guy and, you know, get laid, basically. I met him on vacation—he didn't live here at the time. So I pretty much lied to him. I told him we would see each other again, and that we could date and stuff. I really didn't expect it to go anywhere. And then we just really clicked, and things sort of went in the same direction.

She fooled around and fell in love. Hmmm. We ought to write a song.

As a relationship deepens, both partners watch for signs that the other may not be as committed.

Whenever one partner is unsure or simply insecure, there's jealousy. And fighting. Amanda, a 21-year-old student in Maine, described what is probably a typical argument among young couples.

> This girl came on to him—it was really obvious—when we were out together. He just stood there and talked to her like I

wasn't there. I was like, "You've got to be kidding," because if I had done that, it would have been the worst thing in the world. So we fought about that for a good hour. He told me it was my fault because I should have been up there with him anyway.

When we asked, "What was your last fight about?" most of the answers provided by young women revolved around the issue of commitment. Often, but by no means always, she wants more commitment than he's willing to give. If you look back over the big fights in your relationship, you'll probably see a pattern there. If you're unusually quiet and withdrawn, a woman might start a fight just to get a rise out of you—to see you show some passion or emotion. But that's the exception.

> "Do not force a relationship if there are too many little things wrong with it. They only get bigger."
> —JANET, Louisiana

Fights are usually about commitment. Specifically, your lack of interest in it.

"My last fight was about commitment," said Edith, 23. "I wanted more. I still do. I want more in this relationship than what he's willing to give me right now. I gave him an ultimatum: He has just a couple of more months, and if he doesn't make up his mind whether he wants me or not, then I'm walking."

For some women, commitment means "When are you going to put a ring on this finger?" For others, as for Amy in Pittsburgh, it's simply about exclusive sexual behavior. As she put it, "I'm at the point right now where I've done the non-monogamy thing, and now I'd like to try the monogamy thing." And for some young women who don't know where they'll be next year, commitment isn't about a promise to love her forever. It's about loving her right now, this very hour— and where did you leave your head, boy?

Just listen to this description of Markie's break-up fight with her boyfriend, and tell us you've never been guilty as charged.

He had borrowed my car and went to work, which was fine. He worked pretty late. And it was right before I was getting ready to leave town and return home. So I wanted to spend some more time with him. It was valuable to me; he was valuable to me. So he was supposed to get off work around 11:30 or 12:00 and, of course, return the car; and we were supposed to hang out at that point. Well, 3:30 rolls around, and I haven't heard from him. I'd gone to bed. He calls me, and he's like, "So, I'm at an employee party, and the boss came . . . and the managers; and I'll be home in a little while. Everything's fine."

The biggest problem that we had was lack of communication on his part as far as time frame. I think guys are on a different time frame. I think 'a little while' to him is like a couple of hours, and 'a little while' to me is like 15 minutes to a half-hour. So he's consistently late and, like, very forgetful. And I don't think any of it is malicious and done on purpose. But this was my final straw. I really couldn't deal with it. So I was like, "Yeah, you're coming home right now. I want my car right now."

I pretty much broke up with him over the whole thing. I was getting ready to leave anyway and start a new life. It was good timing for me, and I couldn't handle it anymore. I guess my last argument was about punctuality and courtesy and respect for other people's things and feelings.

Of course, we're not saying that all fights are really about commitment. Sometimes, they're about the way you drive or that raw chicken that you left in the fridge for 3 weeks or the fact that you're, you know, a total chowder head, basically. Like Markie's ex-boyfriend.

But if you're having a lot of fights about the commitment thing and she's always hammering you that way, it sort of makes us wonder too: Are you committed? Do you still love her? And even if you do, do you already know you'll probably never marry her?

Not everyone you love will be the right partner for you.

If that's the case, then here's what a woman wants.

She wants you to break up with her.

As a *New Woman* magazine reader scolded us all, "If you don't love someone, don't lead them on just because the sex is free and available. It is a cheat to her and you. Don't tell someone that you love them if you really don't. Be honest."

There's that word again.

Your frail little cupcake may be more ready for a split than you think.

Many men have a tough time calling it quits because of our low-down reluctance to give up the sex.

But she may have a sense that this thing is going nowhere even before you do. In which case, it's time to say bye-bye, said Rebecca in Montana.

> If you have lost that lovin' feeling, then get out of the relationship. Tell your partner the truth and get out. Don't play silly head games because you don't want to hurt her feelings. Feelings suffer a much longer period of recovery if you let your partner believe you still care. I don't want to expend my time and efforts pleasing you if you're not interested, because there will be someone after you who will love and appreciate me for who I am. So don't waste our time."

The don't-do-us-any-favors argument was also made by Carolyn in Chicago.

> I think the best way to break up is to be really honest about what you're feeling, and if you don't want to be with someone, you just need to tell them that. And that's not something they can't hear. I mean, they'll get over you.

If it's over, it's over. Face it. Say it. End it with respect and dignity.

The painful truth is better than candy-coated lies. Sooner or later, she'll find out that you lied, and then she'll feel like an idiot. And then all of her girlfriends—and some of yours—will know that you were an idiot.

We also heard a few other examples of how *not* to break things off. Don't be cold and cruel and nonchalant, like the last guy who dumped Dana in Texas. "Basically, he told me, 'I'm in four bands. I don't have time.' I knew he was in two bands; I don't know where those other two came from." (The truth is, he wanted to pursue his ex-wife.)

On the other hand, don't be so afraid of confrontation that you come off like Super Chicken, leaving a message on the answering machine or a note and, worse yet, not letting her talk to you afterward. (This is the more commonly male break-up method. Guys flunk most episodes of emotional confrontation.)

Falling into this same category is the kind of guy who, as a boss, never fires anybody—he just makes them quit. As a boyfriend or husband, he'll do the same exact thing. He'll treat her like dirt, hoping she'll leave him. That's what happened with Markie and her first boyfriend. "I ended up being the stronger of us both. I had to break it off, but I know he wanted to break up with me, and I just think he had no balls." Ouch.

No, it's never easy. As Amy said, "Of course, you can't break off a relationship with me and have it be good. I mean, that's rejection! There's hurt in every breakup. But there are ways to do it that are better or worse. It should be talked about. It should be respectful."

Lisa in Arizona adds this: "Most girls need a closure. Not necessarily a reason, but a 'Look, this isn't working out for me. Sorry.' Some girls can't handle the we-just-fell-out-of-love business, but more girls, on average, can handle that.

You learn to accept that maybe we weren't the greatest match. And you get over it."

She may call you many names. But "coward" won't be one of them.

CHAPTER ELEVEN

She's the One

SHE WANTS TO FEEL ROMANTIC LOVE
AND COURTESY AND RESPECT—FOREVER. She's
on the lookout for any clue that you are only
pretending to be that wonderfully romantic bloke
and that the romance will disappear as soon as
you are married. Oh, and pop the question in such
a wonderful, inspiring way that she'll be happily
telling her friends about it 30 years from now.

Amy, a 26-year-old from Pittsburgh, speaks for her generation when she told us: "I'm really afraid of regretting who I'm with. I'm afraid of ending up with someone and then it turning bad. And being so emotionally invested in something that I'd stay, even though it's not the right thing."

When the subject is marriage, men don't have a monopoly on fear and indecision. We heard many young women voice their fears of making the wrong choice. How do you know for sure that, out of the six billion people on this planet, you've chosen the right one for you?

This may be no consolation, but we heard middle-age women look back on their decisions and marvel that it all turned out all right.

Two married nurses in their forties got to talking about this. Ann asked, rhetorically, "How do you know who you marry, anyway? You don't really know till you start living together. They could turn out to be anything. All you do is fall in love or lust. You fall in lust, you get married, and you don't really know what they're going to turn into. And then you throw each other challenges, like kids. My husband says, 'If you had any idea what life would be like at 6 o'clock every night in this house, who would ever do it? Who would want this?' "

Ilene replied, "And yet it seems like everybody who doesn't have it, wants it, which is really interesting. We're in nursing, so we work with a lot of single women, and some of them are miserable because they think they're missing so much. They don't have the husband; they don't have the children; they don't have the picket fence. And it's easy for us to sit back, because we have it, and say, 'What's wrong with you guys? Just enjoy your life. Enjoy what you have.' But they're thinking they should have this."

> "The trick is to marry a nice person."
> —CHERYL, 51, Philadelphia

Whether they're single or married, young or old, virtually all heterosexual women continue to pursue an ideal that is brand-new in human history: romantic love within marriage. They're trying to find it, keep it going, get it back, or get it somewhere else.

At a late-afternoon gathering in Brooklyn, we heard Kay, a 55-year-old librarian, ask a half-dozen other women, "Have all of you figured out why you married your husbands? A friend of mine who's a psychologist, I remember once, we were walking and he said, 'You know, you marry whom you deserve.' I've struggled with that, but in many ways it is true. You think that you marry for reasons that are up here. I suspect it's mostly for reasons that are way down here, for reasons that you're mostly unaware of. And it's that current that continues through a marriage. Hardly anybody makes a mature choice. It's just undercurrents."

We're awfully sorry. If you think you're going to have your big problems solved by women who've gained wisdom and maturity, you'll be disappointed. They're still puzzling over the mysteries of their own lives. They did not say much about yours, other than, "What's the hurry? Make sure she's the one for you."

For example, here's some free advice from an anonymous woman who answered our Magellan Poll.

> Don't propose to a woman unless there are no doubts in your mind that she's the one, or 10 years from now you'll be the man at work who never wants to go home to his wife.

Okay, that's good, you can go along with that.

How do you know when she's the one?

It must be wonderful when the heavens seem to open and place your lifetime partner before you, all radiant and shimmering. Some vision like that must have happened to Lana's husband.

> We only dated for a couple of weeks, and we decided to get married. We got married in 4 months. He had two children and I had two children, and we just hit it off. We were not even looking for anybody. We decided that we didn't need a man or a woman in our lives. It was too much of a hassle. Then we met each other. He told me the first night we went out that we were going to get married. I told him he was a fool.

Eighteen years later, they're still married and living in Ohio. And we all envy their clarity.

Especially when so many people think they know their partners, then get married and find out that they really don't know their partners.

In researching this book, we were struck by the anger and resentment of so many married women who answered our Magellan Poll.

But the numbers seemed to belie the bitterness: Two-thirds of the married or paired-up women answering our poll gave their relationships overall scores of 8, 9, or 10 on a scale of 1 to 10. But, given space at the end of the survey to impart some final words of wisdom, many women grabbed the chance to vent. Some felt particularly deceived by the court-ship process. Okay, so not every guy can be as wonderful as we are, personally. But we had to wonder what, exactly, they were expecting.

Did they really believe that the rest of their lives would be a Harlequin romance?

Listen to this diatribe from Lois in Michigan.

> You should be yourself right from the start. You shouldn't spoil a woman with attention if you're not like that at all. All too often, men spoil women with attention and affection until they win them over. Once they know they've got you hook, line, and sinker, they stop and tell you that they are not really like that, nor do they even care to be. All the "just because" gestures that you thought meant everything were nothing more than planned plots to win you over. The only time you're wanted or needed is behind closed doors as a sexual partner, and that's it. Wow, isn't that fulfilling?

Do we detect a note of sarcasm there, Lois?

Both men and women change after marriage. Both sexes are on their best behavior during the courtship process, and neither has a lock on the age-old gambit of self-promotion. But you would not know that to hear complaints like these:

• "I had the perfect boyfriend. He loved everything I loved, was sweet, caring, and romantic. He complimented me constantly and was very loving. He is now my husband, and there is absolutely no romance in our lives. He is only con-cerned with himself and what's important to him. So be who you are from the beginning so women know what they are really getting in a mate."
• "The biggest error men make is when, at the beginning of a

relationship, the man tends to put on airs or even over-impress her just to bait the hook, and tends to hide the real him. Once the impression stage is over and the comfort-ableness stage begins, he becomes less understanding, less romantic, shows less courtesy. He doesn't try as much to look attractive for her anymore."

We don't know what's behind these tales of woe. We're only hearing her side, and it's all his fault. Yeah, maybe. We also know that men feel deceived too. But they make jokes about it. Like this old chestnut: "Scientists have discovered a food that diminishes a woman's sexual desire by 90 percent. It's called wedding cake."

Here's the best, bitter-free advice out of all that: "What men do to get a woman interested, they should keep doing to keep a woman interested," said Gail in Pennsylvania. "A life-time full of mutual common courtesy and understanding goes a very long way."

There will be disagreements and moods and change and fights, but you'll fix that if you actually like each other.

"In the end, you want to know that you're dealing with a respectful, decent, loving, fair human being," said Sunny, a 45-year-old teacher in Brooklyn, "despite the misfirings in communication. And I think you can handle the misfirings in communication if you think that at heart he's caring, loving, respectful. Right? Because you expect the blips and the misunderstandings. They're annoying, but I don't think you get divorced because of them. You get frustrated, but not divorced."

If male deception during courtship were really pandemic, you might get more women wanting to live together before marriage just to see whether the SOB shows his true colors. It's a solution that enjoyed a heyday in the 1970s and 1980s, but a new generation of women is wary of it. We asked 10 women in their twenties, "Is it a good idea to live together before marriage?" Only 1 in 10 responded with an unreserved "yes." The others were politely respectful of differing opinions—but when they got down to it, they were adamantly opposed to the idea, personally. They called it a cop-out and a really stupid move if done just to save on rent. Markie, 24, spoke eloquently:

> This is a big, big, issue that is really part of our generation right now. So many of my friends have either lived with a long-term boyfriend or have just started living with one. It's very much a part of my surroundings. That's great for some people. They need that extra security of feeling like they really know, maybe, how things are going to be. But do you really know, even after you live with someone? Some guys, from what I've heard, end up being completely different. Maybe you just didn't see these things when you were living with them, and then you get married, and suddenly it's like, "Ohhhh."
>
> I don't think I have to live with someone in order to figure that stuff out. Personally, I do not want to live with someone before I get married. It's not even for, like, moral or religious reasons. I kind of feel like he's trying to have his cake and eat it, too—like he can't really make a commitment. I mean, if you're ready to commit that much to me, then aren't you . . . ? It's playing house. "Oh, we'll just commit this much, and it'll be really easy for us to get out of it."
>
> Personally, I think that's weak reasoning and you're just kidding yourself—pretending that you're really together when you're really not. And what do you do when you break up? How crappy is that?
>
> I want that newness. I want it all to be new. I want him to carry me across the threshold, and I want it to be our first time in a new house together.

Who says romance is dead? It springs eternal in the young heart.

THE SHORT ANSWER

WHO'S MORE AFRAID OF COMMITMENT?

We asked women in their twenties, "Do men fear commitment more than women?" There's plenty of wariness in both camps.

- "A lot of my female friends are ready for a commitment, and their boyfriends won't commit to them in the way that they want. I mean, they're loyal and everything, and there's talk of a future, but there's not the ring."
- "I think I know more women who are afraid to commit now. I'm still struggling to get where I want to be in my life, and a lot of that has to do with graduate school and traveling."
- "Guys want someone to take care of them. They want to go right from mom to wife and it's all going to be okay. It's the men who are drowning, almost. It's like, 'Back off, buddy. Slow down, there. There are other fish in the sea.' "
- "I don't like commitment at all. And it's not just a stage in my life. I can be with someone for a year or two, and after that I freak out. I'm sure it stems from my parents, like, getting divorced. Commitment has all these things that go along with it, like, you have to open yourself up and trust that other person. And that's very scary."
- "I enjoy depending on someone and having someone be able to depend on me. That's a wonderful feeling."
- "We all want to find that one—and if you haven't found that one yet, it just looks like you fear commitment."

We can't tell you who to marry, but we can tell you how to marry. That's a largely practical matter, and as it turns out, we can offer a little practical advice.

You're aware that people are finding ever-zanier methods of proposing marriage these days. Men have arranged to have diamond rings dropped from helicopters, delivered via motorized boxes of Tide, and tucked in such odd places as a trout's mouth, a fortune cookie, and a cupcake. We have a modest suggestion: Don't let the zaniness overwhelm the romance. Keep in mind that, 30 years from now, she'll be retelling this story, and it will be much nicer for you if you can stand there feeling loved and appreciated.

That's the lesson we hear in this long story told by Susi, who's now a 42-year-old mother of two living in Pennsylvania. She recalled the night back in Chicago when her husband proposed.

> Our engagement was the most romantic day of my life, without a question. He picked me up after work on a Friday. He said we were going to downtown Chicago to a new fish market. Now, does that make you feel excited and romantic? I thought, "Oh my God, the aroma of fish on a hot night in Chicago." Anyway, we drove downtown to the warehouse district and parked in a parking garage. It was just gross. We come out of the stairwell onto a dark, dingy street—and there's a white horse and carriage waiting for us. We go on this great ride, out of the warehouse district to the cool district downtown. And we get dropped off outside a restaurant called the Pump Room.
>
> In the Pump Room, there's one table that's up on a pedestal, and there are strolling violinists. We go in, and the maître d' knows exactly who I am. He escorts me to the pedestal table. There are my favorite white roses, already on the table. And once we get seated and have a drink, Kirk gets on his knee. They stop the violins. He asks me to marry him in front of 300 people. The restaurant is silent. Now, what

am I going to say? No? He was definitely hedging his bets here because we had spoken of marriage five or six times before this, and I was always, "No, no, no, no. Absolutely not; not ready." So he was really taking a chance.

But I wasn't in the mood to say no anyway, so I said yes. Everyone's applauding us, and it was just bizarre. We finish dinner; I've got a ring on my finger; my ring is beautiful. We leave, and the horse and carriage picks us up again. We go to the top of the John Hancock Building, where a set of red roses is waiting, and the maître d' is expecting me again. We have after-dinner drinks overlooking the lights of Chicago. Is that, like, unbelievable? That was, without question, the most romantic day of my life.

I very seldom tell that story in a large group of people because, inevitably, it ends up with people fighting. Some woman will turn to her husband and yell, "Why weren't you like that? You stuck my ring in an old gym shoe and told me to put it on, you asshole!"

Put some thought into it. Run the idea past your mom or her mom or somebody's mom. Thirty years from now, you really don't want your wife punching you in public when somebody else tells the story of how they got engaged.

CAN SHE EX?LAIN IT

Maybe She Wants to Meet You Too
—MONICA MOORE, PH.D.

You're at a bar or a party or a poetry reading. You see a woman you'd really like to meet. You wonder whether she feels the same way. If only you'd pick up her cues, you'd know.

In those situations, women often use wordless cues, or nonverbal courtship behaviors. And for two decades, they have been studied by Monica Moore, Ph.D., associate professor of psychology at Webster University in St. Louis.

Dr. Moore and her research assistants posed as boring couples in singles' bars and began taking notes. They observed more than 200 single females, and the result was a research paper that described 52 "flirting gestures." In 1998, Dr. Moore published more research—this time, on 17 rejection behaviors. Once again, more than 200 single females were randomly selected for observation in places where singles mingle. Here are the highlights of her research.

Q: *How does a man know when a woman is interested?*
A: When a woman enters an area, whether it's a club or a classroom, the first thing she does is scan the room. My graduate students say she "cases the joint." If she sees a man she's interested in meeting, she will engage in several nonverbal cues to get his attention.

She will attempt to make eye contact with him. She will look at him and look away, look at him and away, with a series of short, darting glances. While she is doing this, she may smile briefly. She will primp—that is, she will smooth her skirt or flick an imaginary piece of lint off her sweater. She will flip her hair or play with it in an exaggerated way since, as we know, hair is regarded as attractive in many cultures. She may play with her car keys or other objects on the table. She'll talk with her friends and generally have more animated expressions on her face. This makes perfect sense: Who would want to approach someone who sat there looking depressed?

In what I call the parade, she may walk by him to go to the rest room or to get a refill at the bar. But she won't try to establish eye contact with him while doing so. When she gets back to her seat, she may sway her body to the beat of the music.

Q: *So if he sees these nonverbal signals, he can approach her without feeling nervous?*

A: I advise men to wait for a constellation of cues. Don't approach her just because she looked at you once. It's a dark room; maybe she was looking at the guy next to you. Maybe she was staring off into space.

Q: *But if you get several signals, then it's okay? And you won't get rejected?*

A: If there's one point I want to stress, it's that courtship is a process. Men sometimes talk about all this flirting and rejection as teasing. I don't want to say that men don't risk more rejection; they do. The onus is still on them to walk across the room and make the verbal approach. But both genders have the power, at any point, to change their minds.

He may bring her out on the dance floor only to decide she's not as pretty as he thought, or she's just completely different from him. So he'll return her to her table after the song ends and thank her very much and walk away. He has rejected her, and she will spend the next hour sending more nonverbal cues his way. Similarly, once he approaches the table, she may rethink her strategy. Maybe he opens his mouth, only to insert his foot. Or she decides he isn't really as attractive as she thought.

Q: *Because she gets a good look at that tattoo.*

A: Exactly. Or he'll make a tactical error.

Q: *What's the big tactical error that men make in these circumstances?*

A: He touches her. Maybe the music has slowed down and he asks her to slow dance with him, and she's not ready for that yet. So, in addition to refusing to dance, she may start sending out rejection behaviors. She will look away. She'll stare at the ceiling, fold her arms across her chest, cross her legs, or otherwise exhibit "closed" body positions that are the opposite of the "open" body language we see in flirting behavior. She will pick at her nails or examine her hair for split ends.

In our research, we saw some women use only flirting signals, and some women use only rejection signals. But the most interesting thing is, some women used both. They mixed these signals. I don't have any data on this, but I believe they used mixed signals in an effort to slow down the courtship process or because they were still making up their minds.

Q: *So when men sometimes complain, "She was giving me mixed signals," they may be right. But why would women want to slow down the courtship process at this point?*

A: I don't think men can fully appreciate how much fear women feel in this society. From the time they're very young, they're told, "Lock your doors. Go in groups."

Women want to go out; they want to be able to meet available men. But they're also afraid of what can happen to them.

Q: *Do women engage in nonverbal communication because they don't want to be rude or hurt men's feelings with words?*

A: Perhaps. Many women would not want to say hurtful things. But a few women are not hindered that way. I've been close enough to these encounters to hear women say, "Get away from me" or "Why would I want to dance with *you*?" And this was immediate; there were no nonverbal rejection cues that the men had just ignored. Some women aren't very nice, just as some men aren't very nice.

Q: *How important is nonverbal communication, generally?*

A: It's not something that's limited to singles' bars, by any means. I see it in my classroom. I may figure out, by watching nonverbal behavior, who's going to be dating weeks before they start dating. It's used in the workplace. It's everywhere. I've heard what I consider to be outlandish claims that nonverbal cues are 70 percent of our communication. I can't agree with that. But they are important. In fact, now that people communicate via e-mail, they miss the nonverbal aspect so much that they incorporate it into their messages with little symbols for frowns, smiles, and winks.

Q: *Any final words of advice for men who are trying to meet women across a crowded room?*

A: Men can do better in these situations if they pay attention to the women who are signaling them. Mostly, men don't. They choose to approach the woman whose looks they like. She may not know they exist, yet. So they should not be surprised if her reaction is "Who are you?" They could give it one more polite, respectful shot. But then they should get the message.

PART FOUR

The Husband
She Loves

CHAPTER TWELVE

Advanced Romance

RESCUE HER FROM SOMETHING.
Call her boss and "kidnap" her from work. Take
her for a run through the sprinklers. Wash her
hair. The best news is, being romantic can
be as simple as having fun.

Among the hundreds of questions we posed to women in the course of writing this book was one that we doubt you've ever posed to a woman you've never met.

"What's the most romantic thing your husband or lover has ever done for you?" we asked. What follows are the best of the hundreds of responses we got—a long list of winners in the triathlon of love. Some of these romantic interludes required days or weeks of planning and big bags of bucks; others, just a bold stroke of genuine feeling. But all of them scored high marks with our panel of comely female judges in the categories of imagination, technique, execution, and of course . . . results.

Feel free to shamelessly pilfer as many ideas from the following list as you want, because we figured that (if you're like us) you just don't have that many great ideas on inventory in the romance department. If you do swipe somebody else's swashbuckling idea, just make sure it's something that your lady would like. And, oh, one other thing: If you're just doing this as a way to get sex, she'll almost certainly see right through it.

Then you'll be in bigger trouble than you're in right now.

A romantic gesture says: I love *you*—not your sister, your girlfriend, or women in general. That's why, believe it or not, sometimes she'd rather receive chew sticks for her poodle than a rose.

A dozen red roses certainly have their place in the pantheon of romance. But the trouble is, they're so . . . predictable. They're almost a generic romantic gesture, something you could buy in bulk in the romance department at Sam's Club. But if the gift you give her shows that you're sensitive to who she is and what she needs, that you're really paying attention to her and her alone—well, that's practically guaranteed to ring her chimes.

What? You don't believe that chew sticks would work? Listen.

- "On the night of our first date, my husband brought me a single rose and a bag of chew sticks for my dog (whom he'd never met)," said Kathleen in New Jersey. "I was impressed with the chew sticks more than with the rose because it showed the kind of thoughtfulness that I think every woman appreciates and wants in a mate."

- "I love the little things in life,"

> "You've got to be more <u>passionate</u>, Ross—what all women want to hear is, 'The only thing that matters to me is seeing you and being with you.'"
>
> "But I've never even met her!"
>
> "I don't care, Ross! Passion is the only thing that matters! You must say to her, 'You are the only woman to me; I live for you, I breathe for you, I would die for you, please for God's sake be with me!' It doesn't matter that you haven't met her. What matters is the quality of your passion."
>
> —CHARLENE, trying to fix filmmaker Ross McElwe up with a girl, in the wry documentary film SHERMAN'S MARCH

said Diane in West Virginia. "One guy I see regularly brings a bottle of Diet Dr. Pepper for me and a Pepsi for himself when he visits. He knows I love Diet Dr. Pepper more than almost anything in the world. It's a sweet gesture that says he's thinking about me and what I like."

- "Real romance is all about listening and hearing what I say," said Carolyn in Vancouver. "For example, one night I mentioned that potatoes are my very favorite food. The next day, he came home with a present in a little bag: a raw potato. When he saw my puzzled look, he reminded me of what I'd said the night before, adding that he wanted to bring me something that he knew I would really love."

- "This sounds crazy," wrote Connie, "but I had a lover . . . we worked together and he knew how much I loved fresh tomatoes from the garden. He grew tomatoes, and every day he would bring me one. At lunch, he wouldn't even mention it—just open his bag and get out this fresh tomato, cut it in half, hand me half, and smile."

Wow.

Pretend you're in a fairy tale and rescue her from something.

In most decent, self-respecting fairy tales, there's a damsel in distress. And you, you big palooka, are supposed to come along and slay the dragon. Well, okay, maybe you haven't spotted a dragon in the neighborhood lately. But every day, there are damsels in distress—women having a rotten day at the office, on the road, or in a Volvo crammed with kids.

Rescuing her from all this gives you a big testosterone buzz—and it makes little hearts go fluttering up above her head like butterflies. In fact, some variation

> "Romance sometimes—but not always—leads to sex. Romance is always about love, but only sometimes about sex."
> —GREGORY J. P. GODEK, author of 1,001 WAYS TO BE ROMANTIC

JUST DO IT

ROMANCE 101: A NUMBSKULL'S GUIDE TO LOVE

Okay, pal, so you think you're some sort of Romeo of romance, a regular Lothario of l'amour, a guy whose instincts in the sport of love are so impeccable that you can make a woman eat out of your hand. When it comes to romance, you know what women respond to, what they would do anything for, what they crave from the bottoms of their hearts.

So prove it. Have the guts to take this simple little romance test.

Which of the following spontaneous gestures do you think a woman would find most romantic?

- A bouquet of flowers
- A surprise date
- A hidden note
- Chocolates or candy
- A greeting card
- Jewelry
- A surprise phone call

If you answered "a hidden note," we'll concede the point: You are a regular Romeo of romance.

When we asked more than 1,100 women this question on the scientific survey conducted for this book, more than 40 percent—far and away the greatest number—said a hidden note was the most romantic gesture on our list. The next most common answer, "a bouquet of flowers," drew only a 28-percent response. Ten percent said "a surprise date." Seven percent said "a greeting card." And everything else, including—amazingly—chocolate, wound up at the bottom of the heap.

on the following was one of the most common "most-romantic-moment" stories we heard. Though it may not be wildly imaginative, we like it because so many women remembered it so fondly.

This conveys the same general message that we got from women over and over again in all of the surveys we conducted. A woman wants to feel that you love and cherish and care for her and her alone, out of all of the other women in the world and all of the other fish in the sea. Writing her a little personal, romantic note is just another way of conveying that message.

Flowers, cards, candy—all of that stuff is fine in its place, but nothing seems quite so personal, aimed quite so directly at *her*, as a note. (And a note scribbled on a napkin, need we add, is considerably less expensive than a dozen roses.)

"I'm still nuts about you."

"Wanna go steady?"

"You knock my socks off."

"You're the best thing that ever happened to me."

Whatever.

And, as we've mentioned before, you get extra points for the element of surprise. Use your ingenuity. Make her gasp with surprise before making her . . . well, gasp with surprise. Here's a handful of hiding places that are worth a try.

Carefully open various product packages, insert note, and reseal the packages. You can use cereal boxes, ice cream cartons, candy bars, or (of course) Cracker Jacks.

Freeze a note in an ice cube and float it in her drink or in a punch bowl.

Stick one in a clear bottle, with the message visible, in her medicine chest.

Tuck it someplace where she'll find it later—in her briefcase, in her car, in her glasses case.

Hide one in a bouquet of flowers.

Tie one or several to a bunch of helium balloons.

- "A few weeks ago during a heat wave, he called me on my mobile to see when I would be home. I was cranky and hot, and told him so. When I got home, he had a nice cool bubble bath waiting for me with candles lit. When I got into the tub, he washed my back for me. Sweet."

- "I was on a business trip and I was having a very bad day," wrote Stephanie, in Tallahassee, Florida. "I had to buy another outfit for another unexpected day on the road, and I got lost trying to find the mall. Then my wallet got stolen. I came back to the hotel with a bad headache and soaked with rain. When my boyfriend called, I told him about my horrible evening and he was very sympathetic. He suddenly said he had to go and would call back later. Fifteen minutes later, there was a knock at my door. He had called room service! They were delivering a seven-layer chocolate cake and a quart of milk to my room. I love him so much."

- "It doesn't sound like much, but he bought me my favorite flowers (yellow roses) just because I had had a bad day," related a woman in London. "He cooked dinner and washed up; then we spent the evening curled up on the sofa, just talking. It was exactly what I needed—it meant even more than the weekend in Paris for my birthday."

We hate to belabor the obvious, but before she wants to have sex, she wants to be romanced.

Romance and sex are two ideas that are so inseparably linked in most women's minds that they're practically the same thing. To most men, most of the time, this is a genuinely odd connection, one that requires lots of quiet time and concentration to figure out.

Well, take our word for it: It's true. And it really, really matters. If you learn nothing else from this book but that, you'll be a happier man.

- "Women really like romance and sex," said one woman. "Surprises like flowers or even sneaking up from behind to give a kiss on the neck or a squeeze in the butt are great. I could easily enjoy sex four or five times per week. I can live with less, but then it better be longer than 5 minutes, with lots of kissing and foreplay beforehand. When my husband notices what I'm wearing or tells me I look sexy, wow, I really feel sexy. And that's one of the best things that a man can do to make you feel sexy even after you've been with him for years."

- "Take more time to be romantic instead of, 'How about you and me go upstairs.' If there was hugging, touching, and kissing ahead of time, he wouldn't have to ask to go upstairs. It would happen where we were," said another woman.

- Teri in Knoxville, Tennessee, told about the time her boyfriend picked her up from work unexpectedly. "We drove to a park and watched the sun go down. He just held me and we didn't say much. We both just relaxed. Then we went to dinner at a favorite restaurant. We drove back to pick up my car knowing we couldn't wait to get back home. It was during the middle of the work week. I swear, we both grinned for days afterward!"

We get your drift, Teri.

Sometimes—brace yourselves, boys—women consider not having sex more romantic than having it.

One woman said that her boyfriend "ran a bath, got in with me, and washed my feet. We didn't make love that night," but she remembered it as the most romantic thing he ever did for her.

Another said her husband once "said no to sex because he didn't think I was ready."

Look, sometimes you're just going to have to think about car wrecks or how your grandmother looks naked in order to keep the temperature under control.

The public profession of love and devotion seems to get 'em every time.

- "One month after we were married, on Valentine's Day, my husband (a military officer) hand-delivered two dozen red roses to my office," one woman said. "He waited while I read his 'little' love note in front of all my very envious coworkers. It reminded me of the scene from *An Officer and a Gentleman*. It took all I had to keep from bursting into tears."

> "My boyfriend blindfolded me and undressed me. Then he dressed me in a new outfit, which was gorgeous. Of course, that led to a night of beautiful and fun sex."
>
> —ANONYMOUS

- "It may sound very simple, but he sends me flowers at work," wrote Jennifer in Alberta, Canada. "Not only are the flowers nice but the attention received by others makes the gesture that much more pleasurable."

- "He sent 40 red roses to my work. It was beautiful," a woman from Kansas wrote. "Even other men would come by and say, 'Now that is real love.' It made me feel so very special."

This one wins for the sheer audacity of its tackiness. Leann told us that, though she hates going to those hardware superstores, her boyfriend managed to convince her to come along on an errand on her birthday. When they got to the lumber department, she realized that he had convinced the management to play "This Guy's in Love with You" over the intercom. "Then he struck into the worst lip sync and pulled a gift out of his pocket. We got out of the store and started a very romantic evening. . . ."

You get extra points—lots of extra points—if you do something romantic when she doesn't expect it. Turn an unexpected day into Valentine's Day. Surprise her.

Sure, it's great to give her flowers or take her out to dinner on her birthday, your anniversary, or whatever. But if you do that tonight, for no special reason, it's like getting 10,000 free frequent-flier miles.

- "The most romantic thing my fiancé did for me was send me a half-dozen roses for no reason," said Leigh. "Sorry, girls, but I got the best guy in the world and he's not available anymore."
- Glori, a businesswoman, told us that "the most romantic thing someone ever did for me was hiding a card and a rose in my briefcase so when I arrived at work I would find it. The best part was it was 'just because.' "
- Another woman reported that her boyfriend "called my boss and arranged 3 days of vacation time for me, then 'kidnapped' me from the office and whisked me off to an unexpected getaway that he planned right down to the packing and Swedish massage."

It's not so hard to understand the appeal of surprises, really. Surprise parties, gift-wrapped packages, winning 20 bucks on a lottery ticket . . . somehow, the shock of the unexpected adds magic to your life, like an explosion of glitter settling over your day. Yet most men still don't seem to grasp how effective a truly excellent romantic surprise can be—or how easy it is to pull one off.

- "Most women, married, with children, don't expect a lot," another woman told us. "Just every now and then surprise us with a little something. Say I love you when least expected. A hug when least expected. It can last a long time. Let me know I'm doing a good job as a mother, wife, and friend."

- "Women, no matter how long they have been married, still love to get unexpected gifts from their husbands—flowers, candy, or taken out for no special reason or occasion. Always take the time to tell them how much you appreciate them for all they do, and that you love them."

- "My advice to men would be that it's the little spontaneous gestures that keep a woman coming back for more," said Tricia in South Dakota. "Surprises are wonderful even if it's as simple as an I-love-you note tucked in her daily planner or a walk in the rain or running through the sprinklers or a motel-room key tucked in your pocket with a note attached promising a night full of passion. . . ."

The romantic getaway is an old standby because it works.

Marriage therapists are forever telling couples whose sex lives have settled into a dull rut to get out of the bedroom—get out of the house, even—to spice things up. They keep saying this because, wonder of wonders, it often works. How come? Well, who knows? Maybe the newness slaps your senses awake, drags you back into the moment, creates the memories that are so much a part of a rich, exciting life.

All we know is that lots of women say it works. And it works especially well if you demonstrate a capacity for exceedingly elaborate planning (having left the planning of your own wedding entirely up to her and her mother).

- "One weekend, I had a ton of homework, but my boyfriend wanted to get out of the house," wrote a student in North Carolina. "So he forced me into the car, with me whining about my homework. After picking up Chinese, we drove to the Blue Ridge Parkway. He spread out a blanket, got out a picnic basket and a copy of *The Invisible Man*, the book I was supposed to be reading. After eating, we lay on the blanket, and he picked up the book and started reading to me. There we were, taking turns reading, changing our voices and expressions to fit the story. This was so sweet coming from a college football player, and I'll never forget it."

- "Dan took me to a bed-and-breakfast in Vermont," wrote Karolyn in Connecticut. "The room was adorned with antique furniture, a canopy bed, and a Jacuzzi. He brought warm, soft, matching robes for us to wear after skiing during the day. After 3 days of the most incredible romance I ever experienced, he presented me with an Irish Claddagh ring, which signifies our commitment to each other."

Make her homecoming something special.

They say absence makes the heart grow fonder. But with a little effort, you can greatly enhance the absence effect by throwing some sort of romantic shindig to celebrate her return. It's fun, for one thing. And for another, when you create fond memories like the ones the following women describe, it's sort of an emotional version of saving up for a rainy day. Because some day in the future, your marital kingdom may not be so peaceable. In fact, you may be fighting like junkyard dogs. But if she can look back and remember the time you left a trail of petals to the bedroom door when she came home from a trip, well, that has an amazing way of softening up the whole situation.

> "The most romantic thing my fiancé did for me was send me a half-dozen roses for no reason. Sorry, girls, but I got the best guy in the world and he's not available anymore!"
> —LEIGH

We're not just making this up, pal. One of the best tests of a successful marriage is the way a couple views their own past, according to John Gottman, Ph.D., a psychologist at the University of Washington and codirector of The Gottman Institute, both in Seattle, who has been studying marriage for more than 25 years. "I've found 94 percent of the time that couples who put a positive spin on their marriage's history are likely to have a happy future as well," he writes. Celebrating her homecoming is just one more way to put a positive spin on your past and, of course, your future.

- "After being married for 6 years, you would think the romance would fizzle out," reported Kelly in Laguna Hills, California. "On Valentine's Day a couple of years ago, I learned that's not always true. I came home from work to a dark house. As I walked in, I noticed rose petals scattered throughout the house. I walked into the kitchen and the table was set with the best dinner I've ever had. (I think he ordered out, but that's okay!) We continued the evening in the bedroom with dessert: hot fudge cake with a raspberry sauce. He even brought our son to a friend's house. It was a wonderful evening I will never forget."

- "I went on vacation with a girlfriend and when I returned, he had 'welcome back' and 'I missed you' signs hanging throughout the house," said Paula in St. Louis. "Then he cooked a spaghetti supper, served with wine, by candlelight."

- "He left love notes around for me, flowers, and a romantic night when I returned from a trip."

- "I had to go away, 3 days before my birthday, to a funeral," recalled Tami in Santa Rosa, California. "I came back home the day of my birthday. I walked into our apartment to find the whole house decorated. Balloons, streamers, a stack of presents, the whole bit. What made this even more special was that he wasn't home. He left me a note saying his sister was in the hospital about 8 hours away and he had to go see her. It was so special because even though he was having a family emergency, he took the time to make sure my birthday was special."

Use your imagination. Put diamond earrings on her while she's asleep, or answer her door with a rose in your teeth.

The problem with predictable romantic gestures is that they're entirely too forgettable. You don't get long-lasting benefit; the memory quickly fades, like a tulip petal in the sun.

But a romantic gesture that demonstrates boldness or imagination or wit or outrageous daring or something lodges in her heart and mind and stays there without fading, sometimes for decades.

The following grab bag of romantic gestures all seemed to have something about them that touched a woman deeply. And a

> "Real romance is listening and hearing what I say."
> —CAROLYN, Vancouver

woman deeply touched is often a very interesting creature, indeed.

- "My boyfriend had just come back from a trip to Italy. My gift was a surprise. He blindfolded me and undressed me. Then he dressed me in a new outfit, which was gorgeous. Of course, that led to a night of beautiful and fun sex."
- "While I was in the hospital after giving birth to our son, he gave me a certificate that he had made on our computer that said I was the most wonderful woman in the world for giving him two wonderful children and for putting up with him."

The psycho-killer approach occasionally works, if done with flair. Claire in Surrey, England, told us, "One of the most impressive things I ever got at work was a ransom-style note made from letters cut out of a newspaper, which read, 'Lunch tomorrow or the rest of the packet gets it!' Stuck to the bottom of the note was a jelly baby with its head bitten off."

Surprise is always cool. It doesn't always have to be funny; it can simply be surprisingly thoughtful—like this.

Just before Christmas last year, we went with some friends to an annual Christmas bazaar that has beautiful, handmade crafts. I saw a lovely jewelry box, and I fell in love with it. Mike saw me admiring it. But it was pretty expensive, so I didn't buy it. I wandered off to look at something else, and about 5 minutes later, I went back to look at the box again, but it was gone. I couldn't believe someone had bought it so quickly.

It turned out that Mike had bought it as soon as I'd left, barely managing to get it in his coat pocket before I got back. He had trouble keeping it a secret from me that night, since I kept trying to put my hand in his pocket, so he had to hand it off to his friend. Mike finally gave it to me for my birthday in January, and I was so surprised. I love the box, but even more important is the time and effort he put into getting it for me.

Here are the token gestures that some other guys came up with. Think you can outdo them? She'd sure like you to try.

- "Last year, I got a dozen roses and a note saying, 'Today is the day you have been in my life for half of my life,' " said Barb, a magazine ad saleswoman who's been married for 20 years.
- "We'd had a couple of dates, and I blew him off. I found a note he'd written stuck in a book he'd lent me, pouring his heart out about his feelings for me. I called him pronto."
- "He put diamond earrings on me while I was sleeping."
- ". . . answered the door with a rose in his teeth."
- "My boyfriend sent my mom flowers for her birthday."
- "I don't know if this is classified as romantic, but it certainly was the most touching thing anyone (male or female) has ever done for me. My cat of 17 years recently died. Naturally, I was devastated. Cried for days, in fact. My fiancé dug out an old picture of her sitting on my old house-coat and had it blown up and framed, with a little name

plate on it. I cried for a few days more, the gesture meant so much to me."

- "My husband took me to a nature park and celebrated my birthday. He had wrapped my gifts individually and composed a poem to go with each. The poems were risqué, and I had to guess a rhyming word that he left out before I could open my gift. He is so sweet!"

- "With money being a consideration last Christmas, we decided to give gifts that did not cost money and could not be bought. As a coupon clipper, my partner made me a coupon book with coupons for back rubs, bubble baths, a walk on the beach. My favorite was 'Your wish is my command.' We have enjoyed them."

- "The most romantic thing he does for me is wash my hair. When I'm tired or sore and taking a hot bath, he will lather my hair and massage my scalp. Think about how good it feels when your hairdresser does it. Now imagine your lover doing it. It's thrilling!"

- "We met while salsa dancing (I was the beginner). My boyfriend bought tickets to a special evening dance and booked us into the hotel for the night. We spent an evening of hot salsa dancing, followed by his giving me a sensuous hot-oil massage by candlelight (with soft new-age music in the background) in our room afterwards. He had thought of and brought everything we needed. Needless to say, we didn't get much sleep that night, but it was the best night of my life!"

CHAPTER THIRTEEN

Intimate Communication:
Touching the Essence of Her Soul

FOR WOMEN, HAVING AN INTIMATE
SENSE OF COMMUNICATION WITH THEIR
MATES IS ONE OF THE ESSENTIALS
of a happy, long-lasting relationship. Most guys
have trouble understanding this—understanding it
the way women do, that is.
Men and women view the whole purpose of talking
(and listening) differently.

What do women really want? (At least, what do they want from us?)

Well, this book is proof that there's no single answer— there are zillions of answers. But one of the most durable and recurring themes in everything we heard from women is something that it's a little difficult for most guys (ourselves included) to comprehend.

It's not concrete and physical, like meat on the table. It's metaphysical, like mist. Yet to women, it's as real and as vital as breath.

Cathy, a 44-year-old business consultant from Colorado, put it this way: "I think what women want is that intimate sense of communication—the sense that I have made contact with somebody, that I am understood, that someone is paying attention to me. I think men probably have the very same needs, but with women, it's almost an imperative. Knowing that I am heard and understood is the ultimate goal.

"There's a voice inside you that wants to say who you

148

THE FACTS OF LIFE

TALL, DARK, SILENT . . . AND DIVORCED

In our national Magellan Poll, when we asked women what most of their marital fights were about, we figured the answer would be either sex or money. Wrong! Look at how they actually answered.

His inability to communicate	19%
Household responsibilities	15%
Money	15%
Kids	13%
Conflicting interests	9%
Jealousy	4%
Ex-spouse/partners	4%
Staying home versus going out	4%
In-laws	3.4%
His spending too much time watching sports on TV	2%

Frankly, the fact that male silence topped the list of female gripes came as a genuine surprise to us. Then again, we're just a couple of guys who tend to think that Arnold Schwarzenegger is really waxing eloquent when he says stuff like, "I'll be back."

Apparently, when she asks how your day went and you say, "Fine," this is not sufficient. Women do not think this qualifies as communicating. In fact, women's longing for deeper, more frequent, and more meaningful communication with their mates was one of the most oft-repeated refrains in everything we heard from them.

are—the intrinsic self, the creative self. It's the me who is me. And it's that intrinsic me making contact with another human being that's so important. For women, who are so often just functionaries, simply serving others, who don't have a voice, to know that in a relationship they are understood—that validates their lives."

Do you get that?

Maybe you ought to read that through one more time. Because if you could really understand what she's saying, in a deep way, you'd be on your way to a beautiful thing. After all, it isn't just Cathy who feels this way. The woman you share your bed with very likely longs for the same thing.

> "The most important issue between men and women in regard to a satisfying relationship would have to be communication. That is at the core of everything else."
>
> —ANONYMOUS SURVEY RESPONDENT

Being somebody's soul mate means making contact with them on a profound, almost metaphysical level. It's like angel-to-angel communication. Or as Laurie in British Columbia, Canada, put it, "Loving and being in love with someone means sharing even the deepest or most painful feelings, being totally vulnerable, and trusting your partner to hold your heart gently, with tenderness, and never use that information against you."

It has nothing to do with what you look like, how much money you make, or even what gender you are. It's also next to impossible to do this without deep and honest talking and listening—probably lots and lots of both.

This is the thing women say they crave the most from men, and the thing they're most likely to report men don't provide.

Women long to be listened to, to be heard, to be understood—so deeply it's hard for men to understand it.

What Cathy described is kind of like the pinnacle of communication—the Mount Everest of human intimacy. Ultimate contact, as if someone had actually reached out and touched the essence of her soul. In the course of day-to-day life, women's longing for intimate communication plays out on a much more mundane level, of course. But the underlying principle is the same: a desire to make genuine, heartfelt contact with another person. Listen to how other women described how important this is in their relationships.

- "I think the most important issue between men and women in regard to a satisfying relationship would have to be communication," one anonymous survey respondent told us. "That is at the core of everything else in the relationship. I feel that if two people in the relationship deeply love each other, trust and respect each other, and want to please each other, communicating with each other should become easier, with satisfying results. Both people must work at the relationship. Just one person cannot hold it all together."

- "I feel that communication is the most important part of any relationship," another woman told us. "You must be able to talk openly and honestly for it to last, and think of each other as friends. Long after the first romance and maybe youth has gone and you're much older (70 plus), you will still enjoy each other's company; and that kind of companionship is a love that lasts."

- "Communication is the key to a satisfying relationship," echoed Susan, another survey respondent. "If I don't feel connected or in synch with my partner, I won't be interested in sex. If we are sweeping issues under the carpet and just going along with only surface conversation, I check out."

To many of these women, guys' way of operating is an unfathomable mystery. To them it seems cold, impersonal, detached. They are as mystified by us as we are by them.

"Men don't understand our need to talk things out, and we don't understand how they can have friends that they never really open up to," said Jane in Homeland, California. (Nevertheless, she adds, one other thing she wanted men to know is that "despite all of our differences, we love them and need them." Thanks, Jane.)

Other women put their fingers on one reason that men may actually be *afraid* to communicate the way women do: We associate it with being feminine. After all, male movie stars basically just lock and load. Sometimes, they'll grimace meaningfully. Or they'll say stuff like, "Take 'em to Kansas!" But almost never do they have meaningful conversations with anybody, male or female. (Then again, movies—especially guy movies—provide more useful advice about how to reload an AK-47 than about how to have a successful relationship with a woman.)

> "Many men honestly do not know what women want, and women honestly do not know why men find what they want so hard to comprehend and deliver."
> —DEBORAH TANNEN, Ph.D.

But women generally don't consider guys who talk to be wimps. Anita in St. Joseph, Tennessee, told us that "men should know that most women like just a tad of femininity in a man. Meaning: men who keep a clean house, can cook, and are brave enough to show their feelings and emotions."

Even so, just to make sure we weren't hearing only from isolated members of the Ladies' Lonely Hearts Club Band, we decided to ask a few questions of a broader national sample. What did we find? See The Facts of Life sidebar "Hello. My Name Is David. How Are You? I Am Fine" on page 155 for one example.

Even John Gray, Ph.D., though badly handicapped by his

THE FACTS OF LIFE

FORGET THE MONEY—SHE WANTS A SOUL MATE

Question: "Of all the roles he needs to play, what is the most important role you want the man in your life to play?"

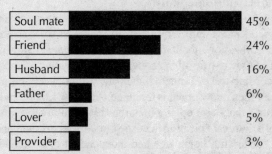

Soul mate	45%
Friend	24%
Husband	16%
Father	6%
Lover	5%
Provider	3%

Soul mate? Yeah, we were pretty amazed too. Just a wild guess, but we figure that the chance that guys would have ranked that choice first is something very close to zip. Yet women were more than four times as likely to say they longed for a soul mate or a friend than they were to say they wanted a husband. A lover or a provider, the roles men cherish so deeply? Forget it, pal. Women ranked them so low they barely registered on the scale.

maleness, confirms what these women say. "The most frequently expressed complaint women have about men is that men don't listen," he writes. (He goes on to add, "The most frequently expressed complaint men have about women is that women are always trying to change them." Hmmm. Could it be that they wouldn't always be trying to change us if we'd learn to listen a little better?)

How on Earth are men and women supposed to talk to one

another across the Great Divide of gender, where women want soul mates and men don't even know what that means? The more you study cross-gender communication, according to Deborah Tannen, Ph.D., professor of linguistics at Georgetown University in Washington, D.C., and author of *You Just Don't Understand*, the more you realize the following truth.

Men and women have a tendency to view the whole *point* of talking differently.

Like all books about cross-gender communication (or cross-gender anything), Dr. Tannen's work makes some sweeping generalizations about men and women that are not always true. But they're true often enough to bear repeating.

According to Dr. Tannen, one of the essential differences between men and women is that men tend to see themselves in a world that is set up as a hierarchical social order. Establishing a dominant position in this world—being in command, being successful, being free and independent of someone's else's power—is paramount. The usual point of talking, in the male world, is "primarily a means to preserve independence and negotiate and maintain status in a hierarchical social order," she said. We talk in order to make plans, impart information, and accomplish things, and to draw attention to ourselves and thereby establish our status in the world. Men talk in order to rule, more or less.

A woman, on the other hand, approaches the world "as an individual in a world of connections," Dr. Tannen explains. To women, closeness and intimacy are the most important goals. "For most women, the language of conversation is primarily a language of rapport: a way of establishing connections and negotiating relationships. Emphasis is placed on displaying similarities and matching experiences." Talk is the glue that holds women's relationships together. They talk in order to feel a sense of closeness and to avoid isolation.

In women's world, where intimacy is key, sameness is important. From a young age, girls criticize other girls who

THE FACTS OF LIFE

HELLO. MY NAME IS DAVID. HOW ARE YOU? I AM FINE.

Just to make sure we were hearing what these women had to say about the importance of communication, we asked them, "If you could send your partner or husband to an adult education class of your choice, which one would you choose?" Their answers:

Interpersonal skills	38%
Massage	17%
Ballroom dancing	11%
Money management	11%
Cooking	9%
Minor household repair	7%

So there it is again: Women think men don't know how to talk (or listen). Or maybe we do, but we won't. Or maybe we do, and we will, but we don't do it the way that they want us to do it. Anyhow, these women were twice as likely to say they'd prefer that you learn to communicate as to give a good back rub. Hoo-boy! Is there a good community college near you?

try to stand out or be different. Women say to each other, "That very thing happened to me; I know what you mean," as a way of saying, "We're really the same; you're not alone; I'm no better or different than you." In men's world, where status and independence are key, differences are important. We are driven to distinguish ourselves, to be better, to be different than our peers. We tend to talk in order to establish our greater expertise or power or status (our difference) from other people. Giving orders or instructions or offering solutions are age-old indications of high status because they suggest that we know more than whomever we're talking to. So we do that a lot. (By contrast, taking orders or asking for directions are age-old indications of low status, hence, our famous problem with stopping to ask directions.) Dr. Tannen calls male-speak report-talk and female-speak rapport-talk.

Well, so far, so good. Neither way of communicating is right or wrong. It's when they collide that things tend to break down. That's when you look at her in absolute bewilderment and ask, "What on earth are you talking about?" As Dr. Tannen puts it, "Many men honestly do not know what women want, and women honestly do not know why men find what they want so hard to comprehend and deliver." (Does any of this sound familiar?)

All of this results in a couple of common problems. Many women complain that their husbands don't listen to them, nor do they talk to them, Dr. Gray observes. But it's very likely that he does talk a great deal—out in the world of work. That's because men's report-talk tends to be a public affair. We give reports at meetings, make speeches, or exchange information with people at work. This is where we shine. This is where we know how to talk. When we get home, we're relieved not to have to talk anymore. Home is where we have the freedom to be silent.

To women, on the other hand, home is the place where they can speak freely and intimately, where they long to share rapport-talk with their mates. When they're home, they've escaped the world of status-seeking, public report-talk. (Even in a world where most women work outside the home, linguistic studies have shown that women are inclined to talk and ask questions much less frequently in public than men do.) But we guys don't want to talk. We're done talking.

So both we and they have a problem.

Another common problem is that when we speak to each

other, there's a *message* (the actual words we say) but there's also a *metamessage* (the "hidden" message). In reality, the metamessage may actually be more important than the message—and it may be the thing that's likely to provoke the fight.

For instance, when two women are talking and one woman complains that she can't sleep, the other replies, "I know how you feel; I can't sleep either." What she's saying is "We're really the same; I empathize with you; you're not alone." If a man says, as a way of being helpful, "Well, why don't you try a sleeping pill?" what she hears is "I don't empathize with you; you're the one with the problem and I'm not." It seems cold and distant to her. She wants him to empathize with her problem, establish a connection, share a circle of intimacy. Instead, he offers advice. It's report-talk colliding with rapport-talk. So she gets mad. And on and on it goes.

Just listening to a woman is a way of saying, "I love you."

As you can see, women use talk in a way that's dramatically different from the way men use talk. To us, it's usually a way of sharing information, establishing status, or fixing a problem—something akin to handing a guy a socket wrench. To women, talking is a way of establishing a deep personal connection with someone else. In many ways, this is a notion that's entirely foreign to the testosterone-crippled male mind. It's hard for us to understand what the heck women are talking about because most men just don't operate that way and never will. But if you can learn how women operate, there's an awful lot to be gained.

"Men who talk about problems, concerns, feelings, etcetera make women feel much more connected to them," a woman in Winnipeg explained. "If he can talk, she feels more willing to allow him to be closer and more involved in her life. Women don't understand why it is so hard for men to express their feelings, let alone talk about them."

"Men don't understand that women need to share feelings,

both positive and negative, in order to feel connected to their partners. We need to be heard," said a woman in New Jersey.

But the best, simplest comment was this one, from Denise in California, "Men don't understand that listening to a woman is one of the best ways to say, 'I love you.' "

You should read those comments a few more times and really struggle to understand what these women are saying. It isn't easy because when guys get together, we generally communicate by doing stuff together—golfing, fishing, or throwing stuff at the TV on Superbowl Sunday. It's almost as if there's a curious triangulation in male communication: Two men feel close when there's a third thing that's the center of their attention. They're focusing on making the putt or fixing a busted carburetor or cheering for the Jets; they're communicating to each other only indirectly. They're usually not even looking at each other. Women, on the other hand, tend to sit at the kitchen table, face-to-face, and talk (and talk and talk and talk) directly to each other.

One insightful female correspondent from Imperial, Missouri, explained it to us this way: "Women don't get that men need to be physical. If I wanted a man to listen to me, it's better that we go for a hike or walk or catch him doing something to talk to him. This way, he feels like he's doing something as he listens to you."

A woman named Chloe, quoted in the book *Girlfriends Talk about Men* by Carmen Renee Berry and Tamara Traeder, had this to say:

> My husband organizes his friendships around activity. In fact, he's almost critical of the way I do my friendships—you know, how we talk and talk and talk. He told me once that he didn't understand why we didn't go out and live our friendships, rather than talk about them all the time. Doing things together is having a friendship to him.

Maybe that's weird, but that's right. The male mode of communication isn't "bad," as your wife may have you believe. It's just different. The biggest thing is to make a genuine effort to get across the Great Divide that separates the sexes.

Pardon our presumption (and our grandiose generalizations) while we briefly climb up on a soapbox. But here's an observation that is supported, in a dozen different ways, by the responses of the thousands of women we heard from. And it's something that goes a long way toward helping explain the troubles that men and women have in communicating with each other (specifically, with men's penchant for wanting to fix the problem being discussed rather than just listening).

As a general rule, women, by their nature, seem to be much more attuned than men to the invisible world of the psyche and the spirit—the world of thoughts, feelings, relationships, spirituality. They can talk endlessly about this stuff, and they do. Men often feel utterly lost, or utterly bored, in a conversation about the infinitesimal details of a relationship or a blow-by-blow retelling of a specific conversation. We're likely to say something like "Hey, did anybody take the trash out?" and leave the room.

But to women, love, sharing, communication, friendship, and the feeling of intimacy are absolutely real and vitally important—the most important thing in life. Again, this is all in the invisible realm of the psyche. Because they identify so closely with this invisible world, women complain (sometimes bitterly) that men are inclined to view them only as their exterior, physical selves—the outside packages. By contrast, one woman told us, "My ideal man would be tall, sensitive, sweet, caring, spiritual, honest, understanding, and will love me until the day I die." What's interesting about this description is that only one attribute, height, is physical. The rest come straight out of the invisible realm of the psyche, the world of feelings—women's world.

Men, on the other hand, are hardwired to be more attuned to the world of the physical. We feel more comfortable in a world in which things are quantifiable, specific, concrete—and fixable. By nature, we understand the world of fabulous female bods, spreadsheets, and touchdowns better than the world of feelings. We tend to be much more focused on the physical package that a woman comes wrapped in than women are about our packaging (lucky for us). We enjoy the physical act of making love; women like the act of snuggling, the feeling of intimacy after sex.

Sports are a perfect reflection of the world in which men feel most comfortable. Sports are precise. The rules are crystal clear; they're in the rule book. The object of the game is crystal clear. And when the time runs out, the game is over. Everything moves fast; everything is well-defined; and with enough skill, smarts, and resolve, you can win. After all, what's the point, if not to win?

But the world in which women feel most comfortable is a world in which things are hard to define precisely, where things tend to change very slowly, where nothing is easily fixed. You can't just fix a broken heart, for instance. You can't just decide to fall into or out of love. Feelings are never absolutely clear or well-defined. And, obviously, you can't exactly "win" at life.

This is why, when we wade right in and start offering solutions right and left, without spending time to fully hear her out, she gets mad or feels ignored. In the male world, our actions would be appropriate. In the female world, at least most of the time, they're not.

It's that simple.

CHAPTER FOURTEEN

How to Listen to a Woman

SHE DOESN'T WANT HELP—SHE WANTS
YOUR EAR. Don't offer solutions to her problems,
at least not until she's finished complaining about
them—completely finished. Instead, ask questions
and let her scratch and moan. Watch how her
girlfriends do this "attentive-listening" thing.

Women say they really love and long for that feeling of
being deeply listened to, of being heard, of being understood.
In fact, for most women, without this, your chances of carrying on a jolly, spicy, long-lasting marriage are virtually nil.

Fair enough. But how is a guy supposed to give them that
feeling? After all, for most of us, the misunderstandings
begin almost as soon as we open our mouths (or don't open
them).

Here are a few things women told us that may help you
listen to your lady (who's the only one who really matters).

Don't be so quick to offer solutions. Just listen.

- "When we talk about our concerns or problems, we don't
  want to talk to you in order for you to fix it; we just want to
  know that you care about what we're thinking," said Cindy
  from Pasadena, California, echoing a complaint we heard
  so many times that we lost count. "We are, in most cases,

perfectly able to fix our problems ourselves. So it's important for men to just listen to us and acknowledge that they understand what's on our minds. Men don't seem to understand how important it is for a woman to be heard."

- "Most men just don't get that we want to be able to tell you our feelings without you trying to fix them or feel responsible for them," another woman said. "If we say we don't feel attractive lately, we don't want to hear, 'Well, maybe if you started going to the gym . . .' or 'If you got your hair cut, it would make you look thinner,' or have you say 'Well, I'm sorry if I'm not doing something right.' Believe it or not, you are not responsible for all our feelings."

- "Men are very hands-on and need to fix things, and sometimes all we need is a listening ear," complained Jesse, a housewife in Santa Ana, California. "Instead, they feel that urge to have to get involved and offer solutions. But when we are having a problem and they don't see it as one, they stop listening."

THE FACTS OF LIFE

NO WONDER WE'RE NUTS

Question: "When you've had a bad day, what kind of support do you want from your partner or husband?"

Let me vent, but don't offer advice	26%
Let me vent, and offer advice	21%
Make me laugh	19%
Take me for a walk	9%
Be a shoulder to cry on	6%
Leave me alone	5%

- Another woman said, "I have come to realize that in my own relationship, our differences in communication styles does make it difficult for him to just listen without inputting some kind of help."
- "What men need to understand is that we often need just simple comforting," said Teri, a graphic designer in Nashville. "We want to be able to be a little weak and receive some nurturing. . . . Perhaps there is a little girl inside who simply wants her man to become a bit lovingly paternal (not authoritative) and hold her, stroke her hair, and tell her it will be all right. . . ."

> "When we talk about our concerns or problems, we don't want to talk to you in order for you to fix it; we just want to know that you care about what we're thinking."
> —CINDY, Pasadena, California

You get the picture.

And if you look at huge numbers of couples, you'll find the same sort of patterns (and complaints) popping up in bedrooms and at kitchen tables all over the country. When Linda Acitelli, Ph.D., an associate professor of psychology at the University of Houston, was with the Institute for Social Research at the University of Michigan in Ann Arbor, she studied communication patterns among hundreds of dating couples, newlyweds, and long-married couples. She found that women like to talk about relationships at almost any time, whether things are going well or badly. Men, on the other hand, really only enjoy discussing their relationships when there is a problem and the discussion is used as a tool to fix things when the relationship is problematic, but not when things are going well.

Sound familiar?

Actually, it's not always true that she doesn't want you to offer solutions. But you have to let her finish venting first.

It isn't really true that women never want us to offer solutions. Sometimes they do. Sometimes they don't. How do you tell the difference? Well, er, it has to do with communication.

As a general rule, when she's upset and just venting her feelings (rhymes with "snitching"), that's not the time to offer solutions. Just hear her out. Sit there on your hands and do nothing but listen. When a girlfriend is listening to another girlfriend, "she is nonjudgmental at the moment, and might offer a better approach to the problem when you have cooled down," observes Jacki, who runs a day-care center in Blue Anchor, New Jersey.

Again, this is not such a difficult concept to understand. After all, men are kind of the same way. "I have found that the easiest way to break through to him is finding the right time to talk to him," said Teri in Nashville. "Obviously, he isn't giving me his full attention directly after work or during his favorite TV show. But during dinner, I usually say something like, 'I've had an awful day; maybe we can talk about it later?' That way, dinner doesn't turn into a gripe fest, and he has a chance to unwind. Later, he'll come to me and we'll talk the situation through."

Finding the right time to talk is critical because a woman's mood swings are similar to a wave, explains John Gray, Ph.D. For a time, she'll ride the wave up into feelings of love and fulfillment and happiness. Then—for who knows what reason—her emotional wave peaks, and she begins descending into vague, diffuse feelings of hopelessness, sadness, or loneliness.

"The last thing a woman needs when she is on her way down [the wave] is someone telling her why she shouldn't be down," Dr. Gray observes. "What she needs is someone to be with her as she goes down, to listen to her while she shares her feelings, and to empathize with what she is going through."

But here's the mysterious part, according to Dr. Gray: A woman has to go all the way down to the bottom of her emotional trough before she can come up again. That's why you may discover that, even though you're listening to her and trying to support her, she may actually be getting more upset and irritable.

"A man needs to remember that sometimes when he is succeeding in supporting a woman, she may become even more upset," Dr. Gray explains. "Through understanding that a wave must hit bottom before it can rise again, he can release his expectations that she immediately feel better in response to his assistance."

You just have to be patient, keep listening, and try to forget about the Colts game. (You can always tape it.) Though it may not seem like it at the time, her irritation and unhappiness will not last forever. And she won't go on talking forever, either (though it also may sometimes seem like it). Eventually, by some mysterious female alchemy, she'll hit bottom, start coming back up again, and begin to feel better all by herself.

Even so, let's face it: The whole idea of just sitting there listening to a woman venting, without offering solutions, without being condescending, without being pushy, but remaining attentive and sympathetic for seemingly interminable periods of time . . . it's, well, not exactly something that comes natural to us.

This classic male-female conflict seems to grow out of a fundamental male-female difference in our understanding of why people talk at all. After all, when a woman tells us about a problem she's having, in our warm, wonderful, generous, bighearted way, we simply want to help her fix it. We base this largely on our experience with other men. In the rare event that Dude Number One tells Dude Number Two about a problem he's having, he's generally asking for advice. He's trying to fix the problem. If he thought he could handle it himself, he wouldn't mention the problem. Why should he?

But women, as we all know, operate in a whole different way. They would mention it—probably in great detail—for reasons that it's difficult for either Dude Number One or Dude Number Two to comprehend.

The difference between male talk and female talk is sort of like the difference between the way men and women go shopping. Guys generally go to the store only with a specific need (a warm shirt, a decent socket wrench) in mind. They buy it, and go home. They have no interest in hanging around a store for any longer than is absolutely necessary. Women, on the other hand, actually *like* to go shopping. They take a friend, stop for lunch, go to 10 stores, and come home with one sweater.

> When women get together and talk, "most women already know what they are going to do about a problem. We just like to, well, bitch about it first."
>
> —JACKI, Blue Anchor, New Jersey

To us, shopping is merely a form of problem solving. To women, it's entertainment, a social event, a way of life.

Look, if you want the love and understanding of a good woman—and what on Earth could be better?—you're going to have to learn a little bit about how to talk and listen to women. It's important. Really important. In Dr. Acitelli's study of 300 couples, she found that spouses who communicated well in their first year of marriage were much likelier to still be happy in their third. Not to mention their 30th.

So we asked women for help on this point. We asked, "When you're talking, and you want us to listen but not offer solutions, what, exactly, are we supposed to do?"

Our question was innocent and well-intentioned. But some of our comely female respondents took this as an opportunity to rack a couple of shells into the chamber, take aim, and commence firing.

"All a man has to do is realize the woman just needs to get it off her chest," one woman told us. "He can listen and perhaps hold her, telling her he loves her and is there for her. This shows a lot of love when a man gives his precious commodity: time. It may be only 30 minutes. But is that so much in the big scheme of things? Is that Steven Seagal movie or football game so important that showing love and concern has to be quickly brushed aside? Would you want a woman to make you feel that she has little time or patience for what's bothering you?"

Well, excuuuuuuse us.

Other women had a few suggestions that were a little more helpful.

You can actually learn something from her girlfriends.

Over and over again in the course of writing this book, women asked things that really sounded to us like the same question: "How come men can't be more like women?" And when it comes to the sort of communication problems mentioned above, what they seemed to be saying was "How come men can't listen to my problems like my girlfriends do?"

Well, ladies, it's not gonna happen—ever. But if we're going to communicate with one another, we have to learn from each other. And guys could actually learn a lot from her girlfriends.

When women get together and talk, "most women already know what they are going to do about a problem. We just like to, well, bitch about it first," said Jacki in Blue Anchor, New Jersey.

Offering solutions won't help in this case because she already knows what the solution is. She's just getting to it by means of her mouth.

"When a girlfriend listens, she agrees with you, giving your feelings validity whether or not she agrees with the way you handled the situation," Jacki continued. "The worst thing men do is not acknowledge our right to be angry at someone or something that did us wrong or caused us problems. Women like to get it all out, and then usually they go and resolve the situation—whether it be just swallowing it and continuing to be nice to the person or doing whatever has to be done to correct the problem."

This sort of sympathetic listening is not really all that difficult to comprehend. Somebody (probably a woman) has surely done it for you, and you know how good it feels.

Ask questions.

- "Men can help by making such comments as 'No way!' 'You're kidding!' 'Wow, that's terrible!' and 'What are you going to do now?' " said Jacki. "Also, nodding your head and making eye contact show that you are listening. Asking a man to put his hands on his hips and shake his head in disbelief is a bit much, but the masculine version of this would be helpful!"
- Another woman told us, "It's really simple. Just listen, ask questions about how we feel, what we think (*really* think), what we are thinking of doing—instead of telling us what to do. Give support, say you understand, even if you don't. And repeat back what we said, just for clarification."
- "When we talk, I let him ask me rhetorical questions," another said. "In this, I feel that he is really listening to what I have to say because he is basically feeding back to me what I have said. He doesn't expect me to answer him, but at the same time, he feels he is taking an active part in solving whatever problem I am having. Perhaps it's just my need to be heard that is being met, but many times his questions give me a new perspective to the situation . . . and I am able to see it differently."

Be sensitive to her need to speak—and then shut up.

If you talk about yourself so much that you force her to say, "Now I want to talk about me," that puts her in a terrible spot. It feels awkward, and she hates it.

Susan, a 49-year-old writer from Michigan, shed some light on this problem for us.

> Once, my husband and I got a babysitter and went out to dinner and the whole bit. At the time, David was doing mechanical contracting, and he was going on and on about the piping system in this building he was working on. And it was only halfway through the dinner before I let myself notice how boring it was. I was just being a good wife, listening. But that was a turning point, realizing how miserable I was.
>
> After that, though, when David had been talking awhile, I would say, "David, now it's time to talk about me." And he would say, "Okay, great!" And my mind would go completely blank. It was like stage fright. I thought, "I'm not supposed to do this!" You know, I'm not supposed to overtly call attention to myself like that.

For most guys, this sort of conversational stage fright is very difficult to comprehend. We need assertiveness training like we need a hole in the head. But Susan wasn't the only woman we heard this from.

"Men will just start talking about themselves—it's not like the woman has to give him the floor. He just takes it," said Joan, a bookkeeper from Arlington, Virginia. But for many women, being specifically asked to take the floor can make them feel foolish and uncomfortable, she said. "It's like, I can sit over here in the corner and sing and enjoy myself, but if somebody turns the spotlight on me, I freeze. I don't want anybody to know I've been singing."

Getting this one right is not as difficult as it may sound. It's not necessary to put her on the spot by asking her directly what she has to say. Just don't go on talking about yourself forever. Be sensitive to her need to speak. Then shut up.

She needs to change too.

A fair deal is when both parties get something they want but neither party gets everything they want. The same is true of communication. Women tend to think that if men learned to communicate like women, all of our problems would melt away like the snow in spring. There's one problem: Men are never going to learn to communicate like women. Nor should we have to. And some of the women we heard from were good enough to acknowledge this.

"I believe that when a woman just needs to be heard, she should make it clear at the start of the conversation," one woman told us.

This, to us, was a rather startling admission. But why not? Surely, there's a nice way to ask her, "Are you just venting now, or do you want me to try to help you figure out what to do next?"

Learn attentive listening.

Much of what these women told us has also been described in the scholarly literature by communications experts (no, not your wife—people with Ph.D.'s in linguistics). It's generally called attentive listening, and it has four basic parts.

1. Ask for clarification. Just asking friendly, nonjudgmental questions while you're listening to her helps her know you're interested, and it also helps you understand what she's saying. "I'm not sure what you mean by that." "Can you give me an example?" "Tell me more about that." Stuff like that. "Why" questions tend to sound a little judgmental, so keep them to a minimum. Instead of asking, "Why do you want to go back to school?" you could ask, "Is there something special you want to learn?"

2. Reflect content. Along with gentle questions, it's a good idea to give her a sort of creative summary of what you've heard her say. Don't just parrot her words back to her— briefly paraphrase what you heard (or what you *think* you heard). "So you're saying you really think you've hit a wall at work and can't get any further without a higher degree? Is that what you mean?" Maybe you're getting it all wrong. Maybe you actually do understand her (for once). Reflecting content will help you figure out if you're getting or missing her point.

3. Reflect feelings. Okay, here's the hard part. For women, it's important that you hear not only her words but also the feelings behind the words. She wants you to listen between the lines. She wants you to sense what's in her heart. What is she feeling but not saying? Watch her body language, her expressions, her gestures. (Communications experts say that more than half of what we communicate is conveyed by body language.)

Try to empathize with her situation. Ask yourself, "If I were going through something like that, how would I feel?" Again, you can find out if you're getting it right by asking her questions. "Boy, sounds like you're really angry and frustrated. Are you?"

This, of course, is the part that guys don't get and may never get. For us, picking up the cues about a woman's feelings and talking about them is the equivalent of the ropes course at Camp Lejeune. So just do the best you can—a passable job will do. If you can just scramble under all that barbed wire, clamber over all the obstacles, and avoid the major land mines, you're golden, pal.

4. Reflect meaning: If you put together everything she's feeling, everything she's saying, plus all the facts of the story she's telling, you're getting close to what she actually means. Again, you can ask her gentle, nonjudgmental questions—tentative interpretations—to see if you're on the right track. "What you're trying to say is . . . ?"

If you can figure out what she actually means, you've seized the Holy Grail of cross-gender communication.

That's amazing enough. But more important, she'll love you for it.

CHAPTER FIFTEEN

Do I Look Like a Psychic Hotline to You?

YOU KNOW THAT THING SHE DOES WHERE YOU'RE SUPPOSED TO KNOW EXACTLY WHAT IT IS THAT SHE WANTS but she won't tell you what it is . . . and if you ask you're in big trouble, buddy? You're never really gonna understand that one. But you can head it off by being a bit more attentive.

We have a male friend who works as a magazine editor in New York City, who once made an interesting observation as we were strolling down one of those windswept urban canyons in midtown. It was a dark, overcast day, and we were talking about the psychological weather in our (mostly happy) marriages.

"A lot of times, it's kind of like this," he said, gesturing toward the gray sky. "It's not actually raining, but you feel like it might start raining any second. There's the threat of rain in the air. On the other hand, it's just as likely to clear up. But you never know which it's going to be."

Frankly, we thought this was a pretty fair assessment of the situation a lot of the time, in a lot of relationships (at least from the male point of view). Chances are, it's one of the reasons that you bought this book.

THE FACTS OF LIFE

ACCORDING TO WOMEN, THEY *DON'T* DO THAT

We posed the following question to women who participated in our nationwide Magellan Poll: "When you want your partner or husband to do something for you, what is your typical pattern of behavior?"

Their *least* common answer (less than 5 percent of them checked this box) was "I expect him to know what I want or need and get angry when he doesn't."

Are we nuts? No doubt. Though it seems like that happens all the time around our houses, here's what the women said.

I ask him once and only once ➪ 39%

I ask him and then keep asking him till he does it ➪ 36%

I hint, hoping he will eventually catch on ➪ 15%

I expect him to know what I want or need and understand when he can't ➪ 6%

There's something going on with her, or there's something she wants from you, but she won't tell you what it is. You care, you're concerned, you want to be her hero—but, not being blessed with the psychic powers of the Amazing Kreskin, you really don't know what she needs, wants, or is feeling. So you just flat out ask her. Big mistake. To her (and her girlfriends) what she needs and wants is so transparently obvious that only a doofus would have to ask. But to you, poor guy—well, the sky is gray, and even the weatherman doesn't know why.

Why do women do this? Men tend to have their dark suspicions. One male friend told us, "That thing they do, getting mad and not telling you why? Well, I'm convinced it's just a control thing. And it works. So why would they give it up?"

Another laughed and told us that when she's angry but won't tell him why, "I know I'm going to have to dig it out, but it's like unwrapping a gift that contains something bad— you know, like a bomb, or your picture with a knife in it. There's a real disincentive to unwrap the package."

Women, of course, have a considerably different view.

Consider the following excerpts from a conversation between a befuddled male interviewer and two women. Lisa is a 41-year-old theater publicist from Boston; Cindy, 50, is an artist from New York City. It was evening, and we were all sipping wine in the kitchen.

STEFAN BECHTEL: A woman named Leann, who responded to one of our surveys, said this: "I find that many women want their partners to just know what to do or say at all times. The man may ask, 'What should I say?' or 'What should I do?'

WHAT THEY SAY THEY WANT, AND WHAT THEY REALLY WANT

"When women let themselves fantasize about what they really want, marriage isn't it," writes author Marcelle Clements in her book *The Improvised Woman: Single Women Reinventing Single Life*. Instead, she says, many women have a fantasy of the "sexy friend, . . . someone you sit around and read with, have sex and sleep with occasionally, but who definitely does not share your living quarters."

One typical woman whom Clements interviewed said she would prefer not to be married "in the married sense . . . not 24 hours a day." On the other hand, she added, "If my doorbell rings and it's Sean Connery, you can cancel this conversation."

and then the woman says she doesn't want to tell him what to do because then he's only doing it because she gave him the words or directions, not because he really wants to."

Okay, so what's this about, anyhow?

CINDY: Obviously, men don't understand this or they wouldn't say, "What do I do? What do I say?" It's like, if I have to ask you to take out the garbage, I could just do it myself. It will cause me less grief to do it myself.

SB: Whoa! Wait a second! I did it. You asked me to do it and I did it. How come that doesn't count?

CINDY: Why didn't you just know to do it?

SB: Because usually it's not obvious.

CINDY: Well, if I didn't just *know* to empty the garbage, what would happen? The garbage would pile up to my eyeballs. But it's a key point—it's an awareness. It's an awareness of your relationship with everyone around you. For the man to say, "What do you want me to say?" is a surefire way to throw a woman into a fury. I think, in general, men don't think as much about how their reactions will affect the people around them. The guy says, "What do you want me to do?" But she thinks, "If I have to tell you to do it, it's meaningless." You're just doing it because I'm going to get mad if you don't. It's like giving a line reading in theater. A bad director says, "Don't say it like that. Say, 'But I love you.' Say it like that." That is devoid of meaning and devoid of coming from any true place.

> "We want men to be more aware—more aware of what we want. We're aware of what you want. Women spend a lot of time trying to figure out what men want, and men don't spend 2 seconds thinking about what we want."
> —CINDY, New York City

But the gallant interviewer, still mystified, keeps probing. As a way of explaining herself, Lisa told a story. She's stuck at work because her car is in the repair shop while her husband, Willie, takes their small daughter, Carmen, to the balloon shop on the way to a birthday party. Willie calls to tell her they're at the balloon shop and running late. He says, "What do you want me to do?" She says, "Nothing, I'll be fine. Go to the party! Have fun." Actually, though, she doesn't mean this. She's angry and hurt. She wants him to come pick her up. She thinks this is obvious. But she doesn't say so.

SB: I don't understand this. Could you help me with this? Because to me, you didn't say what you meant; what you said was in code, and he didn't get the code. Why didn't you say what you meant?

> "For the man to say, 'What do you want me to say?' is a surefire way to throw a woman into a fury."
> —CINDY, New York City

LISA: Because my realistic side said that was stupid. It was too far for him to drive. It would have made Carmen late for the party.

CINDY: It would be more work for him. But . . . [and here she switches to a sexy, come-hither voice] wouldn't it be *sweet* if he wanted to do that?

SB: Wouldn't it be sweet if he picked up on that and you didn't have to *tell* him this?

CINDY: Even though I can't really suggest it, because it would be way out of his way, wouldn't it be *darling* [that voice again] if he did it . . . ?

LISA: Of course, I would have felt totally guilty because he and Carmen would have been late.

CINDY: But then you'd say [come-hither voice], "Oh, did I make you late, honey?"

SB: But the guy has every right to say, "Why don't you just tell us what you want?" What *do* you want, anyhow?

CINDY: We want men to be more aware—more aware of what we want. We're aware of what *you* want. Women spend a lot of time trying to figure out what men want, and men don't spend 2 seconds thinking about what we want.

SB: No wonder guys are confused.

CINDY: We should be the ones that are confused. We're thinking all the time!

Touché. Her point is one that men have a lot of difficulty hearing.

We need to make more of an effort—like women do—to figure out what our mates need, want, and desire.

Most of us aren't very good at figuring out what women want—at least partly because we don't try. It's not that men are selfish slobs (well, sometimes we are).

Women, by contrast, are socialized to be attentive to other people's needs, to the point where they're almost intuitively aware of them.

It's also important to remember that this whole deal works both ways—it's not only women who think that men ought to know things without being told. Listen to Danielle, a 23-year-old account executive at an advertising agency in Philadelphia: "Men always say to women, 'I'm not a mind reader. If you want something, you have to tell me.' Well, women aren't mind readers, either. Do I know if he's in love with me if he doesn't tell me that? Do I know if he missed me if I was away? I have no idea."

We have to admit, she has us there.

So making progress on the whole problem of marital mind reading is one of those things that requires both parties to work a little harder. Women need to do a better job of expressing their needs to us in ways that we can understand. (Hey, what's the big secret, anyhow?) And men need to be more sensitive to the cues that women put out there. We need to try harder to figure out what women want.

It's not impossible. In fact, the kind of relationship that Leann described to us was not as unusual as you might think.

"I feel very fortunate that my partner asks me what he can do or say—what I need—and then does it," she told us. "His asking and then doing shows me how much he loves and adores me, and it only helps him learn more and more about me. We've been in love for over 8 years, and just when I think I can't love him any more than I do, he asks, 'What can I do for you, pal?' and I feel my love for him compound."

Just because she wants to talk about her problems doesn't mean she's criticizing you.

There's another, related marital hot seat you may be familiar with. You find yourself sitting in it when your wife lets it be known that she wants to talk—about problems.

The moment you hear that word "problem," a red flag goes up. "Uh-oh," you think. "The problem she wants to talk about is me!"

"When women talk about problems, men usually resist. A man assumes she is talking with him about her problems because she is holding him responsible," points out John Gray, Ph.D. "The more problems, the more he feels blamed."

Maybe that's why Herb Goldberg, Ph.D., a psychologist in Los Angeles and the author of *What Men Really Want*, says that in long-term relationships, men are inclined to wind up feeling guilty and women feeling angry.

This isn't just touchy-feely psychobabble. In the real world, men tend to hear stuff like the following, contributed by a woman named Rhonda.

> Men should listen and take notes if necessary. They don't seem to remember the things you say or want. What is even worse is, they will give you something totally different because they think you will like what they pick better. They are usually wrong and would benefit greatly if they would do what was asked and not amend requests.

(Let us take a wild guess, Rhonda: You're divorced.)

Still, by getting so defensive so quickly, we're missing a lot. Here's what one of our female correspondents told us about that.

When women address a problem with their mates, they are usually doing so because whatever he did or didn't do made them feel unloved or unappreciated. They want their partners to understand how it made them feel, show concern and empathy, and reassure us of their love.

Rather than being defensive and getting angry back at us because they think that our only motivation for saying anything to them is to tell them how bad they are, if they could only listen—without being defensive—and hear our need for love and validation, we would once again see them as our wonderful partners because they cared, listened, empathized, and validated us, making us feel important, loved, and cherished like in the good old courting days.

And if you can make her feel like that, you know that something good is going to come of it.

You'll never learn to communicate the way she does—and you don't have to.

What an experience! Here we are, a couple of craven males sitting in our shabby offices, poring over the whines, praises, complaints, and instructions of women from all over the United States and Canada. Piles, heaps, tidal waves of them, pages and pages of lilac-scented stationery and faxes and e-mails and notebook paper and yellow legal pads. Man, these women had a lot to say.

And fellas, we gotta tell you: There are certain repetitive themes that emerge from all this that are never quite spoken aloud. These women don't actually say them, yet they say them loud and clear. Know what we mean?

One of the most persistent of all of these spoken-unspoken themes is this: "How come men can't be more like women?" Know what we mean? For instance, the following complaint is something we heard over and over again—and we reckon you have too.

Men just don't get that women want details. Women want to know when you went, who you went with, why you went, how you got there, if it was fun, what you wore, etcetera. Women want to hear, "I went to dinner with Fred; and we went to McDonald's; and I had the Big Mac with fries and a Coke; and we took Fred's car because mine was low on gas; and I wore my white shirt, which I spilled my Coke on, so I didn't have a good time."

> One of the most persistent of all of these spoken-unspoken themes is this: "How come men can't be more like women?"

In the unlikely event that the guy mentions he ate at all, he's inclined to mumble something like, "Burger and fries."

This is, perhaps, the way that nature intended it. There are certain fundamental differences between male speak and female speak, and it will probably ever be thus. You'll never learn to communicate like a woman, and even if you wanted to, you probably couldn't.

For instance, the next time she complains that you can't give her the precise blow-by-blow of a conversation you had last Thursday, pull out the following handy rodent study. It suggests that there are innate differences between male and female brains that could have a direct effect on the way we communicate.

Human volunteers, male and female, were set loose in a big maze and were asked to find their way back to the starting point. Most of the men did it much more quickly than the women did. But when asked to describe the trip, many of the women could recall the landmarks in great detail; the guys could hardly remember anything. All they knew was that they had reached their goal and done it fast; everything else was a blur.

Sound familiar?

Probing this gender difference further, Steve Gaulin, Ph.D., professor of anthropology at the University of Pittsburgh, set up a study to compare two species of small, hamsterlike rodents, the meadow vole and the pine vole. Male meadow voles, it turns out, are promiscuous Don Juans who range far and wide in search of mates. Pine voles, by contrast, tend to be dull, monogamous homebodies.

Dr. Gaulin subjected both kinds of voles to the old vole-in-a-maze trick. He discovered that the horny, testosterone-crazed, far-ranging meadow voles were very adept at finding their way through the maze. Male pine voles, by contrast, took much longer to figure their way through it (so did females of both species).

When he dissected the brains of both kinds of vole, Dr. Gaulin discovered that a brain structure called the hippocampus was about 11 percent larger in the philandering male meadow voles than in male pine voles or females of either species. The hippocampus is believed to be the place in the brain that helps you form mental maps of places you've never seen. And evolutionary biologists now speculate that our male human ancestors, who had to roam across vast distances in the unending search for game and girls, became exceptionally adept at making mental maps. Home-hugging females and homebody males had a much harder time finding their way around an unfamiliar place.

In other words, it now appears that there may be an actual structure in your brain that causes you to believe you know where you're going (even if you don't)—which is why guys hate to ask for directions. And why, when we get there, we can't remember as much as she can about how we did it.

Try as you may, you will probably never remember as much of Thursday's conversation as she can. All you remember is the bottom line—what was decided, what came of it, the end result.

So just listen as well as you can. Make some effort to communicate in your own humble, mumbling male way. Just don't be too hasty about it. As Janine from Kennewick, Washington, told us, "We will never understand each other, so we should all think before we speak."

PART FIVE

The Lover She Wants

CHAPTER SIXTEEN

Are You Missing the Link?

MEN DON'T CONNECT ROMANCE AND SEX.
Women do. They need to be wooed. It doesn't take
much, and a better sex life is the immediate reward.

You've just turned to this section thinking what all guys
think: "Here's the good stuff." And now you're wondering,
"What's this?"

This is about a woman's answers to the questions "What is
sexy? What turns you on? What gets you started up?"

Very often, a woman's answer is nothing like yours.

When we surveyed the readers of *New Woman* magazine, we
asked 15 open-ended questions. Question 12 brazenly inquired,
"What consistently enables you to reach orgasm?" Being guys,
we were expecting an exchange of technical data. We thought
we'd hear about moves and positions and body parts. Instead, we heard from a lot of women who said, "Sweet nothings
are everything." Without romance, their boats won't float.

In fact, in nearly one out of four cases, the responses to
question 12 went something like this.

- "Feeling totally loved and wanted and caressed"
- "Concentrating on how excited and loved I feel"

- "Being totally open and trusting him"
- "The way he makes me feel like I am the only woman for him"
- "Loving words and actions; romance; sincerity"
- "Just being with someone I really love"

This is how they reach orgasm? A guy wouldn't say stuff like that in a million years.

That's why we're starting this section with a chapter on romance. To understand what women really want from their lovers, you have to understand where they're coming from. It's not where you're coming from. This is a bedrock issue, if you will, that will always bedevil the genders. Men don't get why women wrap sex in romance, and women don't get why we don't.

Patty in San Diego said, "A woman has to know she is loved before she makes love."

A Florida woman wrote, "I need more respect and attention outside the bedroom to be better in the bedroom."

And from Valerie, a married 32-year-old in Forest Falls, California, this eloquent e-mail:

> I feel very strongly that men don't realize how closely our sexual desires for them are linked to the amount of non-sexual affection we get the rest of the time. This doesn't always hold true at the beginning of a relationship or with a casual-affair type of thing, but with the men we love, most of us need to feel listened to, wanted, loved and respected. A hug and some kisses (nonsexual) now and then on a daily basis let us feel we are truly loved and appreciated.
>
> In the absence of this, our sexual desire can start to just fade away. So many of the women I know try to tell this to their men when the men ask why their desire isn't what it used to be, but they (the men) just don't seem to want to hear this or believe it. It's a shame. You guys have the key to getting so much more sex. If only . . .

Valerie spoke for the vast majority of women on this point. In fact, if you remember only two or three things from this book, remember Valerie's last words. Nearly every woman in our surveys and discussion groups and one-on-one interviews touched on this point.

We heard from Lennette in Michigan, for example, "No matter what a man thinks, women need romance. Simple things like holding hands, hugs without sex, flowers or a card for no reason, or a romantic dinner in a place that he may think is silly but she enjoys."

"All these things will make a woman a more willing sex partner."

The women who really complain about this tend to be married for a few years. Once upon a time, their husbands were romantic, adoring, and spontaneous boyfriends. All that gradually faded away after the wedding, and now they're feeling just a little cheated, a little tricked. Like the woman who wrote anonymously on her survey response, "My partner worked so hard to get me. Now that we are married, I have to jump-start him and keep reminding him about romance. The result always benefits him in the end."

Other women simply give up; their hearts harden, and they get divorced. Pam, 34, in Dresden, Maryland, wanted men to know that most women are not asking for the moon. In fact, she would be turned off by a man who was romantic all of the time. "I just need, like, the middle ground," she said. "I don't want him to be overly sensitive. I would like a little more than what my ex-husband gave me. There has got to be a balance."

"If there is no romance, it just turns into a routine."

The reason we're like this is probably buried in our genes. According to evolutionary biology, a great deal can be understood about human mating strategies if you think of things this way: Each of us is here because our ancestors were particularly good at passing along their genetic heritage. Since the sexes are innately different, a guy's inherited tendency is not the same as a woman's inherited tendency. Men can have more offspring than women, thus the male mating strategy involves sowing your seed far and wide. But women, who must bear all of their offspring, have their limits. So theirs is a different strategy, one that stresses quality over quantity. Women's genetic heritage is to find a mate who will stick by her and her alone, swear his undying devotion, and help support and nurture the children who are carrying her genes. She needs assurances that he will not simply disappear with the next band of Visigoths that rolls through town. In short, she needs to be romanced.

Hence the candy valentine.

These innate gender differences are reflected in our deepest desires and longings. Psychologists who have done con-

---

THE FACTS OF LIFE

SO THAT'S WHY SHE WEARS FLANNEL PAJAMAS

We asked the question "In your own life, what do you feel are the biggest barriers to enjoying great sex?" The responses were split: Women who are basically happy with their relationships complained mostly of fatigue and lack of time. But among unhappy women, the number one problem is, you guessed it, lack of romance.

What's Standing in the Way	Unhappy Relationships	Happy Relationships
Lack of romance	39%	30%
Fatigue	18%	22%
I'm not interested	16%	14%
Lack of time	11%	12.5%
Partner not interested	10.5%	10%

tent analyses of men's and women's sex fantasies have found that women's fantasies tend to focus on tender, gauzy romantic attachments to a single caring individual. In two words: romance novels. Men's fantasies can generally be summed up in two different words: nude blondes.

According to an old adage, women trade sex for love, and men trade love for sex. There's a grain of truth in that, but the adage makes it sound as if

> "The more he goes out of his way and plans ahead and does nice things, the more turned on I get."
> —KELLY, San Francisco

women draw a distinction between sex and romance, just as we do. They don't. They're not negotiating a preseason trade. There's no quid pro quo. It's all part of the same thing. Maybe that's why men call it sex and women use fuzzier, more encompassing words like "sexuality" and "intimacy."

Whatever. Here's the key point. Lorri in British Columbia, Canada, wanted each of you to remember this:

> The more attention, love, affection, caring, etcetera that you show your partner, the more often you will find yourself making love, and it will be far more fulfilling for you both.

Question 5 in our *New Woman* survey asked, "What's the most romantic thing your husband or lover has ever done for you?" We asked the same question on the magazine's Web site. Other chapters examine the answers in depth, but here we want to highlight the answers that connect the dots and make explicit the link between romance and sex. Many a description of romantic gestures ended with a memorable night in bed. Marva in Sacramento wrote the following:

> I was fortunate to have a man honor me with his romantic side. I found myself going to a local very expensive hotel on Valentine's Day. He opened the door to this luxurious suite, which he had apparently spent most of the day decorating. For the bed, he had designed a red-and-white four-poster

canopy—and in the center he had placed a red fold-out heart. Around the mirror over the vanity, he decorated red streamers and hearts, and on the mirror he wrote, "I love you" with red lipstick. In the hotel's water pitcher, there were two dozen red roses, and in an ice chest he had chilled two bottles of champagne. When room service delivered our dinner, I was completely swept away. Needless to say, Valentine's Day turned into the Fourth of July!

Especially when the guy pulled out his bottle rocket. Marva's man went to a lot of time and expense, but that's

---

THE SHORT ANSWER

WHAT A GUY!

We asked women, "What was the most romantic thing he ever did?" Many women answered, "Pass." But the answers we got make us realize that romance doesn't take tons of money. It just takes a little thought.

- "One time when we were at the food store, he just dropped everything and started dancing with me— we were dancing to some kind of cheesy love song."
- "He left me a peach Snapple with a little note that said, 'I know you're having a rough day. I love you.'"
- ". . . a homemade valentine."
- ". . . a bed-and-breakfast for Valentine's Day. And he didn't tell me until we got there."
- "He didn't do that many romantic things because he was too young and stupid."
- ". . . when he asked me to marry him. It was the way he looked at me—he was making that life decision right there, and he was so secure in the fact that he wanted it to be with me."

not the only way to romance a woman. Listen to Diane, a single, 24-year-old teacher in Philadelphia.

> A lot of romance is not, like, roses every week or that type of thing. It's just the things men say and do. They're thinking about you. You know they are looking at you as a lovely person. So they don't have to buy you anything to be romantic. It's a style, a way of being.

Sheila, a 33-year-old single parent, told us the same thing.

> It's not always about buying stuff. It's not always about presenting something to the other person. It's letting that person know, either physically or verbally, that you care.

So if you're the type of guy who thinks of "romance" as just plain corny, if you just can't bring yourself to buy her flowers or a box of chocolates, don't. Plenty of women will understand your reluctance to be "romantic," as long as you can be romantic in ways that take the quote marks off that

---

JUST DO IT

SURPRISE HER

There are a million romantic gestures in the book of love, but they all have one element in common: surprise. And not necessarily a huge, gigantic, get-out-the-camera surprise. We've seen something as simple as a single acorn, placed in her hand, become a lifelong memory—because it was done while he said a few thoughtful words in an unexpected moment.

So surprise her. Light candles. Bring flowers. Write a note. Buy a card. Meet for lunch. Get tickets. Throw a party. Plan a weekend. Pick up that CD. Tape her favorite show while she's at choir practice. If she doesn't die of a heart attack, she'll make you glad you did it.

word. Ways that are just about you and her. Chris, a 39-year-
old homemaker in Canada, explained.

> In all the books and all the TV shows, somebody brings
> somebody flowers. So when somebody in your life does it,
> it's like, "You saw that on TV, didn't you?" You know, the sin-
> cerity of it. Romance is nice, but I always question its sin-
> cerity. I find it romantic when somebody remembers a little
> thing about me that I like or dislike. A man can give you a
> box of candy, and you've probably told him the week before
> that you're allergic to chocolate. You know what I'm saying?
> The fact that he wouldn't give you a box of chocolate, to me,
> would be more romantic because he'd been listening.

Clearly, you don't have to spend hundreds of dollars on a
weekend getaway at a fancy hotel. Maybe all you have to do is
agree to sign up for the ballroom-dancing lessons that she's
been begging you to take with her.

Being romantic is not achieved by opening your wallet. She wants you to open her heart.

Betty in Port Charlotte, Florida, told us this story.

> The most romantic thing was not with my husband. I had
> met this really great guy about 15 years ago, and he showed
> me how to dance. How to waltz, slow dance, two-step, and
> many others so that we could have something we loved in
> common. I had wanted to learn, and he wanted to spend
> that time with me. And for many months to come, I was able
> to be with him with our special time and hold him close
> more times then I could have any other way. It allowed me to
> be more comfortable with him. The lovemaking was unlike
> any I have ever known.

Get the idea? Now, on to the good stuff.

CHAPTER SEVENTEEN

What She Secretly Wants

IF YOUR PARTNER IS LIKE MOST WOMEN,
SHE THINKS YOUR SEXUAL STYLE NEEDS
SOME POLISHING. But has she told you about it?
As one woman told us, "The words don't come out
of my mouth." Maybe it's time for a long, calm talk.

"I put a lot of energy into my lover," said Sheila, a 33-year-old woman in Philadelphia. "I get to know him as well as he knows himself, practically. And I expect you to put the same energy into me. If you're not willing to put in that energy, you've got to go."

Quite the ultimatum.

We're not saying your own wife or girlfriend is about to show you the door. But we are asking, Have you checked in with her, lately? Everything okay in the between-the-sheets department? Has anything changed there? Does anything need to be changed? Just because you two had that long talk 5 or 10 years ago . . . well, that was good, but that no longer counts. Women change with the years. Their most common sexual problems tend to diminish.

They may even get downright horny.

Take Brianna in California, for instance. "Since I got past 35," she told us, "all of a sudden I'll be incredibly horny out of nowhere, no matter where I am, and I am just ready to rip his clothes off."

That's a nice problem. We can't guarantee that you'll hear that particular problem. But chances are, she has something to tell you. So the next time you're engaged in pillow talk, or stuck in traffic, or waiting for a table on a Saturday night, ask her this: "What is the most important thing I don't understand about you sexually?"

We'd give anything to see the look on her face.

We wouldn't ask you to do anything we wouldn't do, so we asked that same question of the readers of *New Woman* magazine as part of a one-page survey in the September 1998 issue. (The magazine has since ceased publication.) We received several hundred replies. Roughly one in eight respondents had nothing but praise for the man in her life. ("He makes me multiorgasmic!" screamed Jessica in Brooklyn.)

Seven out of eight women, however, admitted that their guys had room for improvement. They could identify at least one way, right off the top of their heads, in which their mates could spiff up their sexual techniques.

> "Too much of a good thing can be wonderful."
> —MAE WEST

Most women have no trouble criticizing, say, the way you load the dishwasher. But many, many women have a harder time talking about this stuff. They find it difficult to communicate their sexual needs. In fact, if your lady is at the stage where you can get her to talk about what she wants, you're lucky. She has already zoomed past stage one and stage two. The aim of therapy is a three-stage process, says Beverly Whipple, R.N., Ph.D., professor of nursing at Rutgers College of Nursing in Newark, New Jersey, and president of the American Association of Sex Educators, Counselors, and Therapists. "I try to help couples be aware of what it is they like sexually, and then to acknowledge this to themselves, to say, 'You know, I really do get turned on by that.' And then the third step is the hardest, for most couples—and that is, to communicate, verbally or non-verbally, what you like."

Exactly what your lady likes—well, that's specific to her. Each woman is unique. The simple fact that she may have secret desires is the first thing that you need to understand. The second thing that you need to understand is that sex is important to her. Very important. Nearly half of the women who answered our Magellan Poll said they want more sex in their lives.

Even the women who are the most dissatisfied with their sex lives don't think less sex is the solution. They, too, want more. They just want it to be better.

You can hardly be blamed for assuming that her silence implies equanimity. After all, women are supposed to be talkers. They're always berating men about this; "Learn to talk!" they shout. So what makes them suddenly clam up when it comes to sex talk?

Sometimes, it's just shyness. Other women are more open and outgoing—except in the bedroom, where feelings of guilt or shame prevent them from realizing their sexual potential. And sometimes youth is a factor. Louise is a married mother of two in Denton, Texas. Now that she's 37, she sees, "I was afraid to express myself in my twenties. I just wasn't real confident in myself as a person, so that extended into the bedroom."

Lori is 28; she's a computer consultant in Fort Lee, New Jersey. Her secret desire: "I wish he'd throw me up against the wall and tell me he wants to lick me until I come." She'd like him to be better at expressing his sexual side—and yet she admits she has trouble doing the same. "Sexually, I'm a bad communicator, although I'm a great communicator in everything else," she said. "Sexually . . . I don't know. The words don't come out of my mouth."

As you can see from the box on the opposite page, the words don't come out of many women's mouths. A full third of our Magellan Poll respondents have not yet talked to their partners about their most pressing sexual concerns. If the survey had included more women in their twenties, the percentage may well have been higher.

So let's sort through the hundreds of replies to our *New Woman* survey question about men's sexual shortcomings. Many of these responses will be examined in greater detail in the following chapters. Some of them blatantly contradict each other. As we said, not all women want all the same things. But for now, let's just scan the big, billboard-size messages.

You're short on foreplay.

- "Foreplay."
- "More foreplay."
- "I need foreplay."
- "It's all about foreplay."

This was the loudest, clearest, most frequent request, by far. So frequent, in fact, that we asked a follow-up question on the *New Woman* Web site. And we've devoted chapter 22 to the topic in order to spell out the how's and where's and why's.

Certainly, some women want it rougher or prettier, with a little of this or a little of that. But nobody—nobody—complained that her man spent too long getting her worked up into a frenzy.

Sherry in Nova Scotia, Canada, spoke on behalf of her entire gender when she told you, "When we say we need more foreplay, we mean it."

You're short on desire.

We asked one woman in Cincinnati, "What's too much sex?" Her pithy reply: "I wouldn't know." She went on to say:

THE FACTS OF LIFE

ROOM FOR IMPROVEMENT

We asked the women in our survey, "What is your greatest sexual concern right now?" These ladies, overwhelmingly in their thirties and forties, aren't in conflict with their partners over matters of sexual style. That was *years* ago. Now, their problems are problems of stability and familiarity and routine—or divorce and separation and loneliness. Among the under-30 respondents, however, "too little foreplay" tied with "no complaints" for first place. Tsk, tsk. Young men in a hurry.

I have none—my sex life is great	21.2%
I'm not in a romantic relationship	19.1%
I'm not interested in sex as often as he is	18.5%
Too little foreplay before intercourse	12.4%
I often have trouble getting turned on	8.4%
He reaches orgasm too soon	5.7%
Too little tenderness after intercourse	5.1%
My partner wants sex at inconvenient times	4.9%
I'm interested in sex—but not with him	3.1%
He asks me to do things I don't like	1.6%

Our follow-up question was "Have you discussed this concern with your partner?" Those who rated themselves as dissatisfied with their current sex lives were more likely to answer in the negative. Maybe they've given up hope.

Yes⇨ 66%   No⇨ 34%

Last night, I put on a negligee. Well, he's downstairs paying bills, and I'm saying, "Look, fool, I'm up here with a freakin' negligee on." You know, it hasn't jumped out in, like, 5 days, so he's mine. And he came upstairs at midnight. And I'm like, "Don't touch me." That made me really angry. I wasn't in the mood anymore. The mood was gone.

Frankly, this took us by surprise. Not that women can't have sexual stirrings; that old notion died along with the Vic-

---

THE FACTS OF LIFE

IS IT GOOD FOR HER TOO?

We asked, "On a scale of 1 to 10, how satisfied are you with your current sex life?" A majority are satisfied, with ratings of 7 or above; the rest are either unattached or thinking that maybe they'd be better off that way.

10	16%
9	11%
8	16%
7	9%
6	5%
5	10%
4	3%
3	4%
2	3%
1	5%
No sex life	19%

torian era. But the fact that so many women voiced a desire for more sex seems to defy reports like the recent paper in the *Journal of the American Medical Association* that pegs low sexual desire as the most common form of sexual dysfunction among women, affecting 22 percent of American females.

Our Magellan Poll found that only 4 percent complained of having too much sex, and 46 percent said they wanted more. Low libidos aren't bothering these women.

"I need sex more than once a month," said Amber in Alabama.

"Women get depressed if they aren't wanted," said Heather in Houston.

"I seem to be the rare woman who really can enjoy sex once a day, every day, 365 days a year," said one anonymous reply. "I love the expression, 'A hard man is good to find.' "

> "Men, of course, do have a major objection to their marital sex lives, which is that they aren't allowed to bring home random strangers and have sex with them too."
>
> —JOEL ACHENBACH, in REDBOOK magazine

A woman in Milwaukee is at the end of her rope. "I cannot for the life of me understand why my boyfriend was a sexual banshee the first year I met him and is a celibate for all subsequent years. Women like sex for physical reasons and like it often. If we don't get it from you, we will get it from someone else."

She has a soul sister in New Jersey. "I love sex/making love. I could have sex once or twice a day. Quickies, fellatio, fun places, long romantic lovemaking. And every encounter doesn't have to end with a climax."

But we must tip our hats to Kathleen in New Jersey for reminding us not to confuse quantity with quality. More is not always better: "Having sex with a selfish pig three times a day can't compare with having a wonderful experience once a week. Don't even try to say that frequent sex equals a great sex life. It just isn't true."

Or maybe you're too hot and bothered.

Even if she wants it as much as you do, she wants you to be well-mannered about it and "not to be so darn eager," as Crystal in Tampa put it.

Especially if she's not as overheated as you, she's going to need some warmup time, some sweet-talkin', to get things started. And, as Helen in Alabama reminded us, "Him saying, 'Do you want to f___?' is not a turn-on."

It's not that these women want less sex. They just need more tenderness. They're put off when their men get that glazed look in their eyes and go off hell-bent in pursuit of orgasm. To us, it's a physical need; to them, it's an emotional

---

THE FACTS OF LIFE

"WE'RE NOT HERE RIGHT NOW . . ."

Now you know why you talk to so many answering machines. Our finding that half of all women in their thirties and forties have sex at least once a week agrees with the recent MIDUS (Midlife in the United States) survey of 3,032 Americans that was conducted by the MacArthur Foundation, a private humanitarian organization based in Chicago. Among women who rate themselves as "very satisfied" with their sex lives, 87 percent are finding time at least once a week.

We posed the question: "Approximately how often do you engage in sexual intercourse?"

Once or more a day	2%
Two to six times a week	30%
Once a week	18%
One to three times a month	23%

need. "I'd like smiling eye contact and kisses beforehand, and to be held afterward," said a woman in Fort Collins, Colorado.

"I want him to look at me and connect with me," said Marcia in Seattle. "I've told him, but sometimes he just checks out."

Of course, there are some women who do want less sex. And it often has something to do with the level of stress in their lives at that moment. A 23-year-old who's working on her master's degree complained, "I don't need to have sex every 5 minutes. I would be satisfied with once a month because I'm so busy."

Honey, your fiancé is a very understanding man.

Once a month	6%
Every few months	7%
Once or twice a year	5%
Never	9%

More Is Better

Yeah, baby! Then we asked, "Would you say that amount is . . . ?" We were surprised by the lustiness of the overall reply. We did some extra number crunching and discovered that the women who rated themselves as dissatisfied with their sex lives weren't averse to sex. In fact, they'd rather have more. Two-thirds of them checked off "too little," in contrast with 81 percent of the "very satisfied" women, who checked off "just right."

Too much	4%
Too little	46%
Just right	50%

You're a little too rough.

A married woman in Madison, Wisconsin, had a one-word reply: "Gentleness."

Some guys forget where they are. They think they're back at the shop. And when they touch their women, they treat them like rusted lug nuts.

Or maybe we were yelled at for too many years by feminists who said we were cavemen if we treated women like "the fairer sex." In some circles, it even became a pejorative verb: "Oh, he fair-sexed me." So we all thought, "Okay, we're supposed to treat women as slightly shorter versions of ourselves."

The gender warfare has led to much personal grief.

- "He is just so rough," said Lisa in St. Louis.
- "Be soft when it comes to my breasts," admonished Melissa in Flagstaff, Arizona.
- Angelica in Indiana said, "He doesn't understand why I don't like having sex hard and fast."

Those were common complaints. Less common is the problem faced by Tami in Colorado. "He likes to bite," she said. "I don't mind a little nibbling or some light nipping, but sometimes I think that if he could, he would rip off pieces of flesh and swallow them whole."

We hardly know what to say, except, "Have you tried making love *after* dinner?"

You're a little too gentle.

Don't tell this to Angelica's husband, but some women out there do like it hard and fast. Especially women whose men seem a little too mild-mannered all the damn time, a little like Clark Kent. They secretly long for an occasional display of passion. No, they don't want to get knocked around. They want to feel desired.

"He is a really sweet man, but he is not exactly the most

passionate person," said Whitney, an executive recruiter in Cleveland, about her boyfriend of 10 months. She wished he would throw her on the couch and ravish her more often. "It makes me feel wanted. When I feel that he wants me, that does a lot for my ego and a lot for me wanting to have sex."

Some women enjoyed it as something different, something to be thrown into the mix every now and then for the sake of variety. "I enjoy aggressive, strong sex on occasion," said a woman in Savannah, Georgia.

Other women want it that way all the time. "I need to be controlled—forced," wrote Val in Sacramento. No, it's not politically correct, but for some women it's highly erotic.

You're a little too wild.

More than a few women out there are being pestered to partake of the usual male diversions. Some guys like this stuff; very few women do. And these women are having none of it.

- "I truly and absolutely am not interested in anal sex or bringing another woman into our bed," said Sandy in Morganton, North Carolina.
- "I need to broach the subject to my current partner that some fantasies are more exciting as fantasies," said a lady in Salt Lake City.
- Kathleen in Fort Smith, Arkansas said, "I don't get turned on by his turn-ons, that is, porn, spankings, continual use of toys."

There will be more on women's reactions to these things later.

You're a little too boring.

She doesn't want to limit your sexual repertoire. She doesn't want plain-vanilla, missionary-position sex all the time.

- "If I don't ask, he will do it much the same each time," said Nickie in upstate New York.
- "He doesn't understand how much more creative I wish we were," said a faxed reply from a woman in Calgary, Alberta.
- "I like to do role playing and enjoy being submissive," said Kit in Michigan.
- And in an e-mail, Wendy confessed, "I would like to try new things but am scared to ask."

The good news is, she's ready to spice things up a bit. The better news is, she's blaming herself, not you.

"I prefer sex a little wilder, and it's my fault for not telling him," said Cynthia in Chicagoland. To belabor the obvious, this is her secret desire. She hasn't told him.

THE SHORT ANSWER

GOING SOLO?

We asked 80 women, "Do you want to know if he's masturbating without you?"

- "He does."
- "I'm sure he does and I really don't care. More power to him."
- "There are girls who think their boyfriends don't masturbate because they're satisfied. It really doesn't have anything to do with that."
- "I wish he would. Then he could respond to my needs more than his own."
- "I would like him to masturbate in front of me. That would turn me on."
- "If he wasn't having sex with me, then I'd worry."

What isn't your partner telling you? Or what has she told you that hasn't gotten through?

"Sometimes I like being serious and sometimes I want to have fun and laugh," said another Cindy in Illinois. "It frustrates me that he always does the same things. I should tell him, but I'm afraid he'll want it his way or he'll just smile and continue."

Sometimes she's just not in the mood, okay? You don't have to take it so personally. . . .

"Just because I'm not in the mood doesn't mean I don't love him," said Jennifer in San Jose, California.

We've done it ourselves. She said no, we keep begging, and as part of our campaign to change her answer, we resort to pouting and hurt feelings.

"Sometimes I just don't want to have sex, and it has nothing to do with him," said Bonnie in Pennsylvania.

Bonnie, we know that. We're just hoping that the poor-pitiful-me routine will get us laid.

It may, but unfortunately, it won't get us any respect.

CHAPTER EIGHTEEN

Married . . . with Children

THE YEARS DEVOTED TO CAREER BUILDING
AND CHILDREARING TAKE THEIR TOLL on
even the best of marriages. It's hard to find the time,
but there are some proven ways
to reconnect with that woman who walked
down the aisle to you.

No wonder we're afraid of commitment.

Women with children under 18 are less satisfied with their sex lives. Oddly, they are more likely to say they have feelings of guilt or shame about sex that keep them from enjoying its pleasures. And they're significantly more likely to complain that hubby wants sex too often.

Those were just some of the findings from our Magellan Poll of nearly 1,200 women. After our 68th question, we left some blank space and asked them to use it "to give a final word of advice to the men who will read our forthcoming book." They did not hesitate. They did not stint. They took us at our word. They gave us praise and criticism, thankfulness and despair, tired clichés and brilliant insights. But nothing quite prepared us for the sheer volume of resentment.

Many of our respondents were moms—we were tempted to call this the Soccer-Mom Survey—who may put on a cheerful face for the world, but who secretly are filled with built-up bitterness, and they poured it out on paper to us when given the chance.

These women often feel like their husbands have put their marriages on autopilot. They feel taken for granted, which is easy to feel, considering how hard they work, both in and outside the home. Because they work so hard, they are constantly stressed out. This is supported by the recent MIDUS (Midlife in the United States) survey of 3,032 Americans that was conducted by the MacArthur Foundation, a private humanitarian organization based in Chicago. Among women ages 35 to 44, a full third feel like they have too many demands made on them at home either most of the time or all of the time.

So, you may ask, why are you reading about this in the sex section? Because it became crystal clear to us, as we read those messages, that women's resentment manifests itself in low sex drives and lousy sex lives.

As Toni, a 52-year-old registered nurse and mother of two in Queens told us, "When you're a young mom and you are working, everything becomes a chore."

Because we heard the same basic message over and over again, we think it may be helpful just to replay some of it here. If you see you and your wife in this scenario, that could be useful, in and of itself.

Chances are, your problems are not happening to you alone.

The same stresses color millions of marriages, and the same problems hit couple after couple. You may not realize this because few couples broadcast the nitty-gritty details of their marital difficulties.

Knowing that others have gone through the same predicaments, you may be more willing to try some of the solutions that others suggest. We'll end this chapter with several ideas.

First though, here are some representative voices that articulate the predicament. Because they are so personal and revealing, they are also anonymous.

- "I don't have sexual desires. We have not had sex for over 2 years. We are in counseling at this time. Initially we had sex, but it got less and less frequent. We've been married 9 years now. Our kids are 3 years old and 19 months old. We would both like to have a closer relationship. We get along fine, but definitely not in the bedroom."

- "My husband is very unhappy at work so he comes home miserable, not wanting to be near our two children, ages 2 and 4. This never gives me a break. Also, my husband would like sex more often than I would. Part of it is fatigue, and also I'm home all day watching PBS. At the end of the day I don't feel human, let alone sexy."

- "It just seems that the years of raising children and striving to get ahead take a toll on a good marriage. There are not enough hours in the day, and by the time the kids are in bed, we're exhausted. We both do not have any family that live near or anyone to take the kids so we could escape. I just wish life would be less stressful and demanding for a couple. We really have to try hard to find time for each other, or I'm afraid we will distance ourselves from each other and this will create an even greater stress on the relationship."

- "My husband and I have grown so far apart, I honestly don't know if there's any turning back. Unfortunately, it seems from my experience that only one partner winds up giving most of the time, only to find oneself lonely and sad."

- "I have several good friends at work and we have spoken about our sex lives. We are all about the same age (30 to 35), and we've all been married 13 to 15 years. They tell me they aren't interested in sex, and their husbands can't get enough. Me, on the other hand, well, I can't get enough. Maybe it's because these ladies have children and I don't."

THE FACTS OF LIFE

"BUT WE JUST DID IT LAST MONTH"

We asked the women we surveyed, "What is your greatest sexual concern right now?" Among women with children, hubby's greater sexual desire was the most common concern.

	Women with Kids under 18	Women without Kids
I'm not interested in sex as often as he is	29.1%	18.4%

What we did not hear, unfortunately, was any acknowledgment of the husbands' predicament. You can guess it: These are guys in their thirties and forties who may be facing a crunch time in their work lives. They are busy building businesses and careers. They're not kids any longer; they're at make-or-break stages; they may have been given golden opportunities; they're being hammered to perform. They're trying to build something, and the time is now. They're so busy, and their wives are so busy, that they have just about zero time for each other. And the result is something sad but typical: The only time he's tender is when he's approaching her for sex.

As one woman told us, point-blank, "Often times, sex is the only time my husband will touch me."

How does she react to this? Not well. Not well at all. She gets hurt, and she gets angry. Sex becomes not a point of contact in their busy lives, but a flash point for resentment. Each subsequent approach is viewed with more and more suspicion.

- "The only thing on his mind all the time is sex. I enjoy being in his company, talking, watching a movie, or being outdoors having conversation. He enjoys sex, sex, and sex."

- "If a man is not so nice to you during the day, who wants to have sex? It's about being kind and thoughtful and caring and loving all throughout the day, not just at bedtime. It's about sharing responsibility 50-50. Men usually have a one-track mind."

Women keep gigantic scoreboards. Whether or not that's their intentions, that's how it feels on the receiving end. You know, if you didn't run half of the errands that morning, you get the cold shoulder that night.

Clearly, these women have stopped viewing sex as a pleasant opportunity to reconnect with their mates. Instead, they think of sex as one more incessant demand, one more chore. (If their husbands are selfish lovers, well then, the women are absolutely right.)

The end result is a Mexican standoff.

She withholds sex and he withholds affection.

Both are withholding what the other wants in an effort to gain some control over a bad situation. Listen to this missive we received from Jill in Maine.

> My husband wants sex constantly. If I mention we need to buy toilet paper at the store, he says, "Speaking of toilet paper, how about a little loving?" As for me, I personally could go weeks without it. This has caused a great deal of stress and arguments in our relationship. With two completely different sex drives, the strain on our marriage is very apparent. The more he pushes and complains and finds fault with me over it, the further away I get, and so on and so on. It's a vicious cycle, and it's driving us apart.

Yes, Jill, it is a vicious cycle. The less often we have sex, the hornier and needier we get. We start to pester. We begin to paw. And that turns you off all the more. By this point, most guys can't see how unattractive they've become. But their wives can. "Complaining, whining, and arguing over how few times you have sex is definitely not going to make her want it anytime soon," advised one resentful wife. "If she has sex with you just because you're begging for it, it may make her feel dirty, cheap, and used."

That's great. Just great. Now how do you back yourself out of that dead-end lane?

Here are 8½ suggestions for a happier marriage bed. (The ninth, we offer half in jest.)

1. Meet halfway. Yes, guys, you have to acknowledge that for many women, sex is not as physical. As one woman wrote, "Women view sex as sharing—mentally, physically, and emotionally—as opposed to merely a physical release." You have to romance her. Okay, ladies. If we acknowledge that, will you acknowledge that, for us, sex *is* a physical release? And let's not say "merely," because the belittles the way we're built. Let's face it, you're singing a sad old song.

THE FACTS OF LIFE

NO WONDER YOU'RE GROUCHY

We asked the women we surveyed to fill in the blank at the end of this sentence: "If you could wiggle your nose like Samantha on *Bewitched,* and change one thing about your husband, he would magically . . ." Among women with children, a sour spouse was the top concern.

	Women with Kids under 18	Women without Kids
Lighten up; stop being grouchy so often	25.2%	18.4%

It's called "Why Isn't a Man More like a Woman?" And it's getting you nowhere.

John Gray, Ph.D., has a solution that gets to the heart of the matter. He advises that wives give their husbands quickies to relieve their pent-up libidos. And in return, husbands should take their wives away from it all, once a month, for at least 24 hours of duty-free relaxation, attention, and romance.

2. Date your wife. Does that sound trite? So what? What do you have to lose? Wouldn't you be pleasantly surprised if the solution were really that easy? Maybe it is. After all, "I really don't think women expect that much from a man," one woman wrote.

> "Glamour is just sex that got civilized."
> —DOROTHY LAMOUR

Another one said, "If you are married, don't forget to still date your wife. If you have kids and your wife stays home, it is even more important to take the time to make your wife feel like someone other than a mommy all the time."

Jane in El Cajon, California, one of the 80 women who gave us an in-depth interview, completely agreed. "You have to feel like a woman and not like a mom, because that's two totally different things. Being a mom does not make you feel like a woman. It makes you stressed and crazy. Take me out; let me get dressed up and put makeup on and do my hair and go to a movie and feel good and have other men look at me. It makes everybody feel better."

Dating didn't work as well for Donna, who e-mailed us this note: "After you have children, all your money and time is spent on them. My husband and I still went out on an occasional date, *which I would plan,* because I wanted us to remember we still needed and wanted each other. But the extra attention he gave me when we were dating was not there. It was just a night out without the kids."

"Which I would plan . . ." Did you hear the resentment in that? Make sure date night is not just another item on her

endless list of chores. Ideally, you'd fulfill this young wife's fantasy:

> "Ask me out on a date, make the sitter arrangements, and tell me where we're going. Surprises would be nice. Think of me first, for once. Show me it's me who is most important in your life."

3. Pat each other on the back. "Most women married, with children, don't expect a lot," said Belinda. "Just every now and then surprise us with a little something. Say I love you when least expected. A hug when least expected. Let me know I'm doing a good job as a mother, wife, and friend."

Is it easier to *do* something than say something? Then pitch in with the chores. Most women will get the point. "Good foreplay is when the kids aren't there and we clean the house together," said Jane. "We've got the music playing real loud; and he's vacuuming and I'm cleaning the bathroom or whatever; and we're stripping the sheets off the

---

THE FACTS OF LIFE

MAYBE YOU NEED A VACATION—JUST THE TWO OF YOU

We asked the women we surveyed, "What would be your ideal vacation? Imagine that money is no object and guilt is no obstacle." The vast majority of all women, moms included, would like to get away with no kids in tow. Hint, hint!

	All Women	Women with Kids under 18
Romantic vacation	81%	78%
Family vacation	11%	16%
Girlfriends vacation	5%	4%
Solo vacation	2%	2%

bed and stuff. I love that. It makes me feel like he realizes how much stuff needs to be done around here, that he doesn't think that elves come in the middle of the night and do it."

4. Make nonsexual contact. So many, many women complained that the only physical affection they got was part of a sexual approach—and at that point it felt like too little, too late. We could quote 50 women saying this: "Take the time to hug and kiss when you are not in the bedroom and expecting sex."

"I don't need sex every day," said Tonilynn in Waukegan, Illinois, in her response to our *New Woman* magazine survey. "I like to be held without feeling guilty that he's aroused and wants a blow job." Those few words seethe with resentment. You have to remove that initial resentment before any reconciliation can take place.

5. Change your sexual contact. She may look forward to sex if it is more of a mini-adventure and less of a routine. "I would love it if he would just ask me to try something new, just because we're always looking for ways to make it different and more exciting and fun," said Debbie, a 33-year-old group director of a Westchester, New York, advertising agency and the mother of an infant daughter. "After a while, you know each other so well; you can certainly get into a routine where sex is conventional and it's always the same and it loses a lot of the passion."

6. Change your approach. Instead of putting sex in terms of your needs, put it in terms of the relationship. Sex, after all, is not "just" sex. It's a major glue that holds a marriage together. Studies of happy marriages usually find a lot of happy moments behind closed doors. For example, when psychologist and marriage counselor Judith Wallerstein, Ph.D., of Belvedere,

> "Hot monogamy is no big secret. Part of it is taking the responsibility for keeping my own fire going, and feeling sexy myself. The way I dress or buy lingerie or get my nails done. I'm turning myself on first."
>
> —SUSAN, California

California, studied 50 couples to distill the nine fundamental characteristics of a happy union, sexual love was ranked number six. "A good sex life, however the couple defines that, is at the heart of a good marriage," she wrote in her book *The Good Marriage*.

Put in those terms, asking for a recharged sex life is not merely a selfish demand to have your way with her. It's an expression of concern about the marriage.

7. Seek counseling. In our Magellan Poll, a third of the women with children under 18 have sought pastoral or professional counseling to help deal with the problems in their marriages.

One woman wrote, "I sought counseling to address my decline in sexual drive after experiencing a year of seven deaths in the family. It helped."

Low sex drive, sometimes called inhibited sexual desire or ISD, can be caused by many things, including medications and hormone levels. Some are fixed easily. Some are not. But it's definitely worth a shot.

8. Maintain some perspective. See the forest through the trees. Instead of playing the game of who's-working-harder-here, ask why you're both working so hard and where it's leading you and whether you want to go there.

In the midst of so much unhappiness poured out on paper, we occasionally heard from someone with a refreshing attitude, someone who seemed to have her eyes on the horizon. Like Roberta in southern Indiana, for instance, who proudly described herself as the "wife of Mark, a farmer, home builder, and great dad." She wrote:

"I am truly happy with my husband and he truly loves me. We both know how lucky/blessed we are and we speak of it often. We start and end each day with a kiss and 'I love you,' and we stop for a hug whenever we can. With three children ages 7, 4½, and 2½, and another one coming, we are very busy, but we never lose sight of each other and of what we have together."

Roberta, do you have any sisters?

Here's another snippet of wisdom.

"We all tend to take things and others for granted," said Lillian in Hawaii. "And that needs to stop because without any warning, things can be taken away; and then we live with shoulda, woulda, and coulda."

And one last thought:

"Neither of us is perfect. We enjoy being together. We try to help each other and make this life interesting and uplifting."

There is evidence to suggest that hope and optimism about your relationship will in fact lead to a long-lasting, happier relationship.

9. If all else fails, get divorced. It doesn't mean you have to stop seeing each other—or so we're told. Listen to this story.

> We were married for 5 years, got divorced, but are still involved. He lives in Florida, I live in Ohio. We get together three or four times a year. Our relationship is 100 percent better now than when we were married, precisely because we don't see each other very often. When we do get together, it's wonderful because we're both on our best behavior and we make the most of every minute.

Hey, maybe they're onto the next big thing. Journalist Philip Weiss, who often muses in Manhattan's *The New York Observer* about his wife's misgivings, may be headed down this path. "My wife likes me to leave the house for days," he recently wrote. "Lately, she's come up with the idea of a 'semi-husband.' She had two friends on the West Coast who had broken up with their husbands and were now dating them. 'What could be better than that?' she said."

For some couples, maybe nothing. Nothing at all.

CHAPTER NINETEEN

Setting the Right Mood

MOST MEN HATE ANTICIPATION. It gets in
the way. But women love anticipation. For
them, anticipation *is* the way. A day of phone
calls and compliments and affection is
all part of mental foreplay.

You're about to hear some pure, out-and-out girl talk. At
times, it will be so nicey-nice, so unfailingly polite, that it
will make your teeth ache.

So we're going to cut you a break, right here up front.
We're going to start with the translation into guy speak.
Here's the take-home message of this chapter, as translated
for us by Jane, a 30-year-old mother of two in El Cajon,
California.

> If he's been a jerk all day and then he's only nice for 10 min-
> utes, that doesn't do it.

You have to set a mood.

This is not some minor detail that maybe you can overlook
except on Valentine's Day. Let's put it this way. . . . You know
how important foreplay is to women, right? Well, here's the
point: They think that setting the mood is part of foreplay.

We are not kidding.

"Foreplay starts long before you hop into bed," said Lorri in Washington State.

Do you feel like a deer caught in the headlights?

"Foreplay begins way before the bedroom. If he's understanding and considerate during the day, sex is always better at night."

So said Connie in central Pennsylvania. The women we surveyed indicate that she speaks for women everywhere.

One Vancouver woman even called it romantic foreplay.

And Laura, a 32-year-old Web site developer in New York City, referred to romance as "the mental side of foreplay."

To most guys, the very idea of mental foreplay is, like, out there. But to most women, the idea is right here. That's because, for us, the upward climb to orgasm is pretty much a matter of penile stimulation. But for them, it's not strictly a matter of genital arousal. They claim that the brain is their biggest sex organ. One of our intrepid in-depth interviewers went so far as to say, "Women are sexual from the brain on down; and men are sexual from the dick up."

Maria, a 24-year-old student in Chicago, put it most simply. She said, "A big portion of good sex occurs in my head."

When you realize this fundamental difference between the sexes, a lot of things start to fall into place. As Karen in Hilliard, Florida, made clear in this *New Woman* magazine survey response:

> For most women, sex is between the ears. (In other words, what sets the flame, fans it, and creates the biggest infernos is what happens in the brain beforehand—words, innuendos, looks, small touches, a single kiss, etcetera.) It's like a Christmas present: The longer you have to look at the wrapped package under the tree, the more wonderful the anticipation and the more you want to open it. Why do you think women love reading romance novels so much? Those books are 99 percent buildup, 1 percent action.

The flip side of that is: no buildup, no action. Let's look at the specific components of a good buildup.

1. Touch her in a loving but no-strings-attached way. "Everyone likes being touched," said Wendy, a 26-year-old programmer in New York City. "I really like being touched. I remember one time my boyfriend brushed my hair for about half an hour and I was so wet—I just had orgasms for days. I was, like, crying afterward, and he was, like, 'What's wrong, honey?' "

For some women, it's especially arousing if you display your affections in public. "Public shows of affection make me feel proud and cared for," said Kathy in Peoria, Illinois.

> "Lingerie makes the evening feel different. It's not just stripping down to nothing."
> —OLIVIA, New England

Anna in Huntington Beach, California, agreed. "To me, the sexiest thing a man can do is to make me feel sexy when other people are around—to make me feel like we're the only two people there."

And here's a promise from an anonymous respondent to our survey: "Take more time to be romantic instead of, 'How about you and me go upstairs.' If there was hugging, touching, and kissing ahead of time, he wouldn't have to ask to go upstairs. It would happen where we were."

2. Be an old-fashioned chauvinist—her chauvinist. You know, this stuff worked for eons, and Angela in California is one of many women who thinks it still works. "Opening the door for you, taking your arm as you walk, anything like that," she said. "There aren't a lot of men who do that anymore."

3. Pay her a compliment. "I wish he would be more complimentary about my body," said Catherine in Chicago of her boyfriend. "He isn't. And it shuts me down a little bit. For the most part, I am happy about the way I look, but it would be nice to get some feedback about that. I think he feels a little bit burdened about my insecurity around it."

Laura in New York City really laid it on the line: "The less I hear it, the less I think of myself physically. And if I don't feel attractive around him, I'm not going to want to have sex. If I don't feel like I'm beautiful then, you know, I'm going to be a lot more intimidated when I take my clothes off, when I start to do things to his body. I'm going to feel a lot more insecure. I think more men really need to understand that they have to kiss up, I guess."

Compliments are critically important to women who are not a pert, perky size four anymore. If she has any weight problems or beauty issues or body-image issues, she'll need you to be expressive. Eunice in Louisiana wrote to say, "Lately, I've been feeling self-conscious about my weight. This caused me to have a decreased sexual drive for a while. When I spoke about it, my husband was encouraging. He said he found me to be sexy and likened my body to the women in the famous Renaissance paintings and sculptures. Our sex life became almost immediately better. I still need to watch my weight, but at the same time I feel desirable."

Other women don't want compliments about appearances. Alice, a 46-year-old nurse in Canada, for instance, said, "I love a compliment about something I've done. I'm more of a concrete person in that respect. A good dinner that I've worked hard on ... I love compliments like that, where he's giving me credit. That sets me up. I'm really easy then."

Pardon the shouting, but the overall point is to *make her feel appreciated*. Mandy in Pennsylvania put it nicely: "Don't we all feel a little bit more adventuresome when we feel good about ourselves? We really feel like glory."

As a final thought: Timing is everything. Don't wait until you're in bed to pay a compliment, or your sincerity will be suspect. She'll assume it's your dumb stick talking. One woman gave us this advice: "Never tell a woman she's beautiful when the lights are off."

THE FACTS OF LIFE

YOU'RE GETTING WARMER

We asked, "What is guaranteed to turn you on?" No big surprises here; the fundamental things apply. When we did some extra number crunching, we found that some results were age related. The younger the woman, the more likely she'll enjoy a massage, sexually explicit material, and alcohol. (Percentages total more than 100 because respondents could give multiple answers.)

Candlelight, music, and a roaring fire	68%
A massage	63%
A romantic movie	46%
Showering together	45%
A scent	36%
Compliments about her beauty	28%
Sexually explicit material	26%
Swimming together	17%
Alcohol	16%
Exercise	10%
Other	9%

Hmmm. That could have been the title of this book.

4. Pay attention. Talk to her. When men talk, they share information. When women talk, they share feelings. The act of talking, in itself, is intimate. Maybe that explains why a woman in Waterbury, Connecticut, wrote, "Good foreplay for me is hours of conversation over a really good bottle of wine."

Denise in Massachusetts feels the same. "A guaranteed way to turn me on would be having a completely open, honest, intimate conversation. Being uninhibited with my partner makes me feel real connected to my partner. When the conversation is followed by lots of kissing, stroking, cuddling, and touching, I am totally turned on and ready for a night of wild, hot, passionate sex."

We could continue to quote women saying stuff like, "Foreplay is an all-day, all-night event." Clearly, some women could talk about it all day and all night. Here's the topper: Andrea in Ohio said, "Foreplay is maybe a way of life." This is where most men get lost, because these women have gotten a little too dreamy—their scenarios sound like a daytime soap opera.

But you should see their real lives. Kate in Chicago gave us a glimpse of her reality when she said, "Sitting around, drinking beer, and watching television for a couple of hours makes me not that interested in having sex."

Kate likes to get out in the evenings. But if you do stay home, well, that doesn't have to be all bad. It's what you make of it. Compare Kate's home life to this scene:

"Foreplay is anything that happens before sex that is sensual," said Sarah Jane, a 43-year-old consultant in Michigan. "I mean, I have had dinner where we made pasta puttanesca, and I wore my bra and put a linen napkin in it. He wore his underwear. We had a blast. That, to me, is foreplay."

5. When the mood builds, don't blow it. We may be making this setting-the-mood thing sound like more of a burden than it has to be. You know, most women are like Kate—all you really have to do is go out for a great night with them, and the mood is set automatically. In that case, your only job is not screwing up once you get back home.

Lori, a 28-year-old computer consultant in Fort Lee, New Jersey, made an excellent point:

I have this thing that, whenever we get dressed up and go out for a night on the town, if I'm wearing a skirt and heels, that means it's supposed to be a romantic night. A sexual night because we're dressed up. Those are missed opportunities, otherwise, because I'm always feeling prettier when I'm in a sexy dress. So the trick is, when we first walk back in the door, to keep my mood going and kiss me or throw me against the wall, or pick me up and throw me into bed.

But don't wait for me to brush my teeth and take off my dress and get in my pajamas, because by then it's missed. Don't turn on the lights and check for messages and get on the phone. Don't come home and start talking about the scores of the baseball game. This is not the night for it.

And now that you're both mentally ready for bed, what do you do to get ready physically? We put this question to our 80 in-depth interview subjects: "A lot of men love it when a woman wears lingerie to bed. But what can a man do before he comes to bed?"

The overwhelming, nearly universal reply was "Take a shower."

Remember, "women," as one said, "are olfactory people." Perhaps you hadn't noticed, but their sense of smell is keener than yours. It's not just that they want you not to smell bad.

Women think a freshly showered man smells good. Sexy, even.

"I think it's awesome if a man comes to bed and smells like soap," said Catherine, a 24-year-old Canadian studying in the Midwest.

The runner-up reply was "Brush your teeth."

"It's all in the breath. He needs to brush his teeth, or I can't do it," said Kate, a Chicago attorney.

"It's amazing how many times a man will get into bed and not realize that his pizza-and-beer breath is a turnoff," said Anna from Huntington Beach, California.

We think this is pretty good news, actually. After the demanding tone of the requests for more romantic foreplay, this is refreshing. Women aren't expecting that much of us at bedtime. A bar of soap, a bottle of mouthwash, and thou. That's it. Oh, and if it's your place, not hers: clean sheets. Can you handle that? For women, love is a front-end operation.

> "Good flirting is much
> better than bad sex."
> —AMY BLOOM,
> in SELF magazine

So light a few candles. Put on some music. No, there's no secret sex music that will drive her wild. Most of our 80 interviewees like music in the background during lovemaking, but their tastes run the gamut from rock to reggae to classical. It's not like they all said, "Oh, I'll go down on anyone who plays the Cranberries."

But here's one tip: Now is perhaps the time to play that CD of hers that you really hate. You know, one of those Lilith Fair female vocalists. You may get a reaction. "One of my favorite experiences was Fiona Apple—'Criminal,' " recalled Danielle from Philadelphia. "That song . . . it's a very female empowering song, and I just crawled all over him and completely took control."

What about underwear? Is there any such thing as the male equivalent of a Victoria's Secret scarlet teddy? Not really. Our in-depth interviewees preferred silk boxers over briefs. But they gagged at the thought of you wearing something that you think might be sexy. "Men turn me on," confided Wendy, "but I don't want to look at them in a rubber G-string or anything."

Susi, a Philadelphia mother of two, recalled, "I had a boyfriend once who wore bikini underwear to bed. I was, like, 'Go join the Chippendales.' I thought it was so stupid."

Chances are, the underwear you should wear is already tucked away in your dresser drawer. It's the underwear that she gave you, doofus. "I like it when he just wears his cute little boxers that I buy for him," said Carly, a New York City teacher.

The women we grilled were largely indifferent to cologne. They don't care whether Fido or Snowball is in the room. Whether the lights are on or off is strictly a matter of personal preference. (A 29-year-old Alabama woman told us, "Bright overhead light makes me feel like I'm at the gynecologist's office.")

And although some women think it's erotic if you leave one item of clothing on, most do not. Mostly, they want you to take off your socks. "The socks have got to come off," said Catherine. "Unless it's a quickie, where he's still wearing his pants and you can't see the whole leg/sock ratio. But if he's totally naked except for one piece of clothing, that's ridiculous."

"Get those stupid socks off," said Kristen, a 29-year-old teacher in Chicago. "The last thing we want to see is a guy walking around half-naked with socks on."

"Yes! Yes!" agreed Dawn, a 21-year-old student in Maine. "One time, he left his shoes on. Oh, God!"

CHAPTER TWENTY

Having the Right Attitude

MEN ARE GOAL-ORIENTED. We're intent on
getting to the big result. But to most women,
orgasm is not the be-all and end-all. They love a
guy who simply remembers to have fun.

"Don't be a self-centered slob," cautioned SueAnne in Denver.
"There are enough of those on both sides of the gender fence."

Thanks, SueAnne, for acknowledging that men do not
have the market cornered when it comes to selfishness. That's
a tired image of masculinity. The stereotype of the piggy
male, Mr. Wham-Bam-Thank-You-Ma'am, doesn't ring as
true anymore. If anything, men may be trying a little too hard
to please. We heard more advice directed that way. Women
these days want you to loosen up. Have fun. Stop performing,
start enjoying, and let the pleasure be mutual.

"I enjoy giving as well as receiving," said Kristi in Texas.

You say that you *are* being pleased? Then let her know that.
"Hearing somebody make a sound because they are excited
about something you are doing—that is the most erotic thing
in the universe," said Dee, a 32-year-old professor in Chicago.

This advice applies in spades to young men, many of whom
are inexperienced and anxious about their love skills in the sack.

That's a problem, and here's why.

DOES SIZE MATTER? MAYBE THIS WILL SET YOU STRAIGHT

You can't change your size, but maybe you can change your attitude. That's the lesson here, as we listen in on two Chicago women engaging in girl talk.

"What's your opinion on size?"

"I think size does matter. But everyone's always talking about its length, and I don't think length matters that much. It's girth, diameter. That's what matters. There have been times with guys I've dated where, like, they're on the small side, and that makes a difference. But it does matter, too, what they do with it."

"I think it's possible to be too big. Someone I dated, sex with him was just, like . . ."

"Uncomfortable."

"Yeah. It's almost better to be small because there are things you can do to make up for it. But when you're too big, then . . . Well, you can do other things, too, but when you get to the actual sex, you're just, like, 'Ouch.' "

"It also seems like—and this is from females, like, chatting—it seems that when they're too big, they completely lack any imagination. And that's really why big is bad. It's just so boring. The guy is like, 'I have a huge dick, and so this should be enough.' "

"Actually, with the guy I dated, it was the reverse. He did so much. We did so many things."

"How self-absorbed was he? Because it's been my experience that when the guy is really big . . ."

"Well, because he knew I'd have problems having sex with him, he was more focused on me. He had to get me just so turned on in order for sex to be possible. Otherwise, he'd be left with jerking off. He had to work harder just to make sex possible."

"Okay. Then maybe I had bad experiences."

"I don't know. I think I'm just too tight."

Your anxiety gets in the way of your ability to please and to be pleased.

"I have been with guys with less experience who are kind of anxious, and I end up holding that anxiety for them," said Catherine, a 28-year-old graduate student in Chicago. "When I was younger, my mind, too, was more into insecurities and less in the present moment. So guys should know it feels good to be with someone who is less anxious, and there is really nothing to be anxious about. It feels good!"

Megan in Cincinnati agreed. "I want men to just remain lighthearted and not be insecure. I just love lighthearted sex. I really believe sex can be great when it's just fun and relaxed."

Lighthearted sex. We like that.

"A confident lover is a better lover," said Diane, 24, a teacher in Philadelphia, "because you don't have to worry about them so much. If he's confident in what he's doing or what he can't do, and he knows himself well enough, then it's easier for me. We can just have fun together and everything."

Both sexes gain confidence with age, so this becomes less and less of a problem. In fact, as we learn to give and receive pleasure in equal portions, a magical thing happens. The two become one. Listen to the wisdom of Joanne, 52, a teacher in Texas who has been happily married for 31 years. "The mutuality of it is the turn-on," she said. "To me, the best part of love-making is when you can't tell whether you're giving or receiving. When you absolutely can't decide which one it is, it's so mixed up together. When you get to that place, that is ecstasy."

The reason you're being told to relax is that women don't want sex for the same reason you do. You're furiously trying to achieve two sometimes-conflicting goals—your orgasm, and her orgasm. You have your eyes on the prize. You're trying to accomplish something.

Most women are not.

Most women care less about having an orgasm than you do.

Not all women. There are women like Melissa in Western Pennsylvania, who wrote, "I'm not satisfied with one orgasm. At least six, and it doesn't take that long." Melissa, you definitely need to find yourself a sexually compatible mate. But most women aren't like Melissa. They're more like Wendy, a computer programmer in New York City.

> It's more of a big deal to men. They want to know that they've satisfied you. And because of that, they often stop themselves from coming and it annoys the hell out of me. I mean, come already! It was fun. It was good. We're done. I always enjoy myself. And I always enjoy myself even if I don't have an orgasm. Half an hour isn't going to make me happier than 5 minutes, usually.

A continent away, Kelly in San Francisco told us essentially the same thing.

> It's hard for him to differentiate between what it's like for him to come and what it's like for me. He can't understand that my orgasm is different, and I don't necessarily need to have 15 of them. Sometimes, I feel him holding off on his own orgasm to make sure that I come. And I've reiterated many, many times: Let's just go with it. Whatever happens, happens. If you come first, that's fine. If we have to stop, that's fine, too. I can have an orgasm another way if I want one. Maybe I don't even want one. That's okay, too.
>
> His orgasm is like the end-all, be-all. His is what he works toward. That is literally the climax of the event. And for me it's not that way. You know, the whole event, in its entirety— that's what I live for.

No, this is not a bicoastal thing. We heard from Barbara, a 28-year-old human resources administrator in Chicago.

> It very much bums him out if I do not orgasm. It's like the sex, which was great for him, was then not good for him because

I did not orgasm. So sometimes when I'm really tired, I'll give in and say, 'Okay, we can have sex,' just so he gets it. And I know he gets upset if I don't orgasm, so I'll try purposely not to orgasm, like putting my mind somewhere else. Then he's so upset I didn't orgasm, and why did he even try knowing that I was so tired, so he gets the point. Is that sexual punishment?

Well, maybe, but first tell us who's being punished here. Anyway, guys, your expectations make women feel pressured. They feel like they're onstage. And you know what people do when they're onstage? They act. This pressure leads directly to faked orgasms.

> "It's not true I had nothing on. I had the radio on."
> —MARILYN MONROE

"Sometimes, it is really annoying because he says all these things and tries to make me feel guilty," said Amy in Baltimore. " 'It is really stinky that I can't please you.' It makes me feel horrible. I feel pressured to have one because I feel like he wants me to have one so he feels like he has accomplished something."

And if one orgasm is good, aren't two or three even better?

All the publicity about multiple orgasms in recent years has raised the stakes for men, who can be competitive to a fault.

Besides, there's just something about the fantasy of giving a woman multiple orgasms that appeals to the 11-year-old boy in us. One woman had a perfect image for it: "It's like skipping stones." There we are, standing at the river's edge, and we'll try, try, try all afternoon until we get a fiver.

The pressure that women feel from men to have an orgasm is not limited to intercourse. "Sometimes, oral sex seems more of a pressure to orgasm because he's trying so hard for the big result," said Teri in Nashville.

We'll give you one more metaphor. Although there's lots of

physical contact, sex is actually not a contact sport. Don't keep score.

While we're on the subject of attitudes, let's discuss her attitude. If you're with a woman who has a healthy, positive attitude about sex, congratulations. Don't let her get away. But if you're dealing with deep-seated negativity, all we can say is good luck.

You would think that any woman who sat down with someone for an hour and a half and talked about the most intimate details of her life, with a tape recorder whirring in front of her . . . you'd think that woman would have an open, accepting, guilt-free sexuality. And, truth be told, most of the women were this way.

As Jamie in Baltimore told us, "Sex is a good thing. Sex is fun. Sex is exciting. Sex is important."

But we also heard the voices of a few conflicted women. Women like Andrea, a 29-year-old mother of two in Canada, who confessed, toward the end of her interview, "From the moment I started to have sex, I guess I've always felt like I shouldn't be. I think it's from my mother. I think her sexual attitudes transcended toward me, and I always felt bad."

It was a rare moment of candor on her part. During the rest of the interview, she seemed to be at war with herself. She said she wants her husband "to be a little bit more aggressive," but she evidently turns him down a lot. "Sometimes, I'll just give in to save the heavy sighing at 5:00 A.M." She wants to have "a pleasant time," as she put it, but doesn't want to give a man directions. And in one breath, she said, "I like men who take control"; but then, "I feel resentful toward always being dominated during sex."

We also heard from a 22-year-old student in Chicago who said all the guys she's been with are sexually "boring," but she admitted she's no ball of fire herself. She said she initiates half the time, and yet, "I never probably communicated it verbally." She'd like longer foreplay and more orgasms, but oddly, none of her dissatisfaction is her fault. It's always men. It's their fault.

A woman in Ohio, married for 22 years, is scared to death that her teenage boys might catch her having sex with their father. "I'm a real worrywart," she admitted. "I think he thinks that I'm no fun."

Finally, as proof that this attitude doesn't necessarily dissipate with age, a 59-year-old woman in New England, married nearly 40 years, never wears lingerie for him. "It degrades me." Nor does she wear high heels. "It is an exploitation. It is an objectification of women." She doesn't like oral sex. "I know if I receive, I am expected to give. And I don't want to give." What if she didn't have to reciprocate? Could she just lie back and enjoy it? Hmmm, maybe. But, "if you are going to do something like that, I want your mouth to be clean. And the lights have to be low." She was married for 20 years before she had an orgasm; before that, she faked it. Sex now can be nice, but only if thoroughly wrapped in romance. "Otherwise, it is just fulfilling a physical need, and I am really turned off by that."

> "Being a sex symbol has to do with an attitude, not looks. Most men think it's looks, most women know otherwise."
> —KATHLEEN TURNER

What is this, sour grapes? Is she bitter because she's unattractive? Did she have horrible sexual experiences? Nope. She says she was a hot tamale in her day.

This only helped convince us that people who treat sex as a power trip really hate sex underneath it all.

Before marriage, "I had two wild and stormy years," she said. "And during that time, I both exploited and was exploited. I learned how to seduce the men I wanted. I thoroughly enjoyed the game. I enjoyed the power. I had a beautiful body. And it gave me a great feeling of power just watching men have absolutely no control over themselves. It made me sick, it made me disgusted, and it still does to this day."

So, why are we telling you all this? After all, there's no quick fix. If the problem is more than shyness or youthful uncertainty, if it comes down to a deeply ingrained shame, that's not cured with a page of quick tips.

We're printing this for all the young men who've been thrown for a loop with confusing signals. They may get caught up in trying to figure her out and solve this mess, and say, "Well, if I just do that or we just do this. . . ." Man, we've been there. We're sorry. We really are. She may even convince you that it's your problem.

Friend, it is not about you. It's about her.

CHAPTER TWENTY-ONE

Getting to Yes

A GREAT SEX LIFE DOESN'T JUST HAPPEN.
The world has gotten way too busy for that.
So you schedule "together time," you respond to her
sexual mood, and you initiate with passion—but you
don't pounce. Give her a minute to get warmed up.

Barbara works in the human resources field and lives with her fiancé. She's 28. They recently moved to Chicago, where she has a tough commute to work—1 hour and 15 minutes each way. It makes for a long day. Like most Americans, when she gets home she is tired.

"We have a rule," she said. "If he wants to try something, it's got to be before 10:00 P.M. during the week. Ten P.M. is the rule. So some nights, he'll be rushing around the house to get me to do everything I need to do before 10 o'clock hits. He wants me in that bed by 9:45, so he'll help me do anything I want to do, and remind me about 20 times."

Is 10:00 P.M. an unbreakable rule? Well, no. "Not if he starts giving me a massage or anything like that. If he tries to do things quickly, then I just tell him to leave me alone, I need to go to bed. But if he starts kind of slowly and gives me a massage, or if he kisses my back . . . because he has a goatee, I love that. Anyway, those are some of the things I break the rule for."

Barbara and her fiancé are probably on the road to a healthy sex life together. They're flexible. They acknowledge that love-making is important. They appreciate each other's needs. And their 10:00 P.M. rule recognizes a fact of modern life.

More and more couples are finding that they simply have to make a date.

If you wait for sex to just happen, it usually doesn't. One or the other partner is too busy, too preoccupied, or too exhausted.

"Sometimes we plan it," said Vikki, a 37-year-old mother of three in Sandusky, Ohio. "Sometimes we'll say, 'When we get done with all the work we have to do today, let's make a date in our bedroom.' That's a lot of it, getting everything done so you can." And then there's the problem of working it in around the kids. But they do. "When the kids are all right there in the room, we'll say cute little things like, 'You know, I'm really into praise and worship right now.' We mean, 'I'll praise you and you worship me; or I'll worship you and you praise me.' " They're not being sacrilegious. In fact, they often pray together before sex.

Vicki in Illinois sent us this e-mail: "We are both equal when it comes to wanting sex, it's just that we don't have time. Now we pick a day or two each week to spend time to-gether, and we compromise with each other as to what we want to do to each other. It has really made our relationship a lot stronger and more secure!"

Vicki made it sound so simple. But it's not that simple for many couples, to judge by this anonymous response to our Magellan Poll: "When we have sex, it is fabulous and we al-ways wonder why we don't do it more often. But our daily routine is so hectic and stress-filled, it's hard to have the en-ergy or relax enough to get in the mood to begin."

Most people feel as if each new year is more stressful than the last. The pace of life exhausts us. That, more than

THE FACTS OF LIFE

TOO POOPED TO PARTICIPATE

We asked the women in our survey, "In your own life, what do you feel are the biggest barriers to enjoying great sex?" Lack of energy and time are the biggest spoilers. This is especially true for the women who are most satisfied with their relationships and sex lives; the majority of each subgroup checked off "fatigue." By the way, this is true of men as well. We got the same response from readers in our *Men's Health* magazine poll.

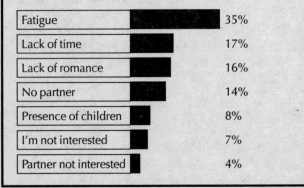

Fatigue	35%
Lack of time	17%
Lack of romance	16%
No partner	14%
Presence of children	8%
I'm not interested	7%
Partner not interested	4%

anything else, affects our sexuality, according to the results of our Magellan Poll.

Women tend to lose all feeling of romance amid the schedules of work, kids, errands, and to-do lists as long as their arms. Although some men can turn to sex as a stress buster, most women aren't like that. Their arousal is much more affected by thoughts, feelings, and overall mood.

What sex experts tell busy couples is to make sex important. Make it a priority.

There are people whose lives are busier than yours, and they find time for fun.

It's because they schedule it. They set aside time. They give their partners the same regard as a client or a community project. Is your partner's response, "I hate to schedule sex"? Well, guess what: The whole world is on a schedule. Does it seem contradictory to have to work at romance? Okay, maybe. But if you're grown-ups now, that's what it takes. Spontaneous sex is great, but when couples reach an impasse and end up glaring at each other in some therapist's office, it's precisely because they've left everything to chance.

Some couples find that making a date gets to be a turn-on. Knowing you're going to rendezvous later that night, you can call each other during the day to fan the flames. You tend to be more affectionate and playful. In effect, you spend the entire day getting slowly aroused. Bernie Zilbergeld, Ph.D., a psychologist in Oakland, California, uses the perfect term for this in his book *The New Male Sexuality*. He calls it simmering.

Making a date doesn't mean that you banish spontaneity from your life. You may still enjoy a quickie every now and then. If it's the exception rather than the rule, it may be a turn-on for her. "I think spontaneity is the key to quickies for us," said Kelly in San Francisco. "Usually, I like it a little rougher when I know it's going to be just a quickie, because it really gets my adrenaline going fast. It gets my juices flowing if it's kind of forceful."

Not many women initiate a quickie. Usually, it's a guy thing, right? We ask for it when we're crazed with desire for her.

Many women go along with the occasional quickie, but you have to ask nicely. If you haven't lost your head completely, a sense of humor helps.

For Dee, a 32-year-old single professor in Chicago, humor helps a lot.

> The quickie is something you do with someone you know pretty well. Like, when you are at the stage when you can say things like, "We have just 10 minutes." You feel comfortable and you can say exactly what you want. For me, I would probably be responsive to a joke at that point. I get really amused when he says, "Oh, I love you, I really, really love you." And it's obvious that he's horny. Not that he doesn't love me, but he makes me laugh. And I think, "Okay." I'm feeling close. We're laughing; that makes me feel much more connected. And if I feel connected, I feel sexually responsive.

Here's another tip: Don't pounce. Whatever type of sex you're initiating, be it a quickie or something more involved, don't come after her like some cartoon Lothario. Catherine, a 28-year-old graduate student in the Midwest, suggested this.

> If I am not in the mood, most of the time—I'd say, 8 times out of 10—I give the guy a shot at getting me in the mood. The key is to go slowly. Just touch me, kind of all over; hold me and give me little kisses. Move me slowly instead of, like, pouncing on me. It is just too jarring to be pounced on. If I am not in the mood, I have got to get those areas of my brain warmed up.

Just seeing your desire will help.

For most women, your desire fuels her desire. It is a powerful aphrodisiac. We were told that time and again.

Asked what might convince her to say yes to a quickie, Anna from Huntington Beach, California, said, "Probably pay compliments, along with hungry caresses. There's something about that hunger that's kind of a turn-on."

In fact, we were impressed by the willingness of most women to accommodate your sexual needs. Some of these women are so bighearted, we wish we could send them a bouquet of flowers on behalf of men everywhere. The first stop on the floral delivery route would be Olivia in New England. "I give in even when I don't want to sometimes, but it's nothing bad. I don't go, 'Grrrr.' I give in even when I'm not in the mood, knowing I will get in the mood."

When they say no and they mean it, not one woman complained that she was being misunderstood or ignored. They feel free to say no without the games that earlier generations have played. So, what does no finally mean? "It depends on how you answer," said Toni, a

> "There's sometimes when I want to be gentle and treated like a lady, and other times when I want to be treated like a biker mama."
>
> —VIKKI, OHIO

52-year-old registered nurse and divorced mother in Queens. "If you answer with a smile and a laugh, of course they're going to keep trying. If it's absolutely, 'No, I'm really not in the mood,' you don't have to give them the headache routine."

All women agree that not all sexual episodes are alike. There's the above-mentioned quickie, sometimes called the nooner if you're coming home for lunch that day. There are longer, more drawn-out sessions of passionate sex, during which you'll move through a variety of positions. And there's making love, the gentle, sweet, face-to-face encounters that arouse her emotionally as well as physically.

If you're initiating, it's wise to remember that she may say no to one type of sex, but yes to another. It all depends on her mood. You usually read these moods pretty well, you'll be glad to know. There were few complaints. "There's just a certain energy that I put out or that he puts out the helps us get connected," said Susan in California.

Still in doubt? Kate in West Bend, Wisconsin, said it's all in the kiss. "If you give him a really passionate, slow kiss, I would think they would get the hint that this is a night when we're going to take some time. Not that you can't enjoy other ways, but that kiss is a pretty good indication of what you want."

Sometimes, her mood doesn't matter. Sometimes, the fact is that you're going out and you have only 10 minutes. In that case, said Jamie in Baltimore, just be glad she's accommodating, and do as she says.

> A lot of times, if we are all dressed up and we are getting ready to go out, I might not want to have sex that is going to make me get messed up. So I will say, "Let me be on top so my head doesn't get messy." Or maybe I'll perform oral sex on him instead.

We asked the 80 women who consented to our in-depth surveys, "Are there certain times of day when you most enjoy having sex?" There was no standard reply to this question. Some women have a preference, some women don't. If you're getting turned down all the time, maybe you're just asking her at the wrong time of the day. That's true for whoever is married to Terrie in Texas. "I don't think there has ever been a compromise in our relationship. He always wants sex in the morning, and I want it before bed at night."

Whereas Kate, an attorney in Chicago, likes an afternoon delight. "I prefer to have sex, like, mid-afternoon. You've been up a while, you don't have morning breath. You're brushed your teeth. And sometimes in the afternoon, it's fun to have a quick one before you go someplace. You know, before you take him to the mall. If you screw him before you take him out, he's a lot nicer."

Aren't we all?

Most women expect you to initiate sex at least half the time—at least. Even among the 80 forward-thinking women who consented to our in-depth interviews, the vast majority

THE SHORT ANSWER

HER NOT-SO-SUBTLE CLUES

We asked the 80 women who consented to our in-depth surveys, "How do you two usually communicate your desires? Do you have any secret cues or signals?" Apparently, we were being a little too cute.

- "The sign is, I grab him and say, 'Let's do it. Get the condom and open the thing up.' That's the sign."
- "I'll stick my hand in his pocket and stroke his penis."
- "Sometimes when we're watching TV, I just jump on top of him."
- "He will go out of the room, and when he comes back I will be naked."
- "I'll flash him. I'll take my T-shirt off. I'll go in front of him and wiggle."
- "If I'm in the shower I go, 'Hey, come here'. He comes in the bathroom, locks the door, and the kids don't know what we're doing."
- "I'll bend him over and bite him on the ass."

said the initiation was equal, at most. They're not necessarily shy or submissive, though.

Women told us the traditional sex roles are the most erotic. When it comes to the mystery dance, they expect you to lead.

"It makes me feel feminine," said Nikki in Maine. "It makes me feel wanted."

That doesn't mean you have to take charge all the time, said Kelly in San Francisco. "You don't always have to decide how fast and where and when. All of those decisions can be either mutual, or you can give up some of them. I think if more men would do that, they'd be more relaxed."

Indeed.

The couples with the most active sex lives seem to be those in which both partners feel free to initiate, and they have a wide variety of ways to initiate at their disposal.

Like Kelly and her husband. They've been together for 7 years. They have sex five to eight times a week. Sometimes they start with words, sometimes with body language. Sometimes they have cues, like lighting the red bulb in the bedroom. Sometimes what sweeps them along is a running game of sorts, like how many dressing rooms they can do it in. Or she'll cash in a coupon for a sexual adventure that he gave her for her birthday. And sometimes they'll come up with something new. "When we lived in Florida, he was working late one night, so I showed up at his office wearing a coat—and nothing else. That was very fun."

Couples can do this if they're on the same page, so to speak. And the key is a ton of respect for each other. Each can say no without damaging the spirit of the relationship. "I know, if he does turn me down, it's going to be in a nice way," Kelly said. "It won't be in a way that makes me feel bad."

Conversely, if one partner initiates all the time, that leads to trouble. The pursuer feels unwanted; the pursued one feels hassled. It leads to arguments. For Brianna, a 37-year-old costume designer in California, that argument ended happily, at least. "I would say I have to initiate it all the time, and he would say he had to initiate it all the time. So I got a calendar. And I kept track. I let him initiate, and in a month we had sex twice. So I told him, "You tell me you like to have sex every day!" Now that he's been made aware of what's really going on, he's trying to make up for lost time."

His response will keep that relationship alive. Unfortunately, not everyone responds so positively. We got a few e-mail messages from women whose stress levels clearly hamper their personal lives.

- "It is very hard for me to relax and want to make love when I've had a tough day."
- "I have to get in the mood. Stress can hamper that mood for weeks."
- "I am not an instant on/off switch. If I'm mad or sad, the last (very last) thing I want is sex."

Show these women a calendar, and they'd probably make you eat it.

How you deal with her low libido is up to you. It's great if you can be hopeful and consider it temporary. And it's hard not to feel rejected. Hey, maybe because you were. But women kept insisting that it's not personal. As in this heartfelt statement from Jamie in Baltimore.

> The only complaint I have about my sex life is that I would be more sexually motivated if I felt sexier. And I don't feel that sexy right now because I am not that happy with my body. And I have a lot of things on my mind that take precedence over my sex life right now. The only complaint I have is nothing that he can help.

We'd be wrong if we left you with the impression that all women are now strong and outspoken and know exactly what they want.

Especially if she's still in her twenties, she may need your help in breaking out of her shell. "Women have a hard time telling men what they want because it's embarrassing," said Shauna in Winnipeg.

Catherine, who's 28, said her shyness can cloud the moments of initiation. "We both initiate sex, but sometimes I think my cues are almost subtle in a way—that he doesn't know if I want to be sexual or just affectionate. I'm kinda huggy, touchy, and playful in my voice. 'Hey, want to get closer?' It is nice if you can find a man who will encourage you to talk about what you want."

Yvonne, who's 47 and lives in Cincinnati, said inhibitions caused her to hide her sexual arousal for years, and she blames it on a religious upbringing. "When we first met, we misread each other a lot," she said of her current boyfriend (she's divorced). "It was difficult, in the beginning, because I was busy playing games. Those stupid girl games that we play. 'Oh, you gotta guess.' I mean I'm, like, sopping wet, but I'm such a little lady that I just can't let you know. You've got to play this keep-him-guessing game. And then I would play, 'How dare you?' I was brought up Catholic, and nice little girls . . . I guess it was okay to feel that way, but you weren't supposed to announce it. It was supposed to be some big fat surprise."

If you misread her, it's no fun for either of you. When the cause is simple shyness, we heard several pleas for greater understanding. Like this one from Nikki, a 25-year-old student in Maine. Asked at the end of her interview whether there was anything else she wanted men to know, she said:

> Men need to know that it's important to talk to us about what you want, what you expect. . . . To be open to everything, but to be able to say what you personally aren't okay with. Likewise, I think it's important for men to get that from women, even if women are shy and reluctant. Because if you want to really be close to a person sexually and really get into it, you have to make them talk to you. I'm not saying sit them down and say, "You're not getting up until you talk to me." But just keep asking the question until you ask it the right way. Even the shyest girl wants to tell you. She just doesn't know how.

CHAPTER TWENTY-TWO

First and Foremost: Foreplay

IT'S A CLICHÉ, BUT IT'S SO, SO TRUE:
You turn on like a light bulb, but she warms up like
an iron. The women of the world are begging you:
Please, slow down. When you grab for the obvious
places right away, you really get on her nerves.

Here's a pithy definition of foreplay from Jaci in Chey-
enne, Wyoming: "Flirting to start, even if you are married.
Kissing and caressing slowly. Then the heat will happen."

Simple enough. We can get that right, can't we?

Apparently not.

In our survey in the September 1998 issue of *New Woman*
magazine, we asked, "What don't guys understand about you
sexually?" Foreplay was the number one reply. But the space
for their answers was small—roughly 2 square inches on a
magazine page. As a result, most simply wrote the word
"foreplay." In capital letters. With two or three exclamation
points afterward. (You know women.)

We, being guys, wanted more details. Are you getting no
foreplay and want some, or are you getting some and want
more? Are you yearning for something specific? Like oral sex?
A slower hand? Or just the feeling of unhurried intimacy?

We asked those follow-up questions on the *New Woman*
Web site. And, you know, this whole Internet thing really is

reducing the world to a global village. It's gotten so that two guys can dream up a bunch of highly personal questions, float 'em out there, and hear back from women all over the world. We heard from Leia in Manchester, England; Kathy in Toronto; Cherrie in Trinidad; Lisa in Cape Town, South Africa; Sophina in Singapore; and Simone in Australia.

And they all said the same thing: slow down.

- As Sophina in Singapore put it, "Men's response to sex is almost instantaneous. Personally, I warm up like an iron; I cool down like an iron too."
- "We generally don't get excited as quickly as you do," said Wendy in Kent, Washington.
- "My body cannot achieve an orgasm as quickly as he can. I need foreplay and time," said Angel in North Carolina.
- "Anticipation and suspense are a big part of the orgasmic process," said Sara in Richmond, Indiana. "If you try to rush, it only turns me off."
- And a quip from Dawn in Massachusetts: "You did not just plug a parking meter. Your time will not run out."

Okay, Miss Smartie Pants. A little constructive criticism would be more helpful. Exactly what should we do?

Susan in Augusta, Maine, had some suggestions. "The best foreplay begins with sizzling eye contact, some flirting, whispering in my ears, then gentle caresses. Then to have him undress me slowly and to take his time. Some bluesy music playing in the background is even better."

We'll be right over.

Adrienne in Tucson had more: "I like a man to let me massage him with some type of fragrance, and then to have him do the same to me. A back massage is very sensual. Then I like him to look into my eyes and kiss me gently for as long as I want. Then I am ready."

Is Arizona anywhere near Maine?

"Nibbling on the ear and neck are great ways to get the

blood flowing," said Janice in New Jersey. "But the most important rule is, slow is good."

If all this sounds totally obvious, then you can skip this chapter. But there are some of you guys out there, and we're not naming names, who act like all this is brand new material. "I've had a lot of experiences with guys who don't know what foreplay is," said Kate in West Bend, Wisconsin. "I mean, they have no clue. They think foreplay is going right for the pants. If you start breathing heavily, a man thinks foreplay is over—that now we can go for the goods. Well, a woman takes a bit longer, guys, and just because I'm breathing heavily doesn't mean I'm all ready."

"Just grabbing my breast a couple of times does not prepare me for an orgasm," wrote one anonymous survey respondent. "I need lots of foreplay—kissing, fondling, manual manipulation."

> "It's even better if you help."
> —LAUREN BACALL after kissing Humphrey Bogart, in TO HAVE AND HAVE NOT

Grabbing. That's it, in a nutshell. It's the word we heard over and over again. We get so horny, it's hard for us to see ourselves. But basically, we lunge a little too much.

"I can't go from a cold start like that," said Anna, a 40-year-old human-development specialist from Huntington Beach, California. "It's really not a turn-on to have somebody start by grabbing my crotch. It's better to have a progression from just a very soft caress, whether it's on the face, the shoulders, the back, brushing the butt, whatever. I enjoy it more when a man starts slow and even somewhat teasing."

If she grabs your crotch, that's different. Then she's already on fire. For once, she's about 5 or 10 minutes ahead of you. Enjoy.

Here's an enlightening comparison. When women get together to have sex, their foreplay is different. It lasts forever—or what would seem like forever to you. Deb, a 44-year-old private investigator in California who left her husband for a woman, shares the benefit of her unique perspective.

> Foreplay in my marriage, and prior to that with men, was completely different than foreplay now. How long it lasted was different. In general, men are not as attuned to foreplay as much as a female would like. I think they're aroused quicker and want to get it on quicker. My foreplay now is a lot more touching, caressing, nibbling of ears—things that are enjoyable.

Are you sure you want to have sex with two chicks? Really, you don't have the time.

Since you'll be taking a lot more time with your foreplay from now on, we'll give you something new to do.

Get away from her genitals. A hard-and-fast rule of human sexuality is that men are genitally aroused, women are generally aroused.

What does that mean? Let's hear from the experts.

- From Teri in Tennessee: "I'm not as genitally focused as he is. I get really turned on by stroking and touching all over my body. . . . A woman's entire body is usually one big sex organ."
- And from Shauna in Winnipeg: "Growing up, I was taught that my erogenous zones were between my legs, and my breasts. Not true! My *body* is an erogenous zone, so have at it!"
- Chris, a 39-year-old homemaker in Canada, summed it up: "As a rule of thumb, men are more genitally oriented than women. And yeah, don't go right for the genitals. Like, with foreplay . . . Foreplay is so important to a woman. Like, the buildup, it's just everything. And the kissing . . . I mean, somebody rubbing their hand up and down your arm can be far more erotic than rubbing your breasts so hard or

going right for your clitoris. You hop into bed, and they start rubbing your clitoris. That hurts. You don't want that. So I think men have to be conscious of that. I mean, they might reach a state of arousal a lot quicker than we do. But in order for the woman to enjoy it, they really have to be slower."

Most of the women we heard from said, in effect, "Explore all of me." "You can't touch a female too much," said Diana in New Mexico.

But other women specifically *don't* want you to touch them in the places they're sensitive about—the places that are the focal points of their bad self-images. Beware: Some women have a microanalytical view of their bodies. Listen to Jamie in Baltimore: "I don't like being touched in areas of my body that I am self-conscious about, like my thighs or certain parts of my stomach that I am afraid might seem fat in certain positions. I will be much more self-conscious if he is touching an area that I am self-conscious about."

Yes, certain parts of her stomach. On the other hand, she might have certain little areas that you've never even considered as a special destination. Listen to Christina, 22, a sales clerk in New Hampshire: "The backs of my knees are pretty exciting, I think. The middle of my back. My neck is a really nice area. I have really nice shoulders. My breasts are not the only thing on my body."

To summarize, if you just grab two or three spots on her body, time after time, then you have two strikes against you. She's not aroused, physically. And she's unplugged, mentally. Sex is a bore. Sex is a chore. "Maybe that is why I get bored with foreplay," said Whitney, an executive recruiter in Cleveland. "Because it's usually the same thing and that is usually why I am like, 'Skip it.' "

Before long, she's saying "Skip it" about the entire process.

Now for one last tip. When you've gotten her all steamed

up and she's building to a climax, stay cool. Remain confident. A man's natural inclination here might be to gun it, to hit the gas and hit that orgasm doing 170 miles per hour. Don't. "Slow things down, instead of speeding up, when I'm on the verge," said Jeanette in Santa Fe, New Mexico. "When he lowers the r.p.m., it creates the most exquisite and memorable moments I've ever experienced—as dramatic as the difference between M&M's and fine Swiss chocolate."

The food analogy is apropos. Think of artful foreplay as gourmet sex. That's what Ann in Seattle called it.

> Foreplay is just connecting. I'll be cooking, and he'll come up behind me and just start touching me and biting the back of my neck, and either it stops there or the stove gets turned off and dinner has to wait an hour. So foreplay can be that, or it can be just cuddling on the sofa watching a movie. The movie will get turned off or paused and then it turns into a blue screen, and meanwhile . . .

> For me, sexuality is something to savor and enjoy, My preference is to make sex a 2-hour experience. Gourmet sex is what I call it. Two hours once or twice a week.

THE FACTS OF LIFE

FOREPLAY IS THE WAY

We asked the women in our survey, "In general, who gets more attention during foreplay in your lovemaking?" Extra number crunching revealed that women who are least satisfied with their sex lives are a little more likely to say their partners get more attention.

Me ⇨ 36.4%	My partner ⇨ 17.4%
It's equal ⇨ 33.2%	I'm unattached ⇨ 13%

We can't end this chapter without passing along the biggest secret to fiery foreplay. You want to know what makes 'em all hot? Kisses.

This turned out to be a surprisingly major complaint. Not a single woman said, "Oh, kissing just isn't that important to me. No big deal."

All women said that guys—especially married guys—don't kiss enough.

At least, they no longer kiss their wives enough. So if you're thinking you can wow chicks with some fancy occult foreplay move, forget it. Go back to first base.

JUST DO IT

IT'S IN HIS KISS

Asked to sum up what men should know about women, Sandra in South Florida replied, "Kiss more."

Chances are, you already know how to wow a woman with a great kiss. So do it. You don't need our help. If we described some whiz-bang new kiss here and you tried it on her, she'd only wonder where you got it from. Forget that. Go with what you have. Go with what you had back in high school, when kisses were deep and soft and done for their own sake.

If she says your kisses lack zing, well, that's another story. Buy the book *The Art of Kissing* by William Cane. It's a little classic. Learn the sliding kiss and the butterfly kiss (you use your eyelashes) and the lip-o-suction kiss.

Kiss more, because it's more important to her. According to Cane, three out of four women think kissing is more intimate than sex.

- "Mike is a wonderful lover, but I wish he liked kissing more," wrote Lisa in Austin, Texas. "A lot of men don't enjoy long, passionate kissing sessions."
- Audrey in Washington State told us simply, "I'd do anything if kissed well."
- For Kristen in Chicago, that's exactly what happened. "There was this one particular guy in my past who was the most phenomenal kisser in the world. And that was probably my primary reason for wanting to sleep with him. He was such an awesome kisser."
- Said Susi, a mother of two on Philadelphia's Main Line, "I love kissing. I'm a real lip person. I like open-mouthed kissing. Teasing kissing. Top-lip-only kissing. Kiss me long and hard and soft and all different ways."

> "He was a great kisser."
> —MONICA LEWINSKY,
> of Bill Clinton

Some women are swept away by this gesture: You hold her face gently between your hands as you kiss her. *Ka-boom.* "He holds my face and he barely touches me. He barely touches my face. And then he kisses me. It's so tender; it's just the way he touches my skin to kiss me," said Yvonne in Cincinnati. "He did that the first time we kissed. He was saying good-bye, and then he reached down and just touched my face and pulled me up to him. I thought that was so sexy. Now, 7 or 8 years later, sometimes I'll just walk up to him and I'll grab his hands and put them on my face."

And here's what not to do: "Nothing is more of a turn-off than when a tongue is constantly probing," said Jill in Western Massachusetts. "The enjoyment is in the lips."

That's definitely on the list of the top-10 mistakes you can make—trying to French-kiss before she's ready. Most women are repulsed by this. Some even call it oral rape. If you begin by shoving your tongue down her throat, you're a dead man.

Let her initiate any tongue wrestling.

"It's all in the kiss," concluded Jill. "If the kiss is right, the mood will follow."

CHAPTER TWENTY-THREE

What Turns Her On?

WANT TO GET OUT OF A SEXUAL RUT?
Would you like to know what makes Megan
scream her head off? Listen in as these women
discuss sweet suspense and sexy talk. Also, whipped
cream, chocolate chips, ice, vibrators, mirrors,
and those little jelly packets.

Susan is 49 and divorced. She's a teacher in California. This is what turns her on: "That take-charge masculine energy that men have. That whole Rhett Butler type of person is very erotic to me. I like intense . . . just . . . holding me real tight. Almost forcing me into sex."

Dee is 32 and single. She's a professor in Chicago. Here's her thrill: "I feel more comfortable being the initiator. I think the most sexually attracted I ever felt was to a guy who was fine about being somewhat passive. That made me initiate sex even more. It is weird. I mean, I know this is kind of unusual, but it makes me uncomfortable to feel pursued."

Jennifer is 29. She works in New York. She likes a gentle man. "I would not want a quickie all the time. I like that softness and prettiness of lovemaking. Some lovemaking is just nice and calm and pretty."

Nikki is 25. She's a student in Maine. To her, good sex is not pretty. "I don't get into mushy, lovey-dovey stuff. I think more of how nasty you can get. Not painful things or rough things, but dirty talk and pornographic movies."

Every woman is different. As Jean, a 50-year-old woman in Pennsylvania said, "Sexuality is a very personal, tailored thing." When it comes to sexual arousal and personal sexual styles, you have to toss aside the whole question of what women want, and simply ask, "What does this woman want?"

That's rule number one. Rule number two is, forget rule one.

Okay, don't forget it, exactly. But don't apply it so predictably, so rigorously, that every sexual encounter is the same old, same old.

THE FACTS OF LIFE

SOMETHING OLD, SOMETHING NEW

Sexually dissatisfied women are either bored or boring. Whereas satisfied women have more adventurous mates, apparently. We asked the women in our survey to complete the question "Does your lovemaking . . ." with one of the phrases in the first column below.

	All Women	Satisfied	Dissatisfied
Vary between two or three scenarios?	54%	65%	36%
Look roughly the same each time?	35%	12%	60%
Always take on new and adventurous scenarios?	11%	23%	4%

"Nobody wants to have sex the same way every single time," said Laura in New York.

It gets to the point where, if you don't do something to make it interesting, then it's not interesting. Who wants that? I mean, it's just, "Okay, I guess you want to have sex again. You're grabbing my nipples again. I'm assuming from your penis hitting me in the butt that you would like to have sex. Okay, well, just let me know when you're done. I'll be here, okay?"

You can tell she's gotten stuck in a rut. So has Ronnie, a 25-year-old bartender in Fort Worth, Texas.

I went out with this one guy who only did it one way. I was on top all the time. I was, like, "Okay, let's try something else. This isn't working for me. I can't just do it one way all the time." So we experimented—doggie style, whatever. Anything that was just different than being on top.

In fact, the longer you've been together, the more she'll appreciate the element of surprise. "My husband is awesome in bed," said Felicia in Houston. "But the best sex I ever had was in the car. The spontaneity!"

He literally drives her crazy.

Surprise is important. So is suspense. Both are key elements of a good romance novel, and they're also important to the buildup of her sexual arousal. No matter what her style, these elements seem to work for most women, just as romance novels themselves appeal to millions.

Listen to Andrea, a 29-year-old business owner in Findlay, Ohio.

It's the anticipation of you moving down that way, feeling your breath on my skin, on the outside of my legs, and your hands touching me, but not right on anything good yet. On skin that seems to be wasted space because nobody pays any attention to it. That is really arousing to me—being near everything but not touching it.

Isn't that cool? You can drive her wild with anticipation, just by the way in which you touch her. "I like to be seduced," wrote Shauna in Winnipeg. "Slow and easy with touching, holding, little kisses and nibbles. A little imaginative oral sex and when just his tongue or finger is touching my nipples (no other body contact at the time)."

That super-light touch does more than build suspense. It's almost a requirement because the more turned on she gets, the more sensitive she is. "He will be kissing my ear and it will be much more sensitive," said Julie in Baltimore. "Or he will be kissing my neck and I can feel my body just kind of getting into it. When he is touching me, it feels better than it normally would if he just touched me when we were walking down the street. In my vagina, I can just feel the excitement building up."

If you can carry this suspenseful buildup into intercourse, you're the man. Ann in Seattle told us how much she enjoys the teasing of initial penetration. "He'll partially enter and then pull out, and he'll keep doing that. Or he'll nudge, and it's just there, but he won't go in. That will drive me crazy. I think it's the anticipation. Oh, that drives me crazy!"

Apparently Ann is not the only woman who is driven wild by this. Megan in Cincinnati told us the same thing. "If you can hold back and you're right at the entrance, and you just do a shallow thrust and you're not going all the way in and then suddenly go really hard all the way in—I love that. I'll just scream my head off."

You know what all this is called, don't you? Sexual tension. And, as Linda in Washington State assured us, "The buildup is worth the wait."

Another favorite way to build sexual tension is dirty talk—or call it sexy talk if you like, since that's a better description of some couples' styles. There's one obvious reason for talking sexy in bed and one not-so-obvious reason. The obvious reason is, it helps her feel aroused and allows her to shed feelings of inadequacy or inhibition. The not-so-obvious reason is, it keeps you fully present. It keeps you from checking out. As one of our Magellan Poll respondents said, "I hate looking at my partner during intercourse and knowing he's thinking about a job he has to do." Women usually know when you've checked out. Several women complained that their mates go through this disconnect in the sack.

Bernice Kanner, in her book *Are You Normal?*, says:

Sexy talk is by far the most popular arousal tool.

According to her surveys, 58 percent of couples include it as part of the fun, whereas only 22 percent have ever rented a pornographic video, 11 percent use toys, and only 5 percent are into some type of bondage.

What do women want to hear? "How beautiful I am. How good my body feels, and my skin. How he loves the way I smell. And how he just can't get enough of me." That's what Melissa, 26, a loan facilitator in Chicago, likes to hear.

Jennifer in New York wanted sexy talk that is more of a "verbal mood setting. Like putting me on a desert island or pretending we're in a hot tub with champagne and strawberries, and just taking me to different worlds. That's very exciting. I need softer, prettier statements. 'I like the way our bodies feel up against each other.' 'You feel so wonderful.' 'I love being inside you.' But not, 'I want to fuck you really hard.' "

Julie in Baltimore felt the same—she wants sexy talk, but not dirty talk. "He always says to me, like when he is kissing me or whatever, 'Oh, I love your body so much' and 'Why do you drive me crazy and how come it is so good?' Things like that. It makes me feel sexier. Sometimes what he says is sexual, sometimes it is much more romantic and sweet. You know, expressions of love, which is what I really enjoy. I am not the kind of person who would enjoy something like, 'Whose pussy is this?' "

> "Sex can cure an asthma attack. I once saved a man's life."
> —ANNIE SPRINKLE, former B-girl

In fact, if you said that to Kate in Chicago she'd probably get up and walk out. "I have this prude thing that zaps in every once in a while. And dirty talk can bring it on."

Whitney in Cleveland sums up the advice that applies to the majority of women. "Don't let it get disrespectful," she said. Name-calling, for instance, would be a big mistake.

But we also heard from women who love raunchy talk—the raunchier, the better. Some like it said with a straight face. And others like it in a campy, ironic way. For them, it's all in the tone. "We like to talk dirty and be perverse together, but playfully," said Carly, a 25-year-old teacher in New York City. "It's very funny."

If you freeze up and don't know what to say, well, you don't need some modern-day Cyrano giving you cues from the bushes. Maybe you'll relax by knowing this: The exact wording doesn't matter. As in the rest of life, she's probably not listening to you anyway. Andrea in Maine said she's merely aware of "soft and loving tones, and I don't know that I necessarily ever hear what he says."

Men tend to underrate this as a turn-on. Maybe because that whispering-in-her-ear thing seems so corny. Buddy, it's corny but it works. Several women say it takes them over the top. Like this woman in Flint, Michigan: "Talking dirty (not filthy) gets me where I need to be reach orgasm about 90 percent of the time."

Let's return to rule number two. Novelty is embraced by couples in their twenties, who are still developing their sexual styles and are exploring the wide world of possibilities. But it can be taken up anytime by couples who are, frankly, bored. They've gotten in a sexual rut, they know it, and they want to get out.

Many women find that, the older they get, the more accepting they are.

"In the beginning, it's more a performance thing, something that guys expect and you're expected to enjoy it," said

Jean in Pennsylvania of her salad days. "But as I've gotten older, I've become more comfortable with novelty, and comfortable with the fact that I find a lot of these things a turn-on. As you mature, you get more comfortable with a lot of things."

Having shed the last remnants of embarrassment, they wander into their local sex shop, or they call a catalog company like Xandria or Good Vibrations, and they start leafing through the pages to see what may catch their eye.

> "Yes, I use a vibrator. I don't know what kind it is; my grandmother gave it to me."
>
> —ANNA, CALIFORNIA

Many couples are intrigued by the use of vibrators. (Okay, we'll admit it: *We* were intrigued.) But they're not really sure what they're supposed to do with them, you know?

Nearly half of our 80 in-depth interviewees use vibrators, but few of them were forthright enough to say exactly how they use one. Andrea in Maine was an exception.

> I used to use it inside of me. I don't do that anymore. I find that I get more excited using it just on my clit. And I don't really move it around much on my clit, either. When I get excited, I either change the speed of the vibrator or apply more pressure. It just doesn't seem to do much for me by moving it around or being inside of me.

We heard high praise for body oils. When you incorporate them into a massage, you end up paying more attention to her body, and that is always a good thing. Body oils appeal to sensuous lovers. "I like oils," said "Trixie," a 28-year-old lawyer in Philadelphia. "I like candles. I like texture. Smell. Taste."

What surprised us, in conducting our research, is how many couples consider the best sex shop to be . . . their local supermarket.

They've tried whipped cream, chocolate sauce, honey. One

couple swears by those jelly packets you get with your breakfast at any diner or pancake house (they mentioned IHOP). And what about a bag of chocolate chips? "Chocolate chips can be a lot of fun," said Brianna, a costume designer in California. "You would be amazed how quickly they melt."

Another old favorite is ice. You put a cube in your mouth, holding it in your teeth so that just the edge of it peeks between your lips, and you kiss her everywhere she can stand it. "I like being teased with ice," said Wendy in New York. "Everywhere. On my breast, on my stomach, and I can't really stand it on my genitals for very long but it's exciting. I also love candle wax on my breasts," she said. "It's hot. But I think that feels really good."

Wendy is only 26, but she's tried a lot in her young lifetime. After we listened to the tape of her in-depth interview, we felt pretty darn naive, especially after stories like this:

> One time, I was with a guy and we rented a hotel room. I think that's fun and sexy, to rent a hotel and just have sex and then leave. And he was a really big guy, which was good because I like big guys, and we were doing 69 and he actually stood up with me and we continued to do 69. And I weigh, like, 160. Yeah, that was sexy. And there were mirrors, too, and I got to see it, so that was good.

Wendy said she's been with about 50 partners, has been tested for AIDS about 10 times, and considers herself to be open-minded. She's tried nipple clamps ("It hurt worse than anal sex") and the clothespins. She likes being spanked. "I bought a boyfriend a paddle once." She and a partner have performed for another couple. "You know, you have sex and they watch, and then they have sex." She likes being submissive. "Not anything too aggressive. I wouldn't say that I like being strangled. But if he pulled my hair a bit—I like that."

No wonder she left Oklahoma.

THE SHORT ANSWER

ARE RIBBED CONDOMS ANY FUN?

Various brands of novelty condoms advertise themselves as being "ribbed for her pleasure," and the like. We wondered: Can she really feel anything different?

- "They're kind of cool. I don't feel, like, ribs, but yeah, it's a different feel."
- "We just bought a box of those, and I didn't feel any difference."
- "They all feel the same to me."
- "That's all crap. That's so a guy can say, 'Look, I'm thinking of you.' No, you're not."
- "It's a marketing ploy."
- "It's the most ridiculous thing I've ever heard in my life."

We thought Wendy was our most adventurous interview. But then we heard from Edna.

Edna lives in Marin County, California, that magical landscape just north of San Francisco, across the Golden Gate Bridge. She grew up on a dairy farm in rural California; she entered early into a marriage that quickly became both sexless and loveless. Both of them were woefully ignorant about sex. The first time her husband criticized her for not having an orgasm, her response was "What's an orgasm?" "I had never even heard the word before," she recalled.

Eventually, she divorced, moved, and met a man 7 years younger. They've been together 16 years now. During those years, she said, their sex life has gotten better. "We try to do things differently," she noted. "The other day, we did a Mexican thing. I mixed Margaritas and we played Mexican music and we put out our rug and got all our toys lined up."

No, nothing by Fisher-Price. These would be their sex toys. She has an acrylic dildo shaped like the goddess Venus; he has an anal toy shaped like a praying monk. And they stay on their rug for hours. "It's our little island."

Theme nights are a big part of Edna's sex life. "Maybe one night it's dancing. We maybe do a leather night. We do so much. We go to swingers' parties, so we've done just about everything that there is to do." And they do it fairly often. "I have a calendar that he puts hearts, big hearts, on every time we do it. And we do, I don't know, probably an average of three times a week."

The only problem is, she's 61 now. "And this is the hard part for him because I haven't really changed so much in how I look. But he still thinks that I'm this girl of 40. So I have to tell him I'm not. That's the worst part about getting older: I don't have that much energy, even though I have a lot of energy. I had to tell him, 'If we want to go home and have sex, you have to think about it as we're driving home.' Say so, and we'll stop for fast food. Then I don't have any dishes to worry about."

All these tricks and toys and games and special sex rugs and full-length mirrors—is that the route to sexual bliss? Does that ensure hot monogamy? Our interviewer asked Edna, "What is important for men to know about women's sexuality?" This was her reply.

> Romance. I like romance. Quickies are fine. A little bit of S and M stuff. But I like lots of touching, constant touching when we're around one another. We hug. We tell each other "I love you" a lot. And I like things being done that you don't expect. Bring home some little thing. It's just, really, paying attention. Paying attention, more than anything. And feeling safe. I love that feeling of being in his arms. Just feeling so safe, so cared for, and so loved.

Paraphernalia was never the point.

Ever. Underneath it all, girls will be girls.

CHAPTER TWENTY-FOUR

Oral Sex: Her Turn

WOMEN'S MAJOR GRIPE IS THAT MANY MEN ARE NOVICES AT THIS. They start too abruptly, they're too rough, and sometimes she wonders if he really knows where her clitoris is. But that's most guys, not you. You're about to become a master.

"Women are simple," said Heather in Columbus, Ohio. "We want the three C's from men: commitment, compliments, and cunnilingus."

You got your money's worth, right there.

For the record, please notice that a fourth C, coitus, did not make the cut.

Men are simple too. We want old-fashioned intercourse. We want entry; we want penetration. But that's not necessarily at the top of her list. She doesn't always climax during intercourse. She's more likely to reach orgasm via oral sex, especially if she's young. Regardless of the fact that it's still illegal in many states, this is the sex act on which she pins her hopes.

Take it from Jennie, a 26-year-old Spanish talk-show host in Manhattan: "I completely think it's better than sex."

Or from Olivia in New England: "It takes a while during intercourse to have an orgasm. They feel different, too. The ones during oral sex are much more intense, so I like those more. If I don't get one during intercourse, I'm not upset, but if I don't get one during oral sex, I am."

And when we asked Tara, a 23-year-old waitress in Cincinnati, what she would like sexually that she's not getting, we think she spoke for millions of women when she told us, "I want more oral sex. . . . And I want it to be perfect."

Tara's great expectations put her at odds with more than a few men out there who flat-out refuse to perform oral sex. In women's eyes, this definitely puts them in the lowest circle of men from hell. They're frying right alongside the guys who say they'll call, then don't. Jennifer in New York told us, "I love a man going down on me and find it quite rejecting if he won't."

Evelyn in Missouri said that her partner has a novel, if flimsy, excuse. "He says it hurts his throat!"

Sheila in Philadelphia had this problem with her current beau: "He won't do the muff. He will not go downtown. That's not cool, guys. Learn how to do the muff."

Barbara in Chicago was leery of her fiancé's intentions. "He's not into oral sex on me," she complained. "He's very into it on himself. He's never given another woman oral sex. None of his friends have. He thinks it's a cultural difference because he's from Spain. I think that he and his friends are inexperienced. He gets into it more now. He sees how much I enjoy it. Still, it's not as common as my giving him a blow job. He thinks reciprocating a blow job is him just touching me."

This is not a strictly male failing. As you'll see in the next chapter, there are plenty of women who hate to reciprocate. But let's not get into that fight. Let's get on with the chief complaint: your less-than-perfect technique.

It's not that most men won't perform oral sex. It's that they do it badly.

If this were a perfect world, women would help you, teach you, guide you. They would have used their supposedly superior powers of communication to make this a nonissue. But the sad fact is, many women won't tell you what's wrong. Tara was complaining that men "don't finish what they started." When our interviewer asked, "Do you say, 'Get back down there?' " she replied, "I don't say, 'Get back down there.' I would never just push his head down there or anything like that. I'd rather have him do it on his own accord. So I usually don't say anything."

Ergo, this chapter. Ergo, this book.

According to our research, presented in the accompanying chart, the clitoris has been voted Her Most Popular Erogenous Zone. She knows where your penis is; do you know where her clitoris is? Oh, really? Tell that to Catherine, a 24-year-old Midwest student who said she has slept with a lot of men. Here's her experience: "There's a lot of guys who don't know where the clitoris is. It just seems like they're all over the place. And even if they find the right place and you're like, 'Yeah!' they keep moving. And you're like, 'No, go back!' "

Susi, 42 and a mother of two in suburban Philadelphia, made the same plea.

> I'm in the field of gynecology, so I can speak for America's women right now, not myself. It is so funny that guys think they have to go into the vagina with the tongue. That is so meaningless. I have to tell you: Get on that clitoris and go! This is a big joke among women. It's like, he's all over the lips, he's into the vagina. . . . Like, "Hello, buddy! Up here! Come on! What are you doing down there?"

Yvonne in Cincinnati speculated on why guys do this. "I think some guys really think they're supposed to be eating it. You're not really grazing down there, you know? There's a job to be done. There's a place to go do it. Get there, and do it nicely. They think they've got to encompass that whole area. They don't stay in the one spot."

THE FACTS OF LIFE

WHAT FLOATS HER BOAT?

In our Magellan Poll, we asked, "What is your favorite erogenous zone?" The answers were virtually uniform across age groups and lifestyles. The only slight variation is that among women under 30, the neck beat breasts by 3 percentage points. Notably, there's not a lot of interest in toe sucking. If you see Dick Morris, let him know.

Zone	Percentage
Clitoris	42%
Breasts	24%
Neck	15%
G-spot	6%
Inner thighs	5%
Ears	3.5%
Belly	0.7%
Toes	0.6%
Other	4%

"And just when they've been there for a while and it's good, they think they've got to move around. And they don't have to move around."

"I'm sorry . . . Because then you lose it. It's gone. And when they go back, you've got to start all over again."

You are not, technically, eating her out. Just forget that expression.

We heard quite a few complaints about guys biting and nibbling and munching too much. That can be fun only for some women, and only if done with utmost delicacy. As

Kana, 48, a schoolteacher in Alaska reminded us, "You are not eating an orange."

Long ago, before shock radio and Dr. Ruth and Lorena Bobbitt and the Starr Report, sexual anatomy was not discussed in public. Back in the olden days, a euphemism for the clitoris was "the little man in the boat." Let's stretch this analogy to the breaking point. You want to get in the boat. But first you have to push off from shore. And once you do, get in gingerly.

The first tip is, don't start cunnilingus too soon. Let her warm up first.

> "As my bowling instructor used to say, 'It pays to hit the head pin.' "
> —ANONYMOUS in Atlanta

"I don't like it when I get a couple of kisses and then he just kind of works his way down," said Kate in Chicago.

"I have to be a little excited first," said Brianna in California. "Otherwise, he might as well be licking my elbow."

The second tip is, do it softly.

"Lick it like an ice cream cone, with your tongue flat and not pointed," said Christina, 22, a sales clerk in New Hampshire.

Remember why you're using your tongue rather than a finger. It's softer, wetter. "If there is too much force, then it is like turning on the TV when the volume is all the way up. It's jarring," said Grace in Des Moines, Iowa.

Jodi, a 26-year-old in Wisconsin, said, "Some guys just start mauling you, and they think that's exciting. I'm sorry, it kind of hurts. They're really stiff and tense, and it's like they're not even thinking about what they're doing. It has nothing to do with you, it seems like. They're just going through the mechanical motions of it, and that really sucks."

But Carol in Missouri had praise for her lover's technique: She loves "his battery-operated tongue! I swear, either it's that or solar powered! He has the best ability with that thing. He can whip it across my clit at lightning speed or he can ever so lightly touch it, and . . . hello, instant orgasm!"

Another satisfied lady is Julie in Baltimore. "He'll do a repeated kind of licking, but fast and then slow—changing the speed. He could do it in the one spot at the top of the clitoris and I would come in a few minutes, and what I really like is if he is doing it and inserts his finger at the same time. That is the most."

Julie brought up a key point about cunnilingus. She didn't speak for all women, not by any means. So, what does your partner like?

You have to discover whether she likes variety or persistence—that is, variation in speed and placement of the tongue, or steady, rhythmic licking until she reaches orgasm.

Some women say, "Keep a good thing going." As in this advice from a *New Woman* magazine survey respondent in Santa Ana, California, "When you find the one spot, stay right there! Don't move on!"

Other women say that's too much. For them, the key word is "teasing." The perfect oral sex technique calls for a variety of sensations. Ronnie in Fort Worth, Texas, falls into this camp, and she has a novel way to get what she needs. "If he's going down on me, I'll give him a trick to do. I'll tell him to spell the ABC's with his tongue. It works, for me at least, because the letters keep the tongue from staying in one spot. And you don't ever make it to Z, which is really cool."

That's great for Ronnie, but not for Amy in Baltimore— she doesn't want direct contact with the clitoris. "A lot of men think they need to twiddle that one spot for as long as they can until the woman gets off, and that might work for some people. But that doesn't work for me. It is more of a nondirect stimulation to that area that gets me going. I mean, you can hit the lip and then that hits the clitoris."

Once a woman is very aroused, there's only one pitfall left. She's excited, you get excited, and you unwittingly change your technique. You do it harder, faster. Don't!

Ann, 34, of Seattle, said that at that point she gets over-stimulated. "And if I become overstimulated, there's no way in hell I'm going to have an orgasm."

"Partners hear me getting excited vocally, and they get more enthusiastic. They increase the pressure, and that's not what I want them to do."

"There's this element of finesse that I don't think a lot of men understand. Just go gentle, be subtle. Tease me. And if I'm making noise, if I'm getting louder, don't up the ante. Don't nibble or suck too hard. Licking is much better. And teasing. Teasing is really best. Circle my clitoris."

We agree that you're hearing some conflicting testimony here. But the bottom line is that if what you normally do doesn't work for her, maybe all this discussion will suggest a new approach. If you're new at this, start with some combination of teasing and steady, direct licking. Said Suzanne, a 29-year-old in Minnesota, "There can be a bit of variety, but there has to be a certain amount of concentration in order to make someone orgasm. At least for me."

Once orgasm occurs, there's only one potential misstep. Some women really do not want to be kissed right afterward. "Don't kiss after you go down there. That's something I refuse to do," said Emily, 28, a social worker in Chicago.

So keep a bottle of sparkling water by the bed.

CAN SHE EX?LAIN IT

Acing the Oral Exam
—SUSAN CRAIN BAKOS

Within the last few decades, oral sex has become part of most men's sexual repertoires. And with good reason: Women love it. But even though it's fairly new among Americans, it's been standard practice in other cultures for thousands of years. The ancient Chinese called it drinking from the jade fountain.

So says sex author Susan Crain Bakos. Bakos began writing about sex as "Carolyn Steele: Dear Superlady of Sex" for *Penthouse* magazine. She went on to become Dr. Ruth's ghostwriter before writing several helpful books of her own, including *What Men Really Want* and *Sexational Secrets*. Her latest, *Still Sexy: How The Boomers Are Doing It,* surveys the sexual attitudes and behavior of America's baby boom generation. Here, we've sought her out as a sex coach—and she told us exactly how to play the game.

Q: *In our surveys, women tell us that oral sex is the most surefire way for them to reach orgasm. Many say they wish their partners would perform it more often, for longer durations, and be a little more skillful. Is there a right way to perform oral sex? Are women as uncomplicated as men in this department?*

A: Women are a little more complicated. Some women have a clitoris that gets hard and stands out. With others, the clitoris shrinks back a little into the fold when they

271

become aroused, and it's harder to find. Some women are more sensitive and they can't stand to be touched directly on the clitoris, and other women want to be. So there's more variation in the kinds of touch that women want.

Q: *The solution to that, for guys, is to find out—to ask, right?*

A. That's the solution, but I don't think you can lay the blame for a less-than-wonderful experience strictly on men. Whenever women say, "I've never enjoyed oral sex; I can't find a guy who does it right," I ask, "Why not? Why can't you help him do it right?" It's up to her to educate him.

Q: *If she isn't enjoying it, what's usually wrong?*

A: There are some women who have real hang-ups about oral sex. And if that's the case—if she thinks it's wrong or it's dirty or her genitals are dirty or she's embarrassed by having an orgasm this way—the man is not going to be able to get past that with her. She is going to have to get past that, and maybe she doesn't want to; maybe she never will. For him, I would say: If oral sex is not going to work out very well, then just kiss her a lot and use your hand. Stroke her and manipulate her genitals manually.

On the other hand, maybe she's never been able to tell a man how she needs this done. If she's just not enjoying cunnilingus, the best thing he can do is to turn the situation into a game and say, "Let's both learn a little more about this. Let's buy a book or rent an erotic video." I think too much pressure—"Well, what can I do to please you?"—makes it even harder for her to tell him. Both men and women have to treat sex like play, not like brain surgery. And it's *not* brain surgery. That's what I tell everybody about sex: This is supposed to be fun. Get back to that idea.

Q: *In* Sexational Secrets, *you said that the first rule of cunnilingus is: Do not perform it until she is already aroused. But won't it arouse her?*

A: Not if she's feeling a little awkward; and a lot of women do, at first. There's always a little bit of do-I-smell-good, do-I-look-good anxiety. Some women need more time to let go of their inhibitions. And for all women, relaxing into pleasure requires taking off a layer, like removing a sweater when you come into a warm room. A man needs to kiss her and fondle her and not just go straight for the clitoris. The guy decides on oral sex, and his head is between her legs already. Always start love-making with a kiss on the mouth. A lot of kissing. As the relationship progresses, men kiss less and less.

Q: *So what is the basic technique?*
A: Arouse her first. Massage her breasts with your palms; then play with her nipples as you kiss slowly down a line from her navel to the edge of her pubic hair. Kiss and lick her inner thighs and the line of flesh between her pelvis and each thigh.

Now you're ready to part her outer lips with your fingers and expose her clitoris. Lick and suck around the clitoris. Finally, cover the clitoris with your mouth. Suck *very* gently. Some women enjoy being lightly nibbled here, but others find this to be way too much. See what her response is; she's sure to be feeling something, one way or another.

If her clitoris is hiding inside her clitoral hood, you may have to take two fingers and place them on either side, lightly pressing down to lift and expose the clitoris. You may even have to keep your fingers there, if that's what works.

You can alternately lick and suck until she reaches orgasm. When you're licking, lick mostly around the clitoris, not right on it. It's so sensitive that most women enjoy only indirect stimulation. When you're sucking, put your lips around the sides and purse your lips as you suck.

Vary her sensations by using your hands. Touch her labia, her inner thighs, her nipples, and her perineum, that spot of smooth flesh between her vulva and her anus. Some women like anal stimulation; they'll want you to insert a finger in the anus. Whatever. Just keep arousing her.

Q: *How long should all this last? How long should a guy hang in there?*

A: That really varies. Some women want a man to perform cunnilingus until she's on the verge of orgasm, and then enter her so she can come during intercourse. And some women want their first orgasms via oral sex. It depends on the women and the circumstances, I tell men, "Pay attention to how she's holding your head. If she's pulling you in toward her and gyrating her hips, you know this is still happening for her. But if she pulls gently away, there's your clue that she wants something else."

Q: *That's a pretty big clue.*

A: Well, women say that men don't pay attention to these things. One woman I interviewed for *Still Sexy* said, "I pull on his ears. When I tug on his ears, he knows I'm ready for sex," as she calls intercourse. I thought that was pretty good. Most women have their subtle signals. I can't tell a man, "You have to perform this X number of minutes every time." But I will say that men have to spend more time on cunnilingus than women do on fellatio, because fellatio works faster. We all know that.

Q: *What if I get tired? What if my tongue muscle wears out?*

A: I would definitely use the hand. Use the thumb or the fingers. And maybe nudge her with your nose or brush your lips across her clitoris. You don't have to be using your tongue all the time. A little variety is good.

Q: *One of the variations that you mention in* Sexational Secrets *is to insert one or more fingers into her vagina while performing oral sex, and possibly massage the G-spot. . . .*

A: Now that's how I prefer it. That's a good one.

Q: *Is that move called the Venus Butterfly?*
A: I've heard many things called the Venus Butterfly. That phrase comes from an episode of *L.A. Law*. The character Stewart, the short, bald guy who had the tall, attractive wife, said he drove her wild by using the Venus Butterfly. It was just something a writer dumped into a script; it meant nothing. But then everyone tried to figure out what it did mean. So for years afterward, you would read, *this* is the Venus Butterfly and *that* is the Venus Butterfly, when in fact there was no Venus Butterfly. The Venus Butterfly is anything you want it to be.

CHAPTER TWENTY-FIVE

Oral Sex: Your Turn

YOU LOVE GETTING ORAL SEX. But you're not getting any. What's wrong with this picture? Maybe you're not following the five little rules.

In the previous chapter, you learned how to help a woman enjoy great oral sex. In this chapter, you'll learn how you can enjoy oral sex.

This is not a joke. So we'll let you get past your initial response, which is, "Doh! Hey, if some guys need to be *told* . . ."

Let's be honest. Are you getting oral sex as often as you want it or as often as you used to get it? Are you counting the days until you can use the birthday-boy line again? Are you suddenly telling your boss you need an intern?

Maybe you're doing something wrong. When it comes to oral sex, unless you do everything right, you can forget about it. With your wife, your lover, or your intern.

The fact is, most women are looking for a reason to say no. Their unspoken motto is "It is better to receive than to give." For all of the complaints that men don't return their sexual favors, we heard from women who don't reciprocate too. Some of the 80 women who gave us in-depth interviews were brutally honest about this.

"I'm totally selfish," said Kate, a 30-year-old Chicago attorney. "He's so enthusiastic about it; it's a privilege for him to give me oral sex. But for me to give it, there's almost always some begging involved. He just has to really want it."

Emily, 28, said, "It makes me gag."

Nikki in Maine is not exactly nuts about it: "I don't like to give a man a blow job until he gets off. It's physically uncomfortable. Your jaws ache; your eyes feel like they're going to pop out of your head. So long as it's a part of foreplay and it's not something you're expected to finish, then it's not bad."

There's a rousing endorsement.

And Julie in Baltimore said, "I would say he gives me oral sex every time that we are together, and I probably give it to him 1 out of 10 times. And if I do it, I usually don't do it till orgasm."

Yeah, that's another thing: swallowing. You're expecting her to swallow? Hah! Hence our first rule.

1. Don't ask her to swallow. Choose your battles.

Bernice Kanner, in her book of surveys *Are You Normal?*, found that only one woman in four swallows. Wherever these women are, they're not married yet. We heard from more than one woman who, given time in a long-term relationship, gave it up. Leaving her boyfriend to wonder, "What happened?"

"Earlier in our relationship, it was an expression of love," said Ann from Seattle, who's 34 and engaged. "So I've done that, and I don't need to do that anymore. And he doesn't ask me anymore, either. I don't know if it's because I've said that if I do that, I'll throw up. But just the thought of it makes me want to retch."

Suzanne from Minnesota won't swallow, either. "I'm afraid of what it's going to taste like. And I'm afraid it's going to shoot down my throat and make me feel like I'm choking. Semen is a funny taste. It's a foreign taste; you don't find that taste anywhere else. And every guy has different-tasting semen. I think men should be sensitive to that. My advice is, men should pull out of a woman's mouth. I do not think a man should ever assume that a woman wants to swallow his come. She's probably not going to want to; and if she does, she'll make the request or keep you inside."

Let's put it this way: We didn't hear one woman praise the taste of semen. (One respondent compared its smell to the household cleansing product Soft Scrub with bleach.) On the other hand, we have heard experts advise you to change the taste of your semen if the act of swallowing means that much to you. Since what you eat shows up 12 to 24 hours later in your semen, you should switch to a smoothie diet—fruits and sweets. Cut out spicy fare, onions, garlic, coffee, alcohol, and highly acidic foods such as tomato sauces. Your semen will taste sweeter. Does it work? Ask her to be your official taste tester.

> "And then I made a joke and I said, 'Well, can I be Assistant to the President for Blow Jobs?' He said, 'I'd like that.'"
> —MONICA LEWINSKY

Then again, swallowing could leave more than just a bad taste in her mouth. As many as 12 percent of women may be allergic to semen, according to researchers at the University of Cincinnati College of Medicine who studied more than 1,000 women. The symptoms include mild itching or burning in the vaginal area to wheezing, hives, nausea, and even fainting. And you thought she swooned because you were such a hottie.

So your semen tastes bad, and maybe your manhood doesn't taste so great, either. But that's easier to change. Most women don't like the taste of a sweaty penis. It tastes salty, at best.

2. Take a shower. Smell good, taste good.

Maria, a 31-year-old married librarian in Cincinnati, made a plea here. "This is serious. Men, do not come to bed without washing your area, okay? Show me a man who has not come out of the bathroom one time in his life without pee on his underwear. Or on his shorts. Please do not come to bed and expect me to go down on you, and you haven't washed it. I have to put my mouth on that and it's got pee on it? Give me a break."

If washing isn't good enough for her, open the refrigerator. As far as we're concerned, oral sex is the reason why whipped cream comes in a can.

Enough said. On to rule number three.

You've probably seen this in a porn flick: Some domineering jerk takes a woman's head in his hands and forces her to give him a blow job by ramming her onto his penis.

That's exactly what you don't want to do.

"Don't push my head to make a deep throat," said Jennifer in New York City. "Let me know if you want it a little deeper, but do not shove it down my throat."

It's obnoxious because you're making her gag. (If she asked for a sip of your beer, would you shove the bottle to the back of her throat?) But it's also obnoxious because you're trying to be in control. Instead:

3. Be paralyzed with pleasure. Give her total control.

Pay attention now. Your job is to lie back in sputtering ecstasy. Because if there's any joy in this for her, it's going to come out of the fact that she's in charge. Only in the classic pornographic fantasy *Deep Throat* did a woman actually have a clitoris at the back of her throat. In real life, there's nothing in it for her other than the power to make your eyes roll back in your head.

- As Kana, 48, a mother of two in Alaska, said, "A woman likes to do it because it gives her the power, and she is in charge."
- Ann from Seattle admitted, "It's a power trip for me. I know he'll completely relax and I can take control of his body."

Her power over you is just part of the fun. The other part is seeing and hearing you get sexual pleasure. As in all sexual interactions, hearing you get aroused gets her aroused.

4. Tell her you're *really* enjoying this.

This is a really easy little thing to do, and yet many guys don't. "Some guys are really silent and then, at the very end, they let out some small little moan," said Pam in Maryland.

Well, whoopie.

"I haven't really enjoyed performing oral sex on all the men that I've ever been with," said Dawn, a 34-year-old coffeehouse manager in Cincinnati. "But with one guy in particular, he made it arousing for me as well. And the way he made it more pleasurable is, he was very vocal. Like myself. He was able to vocalize how it felt when I was performing the oral sex."

Yvonne agreed. "I do like confirmation that it feels good. I like to hear something from the peanut gallery. Just anything. Just, like, 'God, that's good. You're the best.' That makes me feel pretty good, you know?"

So sing her praises. "Positive reinforcement is a good thing," said Sheila in Philadelphia. "Tell me I'm good; tell me I'm making you really satisfied. Let me know how we're progressing here. Give me a little progress report. Talk to me."

And while you're doing so, play with her hair and lightly touch her back. Several women said they liked that stuff.

Talking—or at least, moaning well—is extra important if you're in a new relationship. She may have no idea what you like. Different guys like different stuff, and your silence may imply boredom. "I really like it when guys tell you what's going on with them," said Wendy in New York. "If you play with their balls slightly when you're going down on them, some guys don't like that. Some really, really do."

How else is she to know?

If she has brought you to orgasm, save a few nice words for the pillow talk afterward.

5. When it's all over, tell her again.

"Telling me he really enjoys it afterward is great," said Lori, a computer consultant in Fort Lee, New Jersey. "Like, 'I love that you did that or the way you did this.' The more details he gives me, the more I know he enjoyed it."

And that wraps it up, guys: the five rules of fabulous fellatio.

There is, of course, a way to skip all five rules. Buy her a Mercedes. But what will you do next week?

CHAPTER TWENTY-SIX

Fantasyland

MOST WOMEN HAVE SEXUAL FANTASIES.
Most are afraid to tell you about it, because they
don't know whether you can deal with it.
But if you listen and accept without self-doubts,
your love life can only get better.

"I never told a lover this, but actually, I've never been able to orgasm without a fantasy," said Nikki, a 25-year-old student in Maine. "I have to have one in my head. I don't know if that's a negative thing or not."

Nikki's statement helps to clear up a bunch of stuff about fantasy, right up front. First of all, the vast majority of people, both men and women, have sexual fantasies. That she hasn't told any lovers is not surprising. The sex experts who've studied fantasy believe that only a minority ever share these innermost thoughts, even with spouses of many years. And whether it's a negative thing or not . . . we can't answer that. She has to ask herself:

"Are my fantasies causing problems?

"Do they distance me from my lover?

"Are they out of control?

"How do I feel afterward—better or worse?"

Some women are disturbed by the contents of their fantasies.

But we must say, the women we heard from are not. Nikki's voice the only trace of self-doubt among them. The others who mentioned their fantasy lives talked matter-of-factly about them.

Many of these women use fantasy to reach orgasm, especially during masturbation.

To them, fantasy is truly "like a vibrator for the mind."

That nice turn of phrase comes from a book called *In the Garden of Desire: Women's Sexual Fantasies as a Gateway to Passion and Pleasure*, by Wendy Maltz, a psychotherapist in Oregon. Maltz has talked with enough women about fantasy to discover that it comes in two flavors: scripted and un-

> "Women need fantasy. They need to fill their heads, not their eyes as much."
>
> —Susi, Philadelphia

scripted. Scripted fantasies have settings, characters, plot lines, the works. Unscripted fantasies just zero right in on sexy images, sounds, and sensations. And Maltz quotes another memorable line, this time from the late, great sex therapist Helen Singer Kaplan, who once wrote, "Sex is composed of friction and fantasy." Much has been written about the friction, very little about fantasy.

We heard both scripted and unscripted fantasies described to our interviewers. Here are some unscripted examples.

- "I visualize pretty strange things, like a horse being inside of me, or, like, a rape or a gang bang," said Wendy in New York City.
- "I have a fantasy of two men entering my vagina at the same time," said Robin in Columbus, Ohio.
- "Making love in a meadow while it's raining," said Christina in New Hampshire.

Here are some examples of scripted fantasies.

- "I have this fantasy of an evening out, good food, and dancing or something," said Ann in Seattle. "There's a lot of sexual attraction. And I'm wearing a dress without hose or underwear. And finally, we have sex leaning up against a wall in an alley with the rain coming down."
- "My favorite fantasy involves me being totally bound,

THE TWO-CHICKS THING

Enough of women's fantasies! Now let's talk about your favorite fantasy: doing it with two women.

Apparently, there are a lot of guys—a *lot* of guys—who love this fantasy, because a lot of women report being badgered to act it out. It's such a common request that women sit around and wonder about you. Like, do you think you're such hot stuff that you can single-handedly convert two lesbians to hetero sex?

Other women aren't as cynical about you. They say that men just want to see two women because two are better than one, and four breasts are better than two. . . .

You've probably heard her reasons for denying you this ultimate sexual experience. Now hear ours. Having listened to dozens of women discuss this, we distilled four reasons why this fantasy is best left as a fantasy.

1. You can't handle it.
2. She can't handle it.
3. If she can handle it, somebody is in trouble.
4. If you get your wish, will she get hers?

Think about it, said Whitney, an executive recruiter in Cleveland: "The next day, it could be very awkward. There could be major issues. Major issues."

If you're in a long-term relationship, you've tried to sell your threesome fantasy this way: "It's just sex. That's all." Women's response is "Yeah, phooey. Don't kid yourself." They think a ménage à trois is conceivable only with strangers.

blindfolded, the works," said Carly, a New York City teacher. "Gagged and everything. Just having a man and a woman just totally go away with me. And I'd just have to sit there and take it."

• "While he is, as they say, going down on me, I picture four or five men watching us," said Yvonne in Cincinnati. "And

---

"My feeling—and it's kind of right from the heart—is that I don't think it's healthy," said Jennifer in New York. She's been in a foursome before, so she's not being a finger wagger. She thinks it's asking for trouble. "I don't think I'm strong enough emotionally to handle ever seeing anyone I'm with be with someone else. I would not want to see them give or receive pleasure. And although it would turn him on tremendously, probably, to see me with another woman, I'm not sure emotionally that he'd really be able to handle it. I think he'd always wonder, 'Did she like the way she did that better?' Although it reads great on paper, I don't think it's the healthiest thing."

If she one day suddenly did agree to a threesome, wouldn't you wonder what's up? What's her hidden agenda here? "One time, I put someone in a position where she was in a sexual situation with us, but I did it to prove to her that he was mine," said Jamie in Baltimore. "Yeah, I did it because I was pulling a power trip on her. It was wrong to do what I did, but I got my point across."

Or she might agree to it so that she can start badgering you to bring another guy into your bed. Fair is fair.

"He wants two women and him," said Yvonne in Cincinnati, "which was never on my mind. He said, 'Well, if there's someday that whatever whatever, that's what I'd like.' And I'm thinking, 'That's funny, because I've always thought of two men and me.' You know, maybe one of his friends can come over. He's thinking two women; I'm thinking two men."

You can handle that, right? Yeah, *right*.

they're so jealous. They wish they were him. But all they can do is stand there and watch. And I look at every one of them all the while."

Most women would love to tell you about their fantasies. But they're worried about you. How will you take it? Will you think this is all about you? Will your sexual ego get crushed because you can't be two men entering her vagina at once? Or a horse? Will you feel inadequate? Will you tease her about it, and make her sorry she ever told you anything? Or will you think that, because she has a favorite fantasy, she wants to act it out?

One of our Magellan Poll respondents wrote to plead her cause to all the men of the world.

"Allow your wife to truly fantasize, without thinking that something is lacking in your relationship."

"Fantasizing can be a healthy part of your sex life. Fantasizing is just that—fantasy, not reality."

Tina, a 42-year-old woman in Youngstown, Ohio, wrote to say that she has not told her partner about her fantasies, simply because he doesn't understand "that fantasies are just fantasies. I am inhibited to share them because I wouldn't want him to think I'd like to do them."

For instance, just because a woman fantasizes about other women doesn't necessarily mean she's a closet homosexual. Bobbi Jo in Pennsylvania told us she likes to watch the women in pornographic films. "No, I'm not a lesbo," she said. "It's just a fantasy."

These women aren't confused about the difference between fantasy and reality. Even rape fantasies don't fluster them. "I don't want about half of my fantasies to come true," said Megan in Cincinnati. "I've got plenty of rape fantasies, and rape is, of course, something I don't want in my life. The other day I was in class—a women's literature class—and we had read Margaret Atwood's rape fantasies. All the young women started talking about how they don't know anyone who has rape fantasies and how that's really sad that people would fantasize about it. I had to be the only one in my whole class who raised my hand and said, 'Are you kidding? I have rape fantasies all the time. And I don't want to be raped.' "

You can appreciate why it's difficult for her to tell you. And it may be difficult for you to hear it. There's that initial feeling of "Uh-oh, where is this going?" It's pure sexual vertigo—a moment captured in this anecdote from Kate, a 30-year-old Chicago attorney.

> I said to Rich something like, "Do you ever think about anyone else when we're having sex?" And he said, "What would be the right answer to this question?" Somehow he turned it around so I had to answer first, which is totally fair. So I said, "Well, do you mind if I do?" And he said, "No, I think that would be kind of cool." And I said, "Good, because last night you were Dennis Rodman." And Rich just kind of shook his head and went, "Oh, man." I said, "You were fabulous, by the way, if it's any consolation."
>
> But I'm sure he does. I'm sure everybody does. I don't want him to imagine me as his last girlfriend. I prefer a famous person.

When women relate their fantasies and their partners listen and accept them, women are simply ecstatic. They feel closer to their partners, and their sex lives basically go bananas.

Ginger in Delaware told us her best sex ever was "When my husband and I first started having sex, we opened up about our fantasies and found out they were identical!" Now she has orgasms, she said, just listening to him talk about them being with another woman.

For every pot there's a lid.

Sometimes, women would like to act out certain fantasies. Jane, a 30-year-old mother of two in El Cajon, California, had something in mind for her husband.

Just once, I would love him to, like, sneak in, dressed up with a mask on or something, and totally rape me, basically. The times we have dressed up for Halloween parties— I mean really dressed up, really put thought into our costumes—we've always had good sex that night. Yeah, it was a fun night all the way around, and I couldn't wait to get him alone in the bathroom.

Some women consider the term fantasy to include the sort of role playing that can add zip to a sexual encounter (you know, doctor and nurse, coach and track star, pizza boy and bored housewife). Jean, a 50-year-old woman in Bethlehem, Pennsylvania, who's been divorced for 20 years, recalled a wild night that started with an antique dress.

I was dating an older man, and he was very open about things. We were at a flea market and I bought a Victorian dress. And we went home that night and he was, I think, downstairs cooking pork chops, and I was upstairs looking at this dress. I started getting really turned on. I shaved myself, and we played virgin with this Victorian dress on. I think he ended up ripping the dress off me. But the fantasy, the role-playing, it allowed me to be something other than me, and it was really a turn-on.

For others, fantasies are part of a painful past. Anna, a 40-year-old woman from Huntington Beach, California, explained why she cannot bring herself to do it.

I was molested when I was a young teenager, so I used to fantasize a lot when I was being forced into having sex with this man. Of course, I would fantasize that he was a boy at school or some movie star or rock star or whatever. Now I don't fantasize in a making-love relationship because I really want to be there. I used to escape all the time.

We had never thought about feeling thankful for fantasies until we heard from Anna.

CHAPTER TWENTY-SEVEN

Bigger and Better Orgasms

MOST GUYS ASSUME THAT AN ORGASM
IS AN ORGASM. BIG MISTAKE. You have to
understand the profound differences between
hers and yours. Hers are more mental. And each
one is different. If your masterful technique of
3 nights ago fails miserably tonight, don't be
one bit surprised.

Joanne is ready to admit something. "I don't come from intercourse," she said. "I've had lots of orgasms, but not from intercourse. I've never come during intercourse, and that's okay."

Joanne is a 52-year-old teacher in Texas. She's been married for 31 years.

I went through a time when I was real young and thinking I wasn't normal and there was something wrong with me. But once I had done some reading, I found out that less than 40 percent of women come during intercourse, and I thought, "Oh." Knowledge is very empowering. It lets you know you can be yourself.

I'm curious about what that might be like, I guess. I tried very hard; it hasn't worked. And to me, it spoils the lovemaking to make a sexual experiment out of it. You know, if we push here and we pull there, maybe something will happen? In the meantime, I've lost all the fun, the spontaneity, and the relaxation. I decided it wasn't worth the effort.

Joanne thought she wasn't normal. She's perfectly normal. In conducting our research for this book, we quizzed three groups of women on this topic. We quizzed the 80 women across North America, of varying ages, who consented to in-depth interviews with female graduate students of human sexuality. Then we quizzed the mostly young, feisty readers of *New Woman* magazine, and we got back hundreds of replies. Finally, we mailed a formal, eight-page survey form—our Magellan Poll—to women in their thirties and forties who buy Rodale health books. We received nearly 1,200 filled-out questionnaires.

THE FACTS OF LIFE

WHAT EVERY MAN OUGHT TO KNOW

We asked, "What consistently allows you to achieve orgasm?" The position that guys think should work really works for only one woman in three. Even among women who rate themselves as very satisfied with their sex lives, the missionary position ranks fourth. One interesting finding is that women under 30 embrace oral sex most enthusiastically: 63% checked that answer.

Manual stimulation	50%
Oral sex	47%
When I'm on top	36%
When he's on top	34%
Other	7%
Nothing	5%

The bottom line among all three groups is that only a minority of women report reaching orgasm in the standard missionary position.

Get over it.

Among *New Woman* readers, the most common method for achieving orgasm was oral sex, followed by digital stimulation. Together, these two routes to clitoral orgasm were mentioned by nearly half of the respondents. Others included the woman-on-top position ("riding the donkey," as Tarita in Texas called it), foreplay, emotional closeness, masturbation, fantasies, breast stimulation, and the use of a vibrator. Way down the list was vaginal stimulation—the traditional missionary position, the only position that Bill Clinton defines as sex, the

> "My sister and I live together. She is a nun and I'm promiscuous. Fun, fun, fun."
> —ANONYMOUS SURVEY RESPONDENT

position that gets all the ink in steamy Danielle Steel novels. That would be man on top, thrusting with his mighty blunderbuss until her brains fall out. Only 1 in 12 readers praised this position as the most reliable route to bliss.

Among the soccer moms who buy Rodale's health books, roughly a third say that they can consistently achieve orgasm with their men on top.

As for the 80 in-depth interviewees, granted, this was a self-selected sample of women who were, by and large, more sexually self-assured than the average North American woman. But even among these women, only 40 percent reach orgasm during intercourse. And that's including women who need to be on top to see the fireworks.

Just for the record, only half a dozen of the 80 women spoke of simultaneous his-and-her orgasms. For the vast majority of couples, that happens only in the movies.

"Typically, we'll have intercourse and he'll have an orgasm, and then I'll have an orgasm," Cathy, 30, in California told us. "I prefer to do it separately." She achieves orgasm most consistently when her boyfriend stimulates her clitoris with his hand. But not during intercourse itself. "Physically, it just feels irritating then. This is how I'm built."

She said she's okay with that—but he isn't. "He would like to have it be different. He tends to evaluate himself negatively about that. I think he sort of has a fantasy about making that happen, but I don't see that realistically happening. That's not how it works for me."

Cathy's boyfriend is hardly alone. A lot of men evaluate themselves negatively, as she puts it, about the fact that their sex lives don't resemble the Hollywood version. They start thinking that maybe there's some secret position they're not doing. Maybe if they just learned one trick from the annals of erotic arts or something . . .

For some, those contorted Kama Sutra positions are the stuff of fun and games. A Sacramento woman described this position as her personal favorite: "Him on top froggy-style, thrusting slowly and gently while kissing my breasts."

And Julie in Baltimore, one of our in-depth interviewees, described her recent success in finding a way to orgasm during intercourse.

> Actually, we did it for the first time last week. He was on top, and he sort of sat himself up a little bit and then was playing with his finger, stimulating me, and I had an orgasm. Usually, though, it will be from the back, where I am laying on my stomach, he will lay on top of me and then have his hand underneath me, stimulating me that way.

Olivia in New England took a unique approach.

> Back in our younger days, we used to have this thing we called our position of the month. Some of those positions backfired totally, but they kept it exciting. That kinda died out a couple of years ago, but we should bring that back. It was good.

Nonetheless, her oral-sex orgasms are still the best by far.

Other women dismiss these positions as circus tricks. Asked to describe the best sex she's ever had, one *New Woman* reader in Columbia, California, said, "Slow, caring, loving, and sensual—not 25 different positions."

Even Wendy in New York City, a woman who's slept with more than 50 men, who has done just about everything in every position ever devised, said, "As long as you are really, really open with your partner and having fun and being receptive and responsive, it doesn't matter if you know some little trick that drives me wild."

> "An orgasm for a woman is different every single time you have sex."
> —AMY, Baltimore

We'll say it again: Female sexual stimulation is not just a matter of nerve endings in the erogenous zones. A big component is in the brain.

For women, sex is between the ears. In fact, some sex therapists believe when it comes to orgasmic response, women's emotions have a bigger impact than any physical sensation.

This is exactly what Kaye in North Little Rock, Arkansas, wanted to tell us. "The first time I ever had a screaming orgasm, it was the soft talking and knowing his desires and fantasies that made it possible," she said. "I felt like a sex goddess because of him."

But by now you know this. This is what we've been telling you for the last 290 pages. It's why women connect romance and sex, why they love anticipation, why you need to set the right mood, why many women, not just Kaye, say that what consistently enables them to reach orgasm is love.

Most men have no trouble coming in love's absence. Many women cannot. Here's interesting testimony from Lana, who works in retail in Mount Blanchard, Ohio. When her first marriage ended in divorce, she began what she now admits were some promiscuous escapades. She was very active sexually, but she said:

> It wasn't very good sex. It wasn't all that great because I didn't want to get hurt again, so I wouldn't let my feelings go. And no matter how hard a man would try to please me, it was like, "You're not getting into that part of me." I could not have an orgasm no matter what they did.

Try to picture a man saying that.

If their brains can help them achieve orgasm, sometimes their brains can get in the way.

Women often express a wish to be a little more like men. They wish they could just let go, get into the moment, and enjoy the ride. But for Kathleen, a 25-year-old married woman from Arizona, this is no easy task.

> If there's any excuse for me not to have an orgasm, I won't. I have a really hard time with orgasm and not being present. If I don't have some kind of fantasy going on, I have a much more difficult time. I'm trying to become more physically based, rather than cognitively based.

This may explain a huge difference between men and women.

Most women don't come every time.

Sometimes it just doesn't happen for her. And no wonder. Jane, a 30-year-old mother of two in El Cajon, California, gave us a peek inside her brain.

> When women have sex, I think that men don't realize how much stuff is running through our heads. I don't think anything goes through their heads except, "This feels great. What can I do to make it better? How long is it going to last because I don't want it to end?" And what's going through my mind is "Please, God, don't let me get pregnant. I don't

want another kid. I don't want another baby crying in the house. And if I do want one, I don't want it now. I should have made dinner. There's dishes that need to be done." You hear the dryer buzz. "Oops. Laundry needs to be folded." The phone rings. I mean, you've got so much stuff running through your head, it's really hard to get to the point where you're only thinking about what you're doing. And I would never say that to him—"Oh, by the way, you're really enjoying yourself, but all I can think about is, the dog needs to be let out." It's so hard not to think about that stuff. I mean, I'm grocery shopping or I'm painting the walls, you know?

Let's face it, men would be cranky, miserable SOBs if they came only half the time, but women seem to take it all in stride. Jean, a 50-year-old woman in Pennsylvania, told us why she doesn't mind: "Sometimes it would just take too much effort, and then it can turn into a mechanical you're-going-to-come-if-it-kills-you kind of thing. And that's not the importance of sex for me."

THE FACTS OF LIFE

NO EXCUSES

We asked, "Do you orgasm at least once during a sexual encounter?" As you can see, she's not like you in this department. Even among women who rate themselves as very satisfied with their sex lives, only 46 percent reach orgasm every time.

Yes, every time	29%
Occasionally	20%
Usually	45%
Never	6%

More than one woman used the word "mechanical" as an unflattering adjective. As in this bromide: "Sexuality is not a matter of mechanics but of relationship." For most guys, "mechanical" is not a bad thing.

We like to think of ourselves as mechanically inclined. But the message is that we need to leave that side of ourselves at the bedroom door.

We'll try not to get too *mechanical* about this, but sex does require some mechanics, correct? We're not yet at the stage of civilization where we can just step into the orgasmatron.

So let's go back to the question of what works? As you can see by our Magellan Poll results, masturbation got the most votes. Masturbation was mentioned not just by lonely ladies but also by women with boyfriends and husbands. "Not that we have a bad sex life," wrote one woman in Louisville, "but I can always count on masturbation."

In that department, there's not too much you can do to help.

Okay, how about that close second? Oral sex! That, she can't do without you. "I've read that up to 70 percent of women cannot orgasm without clitoral stimulation, and I'm part of that percentage," said Carol in Missouri. "And the way men feel when they cannot make women come is pitiful. I mean, deal with it. Accept the fact that it's nature and head south."

We have tons of useful advice on how to be a master of the fine art of oral sex. See chapter 24.

You'll note that our survey shows that a woman has a slightly better chance of coming if she's on top of things. One such lady is Kate, a Chicago attorney.

> I almost always reach orgasm on top. That's just the way it is. Yep. I don't know why it is, but I can make myself come in a minute, easily, if I'm upper that night. And when I feel that it's somewhere within reality, I'm willing to chase that little bunny until I catch it.

Still holding out hope for the missionary position? Here's one circus trick to try: the CAT position. CAT stands for coital alignment technique. Her ankles should be resting on your calves; you slide forward so that you're "riding high." Your head is above her head; your pubic bone is atop her pubic bone above her vagina, putting the base of your penis in contact with her clitoris. Relax your upper body, lowering it onto her torso. This helps to keep your pelvis from sliding back down. She tips her pelvis toward you, and the two of your rock rhythmically back and forth. She's pushing upward, you're pushing downward, your penis sliding to a shallow position in her. If you find yourself thrusting, you're doing it wrong. It's not a very sexy name, to be sure, but try it. Maybe you'll start to . . . purr.

Not working for you? Then, once again starting from the traditional missionary position, place your legs outside your partner's, rather than between them. It increases muscle tension in her vagina, "so it makes for a quick come," as one woman said.

The CAT position is intended to combine two seemingly opposite concepts: the missionary position and a clitoral orgasm. More commonly, women who can reach orgasm in the missionary position are getting there via penile stimulation to their cervices or their G-spots. Perhaps you've heard of this G-spot business and wondered what it's all about. Here's the executive summary: It's a sensitive area that can be felt through the front wall of the vagina, about halfway between the pubic bone and the cervix. It often feels like a spongy bean, but when stimulated it swells to the size of a half-dollar. It's named for a German obstetrician, Ernst Grafenberg, who first described it in 1950.

The G-spot may be the biggest news in female sexuality in the last 50 years because it explains why some women experience vaginal orgasms that feel different than clitoral orgasms (via masturbation or oral sex). But despite two decades of heady publicity, it hasn't exactly caught on. If anything, most women have vaguely assimilated the information as one more thing to feel inadequate about. If you and your partner are interested in pursuing a G-spot orgasm, you'll be quite interested in Can She Explain It? on page 302.

In the meantime, if the CAT position doesn't work, don't blame us. And for that matter, don't blame her, either. "Most men approach it with 'Why can't you do this,' versus 'How can I help you do this,' " said Susi in suburban Philadelphia. There's an unnecessary tone of male bashing in her statement, but we'll grant her this, we heard from a lot of women—and they're quoted freely in these pages—who say their partners behaved like jerks in this delicate matter.

THE SHORT ANSWER

G-SPOT? WHAT G-SPOT?

Most of our in-depth subjects answered the question, "Do you have a G-spot?" with a frank "I don't know." Others had these things to say.

- "I have two of them."
- "It's on the outside. Sometimes."
- "Internally?"
- "Someone prior to my husband found that spot. I don't know what happened to it."
- "I hate it when guys think they're supposed to find your G-spot. They hook their finger upwards. It feels like a fish hook. And it's really annoying."
- "It's like, who cares?"
- "He has hit it, but it's not like he's looking for the spot. He doesn't even know what the spot is. I'm not going to tell him, because then he'll just go right there all the time."

"I never reach orgasm with sex," said Suzanne, a 29-year-old social worker in Minnesota. She thinks it may be possible in a theoretical sort of way but, she said, "I think it would get really complicated. It would be, like, he'd have to go down on me for a little while. Then we'd have to have sex, like, doggie-style, so he could touch me during that, and then maybe I would have an orgasm."

The men in her life have made her extremely sensitive about this subject. "I'm afraid they're going to think there's something wrong with me. That's my fear. You know, my second boyfriend was really devastated by me not having orgasms during sex. And then, when he started dating someone new, he told me how she always had all these orgasms during sex. He tried to make me feel really crappy about it."

Dear Suzanne: Send a copy of this book to his current girlfriend. Highlight your last sentence. Wish her luck with him. And we wish you better luck with someone new.

Women may not worry about coming every single time they make love, but they'd like to be given the chance. And they appreciate all your help, especially if it takes them a really, really, really long time. (One woman told us it can take an hour.)

A word of advice: When you're doing something that works, keep working it.

Sometimes you move on before she has time to get over the top. "We call it getting over the mountain," said Amy in Baltimore. "I can be climbing and climbing, and he can move to another technique when I wasn't ready for him to switch, and then I have to start all over again."

So if she's arching her back and moaning and saying, "Baby, baby, don't stop!" that means "don't stop doing exactly what you're doing exactly the way you're doing it right now," explained Jane. "When I put his hand in a certain place or move him a certain way, he can't keep that spot for more than a few seconds. It's like his attention span is really, really small."

Andrea in Ohio made the same complaint. Give her variety early on and the ol' reliable moves later on. "It's after I'm fully aroused that I want them to form some kind of pattern and then stick with it. For me, I want a steady pressure and rhythm right at the hood of the clitoris."

Once again, we must say that not all women go for this. Ann in Pittsburgh praised her boyfriend's red-light method, "when he changes speed on me and totally stops that one thing that got me to that point." She loves it.

Christina, a sales clerk in New Hampshire, hates it. "Sometimes when I'm just so close and he knows that, he just stops. He thinks that's a good thing. He thinks he's making it better, and it's not." That's what guys do to make it last, and some guys get to the point where they like that; they savor being on the brink. But the difference is that guys can always come. Women can't.

As she approaches orgasm, it's only natural for you to get caught up in the moment and clench down or speed up to somehow chase the climax. If possible, maintain the rhythm of what you're doing. "Pace is everything. It's everything," said Dawn in Maine. "A lot of times, he thinks that for me to hit orgasm he needs to speed up; and I keep trying to tell him, 'No, because if you speed things up, it brings me right back to where I was; where if you stay consistent, it will be the strongest orgasm in the world.'"

As if you're not confused enough already, here's one more complicating factor.

Women's orgasms are like snowflakes: No two are exactly alike.

"An orgasm for a woman is different every single time you have sex," said Amy in Baltimore. And many women agree. In fact, some guys may be forgiven for suspecting that they are paired with a multiple personality.

Jamie in Baltimore finds that she's hornier at mid-month. "A lot of times in the middle of the month, probably when I am ovulating, I am extremely wet. And that can be even when I am not being sexually stimulated. There is just more juice down there."

At least she's fairly predictable that way. Jennifer in New York is not. "My body reacts differently on different days. It could be soft. It could be harder. Different things feel good different days. I don't think I can tell until someone's touching me what kind of day it is."

Chris, a 39-year-old homemaker in Canada, explained it all for you.

I find sometimes it takes different things to reach orgasm at different times. What works one night doesn't necessarily work the next. And what's feeling good one night might really hurt the next night. If men can understand that, they will be more confident in their lovemaking. "Oh, I thought I was doing it right." Yes, you are doing right, but right is different tonight. So don't feel offended, guys, if somebody is telling you something new every night.

Finally, a hard and fast rule: Don't ask if she came. She always wonders, "Weren't you here?" It puts distance between you at the very moment when she's feeling closest.

"I hate when he asks," said Jamie in Baltimore. "Every now and then he will, and I am always, like, 'If you have to ask, then you don't know.' Then he says, 'I just want to hear you say it.' Which I think is a lie. Sometimes my orgasm isn't as intense, so maybe he doesn't necessarily feel it."

Good news, guys. Not one woman complained that her man rolled over and promptly fell asleep. The way we figure it, there must have been one guy who did that, once—and we've all taken a beating for it ever since.

How Does She Reach Orgasm? Let Us Count the Ways
—BEVERLY WHIPPLE, R.N., PH.D.

Beverly Whipple, R.N., Ph.D., probably knows more about orgasms than anyone else in the world. Her research in this field began by chance, when she was a nursing professor at Gloucester County College in New Jersey. She taught women to perform Kegel exercises so they could better control their urinary incontinence. In the course of it, she discovered that some women ejaculate a nonurinary fluid during orgasm. She then came across the research paper of a German physician, Ernst Grafenberg, which led to the best-selling book *The G Spot*. Since then, she has conducted pioneering research on female sexual response in her laboratory at Rutgers University in Newark, New Jersey, where she is a professor in the college of nursing. She is president of the American Association of Sex Educators, Counselors, and Therapists (AASECT). Her research has put her foremost among those who differ with the conclusions of the famed sex researchers Masters and Johnson—that the only orgasm in females is clitoral.

Q: *Is a woman's orgasm different? Or is she feeling pretty much what the guy is feeling?*

A: Studies have been conducted on this. Men and women described their orgasmic experiences, and then they've had other people read the quotes and rate whether they think it's a man or a woman. And the readers could not determine whether it was a man or a woman describing their orgasmic experiences.

However, there is a difference in orgasmic experience among women and even within the same woman. And that difference depends on the type of stimulation and the woman's response at that particular time. In my laboratory at Rutgers, we have documented orgasms from various forms of stimulation, including imagery alone.

Q: *You mean these women could lie back, have a sexual fantasy and, without ever touching themselves, reach orgasm?*

A: Yes. Some women say they can do this. We invited 10 women who said they experienced these orgasms into our lab, and they had orgasms from both genital self-stimulation and from imagery alone. And when we looked at the physiological correlates of these orgasms, there was no significant difference in terms of elevations in blood pressure, heart rate, pupil diameter, or pain thresholds.

Q: *That's something men can't do.*

A: We don't know. Men have wet dreams. I'm just beginning to conduct studies with males.

But, going back to the different types of stimulation, we have measured orgasms from vaginal or G-spot stimulation, and from cervical stimulation. We are now working with women with complete spinal cord injuries, where the nerve pathways cannot go through the spinal cords. They've been told they cannot have orgasms, and yet we've measured orgasms in these women.

There are many different neural pathways that are involved in sexual response—more, in fact, than we previously believed. And that's what accounts for the difference in the physiological response.

So women do have different types of orgasmic response depending on the area of stimulation, and also depending on many, many other factors—how she feels that day, where her hormonal levels are. There are just so many other things that play into a woman's response. So you can't think you can just push a button, and this is what's going to happen. Orgasm is not a simple reflex.

Q: *Speaking of pushing a button, you have said that your research on the G-spot has been widely misunderstood. You never claimed it was a universal "magic button," and yet the women we've interviewed have that impression.*

A: I never wanted to see the G-spot, multiple orgasms, imagery orgasms, or anything else set up as a goal that people have to achieve. Each woman is a unique individual. And my whole purpose has been to validate the experiences of women—women who said that they didn't fit into the monolithic pattern of clitoral sexual response. Women who said they had vaginal orgasm, who had female ejaculation and had surgery for this, or who stopped having orgasm because they didn't want to "wet the bed." I wanted to validate these women's experiences—not set up another goal.

Q: *Maybe so many people misunderstand the idea because they're so goal-directed when it comes to sex.*

A: . . . When it comes to life. When it comes to everything in our lives, we're very goal-directed. And when it comes to sex, I would say the majority of men are goal-directed, and the majority of women are pleasure-directed. Problems occur when people do not realize this, or they do not communicate this to their partners. It's very important for men to realize that women may have a different goal, and that goal may be pleasure.

Women can have orgasm from stimulation of other areas of their bodies than just the genitals. Primarily the breasts, although there are women who have orgasm from stimulation of their ear lobes or right behind their ears. It depends on where their areas of hypersensitivity are. We're all different. We're all unique.

Q: *It sounds like orgasms are not one-size-fits-all. Different women experience them differently at different times and in different places.*

A: And different women like different things. Some women love G-spot stimulation; some women don't like it. We all have different tastes in terms of the foods we choose to eat, the clothes we choose to wear, the people we choose to be with. Why should our orgasms all be the same?

Q: *But you can try new foods. Can you try new orgasms?*

A: Sure.

Q: *So women aren't "stuck" with their orgasms? This is a changeable response?*

A: Very changeable. We don't have to be stuck in just one pattern of "Stimulate me here; push that button." Our whole body has erotic potential.

Q: *That will be good news to many women we heard from. Most of them cannot have orgasm through intercourse, and some are almost wistful about that. They say, "I wonder what that would have been like. . . ."*

A: Oh, but they can learn. What I suggest is, first of all, they learn what G-spot stimulation and orgasm feels like, with manual stimulation. Her partner uses a "come-here" motion with his finger to stimulate the area of spongy tissue felt through the front wall of the vagina. And then you find positions of intercourse in which that area is stimulated. Whether that's the woman on top, rear entry, or the man 'kneeling up' in the missionary position, so the penis goes toward the front wall of the vagina. Or maybe the woman is lying on a bed or a table and the man is standing up— you have to find a position in which the penis will hit into the front wall of the vagina. Not the back wall, as it would in the missionary position, and not the cervix. Although we are now documenting orgasm in my lab from cervical stimulation alone.

Q: *Can Kegel exercises help us discover our orgasmic potential?*

A: Kegels are extremely important. The strength of that muscle, the pubococcygeus or PC muscle, is positively correlated with a woman's orgasmic response. That is, women who don't have orgasms have very weak PC muscles. In women who have orgasm from clitoral stimulation, the muscle is stronger, but not as strong as women who can have orgasm from vaginal stimulation or any type of stimulation.

Now, in order to get that muscle strong, we have to teach women how to do Kegel exercises. And here's how I teach it: We all have a muscle that goes from the pubic bone in the front to the coccyx, or the tailbone, in the rear. In animals, that muscle wags the tail. We don't have a tail to wag. So the only time we use that muscle is when it involuntarily contracts during orgasm, or if we're in the bathroom urinating and we're waiting for an important phone call. I teach people to identify the muscle they use to cut off the flow of urination to go answer the phone. And I have them keep that in their heads, and then I have them contract and relax that muscle. Ten seconds of contraction, 10 seconds of relaxation.

You can monitor how well you're doing. I usually tell women, before they start to do this exercise, that they or their partners should put two fingers into the vagina and open those two fingers up. Then the woman contracts the muscle and tries to close the fingers together. Most women cannot do that.

So you do your exercises for a month or so. Do them when you're at a stoplight or when the phone rings or something that will remind you to do them, because you want to get up to about 150 contractions a day. At the end of the month, put two fingers in and see if she can squeeze them together.

Q: *And by the time a woman can squeeze those two fingers together . . .*

A: She may find a change in her orgasmic response.

CHAPTER TWENTY-EIGHT

Why Women Fake It

USUALLY, WOMEN FAKE ORGASM BECAUSE MEN GET ALL BUMMED OUT WHEN THEY DON'T COME FOR REAL. Just remember that at the end of the day, it's her orgasm, not yours.

Laura is a 32-year-old Web site designer in New York City. She's been with the same guy for 3 years—and she fakes orgasms. Every time. "He doesn't know that," she said.

> There's only one way I can have an orgasm, and that's by playing with myself. It's hard enough, even with me faking it, that sometimes he doesn't want to stop trying to keep me having orgasms. Because you know guys, they have this huge policy about women having multiple orgasms. Everybody wants their woman to be the one who has multiple orgasms. Well, I don't want to be the one. It's not going to happen. Because eventually I'm going to get dry, I'm going to get sore. If I don't come, he's never going to stop.

So this is how she gets him off—and then gets him off her. Don't get Laura wrong. She isn't treacherous. She doesn't hate sex. She's not doing this just to keep her man. "There are times when I initiate a sexual encounter where I just want to have sex," she said. "It doesn't mean I'm going to come. It means I want to have his penis inside me or I want to play with him."

But either he can't accept that or she thinks he can't accept that. So she pulls a Meg Ryan. Remember the diner scene? With Billy Crystal. *When Harry Met Sally.*

"Most women are really good at faking orgasms," said Laura.

A *Mademoiselle* magazine survey asked guys if they brought their partners to orgasm every time. Yes, said 47 percent of guys. Yes, agreed . . . 30 percent of women. Hmmm.

Some guys think they're God's gift to chicks. This sort of guy doesn't want to get off a woman until he's seen the whites of her eyes rolling back into her head so that he can then assure himself that, yes, he is Señor Stud Muffin. Guys like that exist, but they wouldn't be caught dead reading this book. You, dear reader, are not like that. If a woman fakes it with you, there's a more charitable explanation than sexual egomania.

> "I will never understand why men can so easily be led by a pretty woman. Attached or unattached, it doesn't seem to matter. If a beautiful woman decides she wants to bed a man, it can almost always be done. They really do think with the wrong head."
>
> —SHERRY, Los Angeles

The trouble here, in a nutshell, may be that unless you come, you feel incredibly frustrated. You assume that she feels the same way. She doesn't.

"The physical closeness—the feeling of being loved, cherished, devoured, whatever—is much more important for women than reaching orgasm," said Susi, 42, a mother of two in suburban Philadelphia.

Other women might say, "Whoa, Susi, babe, speak for yourself. Sometimes I do want to get off." But even they will agree that pure lust is not always their motive for taking you in.

As Dee, a 32-year-old professor in Chicago, said, "Sometimes I am doing it for another reason. Like, I want to feel emotionally close. Or he wants to more than I do, but I want to be there for him."

Some women do reach orgasm every time. Susi herself, for instance. "It's not an elusive butterfly for me," as she put it.

But most women don't. And if it's just not happening, you reach a crossroads. You can both accept that, disentangle your limbs, smooch, and say, "Tomorrow is another day." Or one of you, often the man, but not always, doesn't accept it and presses onward, hoping lightning will strike. He's a guy, after all, and he's there to accomplish something. Before long, it's been too long already. She's drying up; she's getting sore. The easy way out is to have "a little heated event."

"Sometimes, sex for me is just an intimate experience," said Kate, a single attorney in Chicago.

> And that's enough for me. I don't always need to have an orgasm. He's not totally bullheaded about it, but to some extent it's less wonderful for him. He thinks that's the kind of sensation I'm looking for. So sometimes I'll have a little heated event. I don't necessarily fake orgasm, although I have, definitely. Just to finish, because when I get really excited, then he's guaranteed to come. That will pretty much put him over the edge. I've told him I've faked it before. And I've told him why. And I just leave it at that.

Angela, 30, who works in retail in California, went so far as to say, "Every woman fakes orgasm."

Catherine, who's 24, said she has faked orgasms early in relationships, before she has a chance to teach a man what really knocks her socks off. She fakes it, she admits, "because I think it makes them feel better. If I was a guy and I didn't bring a girl to orgasm, I'd be a little sad. I do it to protect their feelings."

That's why Dawn in Maine does it. "I don't want to see him pout," she said. It's as simple as that.

THE FACTS OF LIFE

DOES SHE OR DOESN'T SHE?

In our Magellan Poll we asked, "When was the last time you faked an orgasm?" We'll give those who said "never" the benefit of the doubt. Still, more than 1 woman in 10 has faked it in the last month. And 7.7 percent of women who are dissatisfied with their sex lives say they fake it "all the time."

This week	2%
This month	6.5%
This year	13%
More than a year ago	25%
Never	51%
All the time	2.8%

Of course, faking it is not the politically correct thing to do. When women get up on their soapboxes, they condemn it outright, as one more concession to male dominance. We heard some of that preachiness in written responses. Like this one, from Karin in Minneapolis.

> I get really angry when some women say they have faked an orgasm. Why send the signal that everything is fantastic when it isn't? My thoughts are, I am only cheating myself. What's more, these women send men out into the world thinking they are master lovers, when nothing is further from the truth. What a disservice!

But in our in-depth interviews, women were less judgmental. We were surprised by the number of women who

admit they occasionally fake it, and the matter-of-factness in
their replies.

For many women, and for many reasons, faking it seems to be part of life. Or part of growing up.

Many said it was par for the course back in high school.
Jamie in Baltimore won't condemn anyone for it.

> I don't think it is stupid, because I understand the motivation
> behind it. I understand why a woman might fake an orgasm
> because she is trying to make her partner feel good; but I
> also think, looking back on it now, that it's selling yourself
> short. I think it makes much more sense to be like, "Let's
> figure out a way that I really can," instead of faking it and not
> getting the pleasure in return.

It's in your best interests as well. "A guy said to me that a
man would rather be disappointed than deceived, and that's
why we shouldn't fake that," said Danielle, a single account
executive from Philadelphia.

For years, men were criticized for not caring enough about
women's orgasms. We were all suspected of being selfish
lovers who climbed on and climbed off.

Nowadays, the complaint is that we care too much. "It's a
guy thing, definitely," said Yvonne in Cincinnati. "He always
gets it, so he feels guilty if I don't. He feels like, if he does, I
should. If once or twice I would rather not, he says, 'I owe
you one.' "

Olivia in New England agrees. "Yeah, I have faked it.
I'll admit it. It's when he starts saying, 'Have you had one?
Have you had one?' He means well, but sometimes it's just
overbearing."

We can certainly put ourselves in the place of Yvonne's and
Olivia's lovers—intent on orgasm, and assuming she's as intense as we are. This gets back to the fact that, when it comes to
sex, most men are goal-oriented, whereas most women are
pleasure-oriented. "Men are more orgasm-centered," said

Barbara in Chicago. "They feel really bad if they can't help you achieve an orgasm; and I don't know whether it's an ego thing or if they care for you."

Whatever your motive, the effect is the same. She feels pressured to come. "If they make too big a deal of it, you do feel as if you're onstage," said Kristen, a 29-year-old teacher in Chicago. "And I think that's really what promotes those white lies. It's the fact that there's just too much pressure."

That pressure, by the way, works against you. If it's not happening and you step it up, you "step on it," so to speak.

THE SHORT ANSWER

THE SECRET OF MULTIPLE ORGASMS

We asked 80 women, "Do you ever have multiple orgasms? And if so, how?" Most women haven't. Some did. Here's what they had to say.

- "When I'm on top and I reach orgasm and he hasn't yet, we go from behind and I do again, which is great."
- "The first one will be through oral sex. And then once sex starts, I'll reach it again. And again and again."
- "The time we made love in the hallway downstairs— I don't know what happened."
- "The times I've had them, they were with me, from me."
- "He thinks I have. I fake it pretty well."
- "To him, it's this big prowess thing. I don't care; it's not that important."
- "We did that for a while, and it was getting to be like our sex life was falling into a pattern. We didn't like that."

Her anxiety begins to creep up on the pleasure in her brain, gobbling away at it like Ms. Pac-Man. It's her version of performance anxiety. What would happen to you, after all, if you were wondering how long you could keep that erection? What if your partner were openly wondering the same thing? You'd feel like you were onstage. Indeed, you would be. And you'd wilt.

Said Louise, a 37-year-old mother of two in Denton, Texas, "He tries harder, and the harder he tries, the less chance there is for me to reach it." That's why Louise, among many women, simply finds it easier to climax by her own hands.

> When I'm having sex with him, sometimes it's like I feel pressured to move the right way or feel the right way to him. But when I'm having sex with myself, there is no pressure. I can do anything I want. I don't have to look a certain way. I don't have to smell a certain way. I don't have to answer any questions. I don't have to wonder, "Well, do I look stupid doing this?" I don't have to wonder about anything.

What should we take from all this? Should we go back to not caring?

No way, say these women.

"Sometimes, men give up a little more easily than I'd like," said Jennifer, a 29-year-old single gal in New York. "I get upset and discouraged and just say, 'Forget it,' and it bothers me if they don't argue with me. I'm kind of confusing to men, because a lot of things that feel good to me are not going to produce orgasm, but I'd like it to keep going."

Marie from Minneapolis seconds that emotion. "Just because I take a long time to reach orgasm does not mean he is failing to please me. Quite the opposite—I'm riding the wave."

So, are we damned if we do, damned if we don't?

Not exactly. But we do walk a fine line between trying too hard and not trying hard enough. Women, who have an intuitive radar the size of the North American Air Defense Command, get upset if you give up because you don't care about them. They feel used. They want you to try to please them.

They actually want to please themselves, and they need your help. But if you try too hard, they begin to suspect that the person you really want to please is not her, but you.

As you see, we heard from a lot of young women who fake it out of naïveté or nervousness or concern for their young lovers' sexual egos. Older women aren't there anymore. But some may have a new reason to fake it—to get it over with because some older guys want to maintain rock-hard erections for hours to prove that they're still Mister Hot Rod.

That's been the experience of Deb, a 44-year-old private investigator in California.

> "If everyone truly believed women are responsible for our own orgasms, faking it would become an antiquated practice, like a man asking a woman's father for her hand in marriage."
> —SUSAN CRAIN BAKOS, sex author

> I've been out with guys who, their greatest mission in life is to see how long they can keep it up. And sometimes you would be like, "When is this going to end? This is lasting way too long." And even they are in pain by now, but they think this is their sign of masculinity. They make it a marathon.

We should also note—and this was a surprise to us—that a few women seem to fake orgasm for their own needs. It's not about you at all.

What they're really doing is faking arousal. That sounds like the case with Chantel, 26, a single mother in Arizona. "I have faked orgasms," she admitted. "Maybe in the hopes that if I faked enough, I will actually have one. Or maybe they will think I am so excited they will just really keep at it until I do."

Mary is a Chicago teacher who, at 62, is still faking it. "Maybe to kind of stimulate myself, I guess. You know, maybe it'll get me started."

What it comes down to is this: You can try to please her, and if her heart isn't made of stone, she'll love you to death for your sweetness.

Ultimately, she's responsible for her own orgasm. It may take her 20 seconds or 20 years, but she's in charge. She has to let go of whatever is holding her back and grab whatever it is she needs.

Sometimes it does take time and personal growth—years and tears, even—for people to reach their full sexual potential. One inspiring personal story we heard comes from Andrea in Maine. At 51, she has no trouble achieving orgasm. In fact, she's probably the envy of many a younger woman. Listen to this description.

> "Bad sex is like the flu. Everyone has it, sooner or later; it feels worse than you'd imagined; it doesn't kill you."
>
> —AMY BLOOM, in SELF magainze

I orgasm pretty easily, so I have orgasms with oral sex first, and then I more often than not orgasm again once he enters me. And sometimes I have orgasms, several of them, once he has entered; and usually I orgasm when he does. And there have been times I've orgasmed after he's withdrawn. Him just playing with my clit gives me multiple orgasms. We play in the car a lot, and I can have multiple orgasms by just him stroking me and touching me.

But it wasn't always thus. In her 17-year marriage, she did not orgasm once during intercourse. That may have had something to do with the fact that, as she told us, "my husband was an abusive alcoholic." After she left, she stayed away from relationships for a few years. Then, "the second relationship I had was very liberating because I started to let go of all my old worries and inhibitions and some of the rules that I had been brought up with. I became free in other ways as well, besides in the bedroom. There was a mutual decision about when and where to have sex and how often. And there was talking and laughing and respect there, between the man and myself.

"I remember thanking him for giving me such a wonderful time sexually; and he said, 'I didn't give you anything; you just gave to yourself. You should consider it a gift you gave yourself.' "

CHAPTER TWENTY-NINE

Beyond the Bedroom

WOMEN REALLY WANT TO MAKE LOVE
SOMEWHERE BESIDES THE BEDROOM, for a
change. Some praise vacation sex; some like a
spontaneous quickie on the balcony or in the hot
tub. And some get a thrill out of a dangerous liaison
in a public place.

After this story, you'll want to propose marriage to a total stranger. Her name is Kelly. She's 30. She lives in San Francisco. Too bad she's taken.

"I gave him oral sex last night at Barnes and Noble," she said. "In the very back, behind the shelves. There were people in the store, so it had to be quick, obviously. But it took probably 5 minutes."

So there she was, on her knees, her husband standing up and nonchalantly pretending to read a book about late medieval muskets, maybe, who knows.

And if someone came along?

"We have little signals and stuff worked out. I had a pen on the floor so that, if anybody came around, I could be looking for my pen. We always try to think of some way that it could be legitimate."

But nobody did, so she brought him to orgasm and swallowed. She never leaves a mess.

And then?

"We put his penis away and we got dressed and I got back up and it was, like, very quick that we were back into everyday roles. But I continued to play with him. And of course, he had to go sit down right away. He was so weak. Thus making me completely turned on again—I love the power. That's the ultimate."

THE FACTS OF LIFE

SOMEWHERE, A PLACE FOR US

Are you ready to shake things up a bit? She sure is. We asked, "The next time you make love, what would be a romantic alternative to the bedroom?" Even the floor beat the bedroom.

In front of the fireplace	61%
A charming bed-and-breakfast	52%
A first-class hotel	47%
A hot tub	46%
Outdoors	39%
The shower	35%
The sofa	23%
A motel	17%
The floor	17%
In the car or truck	12%
Other	8%
None	14%

Kelly and her husband have a thing for public places. They've done it by the side of the road and under bridges and on rooftops and in lots and lots of dressing rooms. ("You have to sneak him in. Macy's dressing rooms are not very supervised.") They even did it in the bathroom at her doctor's office. ("Just oral sex was all. It was my fertility doctor's. I guess we figured, 'What are they going to say?' ")

And they've never been caught.

Not that she knows what they'd do if they were ever caught.

> "I think making love in a car is fabulous. I don't know if it is about being discovered as much as just being free. Like, this does belong in our world, and so what is the big deal?"
>
> —SARAH JANE, Michigan

"We might just go, 'All right, you caught us. What are you going to do?' I always think, 'What's the worst thing that could happen?' Well, the worst thing is, we'd get arrested, right? And, you know, we're married. We're a man and a woman. We're normal, red-blooded Americans. What difference does it make?"

It can make a big difference—in your love life.

After a couple of decades of marriage and kids and yadda yadda yadda, things get real routine. Lovemaking gets monotonous.

Everybody wants to believe in hot monogamy, but the people who actually succeed at it are the people who make the extra effort.

And what about those who don't? "My ex-brother-in-law, he shaved every Saturday morning and did it every Saturday night," said Jean in Bethlehem, Pennsylvania. "I thought, 'What a turn-off. How sad.' "

Women have long regarded vacation sex as some of the best sex of their lives. It's a hit on many levels. It's a change of scenery, for starters. She's away from home and feeling free of her usual responsibilities. And if it's a vacation in a tropical resort, the sun and sand and water and those incredibly erotic flowers appeal to all her senses.

This may sound corny, but it really does wake up her sensual side. Ellen in California spoke for many women when she told us, "Find me some deserted beach under a palm tree in Tahiti. I will worry about the sand up my ass in the morning. I don't care. That's where I want to have sex. That's my dream sexual place."

Hillary Clinton once said, famously, "I have often remarked to my husband that we might have had more children if we had taken more vacations." Everyone knew exactly what she meant.

Nobody has made love on the moon yet, but just about everywhere else that people have been, people have had sex. Some places have achieved a sort of folk-legend status. Like the mile-high club, a very unofficial group of those who claim to have been intimate in a rest room during an airline flight. And, since so many people fall in love at work, it's hardly surprising that shenanigans happen at the office. When *Men's Health* magazine did a reader poll several years ago, 56 percent of the respondents said they'd had sex in a place of business—and the most popular spot was on the boss's desk.

Cars have always been about sex, and oral sex in particular is part of the great tradition of American motoring. Put together high-spirited youth, those big bench seats, the long distances required to see the USA in your Chevrolet, and . . . The road wasn't the only thing that was open.

Naturally, we were expecting some good oral-sex-in-the-car stories. And we got them. But we weren't expecting this wrinkle, from Wendy in New York.

One time, I gave him head while driving him back to New Jersey. Eventually, when he was getting close to coming, I pulled over. I was driving. Yeah, it was dangerous. So I pulled over and he came quickly. And as soon as I sat back up, a Jersey state trooper pulled up behind us; and I was like, "Oh my God. Thank God, it just ended." And the trooper was like, "Do you feel okay?" And I'm like, "Yeah, I'm just a little sick to my stomach." And he thought I'd been drinking, but I hadn't been. I was okay. A little bit of danger is always exciting.

A little bit? What does Wendy consider to be a lot of danger?

Most women aren't into the real, physical danger of trying to drive heavy machinery while performing fellatio.

Many women are aroused by the risk of being discovered. We were surprised to find that the majority of our 80 in-depth interviewees like that feeling. The adrenaline rush, as it turns out, is a real turn-on.

This sounds great except for one thing: Exactly what happens if you're caught in the act? In flagrante delicto, as the Romans say.

"One time, I got caught totally in the middle of some knot, and the police came," said Cathy, who's 30 and single and living in California. "And I got carded—to see if I was underage, I guess. I was 22 at the time. That killed the moment."

JUST DO IT

TENDER IS THE NIGHT

Come the next warm night, have sex outside. Get some big pillows, mosquito netting, baby oil, and a few tiki torches. Grab the boom box (and batteries). Put in a CD of Caribbean music like reggae or zouk (from Martinique) or soca (a blend of soul and Caribbean)—something with a hot, driving rhythm. Then pour on the baby oil. Who are those two bodies glistening in the flickering firelight? Why, it's Tarzan and Jane.

Several of our in-depth interviewees told of getting caught in the act. Apparently, the consequences did not rise to the

LOVE IS EVERYWHERE

Our intrepid female interviewers asked 80 women across North America, "What's the weirdest place you ever had sex?" Here's a sampling of the replies.

- On a motorcycle
- On top of a washing machine
- On the hood of a car on a busy street in Phoenix
- On the metal food-prep table in a restaurant
- A church parking lot
- In the synagogue at summer camp
- On a Ping-Pong table in the church annex
- On a pool table
- On a golf course at night
- On a playground
- On the bleachers at a baseball diamond
- On a piano bench
- On the stairs
- In an elevator
- In the library at college
- In the bathroom of T.G.I. Friday's on a Friday night
- On a scaffold
- Under a pier at the beach
- Out behind a haunted house
- In a cemetery
- In a clear plastic raincoat
- At a Grateful Dead concert
- On a mountain, sitting in the crook of a tree, in Bryce Canyon National Park in Utah
- Early one morning in Ghirardelli Square in San Francisco

level of major life mistake; nobody got arrested. It was fodder for bragging rights or a good yarn.

"This is a funny story," said Whitney, 24, an executive recruiter in Cleveland.

> In high school, I was having sex with my boyfriend in his car because, you know, in high school you live with your parents. And we were in a public park and I didn't realize it. A state police officer came up and gave us a warning. He did write us a ticket for being in the park after dark—but no public indecency charges. So it wound up being a funny thing. Like, "Oh my God, I got busted by the cops for having sex in a park."

When we asked Jennifer, a 29-year-old single city worker in New York, what the weirdest place she ever had sex was, she said, "In the Basketball Hall of Fame in Massachusetts. That was pretty exciting," she said, "except we got caught." No big deal—a security guard escorted them out.

Olivia in New England has a novel strategy for avoiding detection.

> If we're at his parents' house and they are in the living room, we might go into the bathroom and have a quickie. It's not like we're gonna have a long lovemaking session in the bathroom. We just pretend we're having a fight or something and go in, shut the door, and come out all disgusted at each other so that nobody catches on. "Olivia and D. J. I don't know how they can stay together. God."

So, to finally answer Kelly's question above—"What's the worst thing that could happen?"—the worst thing isn't getting caught by the police. The worst thing happened to Debbie, a 33-year-old married mom and group director in a Westchester, New York, advertising agency. She was in a park, he was rolling her over in the clover—and it turned out to be poison ivy.

I had poison ivy just everywhere. Everywhere. It was horrible. I went to a doctor and got a cortisone shot immediately.
I recently went back for something else, and I hadn't seen
him in, like, 10 years, and he said, "Oh my gosh, look at your
records! The last time you were here . . ." And I said, "Don't
even say it. Last time, I had poison ivy all over my body from
having sex in a poison ivy patch—and yes, I married him!"

Having sex in the Basketball Hall of Fame may be great
fun when you're young, but as people enter middle age,
they're no longer thrilled by
the prospect of getting busted.
(What would their kids say?)
But there are other thrills to be
had. Yvonne in Cincinnati said,
"I like it on the couch once in a
while. In fact, sometimes I have
to request it. Of course, there's
not a whole lot of room, and

> "My dear, I don't care
> what they do, so long as
> they don't do it in the
> streets and frighten the
> horses."
> —Mrs. Patricia Campbell,
> British actress, circa 1910

we're both too damn big to be on there anyway. But it just
kind of goes back to, like, when you were 16, 17, and you
were sneaking."

And Lana in Ohio, who is 47 and has been married for 18
years, would love to get outdoors. "I'd like to go out and do it
in the rain, but I can't get him to do that."

Julie in Baltimore has a grand plan, and the best part is, it
will take her and her boyfriend many happy years and a few
adventures to carry it out.

A man is going to have an orgasm whatever; in and out, it's
the same. Whereas with a woman, a lot of it is mental and it
takes more preparation. So I do feel that there are certain
times when I want it to be more spontaneous, more exciting,
and different. I don't want to get into a routine; I don't want
to become complacent about it. Because I think that's how
you keep a relationship good.

We have a goal. Our goal is to have sex in all 50 states. At this point, we have Maryland; Virginia; Washington, D.C.; Nevada; California; New Jersey; and we just came back from Louisiana. That's it, but our goal is all 50 states. Just because, why not?

Why not, indeed? Let freedom ring.

CHAPTER THIRTY

The Best Sex She's Ever Had

IT HAPPENED IN HER TEENS OR IN HER
FORTIES OR IN THE 1940s. On a sandy beach or a
snow-covered cabin or a couch in the basement.
With her husband or her boyfriend or her boss.
Or with you.

Question number 13 of our *New Woman* magazine survey asked bluntly, "What's the best sex you've ever had?" And, because we never, ever grew weary of hearing the answers, we asked the same question during our 80 in-depth interviews.

A few replies were downcast—women saying things like, "Still waiting." A few were from finger waggers who take every opportunity to tell men there's no good sex without love. Don't worry, we won't bore you with those. But if you read on, we promise you a grand tour of love, a panorama of moments that range from the lusty to the romantic. Along the way, you'll be taken to just about every spot on Earth. Some of these memories are the stuff of poetry.

But that's only part of why we find them so inspiring. Because they are all unique, we hope you'll get the sense, by the end, that the best sex of your life doesn't require attending a tantric sex weekend with Elizabeth Hurley. (Well, now you know *our* favorite fantasy.) Great sex is not on reserve. Supplies are not limited. It can happen to everyone, anytime. It could happen tomorrow night.

Enjoy.

- "Randy—he treated sex like it was an art."
- "His name was Peter."
- "On a cruise ship when I was 18—with our waiter."
- "An exotic dancer 10 years my junior."
- "With a man 14 years my junior."
- "Out of town in a hotel."
- "Vacation sex."
- "After a formal."
- "Before kids."
- "Husband on bottom and baby sound asleep."
- "Our wedding night."
- "The first time my husband said, 'I love you.' "
- "The morning after the first night I spent with my fiancé. When he wanted me just as bad first thing in the morning, I knew I'd marry him."
- "After we had a fight."
- "After we'd been fighting for 3½ weeks."
- "After we broke up. The only reason I can figure is, it's because I was like, 'Okay, forget it. This is over. So I'm going to care about myself and get what I want.' Truthfully, that is it. The best sex was when we broke up and I could just let go."
- "Shortly after I was divorced. I guess it was very, very different because when you have had sex with one person for 27 years, you really don't know anything else. You don't know if there's something better or worse until someone new comes along and treats you totally different."
- "That time on a train from Madrid to Paris."
- "In a limo after a day in New York. Oh my God."
- "On the rooftop of the Trump Plaza casino in Atlantic City. The breeze, the ocean, and all the lights made it so intense."

- "A moonlit night on the beach in the Caribbean, in and out of the water. Multiple orgasms . . ."
- "At the lake on a blanket under the stars."
- "Doing it outdoors under the stars is always a thrill."
- "In a hot tub on a chilly October evening with billions of stars in the sky and only water between us."
- "Splendor in the grass."
- "We rented a cabin in the mountains and spent the whole day making love and sleeping and eating and bathing and making more love."
- "I was snowed in with my lover and he romanced me from daylight to moonlight."
- "I called him at work and told him I wanted him. He came home. I was ready."
- "In my fiancé's parents' house. The thrill of sneaking around . . ."
- "I had a lover who liked to role play, tie me up, and ravish me. The relationship sucked, but God, was the sex exciting."
- "When I was thrown down on the living room floor and ravished."
- "On the kitchen counter at a friend's house, when everyone else was asleep."
- "I put on a striptease one night to Bruce Springsteen's 'Glory Days,' and the sex was so raunchy! So fun!"
- "Both of us had really bad days at work and we started fighting. We then realized how stupid we were acting and started kissing to make up. It turned into the best sex I ever had—on the kitchen floor. It was so rough and unexpected."
- "By candlelight, on a mountain of pillows, covered in baby oil."
- "The long, slow romantic kind with lots of kissing."
- "In a convertible with the top down."
- "In a convertible on a sunny day by the ocean."
- "On a lifeguard stand at almost sunrise in Miami."
- "On a Harley."
- "On a golf course."

- "In the sauna at our health club."
- "In a hospital elevator."
- "The first time a man gave me oral sex. I passed out."
- "How about the night of my first orgasm? We'd been in bed for at least an hour when he said something about whipped cream, and I laughed and said something about it too. And he got up, got dressed, and was out the door in, like, 15 seconds. He was gone before I even rolled over. It was so crazy. He rode off on a motorcycle. I heard him leaving and I heard him coming back. And he had a can of whipped cream in his hand. That was so much fun. I had my first orgasm; I passed out. He thought I needed CPR. He didn't know what to think. I was out cold for a couple of seconds, probably, and after that I was just . . . I didn't know what had hit me."
- "He sneaked in the women's locker room and we had the most amazing sex on the bench."
- "In my office, in my chair, facing him."
- "Sex with my boss."
- "Philadelphia. Foursome. Wow."
- "I hate to admit it, but when I was high on cocaine."
- "On Ecstasy."
- "On a balcony in January."
- "April 5, 1996."
- "The summer of 1946."
- "The best sex I have had was with a lover I had many years ago. It was the first time I was made to feel so comfortable that I dropped all veils and allowed the real woman inside to show. I did things with him that I have not done since and can't imagine ever doing again; it was as though we were soul mates. But life left us to go our own ways."
- "A quickie in the car, behind a church, en route to a family gathering."
- "We were driving somewhere in the car when the spontaneous thought crossed my mind to climb on his lap while he drove. Incredible."

- "A partner went out and purchased a ton of sex toys, including restraints and blindfolds, a collar, a riding crop, nipple clamps, a spreader bar, etcetera, then tied me up (four-pointed) to his bed and had his way with his new 'sex slave.' We had a safe word, of course, but it was incredibly exciting."

- "The best sex in terms of another sort of excitement was when I initiated dominant sex with my current partner and had my way with him."

- "I just love it doggie style."

- "The best sex I ever had was the first time we tried it doggie style. That was the absolute best. I think that touched the G-spot, if I have one."

- "Fourteen hours of tantric sex."

- "He was on top of me and with one hand he masturbated my clit and with the other hand he was playing around with my anus, and I was paralyzed. I couldn't say anything. I was just paralyzed in such a frenzy."

- "In a graveyard at night. Scary and sexy all at once."

- "My boyfriend before I met my husband. He was one of those bad boys who would never commit to a woman."

- "On a couch, in a basement, with someone I was crazy about."

- "While watching 'The Wizard of Oz.' "

- "I remember one time reconnecting with a lover after things had not gone well between us. We got together and decided to have sex that night. And it was like all the barriers that had come between us just receded, and we lounged and played. I just remember laughing and laughing, it was so much fun. It was one of the greatest sexual encounters I've ever had."

- "It was when I felt really comfortable with the person, and I wasn't worried about whether my thighs were flabby or anything like that. He seemed to be really into it, too, and felt comfortable with himself."

- "I have always associated the best sex with picnics. There's something so peaceful about it. And it's tied up with food and wine and going for a swim. It becomes very sensuous. I remember a cold stream on a farm in California. We could chill our beer right in the stream. We were nude, and some ranch hands rode up. They saw us, turned around, and rode the other way. We weren't about to give it up easily. It was a perfect spot."

- "The best was that one time we reached orgasm at the same time and we were looking at each other."

- "It's going to sound so ridiculous, but the time that, like, we came together, once, . . . a few weeks ago. And I just cried. I wasn't crying because I was upset. I was just crying because I thought it was a really beautiful moment. I sound like such a cornball, but that's what it was. It was knowing that we were in sync and felt it together."

- "The night my daughter was conceived. Incredibly beautiful . . ."

- "It's usually when something's going wrong—we're having problems with the kids or whatever. And it's such a relief. We reassure each other. It's like, 'You and I are okay.' "

- "I'm having it right now with this man. I am 48 and he's 50."

- "There's sex and then there's intimacy with sex. And I would still say, considering all of the really great, wild sex I've had in my relationships, that the sex I have now with that extra connection with my partner is the best sex. He's not the lust of my life. But he's got everything else."

- "There's not one encounter that's above all others that no one else will ever compare to or that is the number one so far and we'll see if anyone can beat it. That's just not how it is for me."

- "When has it been bad?"

- "It's all so different. And it's all so good."

CHAPTER THIRTY-ONE

P.S. Don't Go There

SOME GUYS DON'T SEEM TO KNOW
WHEN THEY'RE BEING A LITTLE TOO KINKY.
Or crass. Or just plain stupid. Here are
cautionary tales that impart wise advice regarding
lingerie, dirty words, food sex, anal sex,
pet names, and pet snakes.

Say, friend, are you feeling a little low? A little confused? Is your sexual self-esteem meter on empty lately? Well, take heart. Whatever your problems, at least you're not as clueless as some guys.

As we reviewed the 80 tape-recorded interviews conducted for this section, we were struck by the stories of stupid moves on the part of current and former husbands and boyfriends. We're talking about plain dumb-ass behavior. As we heard these stories, our mood lightened a little. We thought, "Hey, at least we're not that bad."

Now is your chance to feel the same way.

If you're on the dating circuit, this explains why women seem so skittish. Why they don't want to go back to your apartment on the first date. Why they want to get to know you better.

They *do* want to get to know you better.

But they also want to know whether you keep a boa constrictor in your bedroom.

We shouldn't have to say this, but try not to weird her out on the first few dates.

Okay, compliments are nice. But comparisons are odious.

Never, ever bring up old girlfriends. And the bed, like the dinner table, is the wrong place to be gross.

One survey respondent told us about getting intimate with the wrong guy. After he performed oral sex on her he told her, "You taste good! This is the first time I enjoyed this. The last woman tasted like fish and I thought I was going to lose it."

This time, she lost it.

Another survey respondent wrote to us with this story.

> I was with a man I barely knew who wanted to have sex. I declined his offer, thinking he would understand. The next thing I knew, he was masturbating right in front of me. Embarrassed and disgusted, I offered him a towel and asked him to leave. He was never invited back.

Maybe the guy heard that some women get turned on by watching men masturbate. And that's true. Some women do like to watch their mates. But only after they've been with the guy for a while! Not on the first date, you meathead.

Stupid sex toys are another major turnoff.

This is what drives women to divorce. From Andrea in Maine: "My ex-husband tried playing around with the vacuum cleaner hose on me. Oh, I hated it." If you want sex toys, visit an erotic boutique. Or call a catalog company. But do not, under any circumstances, raid the hall closet.

Or your basement workbench. Dawn, a 34-year-old coffeehouse manager in Cincinnati, recalled the time a guy thought he was being adventurous. "He wanted me to try a paintbrush," she said. "The handle. And I said no. That was not for me." Smart move, Dawn.

Your pets may not be as lovable as you think.

Tara, a 23-year-old waitress in Cincinnati, told about a trip to some guy's personal zoo.

> One time, a guy didn't want to be on his bed, so we were on the floor. And he had a snake crawling around in his room. A big boa constrictor. And I'm not afraid of snakes, but I've never laid on the floor while one's crawling around. The guy is like, "Oh, he won't bother us." But I was just so freaked out. I was afraid the snake was going to strangle me.
>
> It was somebody I really didn't want to be with, anyway.

No more one-night stands for her.

She doesn't want to know what you call it.

Guys like to have goofy pet names for their genitalia. That can be a fun inside joke between the two of you, if she comes up with the names. We heard from one woman who said she gave her boyfriend's testicles the names Hans and Franz, from the old *Saturday Night Live* skit with Dana Carvey and Kevin Nealon as goofy musclemen.

But it's not okay if *you* name it—and then expect every new girlfriend to dig your little joke.

"Guys think it is so funny," said Amy in Baltimore. "But it is really not funny. You know, you don't need to put your Purple-Headed Warrior of Love near me, because I don't care."

Kristen, a Chicago teacher, agreed wholeheartedly.

> I have to say, one of the biggest turnoffs is when I've gone out with guys who, like, have pet names for their dick. And I'm supposed to refer to their dick as this name. That gets into a very sticky image for me. Like, just how well do you know Mr. Happy? Or did your ex-girlfriend name it?

The dumbest move of all is thinking up something cute for her genitalia. Do that, and you're toast, said Danielle, a 23-year-old account executive at an East Coast advertising

THE SHORT ANSWER

PARTING THOUGHTS

At the end of our hour-long intimate interviews with 80 women, we gave them a final chance to say anything else to you, the men of America. Here are 20 answers, woman-to-man advice, straight up and unfiltered. Some of it doesn't seem to deal with sex, exactly. But if you've been paying attention for the past 335 pages, you know that everything affects sex. That's the way women are.

- "We want you to enjoy us for the here and now and the moment. We don't want you looking around for somebody better all the time. We want you to see the good in us."
- "Make a woman feel special. The more special she feels, the more sexual she'll be."
- "It's sexually attractive to talk to women, to listen to them, actually talk and listen. That makes men more sexually attractive than anything else."
- "Listen to the woman."
- "Men shouldn't be afraid to learn more. It is really hard to know everything when they don't have these parts on their bodies."

agency. "I think if he called it anything, I would just have to kick him out of my room. 'Please get the hell out. I can't believe you just said that.' "

Save the dirty talk for later. Much later.

Talking dirty is a popular turn-on. In fact, it can be positively blissful when it evolves gradually in a relationship and takes on the unique, intimate style of those two people and their love for each other.

- "Don't be embarrassed to say anything. Don't be embarrassed to ask anything."
- "Women want more than a guy who gropes them. There's just so many places on the body. Focus on all 2,000 body parts, not just the two you think are the erogenous zones."
- "Be creative once in a while. Dress up in nothing but a tie. Whatever."
- "You kind of know how men like things. But women are definitely more quirky."
- "There's more to sex than penis/vagina."
- "A lot of men, they're in a lot of hurry."
- "Show me who you are."
- "Don't try to be someone you're not, because we'll see right through it."
- "We analyze everything."
- "The little things count."
- "I'm moody. I get stressed out a lot. Don't say my problems are small and petty; they're *my* problems."
- "Take lots of showers."
- "Love each other and show it."
- "Don't be so serious. Have fun."
- "Everybody just needs to step back and relax."

That pretty much rules out the first date.

Kate in West Bend, Wisconsin, recalled this horror story.

I was fooling around with a guy; and we had just met; and we were making out; and he was feeling my chest. And then he wanted to feel my vagina; and I really didn't know him well enough; and I just didn't want to and I said, "No." And that was fine. But then we were going at it again and he whispered in my ear, "Come on, baby, let me touch your pussy." Let me tell you, that pissed me off. I got up and left real quick. That was probably the worst thing that was ever said to me. It was very degrading; it made me feel really cheap.

Just because you're feeling her chest, don't be fooled. She doesn't know you *that* well. And you don't know her.

Want to know the secret to buying lingerie?

If it's Victoria's Secret, keep it a secret.

Catherine in Chicago recalled the time a friend was horrified to get a package of lingerie at work. And it was from a guy whom she'd dated exactly twice. Apparently, she had told him that she had a problem finding bras in her size. So he called Victoria's Secret. How thoughtful of him, if you ignore the fact that a box of sexy lingerie arriving at your desk is very public and embarrassing. "She was a little taken aback," recalled Catherine. "She was just like, 'Oh my God. I wonder if that's for me.' And then it was for her. It was really tasteful and everything, but I think that's too early. I'm sure that on the first date she wasn't hinting for him to buy her sexy underwear."

> "An unscientific poll of my girlfriends found that they would rather have a pill that could change a man's personality an hour after sex. A pill that ensures that he always calls the next day and never gets spooked."
>
> —MAUREEN DOWD, in the NEW YORK TIMES

This guy was in double trouble for being way too public about something intimate and for buying her lingerie too soon. In fact, most of the women we surveyed want to warn you guys not to do likewise.

A good rule of thumb for lingerie is to wait a year.

Even then, most are leery of being presented with lingerie, because if it's the wrong size or color or fabric, or it's just plain cheesy, they'll be highly insulted. You're not just getting her another turtleneck, okay? You're taking a huge risk. No matter how sweet your intentions, they'll be creeped out if it's all wrong. And they'll feel pressure to say it's just right.

"Too much pressure," said Jamie, a 24-year-old theatrical administrator in Baltimore. She's been going with the same guy for 2½ years, and she doesn't want him buying any teddies "because his idea of what I might look good in and my idea of what I might look good in might be two different things."

For other women, a sexy compromise is to shop for lingerie together. "Part of the excitement and anticipation is having him come with me and watching me as I try it on," said Danielle from Philadelphia.

But not on your second date.

It's true that some men can buy lingerie on their own—but either they are very, very good at it or the women are very, very easy to please. Personally, we are not very good at it. We'd bet 100 bucks that you're not, either.

Be tasteful about food sex.

Here's another story from the road-to-hell-is-paved-with-good-intentions department from Ann in Seattle.

> He brought out chocolate sauce and a number of other things. But he brought out a banana he had frozen. That mother was cold. The chocolate sauce and other things were quite effective. And even being tied up. But that cold banana was just painful. I've heard of people inserting ice cubes into the vagina. But anything frozen inside my vagina is not a good thing.

We guess that's sort of the opposite of a Martha Stewart tip.

Most women are not into S and M.

Some guys are into the whips and chains and handcuffs and dominance stuff. Most guys aren't. Most women aren't, either. "I have enough trouble having an orgasm," said Amy

in Baltimore. "I don't need somebody beating the crap out
of me."

It's probably a mistake to think that you can convert
someone to this sexual style. It's not like you're Catholic, I'm
Methodist, let's turn Lutheran, you know? Laura in California recalled:

> This one person I was with, he went to Florida to get his
> Ph.D. He liked that kind of sex—S and M, hitting, spanking.
> He was very handsome, and I was in love with him, but it
> wasn't my kind of sex. He was into doing things like blind-
> folding me. He'd have to go off and run an errand or what-
> ever, and he'd want me to be by his bed, praying. That's just,
> like, too much. Now I look back on it and think, "Why did I
> go along with that stuff?"

By his bed, praying . . . Sheesh.

Don't be cruel.

If you ask a girl for a sexual favor, don't ridicule her
afterward.

That sounds so obvious, but some guys apparently don't
put their brains in gear before setting their mouths in motion.
In his book *Passionate Marriage*, licensed clinical psychologist David Schnarch, Ph.D., director of the Marriage and
Family Health Center in Evergreen, Colorado, has written
about what he calls normal marital sadism. Maybe he's met
Kathleen's husband of 3 years.

Her husband had been asking her to swallow at the end of
oral sex. This she found very difficult to do. "It was, like, gag
reflex from hell," as she put it. But, in order to please him,
she's been trying not to gag. "In the past year or so, I've really
made an effort to learn to do that," she said. (Her trick is to
swallow quickly, like eating a raw oyster.) "And it's really
funny because his reaction to that is, like, initially he'll want
that to happen. And afterward, he'll be like, 'Yuck. I can't believe you did that.' "

And thanks for your support.

Kelly in San Francisco had a boyfriend like that once.

> He wasn't particularly adventurous. I brought this pink feathery thing into the bedroom, and he laughed at me. He just started laughing. I really felt ridiculous. I didn't feel the freedom to experiment with him anymore. I sent him flowers once, and he got upset with me for sending them. He thought that was ridiculous. He was embarrassed at work when they arrived. After that, I was like, "Forget it. You're not worth the effort."

Indeed he wasn't. Kelly, you were casting your pearls before swine.

Guys are intrigued by anal sex. Women are not.

We asked our 80 women, "Are there any adventurous requests you've said no to?" Anal sex was the number one answer.

As one young woman told us, "It is an out place. It is a one-way space."

Some, like Maria in Chicago, have finally consented to an experiment—just once. "I had a boyfriend who asked to try anal sex, and it was so freaking painful," she recalled.

Even those few women who want to like it don't like it. Like Jamie in Baltimore. She really, really wants to like anal sex. She keeps trying. It never works out.

> If I have my period and we don't want to have regular sex, but we are very horny, sometimes he'll try it. Sometimes we will try if we are drunk; and I always think that I will like it this time, I know I will. Because when we are starting to do it, it feels like it is gonna feel good, and when he penetrates it feels fine. It is when he starts to pull out that it hurts. You have to go in and out, and it just feels horrible as he is pulling out. But mark my words, we will try it again. We always go back to it.

A couple of women openly wondered why it is that men are so grossed out by the thought of two men having anal sex, but want to do the same thing to their girlfriends. The usual two-word answer, "That's different," was not enough of an explanation.

If you're insistent upon anal sex, the very best you'll do is finding a partner like Debra, 51, a nurse in Miami. She said, "I like a finger up my butt every once in a while."

Your partner might be persuaded to try rimming, also known as a rim job. Julie in Baltimore defined:

> It's licking around the anal hole. We sort of joked about it for a long time beforehand, and I said, "I don't know if I would ever let anyone do that." And then one time about a year ago, we were staying at a friend's apartment and he was sorta kissing my back. Then all of a sudden, he said, "Do you want me to do it?" And I was like, "Do I want you to do what?" And he said, "You know"; and I said, "Okay, if you want to." So he did it and it was definitely enjoyable. It wasn't the most pleasurable thing I have ever felt, but it was different. Then a couple of months later, I did it to him, and he was ecstatic. I mean he *loved* it. He finds it incredible.
>
> So that is now definitely part of our routine in foreplay. But we always joke about, "Scrub down there." We are both very anal about being clean. No pun intended.

None taken.

PART SIX

The Breadwinner
She Respects

CHAPTER THIRTY-TWO

Is Money Sexy?

THERE'S NO DENYING THAT, IN THE WORDS
OF ERICA JONG, "MONEY IS MONEY
AND IT REMAINS SEXY." But does that mean
that all women are after your wallet? Not quite.
And what's more, success can be a total
turnoff if it goes to your head.

Do you look upon women as sex objects?

No. Well, maybe. A little. Um, sometimes.

Oh, hell, of course you do. How do you answer this no-win question? You know what the "right" answer is, especially if a woman is asking it. For three decades, some feminists have tried to make us ashamed of being physically attracted to physically attractive women.

But you also know what the real answer is. Men are born to look.

That's not to say that all our relations with the other gender are based on our hot little libidos. We know women as neighbors, coworkers, professors, fellow choir members, daughters, wives, and long-time friends.

But we also turn to pudding in the presence of a beautiful woman. Our eyes pick one out of a crowd with the accuracy of a cruise missile. When a gorgeous woman walks by, most of us must make a conscious effort to keep our gaze where we're going and our eyeballs in our heads.

Are women the same way? Not really. Although they can appreciate a buff bod, they aren't instantly aroused and ready for a takedown.

But they do check you out. Oh, yes. It's just that their agenda is a little different. You're being evaluated too—but not as a sex object.

You may be a success object.

It's a rare woman who will admit to this. After all, saying so makes her sound like a gold digger. Like you, she knows the "right" answer, but she also knows the real answer. And to argue otherwise is to argue that, in fact, the sky is not blue.

Not a lot has changed since Cinderella's day; pretty women still marry up. Nor have the fantasies changed very much.

In soap operas, do the gorgeous babes fight over a janitor? No. In romance novels, does the heroine finally win the heart of a housepainter? Nuh-uh.

Money is the bright plumage of our species. It may be no guarantee of sexual success, but it has been a reliable way of getting her attention. "Men are evaluated by their income and professional status as harshly as women are evaluated by their looks," points out Nancy Etcoff, Ph.D., professor of psychology at Harvard Medical School, in her book *Survival of the Prettiest: The Science of Beauty*.

In a less academic voice, here's how boxing promoter Don King summarized the attractiveness of Mike Tyson before he got himself into a world of trouble.

"Any man with $42 million looks exactly like Clark Gable."

The term "success object" was coined by Warren Farrell, Ph.D., a men's-movement guru, San Diego–area psychologist, and author of several books on men's issues, who began as a feminist. He served on the board of the New York City chapter of the National Organization for Women, and wrote

The Liberated Man in 1975. Then he rethought some of the era's unfair accusations against men and in 1984 wrote the bestseller *Why Men Are the Way They Are*. In that book, he called attention to society's "new sexism" against men and some of the double standards at work against us. Like this one: "A woman who supports a man for a lifetime is called crazy, while a man who supports a woman for a lifetime is called a breadwinner."

Dr. Farrell turned out to be a pioneer. In the last few years, some of his ideas have been measured and validated by the emerging field of evolutionary psychology. The general idea of evolutionary psychology is that our brains, both men's and women's, have been shaped by eons of evolution, which eventually rewards the most successful mating behaviors. These behaviors are different in men and women. Today's man is likely to be descended from the guys who did the most diddling around. But the genes of today's woman come from a long line of gals who were determined not to be left in the lurch. They sought out the guys with the brains, the talent, the ambition, and the strength to stand by them, protect them, and help provide for the kids. In the lingo of science, they sought "male parental investment."

> "Two things I never want to hear from a man: that he's broke or that he's lonely."
> —SUZANNE, Niagara Falls, New York

In 1989, David Buss, Ph.D., professor of psychology at the University of Texas at Austin and author of *The Evolution of Desire*, published a study of more than 10,000 people in 37 cultures around the world. It was the largest-ever survey of human mating traits. In 36 out of the 37 cultures, women placed significantly more emphasis than did men on the financial wherewithal of their prospective mates. He found what the theory of evolutionary psychology said that he would find: Men the world over want pretty women, and women want successful men.

More recently, John Marshall Townsend, Ph.D., professor of anthropology at Syracuse University in New York, has published his findings in the book *What Women Want—What Men Want: Why the Sexes Still See Love and Commitment So Differently*. Dr. Townsend has been studying sex and marriage for nearly 20 years. In one of his experiments, he staged photos of guys dressed up in two costumes: either a high-status, white dress shirt, tie, and blazer; or the uniform of a well-known hamburger chain. Then he showed these photos to young women and asked them whom they'd rather meet for coffee.

Women chose the ugly guy in the high-status outfit over the cute guy in the hamburger-chain uniform.

Whereas, in a similar experiment with women in uniform, men always chose the prettier girl and ignored the status signals.

In another study, young women rejected pictures of hunky ne'er-do-wells, but said they would consider a marriage proposal from a homely model who was described as a physician.

> "Ever since I was a little girl, I always had this dream: to marry a zillionaire. I'd like to marry Rockefeller." "Which one?" "I don't care." "I'd like to marry Mr. Vanderbilt." "Is there a Mr. Cadillac?"
> —dialogue in Gentlemen Prefer Blondes, a movie about three blonde women scheming to marry zillionaires

The best material in Dr. Townsend's book is the in-depth interviews that he conducted with 50 medical school students, both male and female. Maybe it wasn't surprising, given the subset, but the women come off as unapologetically arrogant and elitist. Not one woman expressed a willingness to marry a man who made less money than she would (roughly half of the male students said they would). They all wanted to marry up. As one of them said, "I don't think anyone wants to admit it, but when you're on the verge of a successful career, you want a man who's a success himself. . . . I can't see myself having a husband who's a gas station attendant."

In fact, a third of the women medical school students said they wanted a man who made them feel "protected."

Protected from what? From overbearing Range Rover salesmen?

After reading Dr. Townsend's book, we got depressed for about a week and a half. We shook it off, finally, by reminding ourselves that not all women are bratty young med students.

Certainly, Dr. Townsend gives us something to think about. But let's not walk away with a narrow view of the opposite gender. First of all, women aren't puppets to a mating strategy, and neither are we. And let's accept, as a given, that most women are innately attracted to a successful man. Exactly what are they attracted to? His diamond cuff links? Or the signal that he's a guy with self-confidence, a man who can handle responsibility, a man who is at ease in the world? Ann, a 42-year-old registered nurse from New Jersey, put it this way: "I think what's inherently attractive is a really intelligent man who loves what he does. Who can use his intelligence to do what he does every day and love it at the same time."

As it happens, that describes a lot of successful men.

Also, there's something about the success-object theory that makes us say, "Yeah, we *wish*." Wouldn't love be so easy if all it really took was a really hot car? With some babes, maybe that is all it takes. (We wouldn't know; we've never had hot cars.) We didn't hear from them, but we did hear from plenty of women who agree with the lady in St. Louis who wrote to say, "It's not your possessions that count the most. It's your passion for living."

From our research, we've drawn five basic conclusions about women and money. Our first conclusion is that, while success can be sexy, the flip side is the stronger truth.

Lack of money is definitely unsexy.

If you're down and out, you're out of contention. Women look right past you. Aside from the girls who date rebels to piss off their parents, or the women who are hopelessly attracted to bad boys, most women cannot fall in love with somebody who is busted. They know they'll spend the rest of their lives worrying about money. And frankly, they'd rather not.

When we say, "Money is sexy," that doesn't mean that she's literally turned on. She's intrigued. Only intrigued.

That's the hard lesson learned by the guy who dated Whitney.

Whitney is a single, 24-year-old executive recruiter in Cleveland who was interviewed by one of our female graduate students. She recounted a story, somewhat reluctantly, about a guy she'd met, a guy she described this way: "On paper, he seemed like everything I wanted." He owned his own company. And he must have been doing pretty well at whatever it is he did, because he won a free weekend in the Bahamas for his efforts. He invited Whitney. They'd been dating maybe two months.

If Whitney had been totally preprogrammed to lust after success objects, she should have been in heaven. Instead, she was conflicted and confused. Apparently, she was attracted to him as a success object, but she was just not attracted to *him*. Not even amid the palm trees. "When I got down there, I knew I really didn't like him and I didn't want to hook up with him," she told our interviewer. "I didn't want to kiss him at all. And he kept trying. This guy took me to the Bahamas; of course he would want to have sex."

Whitney proceeded to do every dirty rotten thing she could to sabotage this romance. Every night, she got drunk and passed out—or pretended to pass out. Except for one night, when she disappeared with another guy in their group. That other guy, she did have sex with. "It wound up being a very uncomfortable situation the next day," she recalled. "That was really awful." Can you imagine the flight home? Here's a hint: "He ended up leaving me at the airport."

It was a weekend that she will always regret. But regardless of what you may think of Whitney's judgment, you can't accuse her of being a gold digger. A gold digger would have come back with lots of presents. Then she would have dumped him. Lame joke.

Men's preconceived ideas about women and money are unusually whacked. Women are not all gold diggers in disguise. The idea that a woman's goal in life is to spend your last nickel . . . That's just nutty.

We must have been watching too much TV through the years. Remember Jane Jetson plucking money out of George Jetson's wallet? Remember Ricky Ricardo telling Lucy that she wasn't allowed to go shopping in Tijuana, Mexico? But the women we talked with don't want more money for the beauty parlor. They want it so they can send their kids to trumpet lessons or basketball camp or Holy Angels High.

In fact, we heard an unexpected refrain in our interviews. We came away realizing that women don't necessarily want more money in order to spend more money—even though it does get spent. (Americans aren't the thriftiest people on the planet.)

To most women, money is security.

You'll be encountering this theme, our fourth basic conclusion, throughout this section of the book. But for now, we want you to hear one quote. It's from Rosanne, a 38-year-old hair salon owner in Buffalo who makes more money than her husband.

> I wish my husband made more money and so much of the financial everything wasn't on me. I really do wish he did. I would love to have that little bit of security. It's almost like a big chest you could put your head on once in a while.

Success is sexy—unless it goes to your head.

As far as your attractiveness to women is concerned, there may be nearly as much hazard in becoming successful and thumping yourself on the chest for it as in failing to make anything of yourself.

"In the higher echelons of business, you'll get these men who seem to have completely lost their sex appeal," said Carla, a 54-year-old business executive from Connecticut. "They are totally egotistical, totally selfish, totally self-involved. They think they're terribly attractive to women, but they're not."

We want to leave you with a story that takes this whole success-object idea and stands it on its head. This is the story of Patricia, a 41-year-old financial analyst.

Patricia was 25 when she met her husband. Back then, he was the antithesis of a success object. "He was very laid back," she recalled. "No motivation at all." He wasn't a bum, exactly. He was a science teacher at his alma mater, a Catholic high school. But he also played guitar in a wedding band. He had a great sense of humor, he enjoyed life, and as Patricia said, "he did not have a dime to his name. He lived in an apartment that I was afraid to park my car in front of. He wore his dead uncle's old suits. He coached track and basketball. His goals were to have fun and be a good teacher and a good coach. He was a really good coach. I loved the fact that he was so into coaching. He was so into the kids."

And that was the guy she fell in love with, a guy who loved music and kids and wrote her poetry and sent her flowers and cards. "He wooed me. He went after me big-time. One time, he drove to Pittsburgh after classes just to take me out to dinner." At 28, she married him, knowing that, as she said, "I'd have to work, probably, for the rest of my life. But that was okay, because I was doing something I liked.

"I never dreamed he'd be the way he turned out . . . obsessed with success."

Patricia is the kind of woman who you would expect would

seek out a success object. She was and is a traditional gal, the daughter of upper-middle-class parents, who never sought to establish an identity based on an independent career. "I was raised to be a volunteer and stay home and keep the house clean and raise kids and have a social life," she said. "Although I like my job, I do believe I would be happier as a stay-at-home mom." If she married this guy, that wasn't going to happen. But she could deal with that.

Then he got on the fast track. At the urging of his department head, he applied to graduate school, was accepted, and got straight A's. After graduating with a Ph.D. in chemistry, he got multiple job offers. Now he's a corporate hotshot. A success.

So is she happier? No. The fact is, they're separated. The likelihood that they'll get back together, she said, is slim. "He is totally consumed with his job and career."

Does Patricia think success is sexy? Her answer surprised us.

> It is. It is. But there's a fine line. . . . When it's all you think about, when all that's there is this obsession, it's very unattractive. If you lose yourself to that success, if you lose everything that's good about you because success is all you're focused on, that's not attractive at all.

You know by now that a woman's heart can comfortably seat a hundred contradictions. So you shouldn't be all that surprised to hear, from Patricia and others, that no, you don't have to be successful, but yes, success is sexy, but no, not if you go overboard. She's glad you've gotten your "success act" together, but now she wants to see how well you pull it off. Just how do you do that? Find out in the next five chapters.

CHAPTER THIRTY-THREE

Is Money Power?

IN JUST ONE GENERATION, FAMILY LIFE HAS
CHANGED TOTALLY. And the rhetoric
has done a 180. Women no longer feel economically
powerless. Usually, they feel they're in a partnership.
If they don't feel that way, they walk.

"I'm the luckiest woman in the world," said Fran, a 43-year-old stay-at-home mom in Pottstown, Pennsylvania. "I've always had choices about the way to live my life."

She has been a teacher and a pension manager. She has taken good job offers when they came along and left those jobs when they turned into 14-hour-a-day grinds. She's been a working mom and a stay-at-home mom, an independent young career woman and a new mother again at 40. She has not lived her life in one little pigeonhole, and for that she is thankful. She's had a life that her mother and grandmother never envisioned for themselves. She thinks that the gender revolution of the last few decades has served her well.

"I really have benefited," she said. "I feel really, really lucky. I'm not bound by any typical tradition. I've been just following my nose through my life; and I've not been held down by anybody else's standards."

How times have changed.

Nearly 30 years ago, Shere Hite wrote a book that was, in a

way, like this one. She spent the early 1970s sending out questionnaires from the offices of the National Organization for Women in New York. She got back 3,000 responses and turned them into *The Hite Report: A Nationwide Study of Female Sexuality*. A runaway bestseller in its day, it reads now as a somewhat quaint period piece. Somehow, "the Patriarchy" is to blame for everything, including the fact that women don't have more orgasms. In a chapter titled Sexual Slavery, Hite claims that women don't assert themselves in bed because of "economic intimidation," that financial dependence upon a man negates equality in the sack. She quotes women saying things that, today, sound a little scripted. Like, "As an oppressed people, what we women lack is not knowledge, but *power*." Or, "Just as women are used to serving men their coffee, so they are used to serving them their orgasms."

Forget orgasms. Wives used to serve their husbands coffee? Wow. Men *have* taken a beating.

Well, it's surely a different world. The vast majority of women work outside the home, and many women earn more than their husbands. Others have earned more in the past. Women marry later, have children later, and spend more years enjoying a sense of economic independence. The word "empowered" is overused, but it's the perfect word to describe how Fran and millions of other women truly feel.

The question "Who makes the money around here?" has an ever changing answer.

It depends on who has been laid off, who has gone back to school, who is starting a business, who is at home with the kids.

Who is the primary breadwinner at your house? Katey, a 39-year-old manager in Chicago, gave today's typical response.

Since we've known each other, there have been times when he has made more and times when I have made more. This doesn't seem to factor into our relationship. We share all of our earnings.

In preparing this book, we wondered if money and power are still the hot issues that they were 3 decades ago. And so, when we designed the survey that ran in *New Woman* magazine, we included this long-winded question: "Do you earn more than your husband or lover? If so, how has this affected your relationship? Do you agree that whoever earns more money has more power at home?"

Actually, that's not one, but three questions—the first two straight-forward, the third blatantly leading. We phrased it that way on purpose. We invited women to beat up on us. We wanted to make it easy for them to go along with the conventional feminist line of the past three decades—that men use their greater economic power to subdue women at home as well as in the workplace.

> "Insofar as we let money determine status in the relationship, it always corrodes equality and friendship."
> —PEPPER SCHWARTZ, PH.D
> professor of sociology
> and coauthor of
> THE GREAT SEX WEEKEND

Hardly anybody bit. More than 700 women responded to our survey. We counted only 19 who complained that they had less power at home than their husbands; whereas 25 claimed they had *more* power. Of the women who said they had less power, a few, surprisingly, earn more money than their husbands. A few others freely gave up equal power because of religious beliefs. "God ordained the man to lead," wrote one woman.

Of the women who have more power, some earn less than their husbands. But they're still the bosses. "I am a stay-at-home mom, and I still have most of the power," said one.

Others earn more and make no bones about it. One woman, on her reply faxed from a Comfort Inn while on a business trip, freely admitted, "I have more money and it gives me more power."

The vast majority of our respondents said they have equal power at home.

To our question, "Do you agree that whoever earns more money has more power at home?" they shouted a resounding "No!"

And they followed with thoughts like these:

- "Money is not power."
- "I don't believe in power struggles."
- "Equal power is the only way to run a household."
- "We love each other, not each other's money."
- "More money equals more vacations."

Skeptics might argue that these women are all in denial. But most replies recognized what's really at stake here. The question goes to the very heart of a marriage. It challenges the basis of their relationships with their husbands. Are they truly partners? Or are they made to feel beholden? "I think that home should be a safe place and neutral ground for everyone who lives there," said Kaye in Arkansas. "If it's not, then you aren't a family."

That said, power struggles happen. There's usually a tussle over something. When conflicts arise and wills clash, men and women, both, will reach for whatever leverage they can get.

Sometimes, one partner wants more control and becomes more dominant, and the other spouse backs off because he or she has less tolerance for conflict or simply doesn't want control. In a case like that, power has nothing to do with money. In most cases, perhaps, power has nothing to do with money. "Power is held by whomever seeks it—and whomever relinquishes it (which I don't think is ever productive)," wrote Glori, who happens to be a therapist by trade.

YOURS, MINE, OR OURS?

Are couples better off with joint bank accounts or separate accounts? That's a question that every couple faces,
sooner or later. Mary in Denver faced it sooner—she and
her husband debated the matter before they got married.
"Both our mothers said, 'Separate, separate, separate.
You need your own account.' And both our fathers
said, 'Oh my God, get one account, that's all you need to
keep.' "

They got separate accounts, which is the choice of
roughly one in five couples. Separate accounts may give
nonworking wives a greater sense that "this is *our*
money," but it's no magic solution. Mostly, it seems to be
a matter of personal choice, interpersonal dynamics, and
habit. Couples who marry young tend to open joint accounts and stick with them; couples who marry later tend
to keep their separate accounts.

We will say this: It's fun to hear how other couples
manage their money.

Deb is a 39-year-old social worker in rural New York
State. She and her husband have the separate accounts
that they had before they were married just a few years
ago. "He makes more money than I do. He pays the mort-
gage; I pay all the utilities; I buy all the groceries; we split
the car insurance. And it works great for us," she said.
"People say, 'Why don't you get a joint account?' It's not
an issue. I'm not rat-holing his money and he's not rat-
holing mine. We don't worry about it. If I need 40 bucks,
he gives it to me. If he needs it, I give it to him."

On the other hand, we have Amy, a 42-year-old

A Baltimore teacher married to a trucker said, "Power has
to do with who's more assertive." And that assertiveness can
change over time.

Susan in Tampa wrote to tell us her story. "He had all the
power until I finally grabbed him by the *cojónes* and said,

government lawyer in Philadelphia. She doesn't have her own account. "And I don't want it. It would just complicate things." It works for this reason: "I don't complain about what he spends money on; he doesn't care what I spend money on."

Whereas with Stephanie, a 48-year-old corporate counsel, that isn't exactly the case. "My husband would just go nuts to think that he wouldn't have complete control over finances," she said. "My way of dealing with that is, I have my own bank account and my own credit cards. Early on, whenever he expressed an opinion about the way I might spend money on some particular item, he learned, just, not to go there. He'd like to know what my credit card bills are, possibly, but he knows not to even ask. For that he gets to play all the golf he wants."

Kathy, a 46-year-old teacher and mother of two, came up with a workable system years ago, and it's still in place. "All the money that comes into this house goes into a joint account, but we have our allowances," she said. "In spite of the fact that Jon makes five times the amount of money I do, we have the exact same allowance. And our allowances go into our separate checking accounts. We have a joint MasterCard; we each have separate Visa cards. And once the allowances go out, what happens in those accounts are none of the other person's business."

Susan, a 41-year-old gynecologist and mother of two, summed it up: "You find a financial setup that works for you, and as long as your marriage is good and you love each other, it doesn't really matter whether you have joint accounts or separate accounts."

'Hey! I'm not your emotional punching bag! Straighten up or hit the road!' "

He straightened up.

If money doesn't give us power, does it give us anything? Yes. Status. For men more so than for women, money is a way of keeping score. It's the only way to measure our accomplishments and who's where in the pecking order. Whatever we're flaunting, whether it's cars or cuff links, it's just another way of saying to all other men, "Mine is bigger than yours." And for once, we're not talking about sex. This is why women suspect that money is more important to men. Certainly, they see it as a bigger part of a man's sense of himself.

"For the majority of men I know, how much they earn is directly related to how they feel about themselves," said April in San Francisco. "What they earn is who they are." Whereas, she said, women see money as security; "having it means that they don't have to worry about growing old in a park somewhere."

Is money really more important to men? Probably not. But we've come to realize that money is important to men and women in different ways.

The bottom line of this chapter is that few women feel trapped these days. And if you make them feel trapped, you're in big, big trouble.

No matter how angry you get, if you try to assert your power because yours is the bigger paycheck, you're ending the relationship. This is a deal breaker. Just listen.

- "I've seen too many marriages blow from these power trips," said a Seattle woman. "I won't let any man control the money I earn."
- "If he ever threw that in my face, he would find himself at home raising the children and I would go back to work," wrote a woman in Texas who once earned more than her husband.
- "By choice, I am a stay-at-home mom," said Tami in Colorado. "Or should I say, by agreement. And that is a workable solution if the partner who decides to stay home draws a line. My personal line is, 'If you ever hold your job over my head, this relationship is null and void.' "

- "We are equals, no matter what—or I'll move on," said Melody in Jefferson City, Missouri.
- "No one ever has more power—or it's over," echoed Marina in San Jose, California.

We also heard from a woman in Juneau, Alaska, who got divorced over this very issue. "With my ex-husband, when we had our daughter, we decided that I'd stay at home with her. What a nightmare! I wasn't even allowed to drive to town because he paid for the gas in the car."

The changes of the last few decades have affected every family, even those so-called traditional families in which the man trudges off to work every morning at dawn's early light, while the wife stays home with the children. Blink, and you might think it's the 1950s. But in our personal meetings with small groups of women, we heard them explain the difference between appearance and reality. We heard from Penny, for instance, who once was a Wall Street lawyer, but is now a mother of four.

> Functionally, our family setups may look like our parents in some ways. Those of us who are home taking care of the household and working a little on the side, but the husband is basically earning the money—that looks like the traditional family structure. But the difference is in the attitude. So many of us had high-paying jobs; and in my case, I was making more than my husband. So even though it looks to the outside world like we've gone back to the '50s, it's not that way because of the way we relate to each other. And we know the potential we have.

That's it—the potential, agreed Cheryl, who also made more than her husband when she worked. "We all know that if we had to walk out of the house tomorrow and earn a living, within a few years we could probably be earning quite a bit of money. It's a matter of proving yourself, of knowing what you can do if you have to do it. Our mothers' generation never knew that."

These mothers do.

CHAPTER THIRTY-FOUR

If You Make More

DON'T STOOP TO SWAGGERING. You'll look like such a jerk. Instead, be generous. Practice saying "our money," not "my money." Recognize and acknowledge all that she does so that you can go off and succeed. And finally, cope with the stress.

RALPH KRAMDEN: "I'm the boss and you're nothin'!"
ALICE KRAMDEN: "Well, I guess that makes you the boss of nothin'."

Jackie Gleason's character on the early TV sitcom *The Honeymooners* took all the usual male flaws, turned them up a notch, and made us laugh at ourselves. Even in the early 1950s, bellowing about our status as heads of households didn't win any respect. (Quite the opposite.) Try that line today, and you'll be regarded as a psychotic loser.

There are still losers out there, to judge by what we heard from Stacie in Pittsgrove, New Jersey. "I plan to tell my daughters, 'Hey, if you want to turn a perfectly nice man into a domineering asshole, just let him support you while you stay home with the kids.' "

But, to our credit, most women do not feel as if they're married to Ralph Kramden. At least, they don't on most days. And they don't think the old-fashioned family arrangement is guaranteed to cause them pain and suffering. When they were told what Stacie had to say, they dismissed it as the misfortune of a woman who made the most foolish of choices.

Nice guys are out there, too. "He makes in a week what I make in a month," said a woman in Lafayette, Louisiana. "He treats me as a complete equal. Spoils me to death—and I spoil him, just not financially."

Doesn't that sound blissful? Spoiling each other instead of sniping at each other?

Carol, a 49-year-old homemaker in San Diego, has the same sort of relationship with her husband, Bill. It's mutually supportive, despite financial differences. Carol worked as an assistant principal at an elementary school for 20 years, but when she and Bill moved to the coast several years ago, she decided not to look for another job. His new job frequently puts him on the road, and so "when he's home, I'm home. And he likes that. At this stage of life, time together is much more important now; it's more important than whatever stuff an extra paycheck would buy."

Like most women who quit jobs to devote their time and talents to house and home, Carol discovered that not working didn't come easily at first.

> Suddenly, I felt I wasn't contributing at all. If I went shopping and saw a new outfit I really liked, I felt a twinge of guilt about buying it. "Now, Carol, you're blowing his money . . ."
>
> But that came from inside me. He never gives me that idea. He's pleased to support us. It's our money, our payday, our home, our life. He never acts like he's the big cheese, the big boss man. I never feel like he senses that he has more power over me now. I feel like a very equal partner. We share in all the decisions. He doesn't have twice as many votes. He handles it with dignity. I have the highest respect for Bill because of the way he is.

If you want to be the breadwinner she respects, you just read about how to do it.

Bill's attitude doesn't always come naturally or easily to many men. Sometimes, it evolves over years in a marriage. That was the case with Simona, a 38-year-old teacher in Brooklyn, New York.

> My husband at one point was making a lot more money, and it went to his head. He did things the way he wanted to do things, for a long time, without discussing them with me. His life was more important than mine; his job was more important. He did what he wanted to do. He'd walk in at 7, 8, 9 o'clock at night.
>
> Now, his job and his hours have changed, and so the nature of our relationship has changed. And the ego part is not so much there. Now it's my turn. I can make more choices; I have that extra time to myself. Before, if I wanted to do something, I couldn't do it because he was gone, the kids were younger then, and I was stuck. Now, I don't have to always worry about getting home and what's in the refrigerator and the shopping and everything. Now, he does his part. So if there's no dinner on the table, why isn't there dinner on the table? Why are you looking at me? It goes both ways.
>
> We learned that that ego thing, when it comes to money, isn't real. It isn't a real thing. Now he sees how difficult it is to take care of the children, and that money isn't everything. So our relationship is more valuable.

> "Don't you know that a man being rich is like a girl being pretty?"
> —MARILYN MONROE, in GENTLEMEN PREFER BLONDES

Sometimes we excuse "that ego thing" to ourselves by saying it's our reward for shouldering the primary breadwinning responsibility.

But the fact is, we men love the breadwinning responsibility; it's critical to our self-esteem and our identity. It's what we do well. Most women will not fight us for this honor.

At the same time, they will fight with us about helping out on the homefront. And then we get defensive. We start to dismiss what they do as all fun and games. We say it, even when we don't mean it. We're just trying to come up with reasons why she has it easier. Yeah, like that will work.

Susan, a 41-year-old gynecologist and a mother of two, voiced a complaint that, in one form or another, we heard everywhere. "A lot of what I do with the kids is not fun stuff.

THERE'S SOMETHING ABOUT MARY'S EXCELLENT ADVENTURE

Mary is like a lot of women. A 35-year-old former nurse, she's happy to be a stay-at-home mom while her three boys are young, and happy to have her husband work hard at a good job that supports them all.

But she's also happy to take off for a week each year and leave him at home with the kids all day. The week does them both a world of good.

Every spring, she leaves her Kentucky home to join a group of half a dozen women in Florida. They stay at a cottage owned by one of the women's parents. The women are all in their thirties; they're all married, with children. But this is strictly a girlfriends' vacation: No boys allowed.

"Now, to be honest, a lot of our discussions focus on personal relationships—either our husbands or men we knew before we got married. The discussions range from sex—how often, where, when, strangest place, positions, etcetera—to why our husbands can't fold the laundry the way we do. And sometimes, we'll share some trying

He accuses me of going to the mall, as if that's some kind of pleasurable experience."

Don't do that. It's a lousy argument. And it only serves to infuriate her because it shows your ignorance of what she does.

Being the breadwinner has its pitfalls, and this is the biggest: You're not there. You don't know. You just don't know about all that she does.

You act like she does nothing, but you expect her to do everything. You are totally dependent upon her, yet you treat her like your personal chief of staff.

"I never see my husband," said Wendy, a 32-year-old

---

times, whether it be a situation at work, with a relative, another friend, anything. It's sort of a week-long vent session. Other times, we'll do nothing but tell jokes.

"When I go on these trips, I don't have to be responsible for anyone but me. I don't have to wipe sticky fingers or change any diapers. If I want to be alone, I can. If I want to sleep, I can. Last year, two of us were runners, so we'd get up a little earlier and head out for a run on the beach. Some nights, we stay in and play cards or rent a movie. Some nights, we go out dancing. It's, like, total freedom.

"On these trips, I find myself laughing more than I ever thought I could. And each time I return home, my husband notices a little spring in my step. And you know, I feel that spring in my step! He kisses up to me for about a month afterward because he realizes that staying home is not easy. And he says he has a new appreciation for my staying home with the kids full-time. I have noticed that, on his first day back to work, he can't get out the door fast enough.

"Of course, I need to take this trip yearly, just so he doesn't forget."

mother of two who recently went back to work as an architect. "I mean, we pass, literally, in the middle of the night. He owns a restaurant. He works 100 hours a week. The only day I see him is Sunday, and then we end up fighting all day Sunday because we haven't seen each other all week."

Yes, what we have here is a failure to communicate. And that is compounded when you can't let go of the household decision making and you feel the need to nitpick and comment and micromanage. "He tells me to make all the decisions; and then I do make all the decisions, and the one time he doesn't like a decision I made, he gets all upset about it," said Wendy.

This is especially annoying when it comes to spending decisions. Guys who make the age-old complaint that she's spending him out of house and home are, ironically, the guys who also have no idea how much stuff costs. If you make all the money, she's probably more cost-conscious than you are. In that case, it's a real indignity to start picking at her.

"I have a harder time spending money," said Mary, a young mother in Denver. "Part of it's got to be because I'm not earning it."

Penny in Philadelphia has noticed the same change in her spending patterns since she quit work to stay home and raise four kids. "My husband will spend more freely than I will on personal things; maybe that's because I'm still uncomfortable not earning a large part of our income."

Oh, and by the way, if she does any work on the side, in between raising your kids, you'd do well to make a little fuss about that. "If we're out to dinner with friends, people are always asking, 'How's work going?' " said Mary. "And pretty quickly, he'll move on and discuss what I'm doing." (She's writing a book.) "He's quick to tell people what I'm working on. I think it probably is a conscious effort. I'd love to think it's not, and it's foremost in his mind; but hey, he knows it matters to me."

What a guy.

Finally, let's talk about the other big pitfall of being a primary breadwinner. You work so hard, you put in so many hours and so much psychic energy, that your career becomes all-encompassing. You may leave the office, but the office never leaves your head.

You bring it all home with you—the curt impatience, the hypercritical thinking, the bluster, the seriousness, and the stress. Most of all, the stress.

"That was our number one issue for a while," said Sherry, a Michigan mother of three boys.

My husband did not handle stress very well. He'd have a lot of stress, and then he'd come home and stomp around. He'd clearly be thinking about something else, and grunt when you'd ask him something. I pointed this out to him and said, "This isn't good for you; it isn't good for the rest of us; you have to change." He actually got some feedback at work about it as well. So with each successive work crisis, he's gotten better and better, to the point where, now, he's undergoing this huge work crisis and I haven't heard word one about it. That's good and bad. It's almost to where I'd like to hear more about it.

What I felt he needed were other things to think about—something other than work. He'd say, "Oh, I don't have time for this." Well, I'm the sneaky sort. I signed him up to be coach of his sons' hockey team. And then when they called him, I said, "Gee, they really need you." Finally, he saw that he could make time. Yes, it's time that came from us, but he can be with his children. So it's different family time.

I sort of insist that he play golf twice a week. It's sort of a twist on the usual golf-widow thing. And he's now manager of his sons' hockey team. It helps a lot. Sometimes, he gets stressed from the hockey part, but that at least you can say, "They don't own me. I can walk away. I can let go." So all in all, getting outside interests, outside friends, outside things to think about has really made the difference for him.

What a gal.

We'd just like to make one last point. If you don't do any cooking or cleaning and such at home, well, you've cut yourself an exceptional deal. In most houses, doing something domestic when you're home is a gesture, well-taken, that says you're not blind to all that she does on your behalf.

We heard about marketing executives who make dinner every night, and bankers who change exactly half of the diapers. We heard about a lawyer who pitches in his daughter's Little League games while his toddler is strapped on his back. We heard about an emergency room doctor who spends a chunk of his Sundays washing and drying and folding the family's laundry. Okay, he's watching basketball all the while, but he does the laundry.

These are six-figure guys. So don't say it's beneath you.

CHAPTER THIRTY-FIVE

If She Makes More

YOU MAY BE TEMPTED TO EASE UP on the throttle. Whoa there! Her deepest fear is that she'll end up supporting a freeloading bum. Most women don't want to trade places with you. They like being Mom. And they're better at it too.

"A lot of us make more than our spouses," said Marie, a 36-year-old secretary in San Diego. "It used to be the guy's pride would get in the way, and he would want to make more than the woman. But now they don't care. Now they want you to make a lot of money."

Marie is right. It's not unusual, anymore, for a woman to earn more than her husband. The federal Bureau of Labor Statistics keeps track of such things.

Among married couples where both husband and wife are working, 22.7 percent of the women earn more than the men. That's nearly one in four.

We'll agree with Marie regarding her other point: Men don't seem to resent it quite as much anymore. Only a few women complained about that. "My last husband was resentful and became a micromanager of the money to keep me economically strangled," wrote a lady in Salt Lake City.

More often, we heard responses like this one from Morgan

in Manhattan: "He's quite dignified about it. When he wasn't working and trying to start his own business, it was harder on him; and I think he suffered from a lack of self-esteem. But now that he's working, he simply makes jokes about the fact that my check is larger."

Most guys joke about it. It's the women who feel the resentment.

You can judge for yourself, upon reading the following comments and checking out the results of our Magellan Poll, presented in The Facts of Life sidebars on pages 374 and 376. Basically, the majority of women don't want to be the primary breadwinners, and two-thirds of those who are sometimes wish they weren't.

> "I'm tired of being captain of this ship, some days."
> —MADDY, Western New York

Sometimes, they resent being put in the driver's seat. Perhaps they grew up expecting not to have to deal with money and worry about money.

They feel cheated.

"He feels his check should be for fun and mine should take care of the bills," wrote a woman in Tennessee. "I guess it gives me more power, but I don't like it."

Or they feel taken advantage of.

Some women begin to suspect they've paired up with some sort of gigolo, especially if he lets go of any career ambitions as she begins to pull out ahead of him. "Instead of going for more, he rides my coattails," said Cheryl in Long Island, New York.

Then there are the female versions of Ralph Kramden. They make more, they like making more, and it sure sounds like they lord it over their mates. It's as if they set out to not lead the lives their mothers led, and instead they've turned into their fathers. Listen to these ladies play hardball.

- "I have more money and more power, so I think I need more control, which takes manipulation which causes fights."
- "I earn at least twice as much, and I am more than 10 years younger. I wish he would get a real job. I'm disappointed in him, and he knows it. If he never gets a career-path job, that could mean the end of the relationship."
- "I earn more. And yes, I am boss!"

THE SHORT ANSWER

WOULD SHE TRADE PLACES?

In our personal interviews with women, we asked this question: "What would you say if your husband came home one day and announced, 'That's it—you go to work; I'm staying home with the kids'?"

- "I'd say, 'Who are you and what have you done with my husband?'"
- "Yeah! Well . . . yeah. Yes, I would. I'd love it. I might change my mind in 3 months, but I'd definitely try it."
- "We did it. It was an unmitigated failure."
- "I've decided one person in the family ought to be sane and calm. I've opted for that role."
- "Men, from the day they're born, have that responsibility. Everybody looks up to them. It's almost genetic, practically. So why would women want to do that?"
- "If my salary were to double, I don't know that he wouldn't stay home. But if he did, he still wouldn't be the homeroom mom. And he wouldn't be the Brownie Troop leader and do a lot of the things that I take on in my role as mom."
- "I don't really need career satisfaction."

And we received this particularly honest e-mail from Pam, a 46-year-old publicity director in Wisconsin.

> After an exhausting day at work with long hours and lots of stress, I come home to a schoolteacher who's been home since 3:30. I feel entitled to more pampering, fewer household chores, and more deference because I make more money. I know that makes me sound like a stereotypical 1950s husband, but I still feel that way.

As we noted in the first two chapters of this section, women tend to see money as security.

If they work, they feel more secure.

But if they make more than their husbands, they feel *insecure* because if something happened to their jobs, the effect on their families' lifestyles would be much greater.

For them, being their families' sole source of income would mean too much anxiety.

Joyce, for instance, is a 46-year-old strategic planner in

THE FACTS OF LIFE

THANKS, BUT NO THANKS

Gender revolution? What gender revolution? Most women are happy to let men be the primary breadwinners, at least while the kids are young. We asked, "If your partner/husband earns more than you, do you ever want to trade places with him and be the primary breadwinner?" (Note: Women under 30, unmarried women in long-term relationships, and women dissatisfied with their relationships were nearly twice as likely to say yes.)

Yes ⇨ 16%   No ⇨ 84%

Philadelphia who has worked since college. She said that a big reason that she continues to work is the security.

> We've talked about what would it take, how much would he have to earn for me to quit working? And I don't think I'm ever secure enough. I'd be concerned for the long run—for the kids' college, for our retirement. I feel compelled to keep working. I think that with the job changes and everything that happens in today's environment, banking everything on one career can be risky. And I'm too insecure to deal with that.

By the same token, she would never want to be the only source of income. "That would be the worst. Too much pressure on me. I don't need that."

We did hear from women who earn much more than their husbands and who don't sound even a tiny bit conflicted. They must hear the beat of a different drummer. So must their husbands. It's a difficult, lonely choice those men have made. Society frowns on them. Even their mothers frown on them, as we learned when we interviewed Sylvia, a 59-year-old teacher in Brooklyn, New York.

> My son and my daughter-in-law have this role reversal. They live in Israel. She works for an investment banking house, and my son is a scholar and teacher; he has a Ph.D. in theology. She makes three, four times what he does. I'm not happy about it because I want my son to do more stuff. I want him to mix it up. My son is home with the five kids. She is in control. Are they happy? Very. My son never cared much for work. So he found the right person. But it bugs the shit out of me. Back in the '60s, I remember meeting a woman who told me her son was hiking in Nepal. And I said, "Oh, how great!" And she said, "If it was your son, you wouldn't want him hiking in Nepal." I don't want it to be my son who's sitting at home. He imitated me, I guess. I can't pinpoint this. Why, if I'm a feminist, should this bug the shit out of me? I don't know. Why does it bother me?

THE FACTS OF LIFE

GENDER FENDER BENDER

First we asked, "Who earns more money?" The answer indicates that, at least in one respect, our sample of female Rodale health-book buyers is like the overall population.

My partner/husband ⇨ 78%   Me ⇨ 22%

Then we asked, "If you earn more than your partner/husband, do you sometimes wish he earned more than you?" For most women, there's less pride in being the primary breadwinner and more insecurity.

Yes ⇨ 66%   No ⇨ 34%

It would certainly bother the vast majority of women to be married to her son.

For many, many women, motherhood is a choice. They'd choose motherhood over money any day.

Listen to Carole, a 42-year-old mother of two boys in North Carolina, who said exactly that. "My earning potential is greater than my husband's, but my priority is the family. I joyfully sacrifice money for family bliss."

A woman like Carole doesn't quit and go home because she got laid off or is collecting disability or hates her boss or can't decide what to do with her life. She wants to be there for her kids. So it's not as if women feel that they have no other option, that they wouldn't dream of being the primary breadwinner only because they think it's impossible. It's very possible. They just aren't interested.

Ilene is another woman who could be knocking herself out

climbing a career ladder, but chooses otherwise and is grateful she has that choice to make.

> I could be a gung-ho nurse in administration; I don't want to do all that. I want another life. I want the flexibility to do other things. And I'm allowed to do that because I have a husband who makes enough money so that I can do that. Not everybody has that luxury. I mean, that's a luxury!

Ilene has flourished in her stay-at-home role. She has raised two children; she cooks, gardens, engages in volunteer activities, and rows for exercise. Plus, she works a few evenings as a pediatric nurse. And maybe it's the way the world is set up, but many men pointedly do *not* flourish under the same circumstances. They end up like Michael Keaton's character in the 1983 movie *Mr. Mom*—a scuzzy, beery loser who plays poker with bored housewives and makes his bets with food coupons.

Fran, a 43-year-old mother in Pennsylvania, recalled the time her husband tried it.

> When my husband retired from the police department, he took some time off. He took our son out of day care, and I said, "Please, all I want you to not do is *not* to sit around and smoke cigarettes, drink coffee and beer. I want you to do stuff with him. Enjoy it; make it special." Well, he did a few things, but basically he smoked cigarettes and drank coffee. He would drink beer with the moms in the neighborhood; he wouldn't shave or shower for days. He would do nothing all day. After a while, you could see him clearly getting depressed. His world was shrinking in on him. Then we got the tape of the movie *Mr. Mom*, and he saw himself in the tape. And he cleaned up his act.
>
> Meanwhile, I was getting more frustrated because I had my dream house but I couldn't enjoy it because I was gone 14 hours a day and on the road sometimes. I said, "Bag this!" I could see he was getting so paralyzed that one morning I

sat down and said, "I'm giving my notice today. I'm not going to work anymore." And he said, "Does that mean I have to get a job?" And I said, "Only if you want to." And he went and took a job.

Her biggest regret about that interlude: "I wish he would've planned for that time better. He could have gone back to school; he could have done any number of things."

That is the single most important message we got. If her career soars and you decide to take some time off, use it wisely. Start a business or a new career. This is an opportunity to make something more of yourself. Grab it.

Are women expected to be so ambitious under the same circumstances? No. Is that fair? No. Is that life? Yes.

CHAPTER THIRTY-SIX

Two Places at Once

LIFE IS SO BUSY that both moms and dads have conflicting agendas for each other. She wants you to be successful but spend more time at home. You want her to raise a family but get back to work. Are you completely nuts yet?

"You resent them when they're not home, because you're there," said Susan, a 41-year-old gynecologist who's married to a cardiologist. "And then when they come home and they don't do what you want them to do with the kids or about the bills or about something else, then it's worse."

Sound familiar?

The years of raising a family are supposed to be idyllic. But those of us who start families soon discover the truth: Family life, on a daily basis, gets pretty crazy. It's hard work, compounded by the fact that most mothers are working. There's bickering about who has the better deal. If you're not around to help, she's thinking, "Hey, I work too. How fair is this? My job isn't exactly a hobby."

Men are now expected to step up to the plate. And by and large, we have.

But we're expected to be successful too. And success these days is no nine-to-five proposition. In fact, the majority of

American men work more than 9 hours a day. In highly paid fields, long hours are a badge of honor.

Ever get the feeling that you're wanted in two places at once?

She's giving you conflicting signals: Be successful, but get home for dinner and then give your kids a bath.

Psychologists might call it a mixed message. You might call it an impossible dream. It's as if you could be Cliff Huxtable, the character portrayed by Bill Cosby in his hit TV show of the 1980s. Huxtable was actually Dr. Huxtable, a warm-and-wonderful obstetrician/gynecologist whose practice helped house his considerable family in a lovely New York City brownstone. But, by golly, he was around the house every time a minor household crisis erupted. He was around that house a lot.

If you're feeling like you need to clone yourself to make everyone happy, it's not just your imagination. Most women we spoke with agreed that, consciously or not, they do give you conflicting signals. Said Sherry, a 37-year-old Michigan mother of three:

> I see the mixed message that I'm not necessarily intention-ally giving, but that I think he perceives, which is exactly that: "We need more money, but I want you to spend more time with the kids." So I know he feels that, even though I would just rather he spent more time with the kids. And if it meant cutting out a vacation, then I'm happy to make that particular sacrifice.

Depending on your circumstances, you're probably getting one of two versions of this mixed message. If you check off the category called managerial/professional on surveys, if you work long hours and your life is pretty much defined by your job, then you're hearing about your lack of attendance at dinnertime. On the other hand, if you're home a lot but your household budget is stretched like a bungee cord, then you may get the other version: "Gee, wouldn't it be nice if we had more money? Honey?"

Here's what Ann, a 42-year-old New Jersey nurse, said about her husband.

> I would like him to have more of a piranha-type personality. He has no piranha in him. He's not competitive. I think I'd like him, for himself even, to have a more competitive personality. He could stand to be a little more hungry. But so could I. We're pretty alike, that way. Pretty happy with the status quo.
>
> I like him being around at home; I love his availability. I say to people, "I'd rather have him make $50,000 less a year and come home every night at 6:00 and not travel or go away weekends." I'd rather have significantly less money in my life than have him gone. I really would. But I'd rather see him, as the breadwinner, being more piranha-ish. I'm sort of torn.

If Ann's husband got more competitive, then she could commiserate with the wives of highly successful men who dream that someday their men will get off the fast track. One of the groups of women we met with spoke glowingly of a man they know, a guy who was a director of communications for a booming media company but gave it up to spend more time with his family. He now teaches fifth grade. Isn't that sweet? All the women oohed and ahhed. But the fact is, none of them was married to a teacher. Conveniently, all of their husbands had high-powered jobs.

On another occasion, we spoke to a woman whose husband switched careers to become a teacher, and now she earns more than he does. Do we detect a note of resentment in her voice? "When he was unhappy with his job, he quit. I can't do that or we'll have to go live in a trailer."

No. You can't win. So do what you must, and make the best of it. Now, what about your impossible dream?

THE FACTS OF LIFE

BALANCING ACT

Most women respect their husbands for working hard. They just don't want you to confuse your job with your life. We asked, "Would you prefer that he devote less time and energy to his job and spend more time and energy at home?" The mothers, especially, need a helping hand.

	All Women	Women with Kids under 18
Yes	40%	45%
No	60%	55%

After the kids reach school age, some men wonder why their wives can't go out and get jobs.

Guys like this suspect that their wives are sitting at home eating bonbons all day. You know, like Peg Bundy. And their expectations for their wives are, in their own way, as far-fetched as those of the wives who wonder why their husbands can't be more like Cliff Huxtable. She's expected to work wonders, like Kathy Baker's character in the television series *Picket Fences*, who was the village doctor, the mayor, and a mother of three.

Men can be subtly snide and nudgy about this. Or they can be boldly insulting. "He told me straight out, I was a leech," said Francesca, 47, who runs a home-based day-care business in Albany, New York. "Even though I was implementing many cost-cutting tricks in my cooking, cleaning, and my own clothes or lack thereof. I have a very low-paying job—my choice—so I can stay home with my children, for which I get no respect and much derision because I'm not earning enough to help with the big expenses."

Women like Francesca are expected to get great jobs, but they're also supposed to maintain comfy homes and make sure the children's needs don't affect their husbands' lives.

To be sure, most women do want to go back to work after their kids reach school age. If they've stayed home during the preschool years, they're probably eager to spend their days talking to adults once more. But they find themselves between a rock and a hard place. They don't want to turn their kids into latchkey children. And who could argue with a mother who wants to be an active presence in her teenagers' lives? "As the kids get older, the responsibilities just change. They don't lessen," said Cheryl, a 51-year-old homemaker who quit her job as research director for a brokerage firm to be home with her teenage son and daughter.

What's more, these women have spent years maintaining life for their families. The transition to full-time work can be wrenching. Joyce, a 46-year-old strategic planner in Philadelphia, has seen the result.

> People I see in the very worst situation today are married women, married to professionals, who are going back to work after being home for 12 years. They want to start putting money aside for the kids' colleges. But they are totally unequipped to deal with a work life. They want to be able to drop the kids off at school and be there when the kids come home. They want to be able to stay home when the kids are sick and all summer and all holidays. But they want a job that pays well. The stress I see them under . . . They're, like, pissing and moaning about stuff I've been doing for the last 10 years. Normal stuff. Having to get to work in bad weather, having to go to New York for the day. It's not a thought process; you just do it. But for them, it's an awful lot of overhead. A rainy day is overhead. This new job introduces a lot of anxiety in their lives. They feel they're

being unfairly put upon. And I'm thinking they had a 12-year vacation.

The husband is often less than awestruck at his wife's ability to juggle work and the responsibilities of a family. "I sometimes say to my friends, 'There are times when I feel like my husband thinks my job is a hobby,' " admits Christine. "It's on the list of things that I get to do."

And if that happens to Christine, a high-powered tax lawyer, imagine what happens to waitresses and cashiers.

In group after group of women that we interviewed and surveyed, all agreed that men and women sometimes expect too much of each other. And they all pinned the blame on the same villain. Not him. Not her. The era we live in.

> "He told me straight out, I was a leech."
> —FRANCESCA, Albany, New York

- "It's very hectic. Technology is making us wild," said Deb in rural New York State.
- "Somebody who's 20 now wants what their parents had at 50," said Marie in San Diego.
- And Cheryl in Philadelphia agreed: "If we were willing to live the way our parents or our grandparents lived, I don't think the pressures would be as great."

CHAPTER THIRTY-SEVEN

The New Breadwinner

JUST WHAT IS EXPECTED OF YOU? Maybe she craves your time and attention instead of your money. And although the two of you may take on different roles, she doesn't want those roles to rule her life. Most of all, she wants a partner.

We asked group after group of women, "What does your husband do that your father never did?" It always got a good laugh.

Vanessa, a 40-year-old interior designer in California, recalled the handful of chores her father performed. "He did the guy things. He took out the garbage. He mowed the lawn. He let the dog out the back door. He washed the car. He drove, always. I guess that was it."

By contrast, these women have formed families where everyone pitches in and does a little of everything. Sherry from Michigan described life at her house.

My husband's definitely the primary money maker, and what I contribute is sort of the extra. But there's more of a shared sense of responsibility for every aspect of family life from the laundry to the groceries to everything else. He cooks dinner every night. He does half the grocery shopping, probably. He folds laundry. He reads the bedtime stories. And if there's anything else that needs to be done, he does it. My dad took out the garbage—and that's it.

When Joyce was growing up in a rowhouse in Philadelphia, her father ruled the roost—even though her mother earned more money. "Our house now is much more balanced," she said. "Everybody's involved in decisions. It's different."

The old, rigid roles that confined our parents have dissolved.

> "As long as the different roles are appreciated, supported, and mutually respected, who cares who makes the bed?"
> —CINDY, Georgia

It has meant more work for everybody, but for men the upside is this: We're much closer to our kids. More than our fathers, we want to provide for our children—and spend time with them. Surveys in the past decade have shown that, for the father of today, family life is an even greater source of satisfaction than work life. More and more men are turning down promotions and moves on the job in order to protect their time with their families.

For women, the dissolving of roles has led to some frustration. In a recent survey, the *Washington Post* asked this question: "Considering everything, do you think it would be better or worse for the country if men and women went back to the traditional roles they had in the 1950s, or don't you think it would make a difference?" Forty-two percent of women thought we should go back to the 1950s (33 percent said we'd be worse off, and 21 percent said it wouldn't make any difference). The frustration lies mostly in the wake of trying to have it all. Women feel that they have no choice but to work because middle-class life requires two paychecks. Yet they still find themselves shouldering much of the cares of home and family. "I am totally overwhelmed with work and the house," said Sunny, a 45-year-old Brooklyn, New York, teacher and mother of three. "And that's where feminism has really ill-served us."

The good news for women is, they're not trapped house-wives. They no longer feel any need to play the role of "the second sex." And if by chance they do find themselves falling into the old ruts, they are much more likely to shake up the marriage.

There's one word we kept hearing, over and over again. Asked what women want most, they would very often say, "A partner."

" 'Partner' is a good word," said Kathy in rural New York. It doesn't matter whether they're stay-at-home moms or corporate executives. If they feel like there's too much you and me and not enough us, you've got trouble.

Like Rosanne's husband, who didn't know he had trouble until it finally blew up in his face.

Rosanne is 41. She lives in Buffalo. She's been married for 20 years and has two children. Several years ago, her marriage was in crisis. She'd found herself trapped in a role that no longer worked for her. Together with her husband, she rewrote their marriage. They became true partners. This is their story.

> My whole life was geared around being a good wife. I never got a chance to be me. And my husband is a really good guy and he's helpful around the house now and he's respectful of the things I do, but he wasn't before. And I think that, be-cause of the way I was raised, he took advantage of that. I mean, I was raised to be a good wife. I thought my husband would take care of me in one way, and I would take care of him and the home and the kids. I thought I'd work but not full-time—and certainly never earn as much money, or more, than he does.

But that's exactly what happened to Rosanne, as to mil-lions of American women. The girl who got married at 21 moved into her thirties and bought her own business, a hair salon. That little business employed 16 people. Plus, she raised two daughters. She had grown. She had gained immeasurable self-confidence. As she said, "I finally felt like I did this on my own." And she filed for divorce. "I told him, 'I can't do it anymore.' That shocked him. He felt like it was a tragedy that happened in his life, where he stepped outside himself and looked in."

It was killing me. I felt like I had to walk 10 paces behind my husband. Anything I did, it was just not important to him. "What do you mean, you're doing this or that tonight? I don't even have any dark socks in my drawer." And I'd be like, "Oh, I know, I know. Okay, I'm gonna do that first." And I did! This is the way it was. I felt like I was totally losing myself. And I couldn't take it any more.

It was getting worse and worse and worse; and I was real unhappy; and I used to drink, drink, drink and always go out with the girls after work because I was so miserable. It was like, "My God, I can't seem to please this guy no matter what I do." And then after a while, I thought, "Who cares if I do or I don't." I hit rock bottom.

He was totally disrespectful to me. But you know what? I allowed him to do that, too, so he's not totally to blame. It's human nature. If one person keeps giving and giving and giving, the other person is so used to it they accept it. And then you feel horrible about yourself.

It was a change in me. You allow things to happen to yourself, or you don't. It's not until you get up to here that you say, "I'm done." And then, if they love you enough or they want to be with you enough, that's when they'll say, "Okay, I'm willing to change." We worked things out, and I've had a wonderful marriage for 6 or 7 years.

I have a totally different relationship with my husband now. I love my home and really love being with my husband and doing things together and taking care of my home.

And he's right along with me, doing it. It's different now. I
have finally earned his respect.

They've forged the partnership that women really want.

Forging a partnership is not female code for "Now you do
the laundry every other week."

**If she's hammering at you to split every chore right
down the middle, maybe she's given up all hope of
forging a real partnership and is just making damned
sure she won't be put upon.**

If she feels like you're as committed as she is, there's less
chance of hairsplitting. "We are equal partners with very different roles," said Cindy in Georgia. "As long as the different
roles are appreciated, supported, and mutually respected, who
cares who makes the bed?"

If Rosanne felt that she needed more respect from her husband, other women feel that they simply need time. In today's
economy, a segment of society feels they have more money
than time. In that situation, what these wives want from their
husbands is not another dollar but another hour together.
Susan, a 41-year-old gynecologist, said:

I like him to be around. I resent the fact that we have
our own lives too much. That we split up kids and he
goes with one kid; I go with the other. He's become dedicated to spending as much time at the health club as he
can, which in his mind isn't enough time. He's working
so hard, I never see him; but whatever possible free time
he has he spends there. He doesn't walk in until 7:30 or
8 o'clock at night, if I'm lucky, and that's during the tail
end of dinner. And then we're doing homework with the
kids, so the only time we actually get together is generally
around 10 o'clock at night when we're watching a television
program and talking during the commercials and I'm falling
asleep.

We interviewed Susan in the same living room with Kathy, a 46-year-old teacher and writer. Kathy has a little ritual that intrigued Susan. Kathy's solution to the ships-passing-in-the-night syndrome is this: "When Jon gets home every night about 7 o'clock and we sit in here, we have a glass of wine together—and we talk. And we talk about our day. We have half an hour of buffer time."

When asked by another mother what her children are doing all the while, she said bluntly, "We tell them to scram. They will come in to talk, and we will say, 'We're talking grown-up talk. We'll talk later.' My marriage to Jon is not at all like my parents' marriage, except for that half-hour. I love it when we have weekends when we don't have anything scheduled so that we're both in the house together. And we play squash together."

THE FACTS OF LIFE

HER TOP PRIORITY IS NOT YOUR TOP PRIORITY

We asked women, "Of all the roles he needs to play, what is the most important role you want the man in your life to play?" Then we asked, "What do you think your partner/husband considers his most important role?" The overwhelming answers were a reminder that she can't snuggle with your pay stub.

What Women Want	What Women Think Men Want to Be
Soul mate ⇨ 45%	Provider ⇨ 39%
Friend ⇨ 24%	Husband ⇨ 16%
Husband ⇨ 16%	Soul mate ⇨ 12%
Father ⇨ 6%	Lover ⇨ 10%
Lover ⇨ 5%	Friend ⇨ 9%
Provider ⇨ 3%	Father ⇨ 9%

"He's my best friend. I cannot get enough time with him."

Other women in the living room that night discovered they're part of a trend: They've turned the ever-longer American commute into an unexpected opportunity for togetherness.

Said Amy, a government lawyer in Philadelphia:

> A couple of times a week we'll drive home from work together. Bob works at the other end of town, and it would be very easy for him to just go downstairs and get on the train and go home. He will walk down to my end of town, or take a cab, which costs more than the train would, and we drive home together. And in the mornings, we'll drop the kids off and drive in together. That car time is probably our most meaningful time.

Thus do busy couples snatch time together these days. If "transition time" is on the interstate, so be it. At least there'll be some small sense of separation between work and family, a sense that's harder to achieve, given the blurring of the line between home and work. What with cellular phones and laptops, it's getting more and more difficult to distinguish between your job and your life. You have to fight that fight.

"He brings work home; that really upsets me," said Ilene, a 45-year-old nurse, of her husband. "And the whole thing with computers . . . He can get on the computer now, at home, for work-related stuff. I think that's a big problem. This is not an office; this is a home. I hate when he brings work home. No wonder he has back and stomach problems. He lets his job consume him. The fact that he's gone 11½ hours a day is a big enough void.

"So don't bring all that crap home," are her final words to her husband and you. "Come home and do something else."

In sum, we heard a plea to lead a more balanced life.

It was a loving plea, not a nagging plea. Your job ought to be a top priority. But if you keep it from becoming your sole priority, she'll respect you even more.

How to Stop Fighting about Money

—RUTH L. HAYDEN

Most financial experts would have us believe that the answer to all of our problems rests in paying down our credit card debt, or dollar-cost averaging, or the latest version of Quicken.

Phooey. Everyone knows that money problems go deeper than that. And so, when we first bumped into Ruth L. Hayden, we felt like we were finally getting somewhere. Here was an expert who said, "Money is not about counting." Here was someone who acknowledged the emotional side of money.

For the past 2 decades, Ruth L. Hayden has been a financial educator in St. Paul, Minnesota. She's also a media commentator and author of *How to Turn Your Money Life Around: The Money Book for Women.* Her latest book is *For Richer, Not Poorer: The Money Book for Couples.*

Q: *In 1985, you began teaching a "women-and-money" class. Then, in 1995, you began to teach a "couples-and-money" class as well. What prompted that?*

A: Money is the number one reason that couples fight. And according to the Harris Poll (an organization that conducts opinion surveys and other polls in 89 countries worldwide), it's the number one reason that couples break up. As a woman who's been married 30 years, with four children, I'm very passionate about helping couples. Money should not be the reason they split up. It doesn't need to be. It can be worked.

Q: *Are there all kinds of money fights in different couples, or is everyone having the same fight?*

A: I have a chapter in my new book called If You Get Yours, I Won't Get Mine. That is *the* issue for couples. Think about it. It's a pull-push. A couple that's not in a partnership makes a pull-push decision. Their dialogue sounds like, "If you go out tomorrow night with your friends, then I'm going to have to be stuck here with the children." Or, "If you get your way on this argument, then I'm not going to get my way." Pull-push is always adversarial, always. What couples learn in my classes is how to make money work in a creative partnership.

I truly believe that most people—I don't care how many years they've been together—do not know what it means to feel like they're in partnership. It really is totally different.

Q: *How do you describe a partnership to someone who's never felt it?*

A: A partnership is where we both know that we can make our lives work, together and individually. As a partnership, we have three strong entities. I call it an "and" model, rather than an "either-or" model. I watch the couples start to feel less adversarial. And it's really fun. Because I watch their eyes change as they look at each other. And I watch their language to each other change. I teach these couples that they individually can each be strong people and they can develop a strong couple. So it's you, me, and us. And that's powerful.

I believe that compromise is a key to the partnership model, and I use Gumby as a symbol. He's flexible, and he's got big flat feet so he doesn't lose his footing. When I'm in a partnership, I know that my feet are firmly planted while every part of my body stretches. I say, "How far can I stretch toward you without losing my footing?" In our society, we associate compromise with loss. Someone's going to have to give up something. I associate it with stretching. I'm not going to lose me. How far can I stretch toward you and keep my feet planted so we have you, me, and us?

Q: *Do the couples who come to you have power issues in the relationship?*

A: Money and power always go together. Money is the primary power tool in this society. Any time we're talking about money, it's about power. "If you get yours, I won't get mine" is a power statement. Money always has power, and it has safety issues. If you work with money the way I'm comfortable working with money, then I feel safer. But if you spend money in a way that I'm not used to, it makes me very uncomfortable. I don't feel as safe.

Money decisions are a mixture between the rational and the emotional parts of us. That's why money is so difficult for folks.

Q: *Is that what you mean when you say, "Money is not about counting"?*

A: I tell couples, "You didn't come here for me to teach you two to count to 10 and do simple adding and subtracting," which is all personal finance is. Personal finance is not about understanding 9,000 mutual funds. Nobody understands them or even why we need them. Personal finance is counting to 10 and some simple adding and subtracting. I ask couples to take apart the last discussion they had, and divide it into management or money. How much of it was actually about counting? "You didn't count right!"

And how much of it was about management? "How could you spend that much money on that?"

That's money management. And that creates most of the problems for couples. Money management goes back to beliefs. Beliefs are what we consider to be right or true. They're taught to us by our families and our society. Beliefs are the emotional part of money, and this is the part we don't talk about. Beliefs are an emotional conclusion about how we think money should be spent—or how much should be saved.

Here's an example: Shortly after my husband and I got married, his folks were coming over to our apartment for dinner. We had a table and we had plates, but we didn't have water glasses. He wanted to go to a very exclusive place that I'd never heard of. I was scared I would break something; the cheapest goblet there was $15.99, and that was 30 years ago. I asked him to go outside with me a minute, and I said, "Why do we want to spend that kind of money on something to hold water? We could take a trip for that kind of money."

And he said, rather snootily I thought, "Where do you think we should get glasses?"

I said, "There's a new store called Target. It's got good stuff for cheap."

And he stuck his nose even higher in the air and said, "You would go to a cheap store to buy glasses for my parents?"

I thought he was being ridiculous, and I think he thought I was being trashy.

We say that's a money problem, but really it's a value issue. We weren't talking about whether or not we should spend the money, we were talking about what we were going to spend it on. I wanted to go on a trip; he wanted nice glassware because he didn't want to insult his guests. We each thought we had the right answer, but it's just an answer that comes out of our own belief systems.

Q: *Are beliefs about money gender-based at all?*

A: In general, men believe they are supposed to be good at money. And they feel embarrassment and shame when they're not. And women, in general, are socialized in this society to believe that they shouldn't have to worry about money. That if a woman is kind enough, caring enough, loving enough, and giving enough, she just shouldn't have to.

So women who believe "I really shouldn't have to" feel a lot of resentment when they have to go to work. When they have to go on a budget. When they have to curtail their spending and balance the checkbook and pick an investment fund for their 401(k). They do it, and they're very competent. But they feel very resentful, and that's what their partners hear. Because women show their resentment by complaining.

I tell my female clients, "If you feel resentment when you have to do a money task, you have a belief that 'I shouldn't have to do this. This is not my job.' " Understanding this is huge for women. Resentment drains women. They're going against their socializing. Men have to understand this.

I hear resentment in my office every day. "I just wish I didn't have to go to work." Just as, many times, men show resentment when women say, "Could you read a story to Johnny? Could you change Johnny's diaper?" Men get resentful because they believe they shouldn't have to do the relational, home stuff. Men show their resentment as anger or by just not responding to their partners.

Q: *Does this explain why some men seem to thrive on being know-it-alls about money?*

A: It does create a blind spot. When men make a mistake with money, they usually make a big one because men have to pretend that they know. Based on my consulting practice, I could write a whole book of case studies of men who've made a big mistake with money. A wife came in with her husband after they lost their retirement money because of a very bad investment that all the partners in the medical firm made. I said to him, "Before you make another big decision about joint money and retirement money, would you make an agreement with your wife to talk to the accountant first or talk to your financial planner?"

And he looked at me and said, "I'm not going to do that! I'm not just a kid! I have the right to make decisions! And besides that, I don't want to look like I have to go ask Mommy for help." And she started to cry. He was going to do it again.

When men make mistakes with money, it's usually because they don't want to look stupid. They don't want to look like they don't understand. And they are willing to take huge risks to try to make a lot of money fast. It's men who are in the commodities markets.

Q: *How do women mess up?*

A: Women's biggest risk is, we don't get started. Women are taught to be relationship-based, so it's about creating a lifestyle today.

I tell women, "I don't care if you pick the worst-performing mutual fund of the last 10 years. You're still going to have more money than if it's in your savings account or you spend it at Nordstrom's."

Q: *The very next time our readers have money arguments with their wives, what should they do?*

A: There are two languages we speak in. One is emotional and one is rational. Think of emotional as Swedish and rational as German. In Swedish, I might say to you, "I'm really scared we're never going to get out of debt. I really am scared." And you say to me in German, "I just ran off the computer program, and the debt is not going down." We're both right, and yet we missed each other entirely.

I could have written a one-page couples' book, and it would say, "Speak the same language." Emotional language always gets priority, so the other person has to say, "Heck, I know you're scared, but we've done harder than this before. We're gonna do it!" Now we're both speaking Swedish. Couples say, "You're not listening to me!" Yeah, you're listening; your ears work well. It's just that you're speaking a different language and you're not bilingual.

Q: *Do women speak Swedish while men speak German?*

A: No. I worked with a couple the other day who are both accountants. I thought, "This is going to be easy; we're going to have two German-speaking people in here." As she started to pull papers out of her briefcase, he stood up, pointed at the briefcase, and hollered, "Where am I in those sheets? I'm nowhere in those sheets!" He was speaking Swedish. And she wanted to speak German with me.

You know, we marry our balancers. I think we go out and find our opposites because it intrigues us. So almost all couples speak different languages. That's why couples miscommunicate so often. Couples in my classes have money meetings at home, and I ask them to identify which languages are being spoken and to speak in the same language. When they do, their meetings are revolutionary.

Q: *Why does the emotional language get priority?*

A: If I'm afraid and you start counting, what's going to happen to me? I'm going to feel even more emotional. I'm going to start speaking Swedish even louder. You're counting louder, I'm hollering louder, and it's just a mess. So we have to deal with the emotion first.

Q: *Any advice regarding accounts? Joint versus separate?*

A: I am absolutely adamant about couples getting personal money that they answer to no one for.

Q: *Do you have one special message that you wish all men would hear?*

A: Because men have been socialized that they're supposed to be good at money, many men feel they need to be right. I would tell men there are no right answers with money. There's only a wrong answer, which is to let money destroy your relationship.

PART SEVEN

The Father
She Admires

CHAPTER THIRTY-EIGHT

Why Good Fathers Smile

WOMEN FIND GOOD FATHERS SEXY. Caring, involved fathers tend to have lustier sex lives than dads who are distant or detached, say the women in our national poll. Take fatherhood seriously, and it's a pretty sure bet that she will love you for it.

What does she want from you, as the father of her children? What does she really appreciate? What makes her purr with pleasure? What drives her so nutty she'd like to wrap a diaper around your neck?

These are not idle questions—or easy ones, either. Raising young 'uns alongside a good woman can be one of life's most enduring pleasures. Or it can become so fraught with conflict that it drives the two of you into embittered exile from each other.

In this part of the book, we'll enlist the help of women from across the United States, Canada, and the nearer galaxies to help us—and you—find some answers to these questions.

Just to clarify our purpose here: This is not about how to raise your kids, nourish them, discipline them, or ensure that they get into Princeton University. That's some other book (a very long one). What we're interested in here is how you can maintain a rich, rewarding union while also raising kids. It's about successful coparenting. Teamwork. Sticking together.

And just to start off on a high note, we'll begin with one thing that may have escaped your attention.

Having kids is its own reward. But men are also discovering an additional joy of fatherhood: Caring, involved fathers have better sex lives than guys who just pay the bills.

"One thing that attracts women to husbands is the way they are fathers. It's very sexy when they share parenting in a really personal way, when they a have warm, special relationship with the kids, not just helping with childcare chores," said Cindy, a 46-year-old publishing executive from New York City. She recalled one incident in particular.

> I came home one night after working at a job I didn't particularly enjoy, and I was tired and cranky—not really in a mood for romantic adventures. My husband and daughter didn't hear me come in. I walked up the stairs and found the two of them lying flat on their stomachs in my daughter's pink bedroom, playing with Barbies. Now my husband is a big man—6 foot 2, 290 pounds—and there he is holding two little Barbies, and my daughter is holding two, and they're

---

THE FACTS OF LIFE

YOU'RE DOING PRETTY WELL

We asked the women we surveyed to complete the following sentence: "Do you consider your partner/husband to be . . ."

A good partner and father ⇨ 60%

A better father than partner ⇨ 14%

Lacking as a partner and father ⇨ 14%

---

playing schoolteacher. He wasn't using a little-kid voice, he was just using his regular big-daddy voice, and they were having this wonderful, special time together.

It warmed my heart, and I just had to have him. The glow lasted until we put our girl to bed. He got lucky that night!

Another time, Cindy remembered, she found her husband folding the laundry when she got home. "There he was, this huge man, folding her tiny little socks and underwear. I don't know why that should turn me on, but it did!"

Frankly, we were surprised at how many other women echoed this same sentiment, Carla, a 54-year-old business executive, told us, "Guys don't realize that the image of a really buff man holding a baby is tremendously sexy to women. It can't be an effeminate man; it has to be a strong, rugged, classic male. Something about strength combined with gentleness . . . it's great."

"The sexiest thing about my husband is that he is a wonderful father," added Kimberly, in Denver. "To see him transform from a stern, hard-working contractor to a gentle, loving caregiver to our children is beautiful. After 10 years, he's still the one!"

An anonymous respondent to our survey offered the following comment.

Men have come a long way since the days of my father and how men would raise their families. They are more in touch with what goes on in their kids' and wives' lives. Sometimes, men don't realize that when they really get involved in helping raise the kids, it's very sexy to women. I say, more power to 'em.

When we asked women about the sweetest things their mates did with the kids, some of them drew a complete blank. But lots of others immediately recalled the sort of moments that keep marriages alive.

THE FACTS OF LIFE

THERE ARE A FEW THINGS THAT SHE WISHES YOU DID BETTER

Question: "Which of the following roles does your partner/husband play best in the lives of the children?" Guys tend to excel at paying the bills and rolling around on the floor making goo-goo sounds. We're generally most comfortable being a vice president or a 2-year-old. Hey, we can't help it—and what's so bad about that, anyhow?

We also asked these women another question: "Which of the following roles do you wish your partner/husband played better in the lives of the children?"

Roles He Plays Best
Financial provider ⇨ 36%
Playmate and friend ⇨ 24%
An active partner in the childrearing process ⇨ 19%
A role model for the children ⇨ 13%
Nurturer ⇨ 4%
None of the above ⇨ 9%

Roles He Could Play Better
An active partner in the childrearing process ⇨ 22%
A role model for the children ⇨ 18%
Nurturer ⇨ 17%
Playmate and friend ⇨ 11%
Financial provider ⇨ 9%
None of the above ⇨ 23%

Interesting, no? The thing they want most from us, as the fathers of their children, is to step onto center stage and play the role of Father more often (even though, compared to our own dads, we're already playing it pretty well). Paying the bills and making goo-goo sounds don't go quite far enough. But don't forget what this poll also showed: Very involved fathers are also the ones who seem to get the most satisfaction in bed.

• "When we lived in England, I worked very hard, and on Sunday I was grouchy," said Carla, a business executive who spent 20 years in Britain. "One day, my husband and my son, Albie, were out in the garden. Albie had this little mop of blond hair and he had on these Wellies (knee-high rubber boots), and he came in the house with a bunch of daffodils. His father had sent him. Albie said, 'Here, mum!' The fact that I was in such a foul mood, in there cooking, and they were out in the garden and they had thought of me was just so sweet! I was in a much better mood after that."

- "When my son Chapman was young, he had what doctors call malignant colic," said Robbie, 48, a full-time mother in Charlottesville, Virginia. "It's much worse than colic. It's just awful, and we barely slept. My husband and I got him into this terrible habit of rocking him to sleep—if I put the bassinet on the dryer, he'd go to sleep— but all this took ages, and one night I didn't get to bed until 4:00 A.M. Obviously, this had to change. So for 3 nights straight, my husband, David, stayed up virtually all night long, walking him, talking to him, teaching him how to go to sleep without rocking. He had to go cold turkey on this habit we'd taught him. I think this is where men do really well: They're able to see a task, take it upon themselves to do it, and then just do it. He did it quickly and decisively, in a way that would have taken me a month."

> "The sexiest thing about my husband is that he is a wonderful father. After 10 years, he's still the one!"
> —KIMBERLY, Denver

- "Recently, our son started playing the guitar," said Angela, in Longmont, California. "My husband has supported this by practicing on his guitar during our son's practice time. They have mini jam sessions. They also make bread together, which is very cute."

- "When George and I came home from the hospital with our son . . . just the way George was so afraid to hold him because he was so little, but he did. And later, just the way my son loved his dad, that was special. His eyes used to light up

THE SHORT ANSWER

THE DUMBEST THING HE SAID WHEN SHE WAS PREGNANT

- "You know the dumbest thing he said when I was pregnant?" asked Fran, a 43-year-old former teacher and stay-at-home mom. " 'Is it mine?' I just got real mad and walked away. We'd been married for 9 years, and we'd been trying for 2 years."

- "The dumbest thing he did was turn our nice and affectionate cat into a quivering mass," said Nickie in Berne, New York. "He had to do the kitty litter, and this cat sometimes missed the box. He took it as a personal affront and began a reign of terror on the cat that lasted until I took cat-litter duty back."

- "The dumbest thing was he said I looked like a hot-air balloon. The nicest thing he said is that I looked beautiful and I had a certain glow about me."

when his dad held him. There is such a difference in the way a man holds a baby from the way a woman holds him, helping to make him feel secure. It was really nice."

- "My husband has a daughter from his first marriage. She is now 17. There was a long time when they spent close time watching movies and TV together when she was visiting. Now, they share video games and music. The sweetest thing he has done with her is go to her dance recitals. There are one or two a year. He hates dancing and anything to do with dancing; plus, he has to drive to her Mom's town 3 hours away to see her perform."

- "Recently, I was going out the door to visit my mom in California, and my husband Craig said, 'I want you to be sure to have a good time, because you never get away,' "

THE FACTS OF LIFE

YOU'RE A BETTER DAD THAN HER DAD

Question: "Think about your father's involvement in raising his children. When you compare that with your husband's or partner's involvement, which of the following statements comes closest to being true?" The following answers reflect the husband's or partner's involvement compared with the father's.

Much more involved	49%
A little more involved	20%
About the same	21%
Less involved	10%

recalled Martha, a stay-at-home mom in Virginia. "I told him that I really didn't want to go, that I'd rather stay here with our three boys. I just feel desperate to spend time with them because I know it's such a short time that we'll all be together. And I could see that Craig had tears in his eyes, thinking that was really true."

- "My husband, Willy, is always, always thinking of ways to be a better parent, a better person, a better husband," said Lisa, a 41-year-old theater fund-raiser from Boston. "He's an adventurer. He's always thinking of great things to do with the kids, and I think, 'Why didn't I think of that?' "

How important active fatherhood is was also borne out in the Magellan Poll we did for this book.

We asked our tireless statistician to cross-reference two things: women's descriptions of how much hubbies help with the kids, and their descriptions of how satisfied they were with their sex lives. And, big surprise, it turned out that most of the women who say their partners are much more involved in raising the kids than their own fathers were also say they're very satisfied with their sex lives. They also were more likely to be very or moderately satisfied with their overall relationships.

By the same token, women who say their partners are less involved with child rearing than their own fathers were are more likely to be dissatisfied with their relationships.

In a marriage, everything is tied together—your wife, your kids, your yard, your job, your bed. A happy household is, well, you know, happy.

And by the way: Men are more likely to be the beneficiaries of all that happiness than women are. A study at the University of Florida in Gainesville surveyed 323 men and women who were age 35 about their overall satisfaction with their lives. Although women as a group generally scored higher than men, married men with children had the highest life satisfaction of all groups. By contrast, the unhappiest women were those with husbands and children . . . and the happiest were single and child-free.

We'll let the sociologists sort out the implications of all that. In the meantime, though, count your blessings—and change the diapers.

Cheers, guys: Women say we're doing a whole lot better than our dads.

Judging from other national statistics, there are a lot of happy households out there. In terms of our involvement with our kids, most of us are doing much better than our own fathers. Back in the days of *Leave It To Beaver*, when things were considerably more black and white than they are today, moms were not just the "primary caregivers," they were pretty much the only caregivers. Most of the time, dads were simply gone, either physically or emotionally or both.

"What typically happens in traditional marriages . . .

is that the woman makes the children her real emotional community—in place of her partner," observes Pepper Schwartz, Ph.D., professor of sociology at the University of Washington in Seattle and coauthor of *The Great Sex Weekend*. "In a sense, he just seeds the family and visits it."

But things have really changed.

CHAPTER THIRTY-NINE

What She Wants from You
as a Father

SHE WANTS YOU TO BACK HER UP on
disciplining the kids. She wants a fair shake on
dividing up child-care drudgery. She wants you to
pitch in without being asked. Whoa, is that a
biggie. And she wants to be thanked.

What women want from the fathers of their children depends on a lot of things. If they're happy with the job you're doing, they don't want much. (And there are plenty of women who are proud and pleased with their kids' dads.) If they're unhappy, there are all sorts of things they wish for. Listen to Robbie, a 48-year-old stay-at-home mom with two children.

What I want from a coparent is support—emotional and physical, not so much financial. If you have a traditional household where the man is out of the house much of the day, it's very hard for him to understand how draining and automatic and dead staying at home can become, having to do three carpools a day. What do I want from him? It would be nice once in a while if he came home and he said, "Tell me what you did today," and then he said, "Thank you; thanks for taking the kids today." Just an acknowledgement of the small ways in which women spend their hours. These are really important things.

A stay-at-home mom in Saint Cloud, Minnesota, echoed this sentiment when she told us she wanted her husband "to remember that I need as much love and attention as he gives to the kids."

"Consistency, playfulness, responsibility," said Diane, in Rock Springs, Wyoming.

Several others emphasized that they wanted their husbands to understand that fatherhood is forever, that you're still the child's father even if your marriage falls apart.

- "I want him to be there with unconditional love for the kids, even if we aren't together anymore," said one. "I want him to help raise that child financially and emotionally. It's not all my responsibility."
- "I want to make him understand that a father will be for life," said Evelyn in San Juan, Puerto Rico.
- "I want him to be a good provider and a kind soul," said Teresa in Calgary, Alberta, Canada. "I want him to be the kind of man that I would want my daughters to grow up and marry."

> "It would be nice once in a while if he came home and he said, 'Tell me what you did today,' and then he said, 'Thank you; thanks for taking the kids today.' "
>
> —ROBBIE, Virginia

Another woman objected to the age-old tendency of parents to see in their children a vehicle for their own unfulfilled dreams and ambitions. "I need my husband to appreciate our kids as people and not as a focus for his ambitions and desires," she said. "I want him to read *Charlie and His Choo Choo* to my toddlers, not teach them SATs."

"Patience and common sense," said another. "I just want him to be calm and collected when we discipline our children, and not make huge problems out of little occurrences."

Several other women emphasized their husbands' importance as role models.

"Fathers need to be good role models for their children, especially sons. They need to be the spiritual leaders in their homes, realizing death is inevitable, not probable," said one.

Gayle, a Pennsylvania housewife, said, "Since he's my ex-husband, I want him to speak well of me in front of the kids, help them remember my birthday and Mother's Day, and be a positive male role model for my son. In a nutshell, I just want him to give the kids all the love and time he can."

They want you to support them in the way the kids get disciplined.

In our conversations with individual women and in our various polls and surveys, women all over the country agreed on the critical importance of reaching some sort of agreement on how to discipline the kids, and generally present a unified front to them. There's no one right way to do it, of course, though there are plenty of wrong ways. But women told us, over and over again, that if they didn't feel that their husbands were backing them up as codisciplinarians, if they felt his punishments were too harsh, not harsh enough, or too inconsistent, it was enough to drive a stake into the heart of the marriage.

See if this comment from Jody, in Gaithersburg, Maryland, sounds familiar.

My husband and I fight over how our 4-year-old daughter is raised, mostly over discipline. I tend to be consistent on the rules, like if she bites anyone, she's in big trouble. My husband, on the other hand, will let her get away with anything unless the other child got really hurt by it. I say, "No way." If it hurt or not, she is in big trouble with me.

My husband kind of steps in every now and then when things get hot or he feels like being involved, and that really makes me angry. Things should be consistent with our daughter, whether it's Christmas or any other day of the year, not only when he (or I) just feel like putting down the rules.

Our daughter looks to us for guidance, stability, and consistency no matter what day it is.

To me, not keeping the same rules every day is frustrating and confusing for me and for our daughter, and basically means being a fair-weather parent.

Amy in Atlanta told us that "a never-ending point of contention between my husband and myself is expectations and discipline. We have a 12-year-old daughter who is a straight-A student with several interests and hobbies. I am a little more lenient because I think she earns that, whereas I feel he often expects perfection from her."

So Jody is strict, her husband is lenient; Amy is lenient, her husband is strict. Either way, you have a problem. Because if the two of you are not singing off the same sheet, it's hard to have a harmonious household (not to mention the mixed messages you're sending the kids).

> "To me, not keeping the same rules every day is frustrating and confusing for me and for our daughter, and basically means being a fair-weather parent."
> —JODY, Gaithersburg, Maryland

Women suggested various ways out of this particular bind.

"As our kids have gotten older, the main conflicts my husband, David, and I get into is that he wants to be more of the disciplinarian, more of the limiting force," said Susan, a 49-year-old writer from Ann Arbor, Michigan, who has two children. "For instance, my son John always wants to go hang out with his friends, and David got to the place of always saying no. On the other hand, I'd be inclined to always say yes. So we talked it over and got to the plan where our son could go on an overnight or have a friend over every other week.

"It was very much a compromise. John hated it, he would piss and moan, but actually it was great. After he'd pissed and moaned, he and David would get into some building project or other. There would be this childish pleasure about him that you would find only on those weekends when he stayed home. On the weekends when he'd gone out with his friends, he was always sort of surly. It was like he was enjoying being allowed to stay a child. David and I both agreed that this kind of parenting compromise turned out to be a good idea."

"My husband and I have an important but unspoken rule," said Nickie, who works in the real estate business in Berne, New York. "We do not make grand decisions without consulting the other out of ears' reach of kids. We generally do not change direction once the other has set a course. For example, if dad says one sleepover per month, we keep it to that unless I talk it over with him first. My husband is not a Type-A person, which helps. He does not get hyper about too much. I am diligent and persevering enough for the two of us. We do not put each other down in front of the kids. If one thinks the other is wrong or out of line, we discuss it in private. Our kids are used to hearing, 'Mom and Dad will discuss it and let you know.' "

Other couples still struggle with this same issue.

Ellen, 42, a Minnesotan with four kids who, with her husband, makes independent films, said that she and her husband "can never agree on the level of punishment for whatever it is the kids have done. My approach is always more conciliatory. My take on it is that harsh punishment doesn't get to the heart of the problem; it just makes them resent you more. Also, from my perspective, I spend more time with the kids, I know them better, and I resent it when he has a completely different opinion about how to discipline them.

"Over the past 2 years, my husband has been traveling a lot and I've been home with the kids much more than he has. There's lots of tension when he comes home from a trip. He hasn't developed the tolerance I have, just in being around the kids so much, so he'll react very strongly to things that I've learned to let slide. And this really annoys me. It's like, 'You don't get the privilege of losing your temper like that! I've been controlling my temper and dealing with this on a day-today basis, and you can't just lay down the law suddenly because you're pissed off!' These are the sorts of conflicts we get into."

Other women echoed this comment. Linda, a 42-year-old actress from Ohio, told us that "most of the crises happen when mom is there and dad is not, so the woman has to go with it; she has to react, make a decision, deal with it. Then, later on, when things have quieted down, dad comes home and says, 'Why didn't you do this or that?' "

There are at least two ways to deal with this, said Debbie, 49, a military brat who has lived all over the United States and is now married, with one 13-year-old son. "You really have to have a lot in common with your husband so that when he comes home, he recognizes that you were there, you did it, and he backs you up. It's that simple."

> " 'You don't get the privilege of losing your temper like that! I've been controlling my temper and dealing with this on a day-to-day basis, and you can't just lay down the law suddenly because you're pissed off!' "
> —ELLEN, Minnesota

Another important thing, she added, is a simple division of labor. "There are different parts to our life; and in some areas, he takes the lead, in other areas, I do. Since I'm home 90 percent of the time, that's one part of our lives where he just defers to my authority. In other areas, I defer to his. This seems to have worked for us."

Angela, an interior designer in Longmont, California, told us:

The biggest source of conflict in our coparenting would have to be consistency. Fortunately, it is something that is easily enough identified, and we can correct it before it becomes a problem. We have a small child, and our conflicts are over things like, "When should we wean her from the bottle? Do we read her fairy tales or something more moralistic?" These are all things we discuss as they become an issue and solve as they arise. But for that moment when you know it's getting to be an issue, it gets tense.

As with any conflict, communication is how we work through it. We haven't argued at all yet, and as long as we are willing to listen to one another and at least try to understand their view, whether or not we agree, I think we never will. Neither of us expects perfection of ourselves or each other. We try to learn from our mistakes and are willing to bend when things aren't working. In that, I feel we have a strong marriage; and hopefully, we'll attain happy, healthy, well-adjusted children. Isn't that what we all hope for?

Sometimes, of course, it doesn't work out so well.

Kathy, a 41-year-old travel writer, has two children but is now divorced from her husband. "Where I was incredibly frustrated was the imbalance in domestic responsibility," she said. "I felt equal responsibility financially, and 100 percent responsibility for cleaning, cooking, and all of that. I was just incredibly angry about that. I thought it was such a letdown. I was so offended by that! I found very much that that was a common complaint among my female friends; especially when the kids came into the picture, it just became, domestically, this huge imbalance."

Now, after several years in which she and her ex have maintained separate households in the same town, she said, "It must sound strange, but there have been benefits for the children. Now he runs his own house, and I think this is hugely beneficial to both my daughter and my son—to hold this whole different paradigm up to them, where their dad makes their lunches, gives them their baths. I think it's fabulous for all of them. I think he is a much better person and a much better father since the split."

It's a hard way to learn how to pick up your share of the drudge work; but let's face it, lots of guys end up learning that way. This brings us to the other thing that women mentioned over and over: figuring out a fair way to divide up all that drudgery.

Women say it's critical that there be some division of child-care chores that feels fair to everybody.

When we asked women all over the country, "What big thing do you want from your partner that you are not getting?" we got similar answers from Orlando, Florida, to Oshkosh, Wisconsin. Most went something like this: "I want him to have more of a sense of respon-sibility about sharing house-work and child care. I just wish he'd pitch in without being asked."

> "I want him to have more of a sense of responsibility about sharing housework and child care. I just wish he'd pitch in without being asked."
> —ANONYMOUS

Whew! That complaint hits a little bit too close to home. Couples all over the country are struggling to work this one out. In some cases, women (like Kathy) seemed to be so frustrated that they'd simply given up.

"I have one child, 12 years old," one woman wrote. "I don't expect my partner to assume any of the responsibilities in-volving her. Treating her appropriately with patience and un-derstanding and respect is all I expect (which he does)."

That's good, as far as it goes; but it doesn't sound like much of a family to us.

At the other extreme, some guys actually picked up more than their fair share.

"My husband's schedule is fairly flexible, so he is actually more involved with the child-rearing and household chores than I am," one woman wrote. "We try to share those respon-sibilities as much as possible, though."

However you work out the child-care arrangements, many women pointed out how critically important it is because it's amazing how often serious marital wildfires can get started by the tiniest spark. Anna, who's been married for 28 years,

THE FACTS OF LIFE

DIVVYING UP CHILD CARE: HOW OTHER COUPLES DO IT

Women still do more of the child-care chores than men, according to the results of our national Magellan Poll. Even so, this does not have to result in rage, animosity, and divorce.

It's not necessary for couples to split the child care or housework exactly 50-50, observes Pepper Schwartz, Ph.D., professor of sociology at the University of Washington in Seattle and coauthor of *The Great Sex Weekend*. What is important is that both parties feel that the division of labor is fair. "The truth is, what makes a peer relationship is not housework; it's joint purpose. It's creating something together. It's not child care; it's knowing and loving your children and being a team on that."

Linda, a 36-year-old happily married actress from Ohio, put it this way: "That whole thing of 50-50 means that sometimes it's 80-20, sometimes it's 60-40, but it all averages out. The main thing is that we feel like we're a team."

Also, don't forget: These were fairly traditional households, in which the man generally earned more and spent more time working than his wife did. And when we asked women if they'd prefer that he didn't work so hard and spent more time helping with housework and child care, 60 percent of the women said no.

Question: "Who assumes primary responsibility for the following chores?"

Arranging transportation for the kids

I do ⇨ 65%

We share ⇨ 27%

He does ⇨ 6%

Attending parent/teacher conferences

   I do ⇨ 54%

   We share ⇨ 41%

   He does ⇨ 3%

Calling babysitters

   I do ⇨ 69%

   We share ⇨ 18%

   He does ⇨ 2%

Nutritional wellness

   I do ⇨ 67%

   We share ⇨ 32%

   He does ⇨ 1%

Taking off work for illness or appointments

   I do ⇨ 64%

   We share ⇨ 29%

   He does ⇨ 3%

We were also intrigued by the way couples seem to have divvied up the responsibility for discipline. When we asked who assumed primary responsibility for taking the kids to the woodshed, the answers broke down this way:

   We share ⇨ 69%

   I do ⇨ 25%

   He does ⇨ 6%

"Wait 'til your father gets home," it seems, is a line that hasn't been used since *Leave It to Beaver* went into reruns.

told us, "I'm convinced a lot of divorces happen because couples can't resolve conflicts over the little things. Stuff like, 'How come you didn't water my plants while I was away? How come you never put your dirty socks in the hamper? Why do I always have to be the one to find a babysitter?' "

It's amazing how these tiny arguments, fanned with enough force, explode into completely different, much bigger arguments. "We mostly argue about parenting, but very often, wherever an argument starts . . . it usually ends up with us arguing about either sex or the division of responsibilities," moaned Monique in Santa Monica, California.

The devil, as they say, is in the details. Greater minds than ours have made similar observations. Jungian analyst Robert Johnson has written that human love could be called stirring-the-oatmeal love. "Stirring the oatmeal is a humble act—not exciting or thrilling," he writes. "But it symbolizes a relatedness that brings love down to Earth. It represents a willingness to share ordinary human life, to find meaning in the simple, unromantic tasks: earning a living, living within a budget, putting out the garbage, feeding the baby in the middle of the night."

When it comes to sharing the drudgery of raising, feeding, housing, and transporting kids all over creation, it's critical that both of you take turns stirring the oatmeal.

Some of the conflicts, imbalances, and arguments that women describe grow out of something that most guys (ourselves included) are barely even aware of: a sort of blithe, unconscious sense of male privilege. Ouch! Frankly, boys, it took us a very long time to actually *hear* this from women.

> "Who's the 'default parent'? Unless my husband says, 'I'm responsible for the kids now' or I make arrangements with him to be responsible, it's up to me. I have to arrange the babysitter. . . . He has never called a babysitter."
> —CHRISTINE, Philadelphia

We heard them say it over and over again, in a variety of ways—sometimes nasty, sometimes nice—but somehow the words did not stir those little ear filaments that register sound in the brain. Truth is, we didn't want to hear it.

You may not even be aware of it, big guy, but when it comes to child care and housework, women resent our unconscious sense of male privilege.

They'd love it if we'd just pitch in without being asked.

Most of the women we heard from weren't suggesting that their husbands were slobs, oafs, or couch cucumbers. Basically, these were decent guys. It's just that sometimes we don't even realize how much we're acting like some kind of thirteenth-century sultan, reclining on six dozen silk pillows, taking a snooze between dinner and the harem. (Don't sound too bad, does it? But those days are long gone.)

Listen to Ellen, the filmmaker.

> One of the things that gets me annoyed is when I say to myself, "Wait a minute, why does my husband have the time to read the newspaper in the morning and I have to pack the lunches and get the kids dressed for school?" I put the newspaper aside because I'm always saying, "I've got to read that article." But do I ever get a chance? No. The paper winds up in the recycling bin.
>
> It's not that my husband has made a choice to be that way. He's never decided, "Well, Ellen's going to take care of the lunches and whatnot." He's just truly oblivious. All I have to do is ask him to do something and he's right there—but I really do have to ask. He's willing to do whatever needs to be done, and I figure if I just have to give him a gentle nudge, fine. I can't be fundamentally angry, because he's just so oblivious. But I do wish he'd be more aware and quicker to take the initiative.

Or listen to Christine, a 36-year-old Philadelphia tax attorney and mother of two.

Who's the "default parent"? Unless my husband says, "I'm responsible for the kids now" or I make arrangements with him to be responsible, it's up to me. I have to arrange the babysitter. If I want to do something, I have to ask him. I can't just say, "I'll be out tonight; and by the way, if you've got something to do, go get a babysitter." I mean, he wouldn't know where to go. He has never called a babysitter.

"This assumption that the woman is always the 'default parent,' " said Kathy, "is not even an assumption. It's deeper than that. For most men, it's not even conscious. It's not even 'I thought *you'd* do that.' It's that they didn't even think it needed to be done."

It particularly irks women when their own mothers seem to buy into the notion of men as sultans.

"My two married brothers are very active in child rearing, and I'll hear my mom say, 'Oh, Earl baby-sat the boys today,' " said Linda. "And I'll go, 'Mom, you should say, 'Earl's got the kids today' or 'Earl took the boys today' or whatever.' Because if the boys' mother stayed home to take care of them, she wouldn't be 'babysitting.' She'd just be doing what it's assumed she'll do. Or she'll say, 'Oh, he's so good; he's so helpful,' as if he's doing something extra, something special. If the mother 'helped,' nobody would notice."

These unspoken assumptions, said Kathy, are why the male habit of asking, "What should I do?" can sometimes cause a waffle iron to suddenly go ballistic, generally in the dude's direction.

That thing of asking, "What should I do?" is irritating because of the whole foundation that's behind it. It's assumed that I am in charge, that the buck stops here. I'm the one giving out the orders. He shouldn't have to ask; he should be able to see what needs to be done. It sort of comes down to where the man takes ultimate responsibility for the life around him.

Women not only do all this stuff but they also tend to

carry around the whole picture—they carry around the details of everyone's life, their husband, all of the children. . . . As great as my former husband was—I call him my *wasband*—to this day, if you ask him who the pediatrician is, who's the dentist, he doesn't even know their names, has no idea if and when the kids were immunized and all that stuff. Women take all this upon themselves.

Still, many of the women we talked with said they've worked out agreements with their mates that seem satisfying to everyone. Debbie, for instance, said that she "made it pretty clear, early on," that she didn't like the relationship that her husband's parents had because his mother waited on his father to the point where the father was virtually helpless. (As the parents were in their nineties, this was an old-fashioned, almost nineteenth-century marriage.)

Debbie's response to all this was simple. "I don't serve. My husband and I take turns serving. We haven't worked it out precisely, but we do try to take turns taking care of our son; and my husband cooks on the weekends a lot. So it feels fair, and I really don't mind."

Her husband doesn't seem to mind either, she adds, because he's 4 years older than she is and quite independent, having lived on his own, been in the Army, done his own laundry and cooking. "That's why it's better to marry a more mature man," she adds. "They've done things for themselves; they are not as dependent and less likely to fall into the habit of making their wives into their mothers."

Overall, said Kathy, "despite what everyone said, I think it's just so much easier to be a woman today than it was in our mothers' time. It's so easy to see why most of the women of the 1950s, our mothers, were on tranquilizers. They couldn't really complain or bitch about this whole thing of assumed expectations; it was the norm. In those days, it was just expected that you'd stay home and be a happy, blissful mom. It didn't matter if you started out with all these career goals or you were this creative person. Today, women are more able to express their needs, their dissatisfaction. We can whine and bitch about it. We can change things."

And we'd be willing to bet you a thousand bucks, big fella, that you'd be better off helping her change it instead of fighting it.

CHAPTER FORTY

What She Wants from You as a Stepfather

STEPFAMILIES, NOW AS COMMON IN AMERICA AS THE OLD-FASHIONED KIND OF FAMILY, add layers of complication to the job of being a father. If you want to keep her favor and keep the family functioning, don't favor your kids over her kids. She wants to know that your loyalty is focused on her and the marriage. And demonstrate that you understand how strongly your stepkids need you, even if you're not their "real" dad.

It never really existed, of course. But the 1950s sitcom family still persists in the popular imagination. It's the thing that comes to mind when most people think of "family." Mom, dad, sis, and bud, all biologically related, all living in the same house, and all happy (except for each week's micro-crisis, which is always resolvable in a half-hour).

Well, listen to this: According to the U.S. Bureau of the Census, there are as many Americans living in stepfamilies as there are living in old-fashioned mom-dad-sis-and-bud nuclear families. That's because, in the United States, more than one out of two marriages end in divorce; and 60 percent of second marriages also fail. The result is that half of the 60 million kids under age 13 are now living with one biological parent and that parent's current partner.

Wow. If you think it's difficult to figure out what a woman wants from you as the father of children whose DNA you both share, imagine how much harder it is be the stepfather of kids whom you barely even know.

Then again, maybe you're a stepfather already and none of this is news to you. Because one other statistic that's of special interest to men is this: Since the courts award custody of children in divorce cases to the mothers nearly 90 percent of the time, "men are approximately nine times more likely to become stepfathers than women are to become stepmothers," according to Warren Farrell, Ph.D., a men's-movement guru, San Diego–area psychologist, and author of several books on men's issues.

Men who marry women with kids from previous marriages face all different kinds of quicksand: dealing with their ex-wives, dealing with visitation rights, dealing with several sets of grandparents, and, of course, trying to love and satisfy their new wives. But often, the most acute conflict grows out of their ambiguous new relationships with their new wives' kids.

When Dr. Farrell began dating a woman named Anne, who had a daughter named Megan from a previous marriage, the child was hostile, distant, and suspicious. She and her mother had lived alone together for 6 years after Anne's divorce. During that time, Anne had fallen in love once (to a man who lived hundreds of miles away). All that relationship meant to Megan was that mom was gone a lot—and that if mom fell in love again, Megan would be deprived of mom's love again.

When Dr. Farrell came on the scene and he and Anne started dating, Megan thought of him simply as "the man Mommy stayed out with longer than she said she would—the man who made Mommy keep the babysitter waiting." But after he and Anne moved in together, Megan's silence and hostility increased. She had three main responses to him: "I don't know," "I don't care," or "It doesn't make any difference."

"To casually say that it took 4 or 5 months to move out of this stage is to minimize the extraordinary pain I felt with every overture that was unresponded to: the unspoken 'Get out of here—you're just trying to be nice to me because you want to take my mother away from me'; the distrust in the eyes of an 8-year-old who seems to be saying, 'I know what you're up to'; the kiss goodnight with the cheek turning the other way and the hands preparing to wipe away the residue of any possible contact . . . ," Dr. Farrell writes.

Things are considerably more complicated when you enter a relationship with a woman in which there are small people involved.

"If a man enters a relationship with someone who is already a single parent, he must keep in mind that he is getting a package deal and that the child will not suddenly disappear into the background or the woodwork," said Michelle in Detroit. "And he should try to relate to the child as a friend and role model, not a tyrant. Also, he should not try to find fault in everything the child does, because he claims that's how he was raised. Because whether that is true or not, I believe you should always try to make your household and your children's upbringing somewhat better than your own. Believe it or not, making that child a victim will only make the mother defend the child more, eventually making her your victim also and making the love in your relationship disappear."

> Since the courts award custody of children in divorce cases to the mothers nearly 90 percent of the time, men are approximately nine times more likely to become stepfathers than women are to become stepmothers.

Well, it's hard enough to be a parent. But being a stepparent is doubly, maybe triply difficult. And many women we spoke to recognized this. Among them was Cynthia, a 50-year-old art teacher who is the divorced mother of two grown boys.

The main thing about stepparenting, to me, is that there is a very big, huge, gigantic, sometimes overwhelming difference between your own child and a stepchild. There is something in human instinct that's very basic. I can remember my husband and I looking at each other when Davey was very little and very rambunctious and saying to each other, "Isn't he lucky we're his parents?" This is when we halfway felt like taking him 10 miles out of town and dropping him off at the curb. No one but your parents will put up with some of this repetitive, rambunctious behavior.

Yet we heard from plenty of other women who told us that some guys, thrust into the role of stepfather, seemed to get it just right.

> "My advice to divorced men who have a girlfriend or fiancée, with young children in their lives or living with him: Be sure to make your lady in your life feel just as important, needed, and valued as you do your children."
>
> —MARY,
> Jacksonville, Florida

"My partner is the most loving, romantic man I have ever been involved with. He is a father, but not of my children, and is everything you would want the father of your children to be," one woman told us.

Another said, "I have a very sensitive, loving, and caring husband who is a great stepfather to my child. My husband is always there when I need him."

Some of these men even managed to navigate the heavy seas of sharing child custody with an ex-wife. One woman who married a man who had a 5-year-old daughter from a previous marriage told us:

He and his ex have done very well to keep their relations civil and provide their daughter with as settled a life as they can. In order to do that, my husband has not demanded time with his daughter that he could have. There is a very large hole in our spirits when she goes back to her mom. My husband has tried so hard to not let his anger at his ex get in the way of his time with his daughter. I really admire him for it.

Amid all of the conflicting loyalties in a stepfamily, your main loyalty should be to your wife and marriage.

What are the keys to making a stepfamily work? It's important to put your marriage first—even before your kids or stepkids, advise Emily B. Visher, Ph.D., and John S. Visher, M.D., San Francisco authors of *How to Win as a Stepfamily* and founders of the Stepfamily Association of America. It is your marriage, they say, that is "perhaps the most important single factor in how the stepfamily functions." Dealing with a rambunctious kid; winning over a hostile, suspicious child; establishing consistent house rules of discipline—they all flow out of a stable marriage.

Often, new stepfathers are torn by guilt over the breakup of their previous marriage—they feel that they've lost their families, say the Vishers. They're also torn by conflicting loyalties. Should their main loyalty be to their new wives? To their new stepchildren, whose affection they're trying to win? To their own children from their previous marriages, whom they may see only during weekend visitations? The answer, say the Vishers, is simple: Your wife and your marriage should be the central focus of your loyalty. If you continue to put the needs of your kids before those of your spouse, you won't develop a strong couple relationship and the whole family may suffer, they say.

They conceptualize the ideal situation like this:

You begin your life as an individual (I).

You marry and become part of a couple (C).

You have children and become a parent (P).

So the natural sequence of roles in your life is I, C, P.

But if you're divorced or your spouse dies, your role as part of a couple drops out, leaving only your roles as an individual and as a parent (I, P). If you remarry and simply add your role as a couple at the end, you get I, P, C. But that's not the way it naturally happens in life, and putting things together that way can adversely affect your whole stepfamily. Instead, say the

Vishers, it's best to put the "C" of coupling back in the center of your family: I, C, P.

Several women we spoke with complained that, in their stepfamilies, their husbands' devotion to the kids made them feel left out. The "C" of their couplehood had been tacked on to the end of things, like a casual afterthought. Mary in Jacksonville, Florida, was one of them.

> I have lived with my significant other for the last 6 years. Five of those years, his son lived with us; and his daughter lived with us for a couple of those years. They were very trying times when they both lived with us. They came to live with us because their mother (whom they had been living with since their parents' divorce in 1979) decided she didn't want to raise them anymore.
>
> Talk about a complete change of life. . . . Several times, I almost left. My husband really had a difficult time, in my opinion, separating me from them. My needs, I felt at times, were not important, just his kids'. To make a long story short, we're still together; they've grown up and moved out (the girl is 21 years old and the boy is 19). My advice to divorced men who have a girlfriend or fiancée, with young children in their lives or living with him: Be sure to make your lady in your life feel just as important, needed, and valued as you do your children. Children do grow up and go out on their own. A real woman, especially one that really loves you, will be there for you then and when they leave.

Here are some other things we learned from women about what they want from the stepfathers of their kids.

You have to deal with the "2-year syndrome": More than likely, your stepkids will reject you for at least 2 years.

"As a rule, the adults in stepfamilies believe the adjustment period will take place much more easily and much more quickly than is realistic to expect," say the Vishers.

Two years may actually be optimistic. Other studies have

shown that it usually takes 3 to 5 years for a stepfamily to feel settled.

Sometimes, there's just no substitute for patience.

Some stepfathers make the mistake of trying too hard to be good dads.

Said Cynthia:

> One of the fellas I lived with after my divorce tried so hard to be the children's father; but the major problem was, he was trying too hard. He had no children of his own, and he wanted so much to do a good job, which meant that he was thinking about it way too much. Everything that happened had to be reacted to. When you're with little kids all the time since they were born, it filters down like through a sieve to what really needs to be dealt with; and the rest of it you just let it slide because otherwise you'll go crazy. A kid goes running across the room and misses the table by an inch, that doesn't need to be dealt with. Missing the table by an inch while he's juggling glasses on his head, that needs to be dealt with. My boyfriend was dealing with every little thing and it was driving himself and Davey nuts. He was striving to be so good, it was bad.

It's only natural—in fact, it's probably inevitable—but try not to overtly favor your birth children over your stepchildren.

Catherine, in Jackson, Mississippi, had this to say.

> Our biggest problem in our marriage is that my husband is a terrible stepfather. His son was 12 and mine was 5 when we got together. His son was considered an angel and mine a devil. His son received everything and mine very, very little. My son was used to this type of life, but living it and seeing the differences made him very, very angry. When my son turned 10, he started hitting me. My husband also never disciplined his son and would not help me with mine. Now, we

have a 5-year-old daughter together, and I have to be the one
to discipline her.

Still, Catherine's situation sounds all too understandable.
As one stepmom admitted to writer Claire Berman, "I try to
be evenhanded in the way I treat the kids, but my children are
my children."

Perhaps the best way to handle this is to frankly acknowledge it, stop feeling guilty about it, and get to work building
relationships with *all* of your kids. As Richard Gardner,
M.D., clinical professor of child psychiatry at Columbia College of Physicians and Surgeons in New York City, writes in
The Parents' Book about Divorce, "Parents who believe they
should be just as loving toward their stepchildren as they are
toward their own children are placing an unnecessary burden
upon themselves and will inevitably feel guilty about not
living up to this unrealistic standard. I am not claiming that it
is not *possible* for a stepparent to love a stepchild as much as
his or her own; I am only saying that it is entirely reasonable
that he or she may not."

Sometimes, doing your best is the best you can do.

Stepfathers have to try extra hard to listen.

It's widely known that men tend to have trouble listening to
women. But men who are stepfathers often have an especially
difficult time.

One woman told us:

A stepparent doesn't want to feel like they don't know what
they're doing when they're dealing with a kid who is not
their own—but lots of times, they don't. It's difficult to listen
to the partner who does know the child, who has been with
the child since day one. So that's an added listening challenge, which is real difficult for men.

Okay, you're not the children's father. But don't forget how badly stepchildren need a dad—and how strongly they can bond to you.

Carla, a business executive from Connecticut, said:

Something I was slow to notice, and was kind of blind to, was how young children bond very much to a stepparent—and when they're gone, it really hurts them. I was with a man who was not their father for 5 years; and then we split up, and I didn't really think how much it would affect my children. Here we had gone to such great care since my marriage to make sure we didn't do anything to injure the children; and when this relationship that was not actually a marriage split up, it didn't even occur to me that that would be a big deal. Then one day we were driving along, and my son Aaron shouted, "Oh, there's John's car!" And there was such urgency on his face; and I realized, for a kid, 5 years is a huge chunk of his life, and here he is yanked away from this man. It hurts.

Several other women mentioned the unexpected trauma of parting for children, even if the "stepfather" in their lives was only a temporary, live-in boyfriend. Cynthia said:

Unlike in a marriage, where there's so much thought given to what's going to happen to the kids after a divorce, when my living-together situation ended, it was just very unclear what role my ex-boyfriend was going to play in my kids' lives. A boyfriend just tends to disappear. And I underestimated how abrupt it is for the kids, how deeply they would feel this. I was insensitive to that at first. And unfortunately, I don't think I did very much with it, other than explaining to the kids what had happened. I regret not having handled this better.

The kids really need you, whether you're their "real" dad or not. Sometimes love is more important than DNA.

CHAPTER FORTY-ONE

How to Be a Better Father in Your Wife's Eyes

WOMEN REALLY DO APPRECIATE THE ROLE THAT FATHERS PLAY in their kids' lives, even though they may not fully understand it. But don't sacrifice your marriage for your kids. Take and make time for romance. Let her know she's still your girlfriend.

See if you can understand the following. It's one of those deeply felt, not obvious, unspoken things that separate men and women who are trying to raise children together.

Joan, a 44-year-old bookkeeper and divorced mother of two from Annapolis, Maryland, told us about how her ex-husband would sometimes playfully throw their baby girl into the air and catch her.

"This is going to sound so selfish," Joan said, "but I thought, 'I brought her into this world! I *had* her! Don't you take those chances with my baby!' And you could no more get me not to feel that than anything. . . . He couldn't possibly understand the cost of having that baby to me. Throwing her up in the air! That's a man thing, and I just don't get it."

"Yeah," agreed Susan, a 49-year-old Michigan writer with two kids of her own. "My husband used to do that too. And my son loved it! A male friend used to call it acceleration training."

In her own family, Susan continued, the big conflict had to

do with wrestling. Her husband, David, and her son, John,
(when he was between 8 and 12 years old) used to wrestle all
over the house, so violently that her daughter was sometimes
reduced to tears. Susan's mother once accused David of "bru-
talizing" her grandson. "I really worried that John might get
hurt not just physically, but emotionally," Susan said. Once
she became so upset that she stepped into the middle of the
fight and stopped it. Everybody wound up being angry.

On the other hand, John was never hurt. He and his father
both enjoyed it so much that
you couldn't get them to stop.
And when they were through
fighting, they'd always step back
and laugh.

Susan and her husband re-
solved this parenting difference
by talking about it—a lot.

> "Having a family is like
> having a bowling alley
> installed in your brain."
> —MARTIN MULL

> Frankly, I didn't understand this at all. It seemed weird to me.
> But when we talked about it, David was always very ra-
> tional. He said it was a father's responsibility to teach his son
> how to fight and how to fight fair. He also wanted John to
> know that he could still physically dominate him. He felt
> this was important. I've just learned to trust that David
> knows what he's doing.

So there you have it: a complicated crush of conflicting
claims put to rest by a negotiated truce. Many women feel
that they "own" the children in a way that men simply can't
understand. They're protective and possessive of them. Men
view their own role as quite different—and equally critical.
How do you strike the right balance between women's urge to
protect children from harm and fathers' urge to show them
how to play the game a little closer to the edge?

Therein lies many a fight, many a back turned in the night,
many an angry separation.

Some of these differences between men and women are so

fundamental they may not be resolvable at all. Other differences would be better celebrated than resolved. In any event, here's the way women look at it and what they say they want from us, as the fathers of their children.

Though they may not entirely understand it, most women recognize that our role as father is critical in their children's lives, especially in the lives of their sons.

Men have special advantages when it comes to sons because they know how boys operate. Women see this, and— usually—they really do appreciate your help. Because they are keenly aware that there are rock-bottom differences between men and women, and it all begins when we're in diapers.

Lisa, a 41-year-old theater publicist from Boston, told this story.

> I went to pick up my daughter, Carmen, at the baby-sitter; and I immediately got into a conversation with the babysitter. I was kind of ignoring Carmen. Well, she just walked away. She was ignoring me because I was ignoring her. That's an amazingly sophisticated emotional response from a 2½-year-old girl. You'd never on this Earth see that from a boy child. He would march into the other room and knock over a vase.

Cindy, a 50-year-old artist from New York with two teen-age sons, recalled when the boys were young.

> The big challenge with raising sons is getting them to control their physical bodies and not destroy the place or annoy everyone else around them. Whereas with female children, way earlier than with boys, you have to deal with the psychological element. Mind games. You know, "I don't care which color barrette you wear, honey, just pick one of the barrettes and wear it!"
>
> Then she'll say, "I'm not wearing anything then!"
>
> You'd never go through that with a boy. Boys don't play

mind games like that. Women are interested in emotional relationships even as children. Little boys are just interested in this (she makes a ferocious whacking motion). It's very basic, very physical. My two boys would fight all day, but the worst threat was, "I'm going to separate you!" They would rather be together, fighting, than separated. That was the big punishment. Neither one could stand it for more than half an hour.

Whether the children are boys or girls, how should men be their fathers? What do women really want from us? Here's a few things you may find comforting.

Ann, a 42-year-old registered nurse from New Jersey who's been married for 19 years and has three kids, said:

I don't think fathers need to do anything special; they just need to be there. That's all they need to do. And whether it's day-to-day things or special things, as long as they're there, it doesn't really matter what they do. As long as the kids know that he cares about what they're doing and he's going to acknowledge it, that's the main thing.

Each parent has something special—and something different—to contribute, said Ilene, a 45-year-old nurse from York, Pennsylvania, who's been married for 22 years and has two children. And what each has to give doesn't necessarily conform to the usual gender stereotypes.

In the stereotypical family, the father does the roughhousing and the adventuresome stuff. That's not how it is in my family; I was the one who gave more adventure. I would plan vacations; I'd take the kids downtown so they could run the Race for the Cure.

My kids will talk to my husband, Ray; they almost have a calmer or chattier relationship with him. Because I'm always, like, boom-boom-boom-boom. I'm flying like a little hummingbird; and Ray's more calm and present and slow and deliberate. So it probably gives them a lot more time to feel.

"There's plenty of things I can't do for my kids that my husband can; that's the humbling thing about parenting," another woman said.

I have a friend who argues with her son, who is a very smart kid; and she says, "He outsmarts me." Then the father comes in, takes the little boy's hand, and goes for a walk and says just the right thing. I'm not sure you could say it's specifically gender; it's more about taking turns. Each one of you has special strengths as parents.

Many other women echoed this theme. Said another:

My husband and I both bring a great deal of love to our role as parents. We are both very different too. My husband is slow to react, but when he does he tends to blow up. I'm much more on alert and keeping our son within boundaries set by me. My husband is a presence when he is not engaged with our son and a terrific teacher/pal/role model when he is engaged.

Other women pointed out that what women want from the fathers of their children changes over time. Said Carla, a 50-year-old business executive from Connecticut:

I think it changes as the kids grow, but it's really important for the father to be a good role model, especially during those teenage years. It's really, really important to do things with your son and to share the load when they become teenagers.

A teenager needs a safe environment to rebel in, and what you need from your partner is help creating that safe environment.

Other women said that it's not even really up to you to decide what each parent needs to give. "Kids look for different things in their parents," said Ann. "They know what to find out of each parent. They know what to take from each one of us."

Martha, a 42 year-old full-time mom and part-time aerobics instructor from La Grange, Illinois, agreed.

> I think kids choose when the father or mother is important to them. The other night, my 9-year-old, Daniel, kissed me goodnight and said, "I love you, Mommy." And then he said, "That doesn't mean I don't love Daddy too." So that was bringing up the fact that Daddy was significantly important to him this week. Sometimes, they don't really want or need me; they need their dad.

> "I don't think fathers need to do anything special; they just need to be there. That's all they need to do. As long as the kids know that he cares about what they're doing and he's going to acknowledge it, that's the main thing."
>
> —ANN, New Jersey

Martha has three sons, ages 9, 13, and 15. And having grown up associating mostly with sisters, aunts, and female friends, she felt somewhat at sea when it came to raising boys. That's why she feels particularly strongly about the importance of her husband in their lives.

> I want my husband to be a perfect example for my three sons because his example has more meaning than my example. After all, boys have to grow up to be men and not women. They learn lessons from me every day, but ultimately they have to learn to be a man from him.

She told a story to illustrate her point. She and her husband, who is a lawyer, were watching a movie at home with the boys. The movie was about a lawyer, and at one point, he had a fleeting, sexy, romantic moment with a comely female client. "How come that never happens to me?" her husband joked. Martha noticed that her 13-year-old immediately shot a questioning glance at her and then at his dad.

I knew that from my husband's point of view, it was just an off-the-cuff comment to a silly, goofy movie. And if we'd been with other adults, I would have thought it was funny too. But in front of my 13-year-old son, I thought it was just a horrible thing to say. What does that tell him about what it means to be in a marriage? I'm trying to teach him about the idea of faithfulness and fidelity to somebody—the fact that it's important that he respects women and the institution of marriage. And here, my husband is saying something that seems to blow the whole picture I'm trying to create for my son.

> "I want my husband to be a perfect example for my three sons because his example has more meaning than my example. After all, boys have to grow up to be men and not women. They learn lessons from me every day, but ultimately they have to learn to be a man from him."
>
> —MARTHA, La Grange, Illinois

I don't know if he noticed that my son looked at *me*, like, "What does mom think about that? Isn't she a respected person in our family?" You know, he's a young man, growing up; he's trying to figure this stuff out. I think I could joke around and it would have less significance than if my husband did it. So later on, after the movie was over, I talked about this to my husband and he apologized to the boys. I knew he meant it as a joke; but he understood that the boys might not take it that way.

Don't sacrifice your marriage for your kids. If you do, both your marriage and your kids are in trouble.

Said Abbe, who wrote to us from Indianapolis:

My sister and brother-in-law, who have a really good marriage, did not sacrifice their marriage for their kids. What they did was set a good example of what people in love act like toward each other. Now, their kids are all married and away from home, but I so much envy how close they all are and how much joy they have in their family life."

This was another oft-repeated refrain we heard from women. At first, this struck us as odd since in a way it sounds a little cruel: Your own happiness takes precedence over your children's. But think about the last time you got on an airplane. You sank into your seat, buckled up your seatbelt, and before the plane taxied up the tarmac for takeoff, the stewardess ran down her little speech about what to do in the event of an emergency.

"If there's a loss of pressure in the cabin," she explained, "an oxygen mask will drop down out of the ceiling above your seat. Place the mask over your nose and mouth. If you're traveling with children, *cover your own mouth first* before helping them."

> "When it comes to sex, we've had our feasts and famines. After the baby, I didn't want to be touched. My husband had a vasectomy when our son was 6 months old. Then he didn't want to be touched for a while."
>
> —Nicki, Berne, New York

After all, the only way to help your children is if you are alive and conscious. If you try to help your children first, you could pass out—and then all of you are goners.

"I've heard that if a ship were sinking, most people would rescue their kids before their spouses," said Martha. But making your marital partner your first priority can even positively affect the kids, she said. "I think kids are most happy when they know their parents are satisfied."

Another woman told us, a little plaintively:

My husband is a great family man. He loves to play with the kids; and he gets very involved in their athletic activities (coaching, fund-raising, etcetera). All of our vacations are kid-oriented (Disney, Busch Gardens, a tour of roller coasters on the East Coast, etcetera). We spend exactly 1 day

alone all year—our anniversary. Our children are fabulous—
very bright, athletic, well-liked, I could go on and on. But I
think there are times when we must pay attention to our
mates and not only the kids.

Yup. We couldn't agree more.

Once you have kids, women say, taking time for romance is even more important than it was before.

Wrote Roberta in Indiana, who describes herself as "wife
of Mark, a farmer, home builder, and great dad,"

> "My sister and brother-in-law did not sacrifice their marriage for their kids. What they did was set a good example of what people in love act like toward each other."
> —ABBE, Indianapolis

I am truly happy with my husband and our relationship because I know that he truly loves me. With three children, ages seven, four and a half, and two and a half, and another one coming, we are very busy. But we never lose sight of each other and of what we have together. If there was ever any doubt about that, we couldn't possibly have this much joy together. We both know how lucky/blessed we are and we speak of it often. We start and end each day with a kiss and "I love you," and we stop for a hug whenever we can.

That's the way it's supposed to work.

How come it usually doesn't?

Well, in addition to all of its joys and rewards, having kids
ranks right up there with death, divorce, and Hurricane Hugo
on the stress scale. In fact, it's sometimes said that the birth of
your first child is the death of your sex life. That's a little bit of
an exaggeration, but anybody who has kids knows well
enough what a dampening effect they can have on the bon-
fires of the bedroom.

As comic Jeff Foxworthy said, "When you're younger and

you have a choice between sleep and sex, you'll always choose sex. But when you've got kids, you'll always choose sleep . . . and hope you have a dream about sex."

When we asked women what they'd done to keep their relationships sexy and romantic with kids in the house, several told us that you simply have to have realistic expectations. Nicki, who operates an at-home real estate business in Berne, New York, said:

> When it comes to sex, we've had our feasts and famines. After the baby, I didn't want to be touched. My husband had a vasectomy when our son was 6 months old. Then he didn't want to be touched for a while.
>
> When our son was small, we shipped him to Grandma's a couple of nights per month. When our son got older and more independent, I was buggy about his coming in on us. I read an article about sex being normal and so what if the kids know you do it? This calmed me, though I'm much less inhibited when the door is locked or he is gone for the night. When all is relatively normal, we will have sex two times a week. We are very much in love, and we trust that the other is behaving themselves. We tell each other "I love you" many times a day.

This reminds us that marriage therapists strongly advise having a lock on your bedroom door.

- "We've kept our marriage strong through a lot of talking, handholding, caressing, and spontaneous rendezvous in our everyday life," said another woman. "Our lives are hectic, but we don't forget about our love for each other."
- "Take time to stay in touch with the interests you shared as a couple before children arrived," said another. "You can arrange child care for a night out. Fake an important appointment that you need to have with your wife, and spend the day together. (Be sure to clear it with her em-

ployer!) Insist on keeping communication open. Ask questions about her day. Ask her what she wants in the way of sex. Clean up and shower regularly, even though you haven't worked up a sweat. And by all means, bring flowers regularly."

- "Just because you've been with a woman a long time doesn't mean she's no longer your girlfriend," wrote another. "Keep the romance going that got you together in the first place."

Many women made a strong, sometimes wistful plea for the importance of keeping fun and romance in your relationship while the kids are still at home. Lynn, in Salamanca, New York, gave this advice.

My final word of advice to men is to treat their wives always as they did before they were married. Once the children start coming, women need more support and need to hear that they are appreciated for what they do. I work as a childcare provider for four children, but just because I'm home doesn't mean that I don't have very demanding days.

Several others told us what the scenery looks like once you have kids but the romance seems to have seeped out of the house. Said one woman:

I think that when you're married for many years and have children, you really need to make time for your marriage. Time alone together is critical once you have kids. I've found that my husband and I have grown so far apart that I honestly don't know if there's any turning back. Both partners are at fault when this happens, and both partners must be more sensitive to each other's needs and more thoughtful. Unfortunately, it seems from my experience that only one partner winds up giving most of the time. I suggest communicating openly with each other about your concerns. But if there's a situation where one is constantly giving and the other thinks they are while in fact they aren't, the relationship will never flourish, and you're better off going separate ways.

Another said:

My husband and I dated several months before we were married. He took me out, paid for things, and bought me things. He tried to please me, as I tried to please him. That all sort of stopped sometime after we were married. Especially after you have children. During that time, all your money and time is spent on them. My husband and I still went out on an occasional date, which I would plan, because I wanted us to remember we still needed and wanted each other. But the extra attention he gave me when we were dating was not there. It was just a night out without the kids. What I wanted, and still want, is for him to be reminded of how to be with me when we are out. I believe men know how to be gentlemanly; they have just forgotten.

The common motif in all these women's voices is that married women, especially women with kids, just want to be treated with kindness and respect and consideration—"the same way they were treated when you were dating," said Joan. "You know, you hold the door open for me; I'll make dinner for you."

As another woman who answered one of our surveys put it, "There are no great secrets to a successful relationship. All men have to do is treat us decently and kindly. They get that back tenfold."

Joan went on:

So often, things change as soon as the kids come. You're not boyfriend and girlfriend anymore. It's hard to feel romantic toward someone you live with day to day. You tend to get too familiar—you share the same bathroom. But it's possible. I knew an old man who died at age 81 who still loved his wife. I'd hear him talking to her on the phone, and he'd speak to her like a gentleman. He'd call her up in the middle of the day and say, "Want to go to the movies?"

I don't know why that's so rare. But after all, shouldn't you treat someone you live with and say you love the same way you'd treat someone you're taking out on a date?

PART EIGHT

A Hassle-Free Home

CHAPTER FORTY-TWO

Why Fights Always Begin
in the Kitchen

IT DOESN'T REALLY MATTER WHO CLEANS
THE CAT BOX, who washes, or who dries.
What matters is that, however you divide up the
household chores, both of you feel fairly treated.
Because housework is never only about gunked-up
frying pans or dirty carpets. It's about sex, laughter,
lack of resentment, sex, togetherness, power sharing,
sex, and everything else that makes a happy union.

"He does the yard; I do the laundry. I do the cooking and
he'll do some of the cleaning. We both do the vegetable garden. On the weekend, he'll be in one corner of the garden and
I'll be in another corner, but it's like . . . we're still together
because we're participating in the same thing," explained
Barb, a 32-year-old magazine ad saleswoman, describing the
way she and her husband Marty divide up the household
chores.

"We each take ownership for certain responsibilities. I
have my own checkbook; he has his checkbook. I have the
bills I have to pay; he has the bills he has to pay. He doesn't
ask me how I spend my money; I don't ask him how he
spends his money. He knows what his chores are; I know
what my chores are."

Barb said that Marty, a 44-year-old electrical engineer,
rarely has to be reminded of what needs to be done around the
house.

I think it's because we enjoy the time we spend together. We realize that we get done what we need to do and we . . . I don't know, we just kind of get in sync. We thoroughly enjoy each other's company, and I think it's because from the beginning we set these things in place.

We also do something in our relationship that I don't see a lot of our friends doing—and actually, I've gotten grief about it from my women friends. I serve my husband. If he's sitting and watching television and I'm going to the kitchen to get something to drink, I will ask him, "Do you want anything?" He does the same for me. And I get grief from my friends, who say, "His legs aren't broken; let him go get it himself." I love this man. Why wouldn't I want to do these things for him? These are the nice things that you do for each other.

There's always some bit of household drudgery that neither one of them wants to do, so they pay a cleaning lady $60 to come in 1 day every other week. The end result is that, overall, Barb and Marty's marriage seems remarkably free of the petty resentments and recriminations that plague so many households.

What's that you say, bubba? That's not how things have been going down around your house lately? You still squabble over whose turn it is to feed Fido, Chico, and the gerbil? Empty the dishwasher? Water the plants? Pay the bills? She's resentful because she feels overworked; and you're resentful because you do so much that she doesn't seem to notice? (How come mowing the grass or trimming the hedges don't count as real work, but doing the dishes does?) Even couples who are otherwise happy struggle with the issue of household fairness.

Another woman told us:

I feel that I have a good marriage. However, if there is friction in my marriage, it can almost always be attributed to the issue of household chores. It is so customary in our society for the woman to maintain a 40-hour-per-week job and still be responsible for the domestic chores at home. In my opinion, the best policy for harmony at home is to maintain equality between both spouses when tasks need to be done. My personal choice for keeping equality is to have a rotating schedule. For example, this week I may be responsible for laundry, lawn, and cooking. The individual tasks don't even have to be consistent . . . just so the workload is equal. Unfortunately, my spouse tends to classify certain tasks as "women's work," so I'll never achieve this plan in my home. I am very blessed with an open, communicative, loving spouse who has my complete trust. If only I could inspire him to be more helpful around the house, I'd have nothing to complain about.

Hammering out an arrangement that feels fair to all parties concerned is absolutely critical to a happy, long-term relationship.

There are zillions of ways to divide up the humdrum household chores, but the main thing is that it's vitally important for your relationship that both of you feel fairly treated.

"Sharing work at home is vitally linked to marital harmony," writes Arlie Russell Hochschild, Ph.D., a sociologist in Berkeley, California, in her book *The Second Shift*. The title comes from the notion that even though a couple may both hold down full-time jobs, once they both get home, the woman is the one who's more likely to be saddled with a second shift of housework.

Historically, men may as well concede that point. When Dr. Hochschild averaged all the estimates from the major studies on time use done in the 1960s and 1970s, she concluded that women worked, on average, about 15 hours longer each week than men. That includes time spent doing paying work outside the home as well as housework.

But though our dads didn't help out around the house as

much as they might have, we're doing a whole lot better. Forty-seven percent of the women we surveyed said that their partners or husbands were more involved around the house than their fathers had been.

Maybe nobody at your house is about to give you a trophy for taking out the trash, but *we're* impressed. Thumbs up, pal. Our findings are echoed by other recent studies. One survey of 3,551 men and women who held full-time jobs, conducted by the Families and Work Institute in New York City, found that in 1977, men put in about 30 percent as much time as women on household chores. But by 1997, men were doing 75 percent as much household work as women.

The study found that in 1977 men spent around 1.2 hours a day on household chores during the week. Women spent about 3.3 hours. But 20 years later, men were spending almost an hour a day more on chores (up to 2.1 hours), while working women were spending about a half-hour less (down to 2.8 hours).

That's not parity, but it's a lot closer to fair than it once was.

Of course, there are other women out there who would be flabbergasted to learn that their hubbies were leading the pack for their contributions to housework. Take a look at the sidebar "Does He Just Do It?" We'd read that some women are unhappy these days, but when we had the great idea of scientifically polling women, we weren't prepared to be blasted out of the ever-lovin' water. A small but outspoken number of the women we interviewed expressed—how shall we put it?—a certain *discontent* with the domestic performance of their husbands, boyfriends, or live-in punching bags. They didn't give two hoots about fancy-pants sociological studies of "averages" like those cited in the sidebars in this chapter. In their opinion, their men were basically sticking them with all the crap work, and they were pissed. Hoo-boy!

Marva, in Sacramento, said:

I am convinced that men are conveniently blind. They can walk by a penny left on the floor 15 times and not stop to pick it up. They will rinse a dish in the sink, which is right next to the dishwasher, but not put the dish *in* the dishwasher. Unless a woman lives with a clean freak, she should make it easier on herself. Just take money out of the household budget and hire a housekeeper once a week. She will be a much happier person, and so will he.

Have you figured out any good way to divide it all up? One woman responded simply, "Ha!"

Another wrote, "Not!"

Others responded a tad more eloquently:

- "Yeah, I do it all."
- "Good luck (a duplex?)"
- "It's still 80 (me)-20 (him)."
- "Friends of mine nag or command until it gets done. My mother just does it herself. I hope I meet a man who is responsible enough to pick up his share."
- Or even simply, "Don't live with him."

Some women reported that the old boy was quite helpful, overall, but that certain household tasks were like an uncrossable line drawn in the sand. Joyce, a 46-year-old strategic planner from Philadelphia, said:

He doesn't make financial decisions without consulting. He helps clean the house. If I start cleaning the kitchen floor, he'll say, "Shall I go up and clean the bathroom?" I think I'm pretty lucky. He can't vacuum the steps because, I understand, there's something inherently emasculating about vacuuming the steps.

"My husband won't squeegee our new shower," said Vanessa, a 40-year-old interior designer from California. "I said, 'Just squeegee it. Men can squeegee it.' He said, 'You've

---

THE FACTS OF LIFE

DOES HE JUST DO IT?

We asked women to complete the following sentence:
"In general, does your partner/husband perform household tasks . . ."

On his own initiative ⇨ 45%

Willingly, after you ask ⇨ 31%

Begrudgingly, after you ask ⇨ 19%

Not even after you ask ⇨ 4%

Just a wild guess, but we'd say that there is a fair chance
that the guys in these last two groups are sharing their
houses with contentious women (contentious, we'll
readily concede, for a reason).

---

gotta be kidding. I'd die first.' He would not do that. He'd
rather die."

Others said—and here, frankly, we blush—that if the dude
couldn't fix something around the house, he was loath to let
anybody else do it, either. Women, obviously, have no real
understanding of the mind-bending power of testosterone.

"A lot of times, we've argued about fixing something," said
Jane, a 47-year-old cashier in rural New York State. "I'll say,
'Let's just hire somebody and get it fixed.' And he has to draw
it out, drag it out, and find somebody from West Nowhere
who'll fix it for 2 dollars and 50 cents." At the moment, she
reported, she has no electricity on the second floor.

Male landlords tend to exhibit some of these same endearing
attitudes toward household tasks, these women report. Basically, he loves to solve stuff, but only if there's an easy, two-step

---

THE FACTS OF LIFE

ABOUT HOUSEHOLD RESPONSIBILITIES

Question: "Who assumes primary responsibility for cleaning the kitchen?"

I do ⇨ 63%	He does ⇨ 3%
We share ⇨ 32%	Other ⇨ 3%

---

solution. If there is no apparent solution and it's not immediately solvable, the problem simply doesn't exist.

"I live in an upper flat," said Becky, a 48-year-old retail-display designer from Philadelphia. "And whenever I take a shower, the water pressure goes down; and suddenly it's either scalding or freezing. And I told my landlord that. His response is, 'Well, that shouldn't be happening.' So apparently, I'm lying. If he denies it enough, maybe it will go away."

(Ahem, gents, are you getting uncomfortable yet?)

Other women confessed that they had to lay some heavy-duty manipulation on the old boy to get him to help out around the house. Maybe you'll recognize some of the following techniques, including this one from Joyce.

- "I can remember one day riding with a fellow I worked with, and we got to talking about how effective we were in molding our spouses," said Joyce. "I told him how my husband used to make me crazy by leaving his dirty underwear on the floor. After a while, I started taking it and folding it back up and putting it back in his drawer—dirty. And it took him a little while, but he finally figured out that his dirty underwear was in there. So he said, 'What are you doing that for?' I said, 'I figured it must have been clean because otherwise you'd have put it in the hamper.' And that was the end of that."

- "I just quit doing certain things; and after some time, he got it and started doing it," echoed Andrea in Fairfax, Virginia. "It was difficult for me initially, but then it got easier to not want to run downstairs and do all of the laundry. Now, he does 90 percent of it. If I can live with things not done right away, he does begin to take notice, and does it."

- "I simply told him that if he helps out, I won't bitch. It worked wonders . . . and I've kept my word."

Others more or less threw up their hands.

There's only three reasonable solutions for modern couples: (a) Do housework together. (b) Share the cost of paying somebody else to do it for you. (c) Ignore it together until it gets unbearable, then move.

Well, that's enough of that. Consider us nuts, but we have the feeling that you didn't buy this book in order to get snarled at.

Of course, listening to that chorus of discontent only gives you part of the story (as you may well know). Here's another part of the story, which we turned up in our Magellan Poll. It gives some insight into the complexity of the deals that husbands and wives have to work out with each other and the imperfect solutions from which many of us are forced to choose.

Three out of five of the women we polled seemed to say that their husbands are more valuable to the family as breadwinners than bread bakers. That, if push came to shove, they'd really prefer that we focus more on making vice president than on emptying the dishwasher. Ideally, of course, they'd like us to do both. But in an imperfect world, sometimes one thing crowds out the other.

This has been part of the age-old male rationale for not helping out around the hearth as much as women do: "I'm bringing home the bacon. Why do you want me to cook the bacon too?" Of course, one thing that has put ever greater pressure on modern households is the fact that *everybody* seems to be working harder just to stay in the same place. In most households, women don't just run the house, they also hold down paying jobs outside of it.

This pressure cooker is really quite new. In 1950, it was so rare for a woman with a child younger than 1 year old to work outside the home that the U.S. Department of Labor didn't even keep statistics. Today, about 60 percent of women with kids that young have paying jobs. And not only are working mothers working more but so are working fathers. Everybody, in short, is tired.

This makes the hours that we spend at home with our families that much more precious, and figuring out a way to share the drudge work that much more important.

CHAPTER FORTY-THREE

Divvying Up the Drudge Work

BECAUSE IT'S BEEN SAID THAT IT ALL COMES DOWN TO WHO DOES THE DISHES, here are some practical ways to take the rage and resentment out of housework. Like doing what you like and dividing what you hate. Or every-other-week rotation. Or "if you mess it up, clean it up." But whatever you do, avoid a "family myth" of fairness—she's still doing more than you, Buster. And don't make her nag you to "volunteer" to help.

Well, let's just assume that unhappy women are the minority. That things run a little more smoothly in your house. Because, actually, lots of the women who responded to our survey expressed happiness at the arrangements they'd worked out with their housemates.

- "My partner does more than his fair share, so I can't complain," said one.
- "My husband always offers to help when he's here—never a problem," said another.
- "We have a very open relationship; we're each others' lovers, not keepers," added Simone, in Honolulu.

Other women said they'd simply accepted doing more than their fair share of housework because their husbands pulled more than their weight in other areas of life. "Yes, I am more active in household duties," said Cindy in Georgia. "No one ever said that in marriage everything would be shared equally."

Others had figured out a simple solution to the endless argument about who does what. It's called money. Said Samantha, a 45-year-old manager in Philadelphia:

> A lot of women stand on ceremony over what a fella does or doesn't do around the house. If I used that as the basis of my marriage, my husband would be looking for Samantha number four. I knew from the day I met him that he doesn't do anything around the house. I knew that was an area that I could not change; and it wasn't worth it to even try to get him to change. So the question is, can we afford it so that I'm not doing the things that he's not doing? And if the answer is yes, so that I'm not expected to do all those things he doesn't do, we've got a deal. And if you can get that, life is good. And when he calls you at work and says, "What's for dinner, dear," you say, "Would you like Italian food or would you like Greek food?" He picks and you make reservations. That's what you do.

It's too bad that most of us can't afford that solution except occasionally.

But even couples with ordinary incomes told us about ways they'd worked things out so that there was, well, if not marital bliss, then at least a sense of peace, calm, and fairness in the house. Among the many requests that we posed to the women who took our survey was this one: "It's been said that it all comes down to who does the dishes. If you've worked out any good, practical way to divide up the household chores, tell us about it."

We didn't make this request in order to pretend to be sociologists (actually, we flunked that course). We asked it because we were genuinely curious. After all, figuring out a fair way to divide up the dreariness is critical to having a happy household in every room of the house, including the bedroom. Our respondents had this to say about their apparently successful domestic arrangements.

- "Do what you are good at (for instance, I am not a lawn cutter, but I cook well); and the others, well, I guess we just split and do them because we love each other and we know that there are some things the other hates," said Katie, a student at Southwest Baptist University in Bolivar, Missouri. "Put your mate first; that's what love is."

- "If you mess it up, then clean it up; and whoever gets home first or has the time tosses the laundry in or starts the dishwasher etcetera, with the partner completing the project or pitching in whenever he or she arrives home," said Kaye of Little Rock, Arkansas. "We really do work as a team; and we know that we can count on the other person to pick up our slack, so we try not to have much slack for them to pick up. It works great for both of us— no rules, and the house is always clean. (Note: We, however, are both neat freaks!)"

> "When he calls you at work and says, 'What's for dinner, dear,' you say, 'Would you like Italian food or would you like Greek food?' He picks and you make reservations. That's what you do."
> —SAMANTHA, Philadelphia

- Glori, a therapist in Atlanta, had both a practical and a philosophical approach that seemed to work. "Have each chore divided up evenly, such as cooking, dishes (he'll wash pots, you do dishes), laundry (he'll wash and dry, you put away), cleaning (he'll mop and vacuum, you dust and straighten). Outside work do together (he'll rake, you plant or mow). Wash cars together. They key is share, share, share. Contrary to men's beliefs, women don't enjoy housework, either."

- "In our house, the general guideline is 'He/she who can, does,' said April, a computer consultant in Atlanta. "Even though I am an independent woman, I am traditional in that I like to spoil and take care of my husband, which means doing all the housework and cooking because I choose to. However, if I get in a jam and don't have time to finish what

I have scheduled for that day, my husband either pitches in and helps or tells me not to worry about it and to let it go till next cleaning day. This keeps the house running and me sane."

- "My husband and I stopped keeping score long ago, at least well before we were married. The idea of dividing up chores just never would have worked for us. When we see something needs to get done, we do it, be it laundry, cleaning out the bathtub, or taking out the trash. Frankly, I find the idea mentally exhausting, figuring out whether taking out the trash is equal to cooking dinner."

- "If it needs doing, just do it," wrote Laurie, a Canadian in a long-distance relationship with an American man. "This means men also have to see what needs doing. No assigned roles, per se. When we are off (we work in education), we do what has to be done. On weekends, we share chores. He cooks breakfast while I get showered; we eat; I clean up while he gets ready. Or we both do both, then shower together." She adds, "The whole of our relationship is romantic . . . the way we met, how we maintain our relationship, how we keep it alive through e-mail, phone calls, chat lines, snail mail, and, of course, our together times."

As mere male mortals with happy but imperfect marriages, we were also very interested in the nuts and bolts of how these women had managed to work out successful housework arrangements with their mates. Here are some of the ideas these women told us about.

Do something—anything—without being asked.

There's a very ancient, very boring dance commonly performed in American households called the nag dance. She wants something done. She asks you to do it. You say you'll do it. You don't do it. She asks you again. You say you'll do it. You don't do it. She asks you again, this time a little more peevishly. You tell her to stop nagging. She says just do it then. Etcetera, ad nauseam. Both you and she think it's a dumb, boring dance, but somehow you can't stop doing it.

"I hate it when he knows I'll fix it—that if I ask him a hundred times to do something and he doesn't do it, I'm going to eventually do it because I can't stand it anymore," said Marie, a 36-year-old secretary from San Diego. "He knows that, and then if you harp and harp and harp he says, 'You're not my mother, and I'll do it when I feel like it, not when you tell me to do it, and that's why I didn't do it.' "

> "It's not just his big, brown eyes and warm, genuine smile; it's also the way he treats me with such respect, the little things that show he loves me . . . the phone call when he's running late, brushing my hair, the long walks hand in hand, <u>putting the toilet seat down . . .</u>"
> (italics ours)
> —RANDEE HAINLINE, from REDBOOK magazine's Sexiest Husband in America contest

"You know what would be the best thing?" asked Maddy, a 52-year-old utility company employee in rural New York State. "If he took it upon himself to do something that I didn't have to ask him to do, it would make my day. If I had the laundry all folded in the laundry basket and he took it up the stairs, I would be thrilled!"

So just for kicks, try folding the laundry—or anything—without being nagged. You may be amazed by how that improves her mood.

If you and she synchronize your expectations about what the basic standards of household cleanliness should be, you can skip a lot of messy little arguments.

One of the most common reasons that couples go to sex therapists is because of a mismatch in the levels of their sexual desires. He wants to make love a couple of times a week; she's satisfied with once a month. But when it comes to household work, similar problems can occur if there are significant differences in what the two of you consider to be clean enough. If she's a neat freak and you're a pig (or vice versa), this discrepancy can produce no end of domestic friction. It's useful, therefore, to establish some sort of general agreement about what the basic standards of cleanliness should be. How often does the living room carpet need to be vacuumed? How frequently do the bathrooms need to be scrubbed?

As April, a real estate agent in Cincinnati, explained to us, "First, a couple must be able to come to agreement on what the baseline of cleanliness should be. It's no use expecting any half of the partnership to consistently do household chores they would not do if the other partner wasn't around."

Exactly. I'm supposed to make sure that the dainty little foo-foo on the toilet cover smells like a field of windblown daisies at all times, even though if she weren't around, the darn thing wouldn't even be there in the first place? Not fair.

Nickie in Albany, New York, added:

> First, both people need to get rid of 1950s-type expectations of what the house/meals should look like. My husband and I have worked ourselves into a loose system that has changed over the 12 years we have been together (10, married). In general, whoever doesn't cook cleans up. Now that we have kids, I've taken on a greater role in cleaning and food prep.
>
> I think I have the same sense of responsibility to our home life as he feels for being the major breadwinner. I don't tell him what to do about his work; and he doesn't tell me to take on more hours at work or that the house doesn't look good. We do major tasks together. We don't do weekly cleanings. If the family room rug needs vacuuming, someone does it. The doer is usually the person who is the most aggravated by the mess.

Right. If you feel personally compelled to keep the kitchen floor so spotless you can eat waffles off it, well, go ahead. But taking things to that level is *your* responsibility. Imposing this improbably high standard on your mate just isn't fair. Yet many of the women we heard from seemed to be seething with resentment because of just this sort of situation.

"The chores will never be fairly divided," one woman complained. "Never, never! Women will always have to do more. We may as well appreciate the little he does do and try not to think about it too much. Even if they did clean the place top to bottom, in most cases they wouldn't do it right anyway."

You may as well give up before you even start, big guy. Whatever you do, you're doomed.

> "My husband and I stopped keeping score long ago. . . . The idea of dividing up chores just never would have worked for us. . . . Frankly, I find the idea mentally exhausting, figuring out whether taking out the trash is equal to cooking dinner."
>
> —ANONYMOUS

"There is no good way to divide up household chores," wrote another. "If he helps much, it's not the way I like it done."

"My husband and I have worked out a system with household chores," added a third respondent. "He doesn't do them, and I am fine with it. My personal motto is, if you aren't going to do it properly and up to my standards, then don't even try."

And what are these high-falutin' standards, might we ask? How come she's the one to set them? And if he doesn't measure up, though he tries, does that become part of the national men-as-deadbeats statistics?

One no-nonsense woman admitted, "I think the only way to divide up chores is to evaluate what needs doing and do it. But it's hard for me because I am very controlling and I like to do things myself. . . . If anything, I will get in an argument because a man is trying to do too many tasks for me. So, I have yet to find the solution to this one."

The dude is in trouble because he's trying to do too much? Sheesh.

Sherron, a real estate agent in New Jersey, told us this

wistful story about how she didn't know what she had until it was gone.

> My ex-husband and I had a wonderful joint commitment to all chores. We usually shopped together; we each occasionally went alone. We shared laundry, ironing, vacuuming, floor mopping, etcetera. When I cooked, he did dishes; and when he cooked, I cleaned up. Wednesdays were FFS (Fend for Self) night. Each prepared what we wanted, ate whenever, and cleaned up after ourselves. I handled finances, selected his suits and accessories each day—he knew he couldn't coordinate. He was really nice man. I couldn't appreciate him. I was still after the bad boy. Now, 20 years later, I'd love to find a nice guy.

> "The doer is usually the person most aggravated by the mess."
>
> —NICKIE, Albany, New York

If you don't really share the housework fairly, but you pretend you do—thus creating a "family myth" of equality—your mate will probably still be resentful and find unpleasant ways to take it out of your hide.

For her book *The Time Bend: When Work Becomes Home and Home Becomes Work*, Arlie Russell Hochschild, Ph.D., a sociologist in Berkeley, California, spent years trying not to be noticed while she peered into the private lives of couples struggling to hold down two jobs, raise families, and run households without going broke or crazy. One couple she observed was Nancy and Ethan and their rambunctious son, Joey. Nancy held down a rewarding, demanding, not-very-lucrative job as a social worker and considered herself an ardent feminist. Ethan worked in the wholesale-furniture business and brought home the larger paycheck.

But though these two people were loving, hardworking, and well-intentioned, Ethan was quietly tenacious in his

JUST DO IT

YOUR VERY OWN DRUDGE REPORT

Sociologists studying the division of labor in American households have couples fill out detailed worksheets about who does how much of what. It's a revealing exercise because many couples aren't precisely aware of how the household tasks are divvied up. One spouse may be quietly fuming about a perceived unfairness that, on examination, may turn out to be not quite so unfair. Or the opposite may be true: He may feel that he's pulling his weight around the house, but on closer examination, that may not be true at all.

So be a real man and take this test—your very own drudge report. In each case, you can answer "I do," "He/she does," "We generally share this task," or "Other" (as in the chore is done by the maid, kids, or household robot). Then talk with your mate about it, without raising your voices. Ask yourselves, "Is this arrangement fair to both of us? Does it *feel* fair? If not, what could we change to make it more fair?" (Remember, the division of labor does not have to be a perfect 50-50 split, but anything greater than 60-40 generally makes one party unhappy.)

In your household, who generally takes primary responsibility for these?

- Cleaning up the kitchen
- Grocery shopping
- Household repairs
- Yard work
- Laundry
- Making the bed
- Money management
- Dusting
- Vacuuming
- Taking out the trash
- Cleaning the toilets
- Loading the dishwasher
- Unloading the dishwasher

unwillingness to do anywhere near as much work as Nancy did around the house. She nagged. She pleaded. She threatened to leave him. But Ethan barely budged. Most of the time, Nancy cooked, cleaned, and raised Joey while holding down a full-time job. Ethan, meanwhile, held down a full-time job while also operating the TV remote or building stuff in his downstairs workshop.

Finally, there was a breakthrough. They decided to divide the house into two zones of responsibility. Nancy would be responsible for the upstairs, Ethan for the downstairs. And it worked. Nancy stopped nagging. Ethan stopped resisting.

And Nancy, the feminist, could boast to her friends that she and Ethan now shared the house-work equally.

There was just one problem. It wasn't equal at all. The up-stairs for which Nancy was re-sponsible included the living room, dining room, kitchen, two bedrooms, and two baths. The downstairs basically con-sisted of Ethan's ground-floor workshop and the garage. He got to do hobbies; she got to do housework. Ethan had "won."

But even though she refused to openly admit it, Nancy was still seething with rage at Ethan. And she managed to extract her revenge. She began lavishing all her attention on Joey, who had a terrible time getting to sleep every night. Almost every night, after trying for hours to get him to settle down, Nancy began allowing him to crawl into bed with her and Ethan.

They called this Joey's Problem. But it was very clear to Ethan that it had become his problem too, because his and Nancy's sex life was now officially dead and buried.

Dr. Hochschild, observing all this, points out that "at first it seemed to me that the problem of the second shift was hers.

> "In medieval France, the women kept the seeds for sowing the crops; and the men kept all the plows. Without the agreement of both genders about how much to plant, when to do it, and where, no planting at all could happen and everyone would suffer."
>
> —AARON R. KIPNIS, PH.D., and ELIZABETH HERRON, in their book WHAT WOMEN AND MEN REALLY WANT

But I came to realize that those husbands who helped very little at home were often indirectly just as deeply affected as their wives."

Ethan, she said, "had won the battle but lost the war."

"Winning" wasn't worth it at all.

You don't have to split chores 50-50. What you need is a sense of joint purpose and a sense of fairness.

There are plenty of different ways to divvy up the chores so that nobody feels the need to get revenge. It doesn't have to be a strictly 50-50 arrangement. Any arrangement that feels fair to all parties will do.

Pepper Schwartz, Ph.D., professor of sociology at the University of Washington in Seattle and coauthor of *The Great Sex Weekend*, spent a decade studying American relationships and reported that some couples had worked out arrangements that she called peer marriages. In these relationships, she discovered, the partners had worked out something very close to equality. They were deeply devoted friends, companions, and compatriots. They shared equal status and equal responsibility for the emotional, economic, and household duties.

Interestingly, Dr. Schwartz noted, "these partners demonstrate that couples do not have to have a perfect split of responsibilities to lose resentment; what it takes is goodwill and a great deal of effort." Still, she added, "the partners do not have more than a 60-40 traditional split of household duties and child raising. The couples do a lot of accounting; the division of duties does not happen naturally on account of our training for the traditional male and female roles.

"The truth is, what makes a peer relationship is not 'housework'—it's joint purpose. It's creating something together."

Many of the women we heard from seemed to have worked out, if not genuine peer marriages, then at least something that seemed to work for both them and their partners. What follows are some of the insights and arrangements that the women told us about. We present these ideas here because we're hoping you'll find something to steal for reuse in your own house. Tell her you read it in this really great book. Or, better yet, tell her you just made it up.

- "My ex and I were very compatible with house chores," said Sue from Atlanta. "We just rotated weeks for cleaning. I've had some other relationships where hiring a cleaning person was worth not bickering about how messy s/he is and arguing over whose turn it is."
- "The one who doesn't have a job outside the house does all the chores."
- "One week, I will take care of the kitchen; next week, vice versa."
- "You both do them every night—one dries and one washes. Take turns with who does what."
- "I do a load and he does a load. When either one is too busy, the other takes two loads. We don't keep count."
- "Every-other-day rotation," said Rene in California.
- "We made a list of chores, then we each picked one from the list until they were all gone. Now, we have two lists of different chores. We each do our list for that week, then the next week we exchange lists. This way, we both do the good and bad stuff."
- "I do everything for a while, then he feels guilty and starts doing it himself."
- "I think it's only fair that, whoever cooks, the other should do the dishes. And the same person shouldn't have to do all the cooking. It's nice to be cooked for. The least you can do for that person is clean up the mess."

For some couples, it works best if each person just does what they like.

- "Each of us does what we like and know the best. Since I can't cook at all, our deal is that he covers the kitchen, including all the cooking and coffee making, all the cleanup, and keeping the shopping lists. He also does all the dog (new puppy) cleanup, walking and feeding. I clean the bedroom, living room, and bathroom, and do the laundry. One advantage of living room duty: I always know where the remote is before he does!"

- "I do what I do best, he does what he does best, and we share the rest."

- "Just share," said Alice in Woodland Hills, California. "At one time, you did it alone, now split it and spend the spare time together."

> "Make it fun to do the dishes. Whoever does the most gets to be the master and ask for anything, within reason. Sexually, it can be stimulating . . ."
> —JUSTINE, Los Angeles

For other couples, it's more a matter of divvying up the chores they hate.

There are chores that men hate and some that women hate. Find out which chores each would rather do. What about the others? Write them on slips of paper and pick them out of a hat, suggests Sandy.

- Mary in Washington, D.C., said simply, "He irons; I hate it. I cook; I love it."

- "We both hate all of it, so we've each accepted a couple of must-do tasks. He does laundry, garbage, and litter boxes; I do dishes, bathrooms, shopping, finances," said Kim, a 29-year-old writer and editor. "We both ignore other housecleaning chores until we can't stand it any more, then spend a day cleaning like crazy, followed by a reward like dinner and a movie."

- "Discuss your reasons for not wanting to do chores. The person who had the worst day wins. If it's a tie, leave them," suggested Emily in Boone, North Carolina.

- "For the big things (finances, laundry, yard work, etcetera), it comes to what you dislike least. ("I'll do anything if I don't have to do X.") The smaller things we tend to do together. Both have to be committed to being fair and sensitive to the other's schedule."

Some couples have even figured out a way to make housework fun . . . and sexy.

Believe it or not, some of the women we heard from had actually discovered ways to harness the mighty power of testosterone to get the dishes done. They discovered that men, like Pavlov's pooches, generally respond to certain kinds of stimuli even against their will. So to the following foxy ladies, with all due deference and considerable amazement, we officially bestow the Pavlov's Pet Award.

- "Make it fun to do the dishes," suggested Justine, who lives in Los Angeles. "Whoever does the most gets to be the master and ask for anything, within reason. Sexually, it can be stimulating . . ." Just in case you were wondering, she adds that "other than S and M and role playing (dominant and submissive), I enjoy everything."
- "We have two children, a dog, a cat, and a house to take care of," said Susan, who also writes an astrology column on the World Wide Web. "My husband has two choices: Accept that staying at home, for me, is a full-time job, or share in housework equally when I work full-time. I have done both, and the key seems to be in reinforcing his good behavior when he helps out. I frequently grope and fondle him when I catch him doing the dishes. This works like a charm!"
- "My ex and I used to share chores based on half the house. You do this half this week, then the following week you switch. We would also bargain for the stuff nobody wanted to do. For example, 'I'll give you an hour-long back rub tonight if you do the windows.' "

But when it comes to the connection between housework and sex, nobody said it better than Tami, a 36-year-old mother of four living in Broomfield, Colorado.

Hey, you guys, I'll let you in on a little secret. Roses, candy, candlelit dinners, romantic music, and all of that is nice, and sometimes it's even necessary; but if you want into our hearts (and thus into our pants or under our dresses), be considerate. Help us. Don't make us ask you to help out with the kids or the housework. Put down the remote, get up out of the recliner, and don an apron. Take the feather duster out of our hands and say, "You look tired. Why don't you go take a bath? I'll finish up here." Nine times out of 10, we'll be perfumed, in sexy lingerie, and reclining on the bed waiting for you about 45 minutes down the road.

> "Discuss your reasons for not wanting to do chores. The person who had the worst day wins. If it's a tie, leave them."
>
> —Emily, Boone, North Carolina

That's a lot of reward for 10 or 15 minutes of work.

CHAPTER FORTY-FOUR

Guilt-free Guy Time

GOIN' FISHIN' WITHOUT FEELING GUILTY:
Now that's a successful relationship. But how do
you work things out with her so that you can get
guilt-free guy time? Well, women say, it helps a
whole lot if you also give her guilt-free girl time.
You'd be surprised how many women say that they
want you to go fishing. So do it.

Oh, sure. You're married and all that, but you can go off
and do whatever you want, whenever you want to, for as long
as you want to, and come back home whenever you want to.
You don't have to call. You never feel guilty, not even for a
single nanosecond. In fact, hearth, home, and her are three
things that never even cross your mind. The only thing you're
really thinking about is whether the smallmouths will hit on a
popper or a Sneaky Pete. Also, whether or not you brought
enough beer.

Point number one is that that's guy heaven.

Point number two is that it's never gonna happen.

Because if you actually did that, you'd get booted out of the
house in about 6 weeks, and you'd wind up alone, fishing full-
time. That would turn out to be not as much fun as it sounds.

Even so, there *are* ways to go fishing without guilt and also
stay happily married. And figuring out a way to do that is
really, really important. If you can't do what you love from

time to time without feeling guilty about it, what's the point of breathing (or being married)?

Marriage, after all, is a sort of negotiated truce between the wild sweetness of freedom and the deep, gentle pleasures of home and hearth. Figuring out a way to get both is a bit of a trick, but it's worth the trouble.

In our national Magellan Poll, when we asked long-married women why their marriages had survived, 68 percent said it was because "we've given each other enough space to pursue separate activities, interests, and friendships." Women told us they want you to get the free time you need. (See The Facts of Life sidebar on page 477).

You have to give guilt-free time in order to get it. But women say they need your support and encouragement— lots of it—in order to not feel guilty for taking "time off."

Many women told us that, unlike most men, women have tiny microchips implanted in their brains that contain approximately one quadrillion details about household care, child care, and husband care. When they go away, it's hard for them to ignore all this stuff, which makes going away much less fun. That's why they need your support and encouragement for taking time off.

"When I go away, I think about what's happening in that house every hour, every second," said Martha, 45, a former lawyer and mother of three from Philadelphia. "When my husband goes away, it's not that he doesn't miss us, but I know he's not wondering, 'Oh, the kids are getting off the bus now; I hope the babysitter's there; I hope they got a ride to field hockey,' or whatever."

And let's face it, fellas. She's right; we're not wondering about that.

"I just went to tennis camp," she went on. "My husband, David, said, 'I don't understand why you can't just go off and forget it all. Everybody's fine.' I'm like, 'I don't know, but I just can't.' So I call home every day, and he feels like I'm kind of, 'Are you doing it my way?' And that's kind of insulting."

What does she want from him, in order to feel better and enjoy herself? When a woman goes away, said Martha, it's a man's role to not only "let her do it, but you're supposed to make her feel really guiltless about it. When I went to tennis camp, what I really, secretly wanted was for David to say, every day, 'We're fine. We miss you terribly, but we're really hoping you're having a wonderful time.' "

We asked her if David actually did this.

"No. He said, 'I really hope you're having a good time.' But I wanted to hear it constantly. Because in my head, I was feeling guilt, guilt, guilt. If I could've had a recorder that goes,

---

THE FACTS OF LIFE

WHO GETS TO HAVE MORE FUN?

People who own time-shares at a vacation condo manage to do it. But how well do people who are married to each other manage to share the fun time? To find out, we asked women this question in our national Magellan Poll: "Who gets more 'time off' to pursue separate interests and be with friends?" Our female respondents answered this way.

It's equal ⇨ 40%

Me ⇨ 19%

Only one out of five couples seemed to be fighting over the fun time. But one out of five women also said that they actually get *more* free time than their husbands. And three times more women said they'd managed to work out some satisfying fun-sharing arrangement with their partners than said they had not.

'Martha, I'm reassuring you everything is fine and it's really okay that you're doing this,' I would've felt really good."

We were really struck by this because we know Martha well, and she's about as liberated as they come. If even the strongest, most self-assured feminist mom feels this way, imagine the guilt that an average mother would be feeling.

She needs your help. Tell her that it's okay to take time for herself—and tell her that over and over again. If you give girl time to her, you're bound to get guy time back.

You'd probably be surprised by how many women say they really want their husbands to go off and get in some guy time—maybe because they recognize the importance of same-sex friendship more than we do.

It flies in the face of that old stereotype of the married man as trapped adventurer, chafing at the marital bit, dying to get out and howl at the moon (or something even more interesting). But sometimes, that stereotype is as false and useless as any other stereotype. Said Carla, a business executive from Connecticut who lived in England for 20 years:

> Actually, my ex-husband wound up getting very homebound; and it became a big problem in our marriage. Men think they're the ones that want to go out, but often it's the women who want a bit of a life—men wind up sitting home watching sports on Saturday night. My husband didn't need what I would consider real friends. He always had pub friends because pubs are a big attraction in England. Whereas I have to have real friends of the same sex.

Guilt-free guy time usually does have a lot to do with same-sex friendship. Guys all over the world do stuff with other guys in order to spend time with each other and, well, get away from the world of women for a while. Women do the same thing. And it's good for everybody.

Robbie, a 48-year-old mother of two from Virginia, pointed out, "When men go out with each other and then come back, they laugh more, they're much easier to get along with. And if you just depend on one woman for your whole social life, it gets boring."

In Robbie's view, men don't value guy time with other guys enough. She knows this, she said, because of how much she values the time she spends with her female friends.

> Men need friends as much as women, but they're not aware of this. One problem is that men don't know how to make new friends or keep old ones. With women, if you ask, "How many friends do you have and when did you acquire them?" you'd probably find that they'd made these friends over a long span of time. Whereas with men, they probably would have most from high school, a few in college, and one or two from work. Men just have a harder time making new friends than women do. If two couples join up and the guys become friends, they're damn lucky. Because when you're isolated, you're much more vulnerable.

The thing that makes female friendships so rich and satisfying, she said, is talk. Women love to talk. Men, on the other hand, "tend to think of friendship as doing something— hunting, fishing, golf, whatever. But this is kind of time-limited; you can only do that so often. But you can talk anytime, anywhere."

Well, sure, that's true enough. But guys often really don't want to talk all that much. Our ancient tribal custom of expressing deep feeling by doing guy stuff together, perhaps without even saying a word, is something that women will probably never understand. And they don't need to. It's not a crime; it's guyness. And guyness, in its own peculiar way, is a beautiful thing. As if to underscore this point, Robbie told a story.

> My brother-in-law Walt is just great—salt of the earth, the kind of guy you're just grateful he's on Earth. One of his best friends is an ear surgeon at Johns Hopkins. Neither of them

are particularly verbal; if you met them at a party, they'd have little to say. But put them in a truck together, going off hunting or fishing, and they're happy. Once they were driving down from New York State in a truck and the windshield wipers broke in a rainstorm and Walt was driving and his friend had to do surgery the next morning. They rigged up fishing wire to pull the wipers back and forth, and they had to do this for hours to get home. It was that kind of story that cemented their friendship.

Exactly. That is why having guilt-free guy time is so critical. And so much fun.

It's the fun part that men are missing when they get too obsessed with work, other women say. They wish that their husbands would get out and do something, take up a hobby, even go play poker in their underwear with the boys. If they did, they would be more interesting to be around.

Christine's husband is an overworked emergency room pediatrician in Philadelphia. The situation in the emergency room, and hence at home, she said, "is nuts. It's a crazy way to live. He tends to be obsessed with everything he has to do; and so he comes home and he can't sit still. He'll say, 'We've got to do all this laundry.' I just wish he had something that he could go off and do so I wouldn't feel so guilty. Because if he's not doing it, he's complaining about the fact that it needs to get done. When he's home, he's very good with the kids. But he doesn't make time for himself. And he gets really annoyed when I make time for myself."

You may have noticed that this whole thing works both ways: Sometimes, it's the guy who wishes that his wife would take more guilt-free time for herself. "I used to feel guilty if I left my husband home to watch our son while I went out 2 nights a week to pursue my own interests," said Monique in Los Angeles. "Then one day, he told me that it gives him one-on-one time with our son. While I was feeling guilty, he was looking at it as an opportunity."

Very often, getting a break from each other turns out to be a good thing for everybody.

Many women recognize that when you go off with the guys or she goes off with the girls, you're enriching your relationship. Still, it may help to remind her of this.

Linda, a 42-year-old actress from Ohio, observed:

> When a lot of my friends got married, I noticed that they started cutting off all their friends. Those friends helped make them what they are, helped make them interesting for their partners. Then they cut themselves off from that input and started having kids. I thought this was a really bad idea.
>
> So when my husband and I were dating, it was imperative to not get into that tight little circle. That's why I've always encouraged him to do things. He has a beautiful singing voice and wanted to try out for the Columbus Symphony Chorus, and I said, "Go! Do it!" He got in, and after that, Tuesday was his rehearsal night. And whenever I wanted to audition for a play, he encouraged me to go do it too. I think it enriches the relationship. It gives you something to talk about when you get back together. I think it's so important that you not cut off that input to your partner that was so important in making them what they are.

It's possible, of course, that she has no particular interest in learning that the smallmouths preferred the Sneaky Pete. Even so, you yourself are enriched by fishing. And that in itself enriches your marriage. Sometimes, it may help to remind her of this.

Equal time is fine, but if measuring becomes the issue, you've totally missed the point.

Ellen, a 42-year-old independent filmmaker and mother of three from Minnesota, said:

My husband and I have friends who try to parcel out the free time so precisely, I would just slit my wrists. If one of them does something, the other absolutely has to take an equivalent amount of time. Constantly balancing the scale would drive me batty. I'm all for equal time, but if the measuring becomes the issue, then you've just totally missed the point. There has to be generosity, and there has to be understanding of someone else's needs.

My husband went off to Tibet and Nepal for 9 weeks to make a film; and I know he didn't feel guilty about it; and I didn't try to make him feel guilty, because I believed in the film. I felt the film had to be done, and he was the one to do it. Of course, I wanted to go over there with him, but it was just not possible with the kids. This was just my time to be with the kids. I didn't want to be resentful about it; it's so negative and there's just no point in it. Also, I'm always able to take a long-term view of things. This movie was a flash in time, and I'm going to have a long life. But the main thing is this: When he came back from Tibet, I certainly didn't feel that he owed me 9 weeks.

Getting freedom, and giving it, has a lot to do with maturity. This is why it's generally easier if you're older when you get married.

Annette, a 38-year-old Danish physician married to an American man, told us, "It helps that my husband and I were older when we got married. We have had a relatively easy time giving each other freedom. My husband is extremely willing to let me go; both of us made a hard effort to let the other person go. And I don't know that I could have done that when I was 22 or 23."

Another advantage of being older, other women told us, was that it seems to get easier to grant your partner the freedom they need.

Debbie, who at 49 has been married for 25 years, told us:

Early in our marriage, some social opportunity would come up and it would just be assumed that if we had time, we'd want to do it together because we loved each other. But as we've gotten older, you just change. There are things that he might want to do that I'd have no interest in; and I could allow him to do it without feeling resentful.

Sometimes, getting to go fishing gets easier if you just wait awhile.

Don't forget about guilt-free together time, either.

The whole point of taking time for yourself is to enrich your life and your relationship, get a kick out of life, take a break from life, and pursue things that interest you. Since late Paleolithic times, guys have often chosen to do this in the company of their male pals, cronies, and most trusted fishing advisors.

But there are other times when taking your female companion along turns out to be even more fun. And when we asked them, we found out that women would very often like to have you along as much as you'd like for them to come.

- Christine said, "My father's got a time share down in the Cayman Islands; and we both like to dive, but we weren't going to go this year because of money and other commitments. But my husband's work has been so stressful, so miserable, I just said, 'We're going.' I bought the tickets; I called his parents and arranged for them to come down and watch the kids. And we went away and had a great time. It was really fun. Every morning, we'd get up and go diving; and then every evening, we'd take a long walk up Seven Mile Beach, and we'd talk the whole time. It was really great. And we'd say, 'Why don't we do this more often?' "
- Vanessa, a decorator from California, told us, "We have orchestra tickets. I've gotten to the point where I'd just as soon give it up. But you know, it's 6 nights a year that go

into our calendar as soon as we get the subscription renewal. We know which nights they are. He always arranges to be off. Six nights a year I get to go out to dinner with my husband. And I could care less about the concerts—every 2 years I get a great concert. But to have that time, whether it's in a dive Chinese restaurant or a pizza joint, it's wonderful."

• And Joyce, a strategic planner in Philadelphia, remembered this: "A couple of years ago, I went on vacation to the Napa Valley with my husband, for the first time since we had kids—10 years or something. For a week, by ourselves. And I actually thought about it beforehand. I thought, 'What the hell are we going to talk about for a week? What do we have in common?' I mean, it really bugged me. We approached it with a little bit of uncertainty because we really hadn't spent that much time together focusing on anything other than the kids and the marriage and the house and the financing and the this and the that. And it turned out, my husband and I had a lovely time. It was really wonderful."

This is why guilt-free time—guy time or girl time, together or alone—is an absolute must.

PART NINE

Going for the Golden

CHAPTER FORTY-FIVE

What Makes Marriage Sweet Enough to Last?

A HAPPY WOMAN CAN MAKE MARRIAGE AS
PLEASANT AS WARM SLIPPERS and a hot toddy
on a cold winter night. Here are eight things that
women say they want from you in order to make
that warm glow last: Friendship (they say it beats
the pants off passionate love). Shared values
(regardless of what they are). Fighting fair.
Openness to change. Mutual respect. Teamwork.
Listening. And—oh, yeah—lots of laughs.

Probably every little girl, at one time or another, has
dressed up like a bride and acted out her own pretend
wedding, complete with bridesmaids and wedding cake
made of mud or graham crackers. But if a little boy did that,
everybody—especially mom and dad—would start to get
worried. "Is Ralphie, you know, a little light in the loafers?"

Little boys—for whatever reason, cosmic or genetic—just
don't do that. Even when we reach marriageable age, few
men spend much time thinking about or dreaming about or
envisioning themselves as married. There is no male version
of the Harlequin romance novel, which endlessly conjures up
images of the perfect fantasy mate.

But here's the weird part: Once married, most men discover it's not so bad after all. In fact, quite to our surprise,
many men discover that marriage is pleasant. Quite pleasant. As pleasant as warm slippers and a hot toddy on a cold
winter night. In fact, it's now widely accepted among family

therapists that men are often the biggest beneficiaries of good marriages.

"There is substantial evidence that marriage disproportionately benefits men," reports John Gottman, Ph.D., a psychologist at the University of Washington and codirector of The Gottman Institute, both in Seattle, who has been studying marriage for more than 25 years. "At all ages, husbands report higher levels of marital satisfaction than do wives."

Studies have shown that marriage protects men from depression but makes women more vulnerable to it. Married men report greater overall life satisfaction than single men, though the reverse is true for women. And husbands who lose their wives have lower survival rates than still-married men; but widowhood seems to have no effect at all on women's health. (This being an unassuming, down-to-earth sort of book, we'll just skip a big discussion about the more profound implications of all this, thereby fending off yet another skirmish of the sexes.)

Studies at the University of Michigan in Ann Arbor have shown that an unhappy marriage can increase your chances

---

RULES FOR A LONG-LASTING MARRIAGE

1. Jealousy is not a compliment.
2. No whining.
3. I am not your mother.
4. You are not my father.
5. Do not stare at other women when we are together.
6. Accept my strength.
7. Accept my weakness.
8. Be honest.
9. Sometimes use your company manners at home.
10. Extravagance can be a necessity.

—*Dawn Korus, Park Ridge, Illinois*

of getting sick by roughly 35 percent and shorten your life by as much as 4 years. But there's also emerging evidence that marriage can be a genuine tonic for men's physical health. A happy marriage may bolster a guy's immune system, the body's big guns against disease.

In short, marriage suits men very well indeed, especially when compared to eating something-or-other cold out of the can while watching the Bulls game in a shabby apartment. Having a woman in your life who's a sex partner, friend, confidante, coparent, and housemate is, well, wonderful. And fatherhood has joys and rewards of its own. In the end, a good marriage winds up being even more fun than sex with a series of girlfriends.

Okay, okay. That's fun for a while. But other studies have shown that married men almost always have more sex than single guys. The only singles who have sex more frequently than married guys are those who claim to have five or more partners per year, according to one recent study. In the age of AIDS, those guys are also probably nuts. Happy, satiated nuts.

Once little girls grow up and get married, they seem to remain much more interested in the whole subject of marriage and relationships than men do. They spend money on books and magazines on the subject (chances are, they bought this book for you); and they spend a lot of time talking about this stuff with their girlfriends.

Talk about the Great Divide . . . When was the last time you sat down with a buddy and a brewskie and talked about what makes love last?

And yet, it *is* a subject of great interest to you, whether you spend much time talking about it or not. After all, maybe you don't spend much time talking about your health, but the way you feel affects every other part of your life. It's the same with marriage.

The good news is that, despite the well-known fact that in the United States more than half of all marriages wind up in divorce court, there are plenty of others that go into extra innings. It's just not true that there are no happy marriages in America. It's not true that all women are chafing under the patriarchal thumb of men. There are marriages out there— plenty of them—where neither party feels trapped. Where both parties are getting what they need. Where lovemaking is fun and frequent. Where wives love, honor, and laugh with their husbands (and husbands do the same for them). We were pretty amazed at how many of these women we heard from. Like Sue, in Detroit.

WHEN LESS IS MORE

This exchange of letters between gossip columnist Ann Landers and William in Bel Air, Maryland, reveals one man's secret of long-lasting marriage.

DEAR ANN,
   I am 56 years old, have been married for 35 of them, and have been a reader of your column for many years. Now I would like to give some advice to young husbands on how to keep their wives happy with only 15 little words.

   I love you.
   You look great.
   Let's eat out.
   Can I help?
   It's my fault.

   Thanks, Ann
   WILLIAM

DEAR WILLIAM,
   I took a poll in my office and was surprised that "Let's eat out" was more popular than "I love you."
   ANN

I have a fantastic marriage. Our lovemaking is special all the time. We both have respect and understand one another. Some people are jealous of what we have. People need to be open to one another. Real love is hard to find. My husband always makes me feel special. The little things are a real turn-on. I like being touched and told I'm loved. Being thanked for things I do, and helped a lot, lets me know how much he cares.

Another woman told us, "I'm a happily married housewife of 26 years with two great girls and a grandson and, of course, my hubby whom I love dearly, who works very hard to take care of his family. He's everything to me! My love, my friend, my mate, and more."

> "Men have an insatiable desire for variety, and women have an insatiable desire for emotional intimacy. Bearing this in mind will help both partners be better to one another."
>
> —ANONYMOUS SURVEY RESPONDENT

Several other women told us about the amazing power of a good marriage to overcome all kinds of troubles, including physical disability. Sandra, in West Haven, Connecticut, told us:

I'm disabled (multiple sclerosis) and have been wheelchair-bound for almost 17 years. I have one 17-year-old son. He is like his dad. They are both a godsend. Both help me a great deal with grooming, household chores, shopping, laundry—yes, even cooking. In our home, we always laugh, or drown in our tears. We don't need intercourse in our life. Just being home with my family is satisfying for my hubby and me. Twenty-three years and still going strong. Yes, he really, really loves me. Now that's a man.

But our favorite was Jane from Ross, California, who described herself as "the original GI Jane" (and whom we dreamily envisioned looking exactly like Demi Moore, in the movie by that name).

For the past 20 years, I have been working in the field of law enforcement; and for the last 8 years, I have been in the U.S. Army Reserves. So I am surrounded by mostly men. I have had a lot of men confide in me about their love lives and ask what women really want. I just tell them to truly be themselves; don't play games; try not to be so macho; and it's okay to be playful. My husband and I will leave cute notes around the house, even on the bathroom mirror. Right now, we're trying to scare one another with hiding a rubber spider in each other's "space" (coffee can, in the shower, rolled up in his washrag, etcetera). We find this to be very fun, and it leads up to more fun.

We have been married 12 years, but have known each other since 1976 and became best friends first before getting married. I wish I could clone my husband because then many of my friends would be happy in their marriages. I truly lucked out with my husband. He is very patient and not afraid to be silly. He is always thinking of me and takes very good care of me also. He also supports everything I do or want to do. I have had police partners who are so selfish and only concerned with what's best for them. Things are always their wives' or girlfriends' fault. It's a big turnoff for me when men become so self-centered (yes, women can too). I like a man to be secure with himself.

But what, specifically, are the ingredients of these happy unions? What do women want from men, as husbands whom they'll enjoy being married to for 20, 30, or 40 years? Jane and her husband's whimsical spider trick sounds like a lot of fun, but it's not the spider or the trick that puts the humor in their relationship. It's something else. As one survey respondent wrote to us, kind of wistfully, "There has to be more to your relationship than kids, sex, attraction, and romance, or I think the marriage won't last."

What is that something else? In this chapter, you'll hear from plenty of married women, happy and unhappy, about

THE FACTS OF LIFE

WHAT MAKES MARRIAGE LAST?

Question: "If you have been involved in your current relationship for longer than 20 years, please complete the following sentence. Our relationship has stood the test of time because . . ."

We've agreed on basic values ⇨ 84%

We've faced our problems as a team ⇨ 73%

We've learned the art of give and take ⇨ 69%

We've given each other enough space to pursue separate activities, interests, and friendships ⇨ 68%

We take care of each other ⇨ 65%

We've agreed on the lifestyle we wanted to pursue ⇨ 62%

We shared in the raising of our children ⇨ 61%

We respect and admire each other ⇨ 61%

We laugh a lot ⇨ 51%

We've kept the home fires burning and made time for love, sex, romance, and touching ⇨ 44%

what they want (and don't want) from us. And you'll hear from experts who've devoted their professional lives to studying what does (and doesn't) make marriage stay sweet enough to last.

All of these folks have lots of useful things to say. But bear in mind one thing we heard from Lisa, a 41-year-old theater publicist from Boston. She told us she'd had a difficult upbringing and had been in therapy for 4 years, first alone and then with her parents. Eventually, her therapist remarked,

"It's almost like your parents are not even married." But Lisa had a strong negative reaction to that comment. "You know what? It's not for her to say," she said. "Everyone is married in a different way."

That's true enough. And you'll hear more about the truth of that comment later in this chapter. Still, there were certain things that women mentioned over and over again, as can be seen in the results from a broad national sample of women in our Magellan Poll. (Check out The Facts of Life sidebar "What Makes Marriage Last?" to see some of those results.)

> "I have had a lot of men confide in me about their love lives and ask what women really want. I just tell them to truly be themselves; don't play games; try not to be so macho; and it's okay to be playful."
>
> —JANE "The original GI Jane" Ross, California

Many of these themes re-emerged when we talked to women in person or polled them in our *New Woman* magazine survey. The same general themes also tend to come up when people with Ph.D.'s examine the inner workings of successful marriages. For instance, here are eight elements that make for a sweet, successful union, offered by Dennis Lowe, Ph.D., professor of psychology at Pepperdine University and director of The Center for the Family in Malibu, California.

1. Trust.
2. Mutual respect and appreciation.
3. Companionship. You both like doing the same things; you're each other's best friend.
4. Commitment. You're both committed to your marriage and to the institution of marriage.
5. Communication. You've learned to speak each other's language and to listen.
6. Agreement. At least 75 percent of the time, you agree on important issues.

7. Conflict management. You know how to fight fair and resolve your differences.
8. Spirituality. Shared spiritual values become the glue that
   holds the marriage together.

The women we heard from may not have had Ph.D.'s in
psychology, but they clearly had Ph.D.'s in their own relationships. Here's their list of key things that they want from men
in order to ensure long-lasting marital happiness.

Nothing is better than being married to your best friend.

Charlotte in Milledgeville, Georgia, said:

> I think it is very important to like as well as love your partner
> or spouse. My husband is 12 years older than me and is truly
> my lover and best friend. We still share our evening meals
> together, play footsie, laugh frequently, watch our favorite
> sitcoms together, and look forward to seeing each other
> each morning and each afternoon. Every morning, my hus-
> band brings me a cup of coffee and brings his coffee and sits
> on the side of the bed so we can share a few moments to-
> gether before he leaves for work at 5:00 A.M.
>
> I kiss him goodbye at the door. I go back to bed for an
> hour or so and look forward to seeing him again in the after-
> noon. I'm always excited to see him and, if he gets home be-
> fore I do, I'll call him and he has a nice hot cup of coffee
> waiting for me. I love that.

It's not hard to imagine Charlotte and her man still playing
footsie 20 years from now and still having fun. The importance of this kind of easy-going companionship came up repeatedly in comments from women across the country.

Another woman wrote to us, "Love is very important, but
being best friends is a must. Romance should never die, as it
will always keep the sparks alive in your relationship. My

advice to men: Always treat a woman like you would like to be treated."

Another told us this story:

> Both the men in my life are not ordinary relationships. I've been having an affair with a married man for 8 years. I am a widow. My husband was my perfect counterpart and my best friend. I don't want a husband; I want great sex and communication with no commitment. The other man is someone I have known for 28 years; and we are great friends and occasionally have sex (great sex).

After losing her beloved husband and friend, she seemed to long for the friendship that she'd lost more than for anything else. Even fabulous sex doesn't seem to be the main thing she yearns for. (And why is their lovemaking so sweet? Because of their friendship, we'd bet.)

Yet almost everywhere you turn in our culture—in movies, books, and TV shows—you find romantic love, rather than friendship, held up as the Holy Grail of happiness. A torrid love affair makes for a better read or a more saleable story line than a sweet, steady friendship, calm and undramatic as a nice cup of tea.

But people who have studied love with a cold, objective eye (if such a thing is possible) don't entirely agree that passion is so important. One of the greatest skeptics of romantic love, in fact, is one of the most prominent experts on the subject—Helen Fisher, Ph.D., an anthropologist at Rutgers University in New Brunswick, New Jersey, and author of *The Anatomy of Love*. She maintains that romantic love is actually a fierce, unstable force that can lead to lying, cheating, stalking, broken families, and various other species of grief. In one scientific paper, she argued that people in love are actually crazed by an imbalance of brain chemicals, particularly dopamine, the same chemical that floods the brain when you sniff cocaine. Being in love is, literally, akin to being high.

People on drugs eventually come down, and so do people in love. Robert Johnson, a Jungian analyst and author of *We: Understanding the Psychology of Romantic Love*, has written that "romantic love can only last so long as a couple are 'high' on one another." After that, things go downhill.

Another problem with romantic love, Johnson says, is that in some basic ways it really doesn't stand up to its reputation. "When two people are 'in love,' people commonly say that they are 'more than just friends.' But in the long run, they seem to treat each other as less than friends. Most people think that being 'in love' is a much more intimate, much more 'meaningful' relationship than 'mere' friendship. Why, then, do couples refuse each other the selfless love, the kindness and goodwill, that they readily give to their friends?"

> "I think it is very important to like as well as love your partner or spouse."
> —CHARLOTTE, Milledgeville, Georgia

Maybe that's why in one of the Hindu rites of marriage the bride and groom make each other a solemn vow: "You will be my *best* friend."

The importance of friendship in marriage has been observed from a slightly different angle by Frank Pittman, M.D., a psychiatrist and family therapist in Atlanta and author of a book about affairs called *Private Lies*. Very often, he observes, sexual affairs begin as friendships and progress to sex. Once that happens, the whole thing gets too complicated for the friendship to continue. "What is so sad, and seems so foolish about affairs, is that many of them might have been wonderful, utterly unthreatening friendships had they not been so naively sexualized by people . . . who just don't know how to have a friendship with someone of a different gender," he writes.

Just to test this observation against the facts, he chose 100 people (60 men and 40 women) who'd come to see him for therapy because they'd had affairs. Only 10 of these people came from sexually dead marriages, he found. But 30 of them, both men and women, complained that they longed for more emotional intimacy in their marriages. "Affairs were thus three times more likely to be the pursuit of a buddy than the pursuit of a better orgasm," he says. Not only that, he adds, but "the best basis for good sex seems to be friendliness."

Even so, we don't want to sit here taking potshots at the glories of love. That would be like censoring the sunset or outlawing the morning dew. Yet we couldn't get over the fact that women from all over the country, including many who had been married for decades, kept telling us that friendship was more important than passionate love in making a marriage last.

> "Be honest, be loving, be kind. You get more with honey than vinegar."
> —SHERRON, New Jersey

- "This may be a backward way to look at it, but it makes me sadder when couples split who were good friends than those who weren't," said Joan, a 41-year-old bookkeeper and mother of two who is herself divorced. "I think, 'If they can't do it, who can?' It seems like a bigger tragedy. Friendship is number one in my book."
- "After 20 years of marriage, I feel that it is very important that partners in marriage are also good friends," said another woman. "I am fortunate, after all these years, to realize that I am married to my best friend. Learning to share the same interests cultivates a deeper, more meaningful relationship."
- "I think men have to remember to be a friend to their partner first, then a lover," said Gloria in Miami.
- "Men should learn how to be friends first; then you will be a great lover and husband," said Nina in Fullerton, California.
- "We have been married for 24 years! We have a strong marriage. My spouse is my best friend and I love him. We work

at our marriage every day and do not take each other for granted. We feel that we are on our second honeymoon since the kids have grown up. Life is great!"

Many other women made the point that one of the key ingredients of friendship, with a spouse or anybody else, is keeping the channels of communication wide open. You can talk freely with your spouse or partner; whine and gripe, if need be; really express yourself and feel that you are being heard; and expose your doubts and fears without fear that this will be used against you.

> "Affairs were . . . three times more likely to be the pursuit of a buddy than the pursuit of a better orgasm."
> —FRANK PITTMAN, M.D.

To women, friendship and communication seemed almost synonymous.

Another woman said:

> My advice to men is to be your partner's friend. Share thoughts and perceptions from a man/woman viewpoint since men and women think different. This will help you understand what each other expect in a relationship. Communicate with your partner about your wants and needs, likes and dislikes. Be open and honest with each other.

There's something else about friendship that is different from the way many long-married spouses treat each other, said Joan.

> Sometimes, I would lash out at my husband; and I would think, "If this were one of my girlfriends, I would never treat her that way." You know, you learn things about your spouse that you would never dream of throwing back in the face of a friend. You can love a person and say you're going to spend

the rest of your life with them and not respect that part of them, that friendship. It has to do with a certain basic civility, a courtesy, a sense of respect for that person, even if you do share the same bathroom.

Courtesy, civility, and respect involve keeping a certain distance (at least outside the bedroom).

Maybe that's why Katharine Hepburn once remarked, "Sometimes, I wonder if men and women really suit each other. Perhaps they should live next door and just visit now and then."

Others pointed out that women no longer need the same things from men that they did decades ago, before vast—and, to some men, alarming—social changes altered the whole cultural landscape. Women no longer need us to be providers, protectors, hunter-gatherers, or warrior-kings so much as they need plain old friends and companions—equals. Marva in Sacramento said:

> Unlike when I was growing up, young women today don't really need men. Women can earn very good incomes; they don't need husbands anymore to have children; they can purchase their own homes and drive new cars with the credit they themselves have established. So in my opinion, I think men should know that women today are looking for a good friend first and foremost. They are looking for someone to complement their life and not detract from it. They want a man to support their ideas and goals, validate their opinions, and above all, they want a man to actually listen to them when they talk.

Having shared values is all-important.

Cathy and David first met during their junior year in college, at Glacier National Park in the high Rocky Mountains of northwestern Montana. He was tall and blond; she had wide, dark eyes and glossy black hair. They were both working in a park lodge for the summer, she as the dining room hostess, he as a bartender. Cathy—now a 44-year-old business consultant married to David—remembered vividly what a wild time it was back then.

Kids came there from all over the country to work for the summer. It was like college without the classes. Nobody slept. "We'd work these god-awful hours, then we'd party," Cathy reminisces. On weekends, she and David would go hiking in paradise. Out there, they were surrounded by the snow-clad glories of creation.

> There'd be a moment of true, simple appreciation of this in-credible wonder all around us—realizing that the natural world is much bigger than us as people. And to find some-body who understood that made me realize I'd found a partner.
>
> David and I care deeply about the wonder and the beauty of the world, the Earth. He's now an environmental attorney, and we care deeply about making a contribution with our lives. It's so Pollyannaish and so 1970s, I know, but that's where we come from. He sees the same beauty I do. We share this common belief or value about life. I care about what I do with my life in a similar way to my partner—it's almost a spiritual bond. And that shared value has really carried us through, even when I think he's being a jerk. When I think, "How could you be such a jerk, when you were such a nice guy out there on the trail? Why did I ever like this guy?" Those are the times when you have to go back to that fundamental thing that you share. That's what carries you through the dry periods. It helps you get past the petty differences.

For Cathy and David, shared values meant a mutual awe and appreciation of the natural world and a commitment to its preservation. As a practical matter, its importance to their marriage was that it represented an overarching concern, something greater and more enduring than themselves as individuals or even their marriage.

For a great many other women, shared values means sharing an abiding religious faith. This spiritual bond, they say, becomes the central, stabilizing force in their marriages, a point of deep connection with their mates, and a refuge from the storm.

> "Shared values are all-important; everything else is just window dressing."
> —KATHY, Boston

"I think that the most important thing a man can give to a marital relationship is sharing the love of God," offered Cynthia in Athens, Ohio. "The man and wife together should place God as the priority over their family and marriage. It takes three to make a wonderful marriage. Praise God, he is in our marriage forever."

Kay in Moore, Oklahoma, told us this about herself and her husband of 32 years.

> God is the center of our lives. The Holy Spirit directs us in ways to lift each other up. We are very respectful of each other and are best friends. Things haven't always been like this, but we were always against divorce and that was never an option. We have always known things would work out. We knew God had plans for every stage of our lives. We all need to remember that God takes us from glory to glory. We need to take ourselves out of our marriage relationship and put God in it. Only this will keep your marriage exciting. Without Him, we couldn't have lasted this long. We plan on another 32 years.

Several other women mentioned the importance of the regular practice of prayer with one's mate. One woman told us:

> On the really important issues, I'm my husband's confidante and trusted partner. We like to treat each other tenderly. We'll always say a prayer together to try to understand each

other's point of view. Our sex life is great! After three kids, we know it's not just quantity but the quality, fun, and romance we find in each other's arms. We respect and recognize our strengths and our weaknesses. After 23 years of marriage, we realize that character is formed in joys, sorrows, trials, and triumphs. We are always praying and working at being flexible, and caring and laughing too!

For other women, shared values may mean something a little humbler and down-to-earth—just a shared appreciation of what is valuable in life, what is pleasant, worthwhile, comfortable. Susan, a 49-year-old writer from Ann Arbor, Michigan, said:

To me, the term "values" has a little more to do with lifestyle. My husband and I have been building our house for years and years; we've watched it evolve together. There's always some wing that's unfinished. Other women say it would drive them crazy, but I don't mind.

So it's not just that you love this person, it's that we share lifestyles. We value the same things. We enjoy watching the house grow and change. We enjoy making the most out of a little. To me, "values" just means what matters to us, what we enjoy.

Whatever the values that you share may be, the very fact that you share them gives a huge boost to your long-term success.

But what if you don't have shared values? What if you think she's fun and great and sexy and smart, but a perpetual home-repair job would drive her absolutely bonkers? What if you long to go trekking in the Himalayas or fix up an old boat and sail to Aruba, but she just wants to stay home and have another child?

When you and she don't share some fundamental values, you have trouble knocking at the door. In Dr. Gottman's studies of married couples, he found that though lots of problems are small and solvable, most marital conflicts—in fact, by his estimate almost 70 percent of them—are perpetual, recurring, and unsolvable. Over the years, these deep-seated disagreements repeatedly boil over into squabbles, quarrels, arguments, heated discussions, and just plain big old fights.

What's the underlying, insoluble problem? It's that "you have dreams for your life that aren't being addressed or respected by the other," Dr. Gottman says. In short, you don't share the same values.

But you don't have to get a divorce or give up your values or your dreams in order to have a successful marriage.

"In happy marriages, partners incorporate each other's goals into their concepts of what their marriage is about," says Dr. Gottman. If she feels that it's important to go to church, you may go along from time to time, even though you're an atheist, because you want to honor and respect her values. You may long to have a cabin in the woods, so she puts up with the long hours that you have to put in to earn the money for it, because she respects how much it means to you.

> "Women need to get the idea of a soap opera romance or knight in shining armor coming to the rescue out of their minds. Those days are over! It takes years to mold a man into what women want."
>
> —Dawn, Detroit

Sharing values is the best thing. Or as Kathy, a travel writer from Boston, put it, "Shared values are all-important; everything else is just window dressing." Even so, if there are other good reasons why you're together, honoring and respecting each other's values—even if you don't share them—is the next best thing.

Teamwork counts.

Annette, a 38-year-old Danish physician married to an American man, said:

My husband and I both help each other; we work as a team, and that's a big, big key to our success. We have small kids, and my husband will say, "Gosh, they never get up in the night!" Well, that was me, getting up in the night. That was my job. I also cook dinner, and when he comes home I have dinner ready. At this stage in our lives, this is no big deal. But what's also very important is that at other times, I come home and he's cooked up a great meal for me. It's important that we work together in this way.

Actually, said Elizabeth, who has been running the business end of her husband's career as a sculptor for 25 years, " 'teamwork' is kind of a male word. A more female word for this would be 'fabric.' Your lives are woven together, like the warp and woof of a piece of cloth. Everything you do contributes to the overall pattern, the finished product."

The point is this: it's critical that she feels like you're both working together toward the same goals.

What these women describe is similar to something described by Pepper Schwartz, Ph.D., professor of sociology at the University of Washington in Seattle and coauthor of *The Great Sex Weekend*. In her study called *American Couples*, she discovered many same-sex couples and some heterosexual ones in which there was equal status and equal responsibility for emotional, economic, and household duties—genuine teamwork. These "peer marriages" that she found, though relatively rare, had four characteristics in common:

1. No more than a 60-40 split of household duties. There doesn't have to be a perfect 50-50 split so long as nobody gets angry with the arrangement.
2. Both parties feel they have equal say in important decisions.

3. Both feel they have equal control over family economics and discretionary spending.
4. Each person's work is given equal weight in the couple's life plans. The person who earns the least is not the person who gets stuck with most of the housework.

All the way around, both parties are pulling their own weight in order to get done whatever needs doing. If that's not the case—if, for instance, she starts to feel like you're a worthless, lazy oaf—things can get nasty very quickly. Even if she appears to not mind pulling more than her own weight, don't believe it. Resentment is like an odorless, colorless gas that can build up inside a house and then one day, touched off by the tiniest spark, explode. Dorothy, an art teacher in Oklahoma City, admitted:

> "The big thing to be afraid of is not change; it's staying the same."
> —CASS, Virginia

> My way of relating to men is to want everybody to be happy and have a good time, to such a degree that I wind up angry at them. In the end, I've wound up creating a lazy person who is no longer an interesting person or doing anything to contribute because I've done it all for him. I created the biggest couch potato on the face of the planet. And I don't think I'm the only woman who went around making everything rosy and then I look over and say, "Who's this guy? What am I getting from this relationship? Who do I have to blame for that?" It winds up making everybody angry and resentful, big time.

Don't be afraid of change.

"What makes a marriage work?" we asked a small group of women.

"Changing it often," laughed Cindy, a painter from New York City. She wasn't entirely joking. "People change, and I don't see that as necessarily a bad thing. If it means growth, why is that bad? Relationships are not meant to stay the same forever."

Nothing ever stays the same, after all—not the Dow Jones Industrial Average, not the clouds in the sky, and not your marriage. And who'd want that, anyhow?

Whether it's one partner taking a job in a new city, or moving to a new house, or having a child, or pursuing a passionate new interest, change is synonymous with life. And relationships are just two lives, twined together. Things will only stop changing when you die.

"The big thing to be afraid of is not change; it's staying the same," said Cass, a 38-year-old graduate student living in rural Virginia.

Cindy adds:

> I think there should be an openness to the relationship changing, and mutual respect for where that person is going. Actually, in several of the long relationships I had, I left because I didn't think he was growing or changing. He was just turning into this rock, like this was what he was going to be like for the rest of his life. But I was just sort of passing through. I hope there are a lot of men out there who are not like that.

Sometimes, people change so much that they feel compelled to leave the marriage or the relationship. *C'est la vie*. But a much more satisfying outcome, all the way around, is to figure out a way to stay married and still retain your freedom to change. This is so important, in fact, that we devoted a whole chapter to it, chapter 44.

Aretha had it right: R-e-s-p-e-c-t really matters.

We have to confess that we were a little surprised at how vehemently and how often women stressed the importance of respect in relationships. We also have to confess that this probably had something to do with the fact that we're, well, guys. It's not at the top of our list because we just don't have all that much experience with being treated disrespectfully by the guy at the gas station, our supervisor at work, or our wives. Whether we're conscious of it or not, it's still a man's world in many ways, and we tend to get respect for no other reason than our Y chromosomes.

For women, it's often different. They value respect because they so often don't get it.

- "After two divorces and several failed attempts at long-term relationships, I believe I have found the key ingredients to success: mutual respect and trust," one woman told us. "No matter how great everything else might be, if either of these two traits is missing from either side of the relationship, I believe failure is imminent. If these two traits are present on both sides, then the rest start to take their own places of importance. But mutual respect and trust must be at the core."

- "When a man makes his wife feel loved, cherished, and respected, and she knows he loves her above anyone else, then the marriage bed will be heaven, the communication will be open for both, and she will do anything in the world for him and will want to do so. She will even give up things such as her home to move into a smaller home for a smaller house payment. It goes on and on," said another.

- "A lifetime full of mutual common courtesy and understanding goes a very long way—and it's free of charge," added Gail in Hellertown, Pennsylvania.

A few years ago, when one of Dr. Gottman's research studies was published, newspaper headline writers could not resist tagging the story with lines like "Saying 'Yes, Dear' Key to Long-Term Marriage."

Cute. But not entirely accurate. What he actually meant was that "the happiest, most stable marriages in the long run were those where the husband treated his wife with respect and did not resist power sharing and decision making with her," he explains in his book *The Seven Principles for Making Marriage Work.* Saying, "Yes, dear," is not so much a sheepish surrender as a demonstration of genuine, heartfelt respect. His statistics bear this out: Of the thousands of couples whom he and his colleagues have studied, if the man doesn't share power with his wife, there's an 81 percent likelihood that the marriage will end in divorce.

There's nothing worse than phony respect, though— saying, "Yes, dear," when you don't for one second mean it.

Respect means consideration for her sexual desires as well as every other kind of desire. When she says she wants something, or doesn't want it, that wish should be, well, respected.

"The number one thing I would want is respect in all aspects—being treated like a lady when you're in the bedroom," said one woman. "It should be a mutual understanding as to whether you want to be wild, different, etcetera."

Another woman said, "Men need to understand that respect

> "When a man makes his wife feel loved, cherished, and respected, and she knows he loves her above anyone else, then the marriage bed will be heaven. . . ."
>
> —Anonymous survey respondent

and communication are critical aspects for any relationship to thrive and grow. I think many men feel that women are not interested in sex, which is entirely untrue. They need to realize that women are emotional creatures and require more romantic stimulation to enjoy sex more. I feel most women need more foreplay than men do." This sounds to us like a plaintive wish that may well have been voiced, but never respected.

For other women, respect means respecting the other person as an individual, even when you're so angry that you could spit nails. Adriana in Texas is one of them.

One of the most important aspects in a relationship or marriage that still is as true as it was when my parents were young is the notion of respect. My husband and I are always stressing, "When in the heat of anger, relax, stay silent instead, and discuss later." Much more will be accomplished that way. Keeping our respect toward one another is an admirable characteristic in men and women.

Not a few women also pointed out that feeling that men respect them as people can have certain amorous side effects. Diana from Oneonta, Alabama, said:

Men need to realize that what happens outside the bedroom is just as important, if not more important, than what happens inside it. Respect makes a woman respond more than men realize. Men should learn to have respect, consideration, values, and morals for their partners. Values of being honest and kind go a long way in and out of the bedroom.

Of course you're going to fight sometimes; just be sure you learn to fight fair.

Not so long ago, marital therapists believed that couples who fought and argued a lot were bound for divorce court. Simple as that. Case closed. Today, though, in light of serious long-range studies involving thousands of couples, expert opinion on the subject of fighting has changed.

"Fighting, when it airs grievances and complaints, can be one of the *healthiest* things a couple can do for their relationship," writes Dr. Gottman in his book *Why Marriages Succeed or Fail*. There are, he says, "couples whose fights are as deafening as thunder yet who have long-lasting, happy relationships."

No matter how well you get along, conflicts are inevitable, of course. Ron Kessler, Ph.D., professor of sociology in the department of health care policy at Harvard University Medical School, who studied 691 couples over a 3-year span, found that the average married couple has one serious fight a month and lots of little squabbles. What's important is working out the rules of engagement—how to fight fair—rather than simply fighting to draw blood or having the same old arguments year after year without making any progress. Listen to Susan, a self-employed writer living in rural Virginia.

My husband and I need to fight in order to make it a better relationship. Our marriage is stronger because we have been able to get through the ugly times and get all the way back to loving each other. We can say things that are mean and nasty and hard, and in a way that's made us stronger. You decide to confront and face each other, really talk it through, rather than ignore it.

> "Fighting, when it airs grievances and complaints, can be one of the healthiest things a couple can do for their relationship."
> —JOHN GOTTMAN, PH.D.

I think that trust is really important. I think our marriage is stronger for our having hung together through the fights and the hard times. We've had tragedies that have happened to us, periods when we were totally alienated from each other, when one or the other of us was mad at the other. But there was always some underlying trust that this was a marriage that was going to last.

Being able to fight fair, to deal head-on with conflicts, is a critical skill for couples who are sharing their lives with each other. And if the way that Susan and her husband do it works for them, fine.

Today, there is no longer a consensus of opinion that noisy, argumentative marriages are necessarily any less healthy than sweet, docile ones. It's just that each couple has a different "marriage style."

In his research, Dr. Gottman has found three different ways that couples deal with conflict, and all of them "are healthy adaptations to living intimately with another human being."

1. **Validating.** In this kind of marriage, he says, "couples compromise and calmly work out their problems to mutual satisfaction as they arise." Like calm, reasonable Ward and June Cleaver on *Leave It to Beaver*.
2. **Volatile.** "Conflict erupts often, resulting in passionate disputes." Couples who fight like this tend to be "independent sorts who believe that marriage should emphasize and strengthen their individuality. These marriages tend to be passionate and exciting, as if the marital punch had been spiked with danger." Who else but Alice and Ralph Kramden on *The Honeymooners*?
3. **Conflict-avoiding.** "Couples agree to disagree, rarely confronting their differences head-on." Dr. Gottman describes a couple named Allan and Betty who, though happily married for 40 years, have never once sat down to have a "dialogue" about their relationship. If Allan gets angry at Betty, he turns on ESPN; she goes to the mall. Eventually, they come back together and their little spat is never mentioned. For them, this works—and there's nothing wrong with that.

"My research suggests that all three styles are equally stable and bode equally well for the marriage's future," Dr. Gottman says.

One caveat is that there has to be an intuitive thermostat in the relationship that regulates the balance between negativity and positivity.

Couples who fight a lot have to balance that with lots of laughter, passion, touching, and fun.

Dr. Gottman and his colleagues have actually monitored couples' interactions at close range, for long periods, and discovered that the magic ratio is five to one. If there's five times as much positive feeling as negative, there's a good chance the union will survive.

One critical thing that successful couples do is use what the University of Washington researchers call repair attempts to diffuse the anger in a big fight. For instance, if Hal and Joanna are having a big blowup about whether or not they should buy a new car, and things start to get really heated, Hal will suddenly make a goofy face or jokingly stick out his tongue or say something like, "I love it when you're angry." It seems like a small thing. But if she laughs or sticks her tongue out too—if she understands and responds to his repair attempt—it seems to instantly clear the air. Repair attempts are an extremely powerful way to diffuse rage and even save a marriage. But repeated repair attempts that fall flat—Hal tries to make a joke, but Joanna doesn't get it or doesn't laugh—are one key sign of an impending divorce, the researchers have found.

You have to listen, pal. Women's need to be heard, to be listened to, is so great that it's hard for us to understand it.

One woman told us:

> I think men need to listen more when a partner says she's dissatisfied. If he doesn't, she might find someone who will. I did, and now I'm involved in an affair. I'm trying to find all the things my husband is lacking. This man tells me I'm beautiful and compliments me all the time. I now want to lose weight; and I dress better, wear makeup, and keep my hair nice. I enjoy pleasing my man, but once he stops complimenting me, something gets lost in me.

> "If love means never having to say you're sorry, then marriage means always having to say everything twice."
>
> —ESTELLE GRAY, cross-country cyclist

The theme of the guy-who-doesn't-listen came up so often in our conversations with women that we've discussed it in detail elsewhere in this book. But it's so important that we couldn't resist briefly mentioning it once again here.

Obviously, lots of women don't feel listened to, or they wouldn't mention it so often. Mothers of small children spend much of their day in the company of people who are more interested in jelly sandwiches than real communication. Working women rarely get a chance to have at work the kind of meaningful conversations that they crave. So that leaves you, pal.

"I like to feel close to a person by being listened to and feeling I'm understood," one woman told us. "It is important to be able to share stresses and truly feel you're listened to with compassion."

Of all the things women mentioned in this chapter, listening is one of the easiest—and most effective—of all.

A couple that laughs together, lasts.

So there's this old couple, see, and the old guy turns to his wife and says, "I saw one of those commercials on TV about that stuff Vigoro, and how it can pep up your sex life. So I've been taking a couple of teaspoonfuls every night. Don't know if you've noticed."

The old girl turns to the old guy and says, " Vigoro? You mean Viagra. Vigoro is fertilizer!"

"Oh," the old guy says, "that explains the berries."

Being able to laugh together means being able to share the sweetest fruit that life has to offer. It's also a sort of Rorschach Test of compatibility. Because if the same thing tickles both of your funny bones, chances are, you have a fighting chance of staying together—and enjoying it.

"I think having a sense of humor is absolutely critical. It's the only saving grace," said Cathy, a business consultant from Colorado. "The classic marital conflict is where and how you squeeze the toothpaste tube. But if I'm worried about where my husband squeezes the toothpaste, if I can't just laugh it off, we're in trouble."

"Laughter is one of the most important areas of a relationship in order to develop friendship between two people," Diana in Alabama told us. "Being able to accept life and make the best of what you are given helps make life much more enjoyable with that person."

> "Sexiness wears thin after a while and beauty fades, but to be married to a man who makes you laugh every day, ah, now that's a real treat!"
> —JOANNE WOODWARD, Academy Award–winning actress and wife of actor Paul Newman

Several women mentioned that men have a tendency to get overly serious about things, especially work—*especially* work that's not going well. And if they succumb to premature seriousness, it's like throwing a cold, wet sheet over the whole relationship. One woman said:

> My husband and I have withstood the test of time because we take our vows very seriously. However, over time my husband has become disenchanted with life because I don't think he accomplished everything he wanted to be before now. We married young, and my husband started taking life way too seriously. It all became so burdensome. My advice to men would be to do what you think you have to do. Don't let marital obligations prevent you from reaching your personal goals. It has been my experience that my husband put his personal goals aside, and it has taken the spontaneity, romance, and fun-lovingness out of our relationship. It's a good thing we like each other as people.

Their marriage doesn't sound like much fun, though, does it? Maybe they should go out and buy themselves a rubber spider.

Now Get Outta Here

"We've done the feminist thing and beaten men
down, and now we want to lure them back."
—*Stella McCartney*

It's a good time to be a man. The War between the Sexes
has cooled off, and there's a new generation of women (like
Paul McCartney's kid, quoted above) who thinks we're
maybe not so bad after all.

Not only that, but . . .

- Doctors are saying that steak, coffee, fat, and sex are good
for us.
- They're saying we don't have to choke down no-salt
pretzels.
- And the beer! Beer has gotten so much better. Like us.

But unless we've found the Right Woman, and unless we
can keep the Right Woman, all that other stuff is just a pretty
small consolation prize. So let's be sure our newfound mil-
lennial manhood does not go to our heads. Now is not the
time to bellow and behave badly and blow cigar smoke in her
face, so to speak.

Now is the time to kiss and make up. Because sooner or later, you will be at fourth down and 10 with her, and you will need something in reserve.

There's a lot of wisdom in this book. Almost too much wisdom. Let's be honest: Most of us are bears of very little brain, and we'll never use it all. After working on this book for nearly 2 years, your deeply flawed authors are still striving mightily to apply the very basics to our own marital lives. Each time we read it, we find something new. And we keep finding those lines that stay with us, those one-liners that make us smile and that ring so true.

We've come up with a list of the 17 Big Points. Consider this your cheat sheet for a marriage where nobody cheats because nobody feels cheated.

1. We could have written this book with one word in it: *romance*. (We couldn't have sold it for 30 bucks, but that's not your problem.) A woman longs for a sense of psychic intimacy, a feeling of closeness and connection, an assurance that you want to be with *her* and her alone—not her roommate, her girlfriend, Heather Locklear, or your previous wife. To women, that is romance. And almost nothing matters more.

2. So don't dismiss romance. Otherwise, she'll start to dismiss your sex drive.

3. If you're dating, you've probably noticed that many women are suspicious and mistrustful of men. That's because they have a lot to fear. You may know that you're the nicest guy on Earth, but you're still going to have to deal with her past experiences with guys who were boors or bores or creeps or psychos. But here's the good news: Your competition is *so* weak. If you're a decent guy who takes a shower and opens her door, you've already dusted most of your rivals.

4. Many men mistakenly believe that if they can just make vice president, the babes will be all over them. Not quite.

Women told us that they don't want your money; they want your time. They want your attention. They want a soul mate.

5. And they still want you to be a gentleman. That's something that will never go out of style.

6. All women, or all the good ones anyway, have a sixth sense for dishonesty. And they swear by the zero-tolerance approach.

7. Maybe guys have such trouble understanding what women want because we haven't tried very hard. As one woman said, a little bitterly, "We're aware of what *you* want. Women spend a lot of time trying to figure out what men want, and men don't spend 2 seconds thinking about what we want."

8. Listen. Don't interrupt. She talks to feel closer to you. She doesn't necessarily want you to fix her problem. And she sure as hell doesn't want you to belittle her problem. As one woman told us, "Men don't understand that listening to a woman is one of the best ways to say 'I love you.' "

9. To you, money brings status. To her, money brings security. Don't make her feel insecure. Share with her. Never say "my money"; say "our money." Be partners.

10. Women are no longer powerless. You know it. They know it. They are driven, self-assured, smart, and ambitious. If they aren't treated well, they walk out. Girl Power is here to stay, and that's probably a good thing for all of us.

11. To you, good sex happens downstairs, below the belt. To her, it happens upstairs, in her head. "For most women, sex is between the ears," we were told. That explains why they need to be romanced, why they say over-the-top stuff like "foreplay is a way of life," and why they don't reach orgasm every time. It's why sexy talk or fantasies or the mood of the room is so critical to her orgasms. This is not about you. If she needs a long warmup, don't feel inadequate.

12. Speaking of feeling inadequate: Two out of three women cannot reach orgasm in the missionary position. Again, it's not about you. There are other roads to pleasure. To quote one wisegal: "We want the three Cs from men: commitment, compliments, cunnilingus."

13. You can't *make* her come. You can only make her fake it.

14. If she's feeling appreciated outside the bedroom, she'll be happier in the bedroom. Don't save all your sweet talk for the sack. By then, it might be too late. As one woman told us, "Never tell a woman she's beautiful when the lights are off."

15. Slow down. Kiss more. Do something different. Remember to have fun. That's good advice whether you're in bed or not.

16. We couldn't help but notice that women who say stuff like "all men are so-and-so" or "women never do such-and-such" are single or bitterly divorced. Where's that at? What's the point of being "right" if that means you wind up alone? By contrast, women who talk about men as fellow humans, as friends and companions and *people*, are more likely to have happy relationships.

17. And the same goes for guys. So forget about what women want. The only question that matters: What does *your* woman want?

If you rip this out and paste it to the inside of your closet door, we won't mind a bit.

With 2,102 women to help us, writing this book was a fascinating experience and a pleasurable one. But it's over. It's done. The real glory lies yet ahead, and it's yours.

Index

Italicized references indicate boxed text.